Organising Music

Organisational theorists have become increasingly interested in the creative industries, where practices that are commonplace are of particular interest to organisations in other sectors as they look for new ways to enhance performance. Focusing on the music industry, this book sets up a unique dialogue between leading organisational theorists and music professionals. Part I explores links between organisation theory and the creative industries literature, concentrating on practices of organising and knowledge mobilisation, followed by an in-depth discussion of key theoretical concepts by subject experts. Part II provides a diverse range of 'tales from the field', including examples from classical orchestras, folk, indie and punk. The concluding chapter examines the shared dialogue to reveal what practice in the musical field can learn from organisational theory, and vice versa. This innovative book will interest graduate students and researchers in the fields of organisation studies, music management and the creative industries.

NIC BEECH is Vice-Principal and Head of the College of Arts and Social Sciences at the University of Dundee and Chair of the British Academy of Management. His research interests are in management practice, change and the construction of identity in the music industry, health, financial services and creative industries. He has extensively published in the field of organisation studies and is the author of *Managing Change* (Cambridge University Press, 2012) and *Managing Creativity* (Cambridge University Press, 2009).

CHARLOTTE GILMORE is a Chancellor's Fellow at the University of Edinburgh Business School. Before taking up her position at Edinburgh, she was a Lecturer in Creative and Cultural Industries at the University of St Andrews. Her area of interest is the creative industries and her work has been published in *Human Relations*, *Management Learning* and the *British Journal of Management*.

Organising Music

Theory, Practice, Performance

Edited by

Nic Beech and Charlotte Gilmore

CAMBRIDGE
UNIVERSITY PRESS

CAMBRIDGE
UNIVERSITY PRESS

University Printing House, Cambridge CB2 8BS, United Kingdom.

Cambridge University Press is part of the University of Cambridge.

It furthers the University's mission by disseminating knowledge in the pursuit of education, learning and research at the highest international levels of excellence.

www.cambridge.org
Information on this title: www.cambridge.org/9781107040953

© Cambridge University Press 2015

First published 2015

A catalogue record for this publication is available from the British Library

Library of Congress Cataloging-in-Publication Data
Organising music: theory, practice, performance / edited by Nic Beech and Charlotte Gilmore.
   pages   cm
ISBN 978-1-107-04095-3 (hardback)
1. Music – Performance.   2. Organization.   3. Management.   I. Beech, Nic, editor.   II. Gilmore, Charlotte, editor.
ML3853.O74   2015
780.6–dc23

                                                                    2014026360

ISBN 978-1-107-04095-3 Hardback

Additional resources for this publication at www/cambridge.org/9781107040953

For Linda and Rosie
and
For my little one, Esme x

Contents

Contents

x   Contents

List of figures and tables

Contributors

NIC BEECH is Vice-Principal and Head of the College of Arts and Social Sciences at the University of Dundee and Chair of the British Academy of Management. His research interests are in management practice, change and the construction of identity in the music, health, financial services and creative industries. He is a fellow of the Royal Society of Arts, the British Academy of Management, the Chartered Institute of Personnel and Development and the Academy of Social Sciences, and has been voted by HR Magazine one of the UK's most influential thinkers on HR.

CHRIS BILTON teaches and researches on management and creativity at the University of Warwick. He is the author of *Management and creativity: from creative industries to creative management* (2007) and has co-written *Creative strategy: reconnecting business and innovation* (2010) with Stephen Cummings. Chris and Stephen also edited the *Handbook of management and creativity* (2014).

ALAN BRADSHAW teaches and learns at Royal Holloway, University of London.

STEPHEN BROAD is Head of Research and Knowledge Exchange at the Royal Conservatoire of Scotland. Following interdisciplinary studies at the universities of Glasgow and Oxford, he now pursues a range of research interests across historical musicology, music education and arts policy. He is co-author of *What's going on?*, a study of young people's music-making in Scotland that initiated the Scottish Government's £100m Youth Music Initiative. Originally from the Isle of Mull, he now lives in Perthshire.

SHIONA CHILLAS is a lecturer in management in the School of Management at the University of St Andrews. Her PhD thesis was on the changing nature of graduate employment. She is interested in the deployment of skills at work and is currently working on a HERA project researching the supply and value chains of indigenous textiles in fashion. She has published in *Organization and Employee Relations*.

MARTIN CLOONAN is Professor of Popular Music Studies at the University of Glasgow. His research interests include issues of freedom of musical expression, the live music industry and music policy. He is chair of Freemuse (www.freemuse.org) and Reviews Editor for the Cambridge University Press journal *Popular Music*. He has recently recovered from being a band manager.

KEVINA CODY is a lecturer in consumer behaviour and communications at the Dublin Institute of Technology. Her research interests are primarily in the area of consumer culture and marketing communications, specifically the myriad interactions between the commercial world of the market and the social exchanges of groups and individuals. To date, her work has been published in journals such as *Marketing Theory*, *Journal of Consumer Culture*, *Advances in Consumer Research* and *Young Consumers*.

CHRISTINE COUPLAND is Professor of Organisational Behaviour at Loughborough University, School of Business and Economics. She has held faculty positions at the universities of Hull and Nottingham. Her recent publications include articles in *Organization* and *Human Relations*. Her research interests centre on issues of identity and language, drawing upon theoretical perspectives from organisation theory and constructionist social psychology. She currently serves on the editorial boards of *Organization Studies* and the *Journal of Organizational and Occupational Psychology*. She is also Associate Editor for the *Scandinavian Journal of Management* and regularly convenes research streams at the BAM conference.

STEPHEN CUMMINGS is Professor of Management at Victoria Business School, New Zealand. He has published articles on strategy, innovation and the history of management and his books include *Recreating strategy* (2002), *Images of strategy* (2003), *Strategy pathfinder* (2011), *Creative strategy: reconnecting business and innovation*, and the *Handbook of management and creativity* (with Chris Bilton, 2010 and 2014). His latest book is titled *Strategy builder: how to create and communicate more effective strategies* (2015).

ANN CUNLIFFE is Professor of Organization Studies at Leeds University Business School, having previously held positions at the University of New Mexico, California State University and the University of New Hampshire, USA. Ann's current research interests lie in examining the relationship between language and responsive and ethical ways of managing organisations, leadership, selfhood, qualitative research methods, embodied sensemaking, and developing reflexive approaches to management research, practice and learning. Her recent publications include the books *A very short, fairly interesting and reasonably cheap book about management* (2014) and the co-authored *Key concepts in organization theory* with John Luhman (2012). She has published articles in *Organizational Research Methods*, *Human Relations*, *Management Learning*, the *Journal of Management Studies* and *Organization Studies*.

CHRIS CUSACK was born in the relative musical backwater of Stirling in Scotland, and began to actively pursue music from the age of 14, initially fuelled by bands like Nirvana who rejected notions of sexism, homophobia and conformity. Since then he has become immersed in the world of underground alternative music, working as a sound engineer, driver, roadie, journalist, designer and producer amidst the bustling European DIY scene. He has also enjoyed time in a number of touring bands, most notably Hey Enemy and Dead or American, the latter of which was the basis for founding his own label and learning how to operate outside the mainstream industry. He continues to work within music, running an ethical venue and label in Glasgow, as well as freely offering his help to bands and musicians in need of advice on how to navigate the treacherous landscape of the music business.

JANE DONALD has a background in senior management in the arts. A philosophy graduate of the University of St Andrews, her final student summer job was a project for the Royal Scottish National Orchestra (RSNO), and that suggested the possibility of a career in administration in the arts. Following a short period at Scottish Opera, Jane joined the marketing team at the Glasgow Royal Concert Hall. Starting as Marketing Assistant in 1998, she gradually progressed through Media Relations Officer to Marketing Manager and then in 2006 to Head of Sales and Marketing. From 2006 to 2010, she had responsibility for leading the teams delivering marketing, sales, media relations, sponsorship and education. An elected member of the board of the Arts Marketing Association, Jane has both professional and academic interests in the theory and practice of arts management. Jane is currently the Director of External Relations for the RSNO.

MARTIN DOWLING is Senior Teaching Fellow and Director of Teaching in the School of Management at the University of St Andrews. He is a Fellow of the Chartered Institute of Personnel and Development, the Chartered Management Institute and the Higher Education Academy. His teaching interests include human resource management, industrial relations and management development. He has worked closely with colleagues in several universities on a number of HR-related research projects and published in both academic and professional journals. His career in higher education has also involved him in academic management and leadership, postgraduate course development and management, quality assurance systems and external examining at several UK universities.

MICHAEL DOWNES became the first full-time Director of Music at the University of St Andrews in 2008, having previously held a similar post at Fitzwilliam College, Cambridge. He works as a conductor with a number of groups in the area, including the St Andrews Chorus, now the largest choir in Scotland with over 150 singers. Michael read English and music at King's College, Cambridge, and completed a doctorate on the music of Debussy at the University of Sussex. He has lectured on music and opera for organisations including the Royal Opera House, ENO and Glyndebourne, and regularly reviews music books for the *Times Literary Supplement*. He is the author of book on contemporary British composer Jonathan Harvey, which was published in 2009.

CELIA DUFFY was, until retirement, a member of the Royal Conservatoire of Scotland's senior management team, with institutional responsibilities including research and knowledge exchange and the implementation of the new undergraduate curriculum. Career experience ranges from lecturing in music at Goldsmiths, University of London, to commercial software design and using digital technologies in higher education. As the first Head of Research at the Conservatoire she founded the National Centre for Research in the Performing Arts, and led the team responsible for development and management of research, consultancy and knowledge exchange activities. Celia chairs the board of Scotland's foremost contemporary music ensemble, RedNote.

CHARLOTTE GILMORE is Chancellor's Fellow at the University of Edinburgh. Before taking up her position at Edinburgh, she was a lecturer in creative and cultural industries at the University of St Andrews. She has been awarded an AHRC for the Cultural Values Project, exploring the enactment of taste making in contemporary music. Charlotte has also recently been awarded a research grant to explore artistic and organisational practices at Islington Mill in Manchester and the Edinburgh Sculpture Workshop. She was awarded an ESRC post doctorate to develop her research in the advertising industry at the Institute for Capitalising on Creativity at St Andrews. Charlotte's area of interest is the creative industries. Her work has been published in *Human Relations*, *Management Learning* and the *British Journal of Management*.

LANCE GREEN is an English-born trombonist living and working in Scotland. As well as teaching the trombone at university level, Lance contributes to the education of younger trombonists by attending the annual 'side-by-side' event arranged between the Royal Scottish National Orchestra (RSNO) and the West of Scotland Schools Orchestra Trust. He also participates in various brass masterclasses for the same organisation. There are hundreds of recordings by the RSNO available for purchase, mainly from the Naxos Label. Lance appears in many of these as Principal Trombone, of which the most notable is Mahler's *3rd Symphony*, in which he plays the trombone solo. Lance also appears on the American Summit Records release *Big Band Reflections of Cole Porter*, which he recorded with the Jazz Orchestra of the Delta while he was on a year's sabbatical from the RSNO in Memphis TN.

GAIL GREIG is a lecturer in management at the University of St Andrews. Her research concerns collective knowing and learning in and through relational practices in arts, cultural and healthcare organisations, most recently with Nic Beech for the Digital R&D Fund for the Arts and Culture in Scotland (NESTA/AHRC). Recent publications include papers in *Social Science and Medicine* and *Management Learning* (with Nic Beech, and Charlotte Gilmore in the latter), a chapter on improvisational practice (with Nic Beech and Holly Patrick) in the *Handbook of institutional approaches to international business* (2012) and a chapter on improvisational and coordinating practices in film-making (with Nic Beech and Elizabeth Gulledge) in the *Handbook of management and creativity* (2014).

ELIZABETH GULLEDGE is a research fellow in management at the University of St Andrews. Her research areas are the cultural and creative industries, with particular interest in the nature, operation and maintenance of institutional fields, the role of symbolic, social and cultural capital in the economy for symbolic goods and organising practices and their role in creative outcomes. Her current research investigates these issues in book publishing, film and music.

CHRIS HACKLEY is Professor of Marketing at Royal Holloway, University of London. His PhD from the Department of Marketing, Strathclyde University, explored the creative advertising development process in top agencies. His most recent book is *Marketing in context* (2013), and the third edition of his textbook *Advertising and promotion* will be published in late 2014. Current projects include research on children and video games, the production of celebrity and social media, and the culture industry under convergence.

MARTIN JOHN HENRY is a songwriter from Bellshill in Lanarkshire, Scotland. Henry is noted for his success as the frontman of the rock band De Rosa, who released several albums, singles and other recordings on Glasgow's influential independent label Chemikal Underground. De Rosa's music was critically lauded and championed by John Peel and Steve Lamacq. Sound-Scotland recently praised Henry as '...one of Scotland's finest songwriters'. Henry has written, recorded and played with many of Scotland's finest musicians, including Barry Burns (Mogwai), Robert Johnston (Life Without Buildings), King Creosote and Malcolm Middleton. As a solo artist, Henry contributed a track to MOJO Magazine's *Abbey Road Now!* CD in October 2009 and has played numerous shows including SOUNDS Festival, Tigerfest and Glasgow's Merchant City Festival.

PAUL HIBBERT is Professor of Management at the University of St Andrews. His research is principally concerned with knowledge and learning, particularly in collaborative forms of organisation. He has also connected knowledge and learning-related research interests concerned with: how research is produced and used; reflexive practice in the context of management development and formation for leadership; and educational theory. He has published his work in leading international journals and he is an associate editor of *Management Learning*.

CASPER HOEDEMAEKERS is a lecturer in work and organisation at Essex Business School, Essex University. His research interests include subjectivity and management control, financialisation and the psychology of freelance labour. His work has appeared in *Organization Studies*, *Organization*, *Critical Perspectives on Accounting*, and *Ephemera: Theory and Politics in Organization*, among other journals.

R.M. HUBBERT is a guitarist and singer from Glasgow in Scotland. A veteran of the Scottish independent music scene for almost twenty-five years, he is best known for his triptych of solo albums released through the Chemikal Underground label: *First & Last* (2010), *Thirteen Lost & Found* (2012) and *Breaks & Bone* (2013). His solo work is primarily based around a blend of flamenco and Scottish folk guitar dealing with themes of love, death, mental illness and a dog called D. Bone. R.M. Hubbert won the Scottish Album of the Year Award in 2013 for his second album, *Thirteen Lost & Found*.

JOHN HUNT continues to work in investment, and hopes to complete an EP of new Butcher Boy recordings in 2014. Having spent more than a decade cutting, gluing and stitching together club nights, John is taking a sabbatical from DJing – though he is keen to impress on anyone who will listen that this is 'au revoir' rather than 'goodbye'.

PETER KEENAN is Lecturer in Management at the University of St Andrews School of Management. Peter's research sits primarily within the field of strategy as practice, and focuses on how moral legitimacy and human agency shape strategic action and outcomes. He worked as a clinician for many years in community mental health services prior to researching the organisational aspects of addiction services, and youth antisocial behaviour in Glasgow's housing regeneration areas. He frequently debates with others the greatness of The Beatles.

NOD KNOWLES has had a career in senior management and music in the UK and abroad (including at Scottish Arts Council, Bath Festivals and Europe Jazz Network) and now works as a consultant with music and arts organisations and musicians in various capacities: in change management, research, funding, tour and event management, artistic direction and programming.

GRETCHEN LARSEN is a senior lecturer in marketing at Durham University. Her research is located at the intersection of consumption, markets and the arts. In particular, she seeks to understand how the position of the consumer in a socio-cultural world is constructed, performed, interpreted and questioned through the arts. Gretchen has co-written *Music, markets and consumption* (2013) (with Daragh O'Reilly and Krzysztof Kubacki) and her publications have appeared in the *European Journal of Marketing*, the *Journal of Marketing Management*, the *Journal of Business Ethics*, *Psychology and Marketing* and *Marketing Theory*, among a variety of other scholarly outlets. She is the founding editor of *Arts Marketing: an International Journal*.

JOHNNY LYNCH is an Eigg-based singer-songwriter, whose psych-folk-pop solo output under his nom-de-plume The Pictish Trail snaps to a diverse creative grid among a plethora of other outlets for his musical creativity, be it crafting furiously danceable electronica together with London-based multi-instrumentalist Adem in the guise of Silver Columns – whose 2010 album *Yes, And Dance* was hailed as 'a glorious curveball of a record' by *Q* – or making *In Rooms*, a 2011 side-project mini-album containing fifty songs, each thirty seconds long. Or, since the summer of 2013, running his own DIY micro label and musical collective Lost Map, having for ten years before that helmed the cherished and highly respected Fence Records.

RAYMOND MACDONALD is Professor of Music Psychology and Improvisation and Head of the Reid School of Music at Edinburgh University. After completing his PhD in Psychology at the University of Glasgow, investigating therapeutic applications of music, Raymond worked as Artistic Director for a music company, Sounds of Progress, specialising in working with people who have special needs. He joined the School of Music in 2012, having worked at Glasgow Caledonian University previously. He has published over seventy papers and co-edited four texts: *Musical identities* (2002), *Musical communication* (2005), *Music, health, and wellbeing* (2012) and *Musical imaginations* (2012). His ongoing research focuses on issues relating to improvisation, psychology of music, music health and wellbeing, musical identities and music education. His work includes studying the processes and outcomes of music participation and music listening. As a saxophonist and composer his work is informed by a view of improvisation as a social, collaborative and uniquely creative process that provides opportunities to develop new ways of working musically. Collaborating with musicians such as Evan Parker, David Byrne, Jim O'Rourke and Marilyn Crispell, he has released over fifty CDs and toured and broadcast worldwide. He has produced music for film, television, theatre and art installations and is a founder member of Glasgow Improvisers Orchestra.

ROBERT MACINTOSH is Professor of Strategy and Head of the School of Management and Languages at Heriot-Watt University. He trained as an engineer and has worked at the universities of Glasgow and Strathclyde. He has published extensively in top rank journals and played key roles in a range of conferences including the Strategic Management Society and the European Group for Organization Studies. His research focuses on the ways in which top teams develop then implement strategy. He has consulted for the Clydesdale and Yorkshire Banks, Babcock International Group, the NHS, HMRC and a range of other organisations. He sits on the board of the charity Turning Point Scotland. His latest book, *Managing change as enquiry and action* was published by Cambridge University Press in 2012, and his next book, *Strategic management* will be published in 2014.

KATY MACKINTOSH is currently Associate Principal Oboe with the Royal Scottish National Orchestra (RSNO). Originally from Glasgow, she studied at the Royal Academy of Music with Douglas Boyd and Celia Nicklin. In 1994 she reached the woodwind finals of the BBC Young Musician of the Year. In 1999 she was awarded a Countess of Munster scholarship to study with Nicholas Daniel. In 2001 she made her Wigmore Hall debut with Simon Lepper. They have since performed at the Purcell Room, St George's Brandon Hill, Fairfield Halls Croydon and the Bridgewater Hall. As an orchestral musician Katy has worked with the BBC Philharmonic, City of Birmingham Symphony Orchestra, BBC Scottish Symphony Orchestra, Britten Sinfonia, Scottish Chamber Orchestra and Orquestra do Algarve. As a soloist she has performed with the RSNO and the New London Soloists at St Martin in the Fields. When not performing, Katy provides music workshops to a wide range of audiences.

DONALD MACLEAN received a BSc in physics from the University of Strathclyde, a PhD in optoelectronics from the University of Cambridge and an MBA from Kingston University. He spent ten years working in the global optoelectronics industry before joining the University of Glasgow in 1993, where he is now a part-time professorial research fellow. He is currently researching design, creativity and well-being in organisational settings. He has published extensively on strategy, transformation, complexity theory, action theory and research process in a range of journals including the *Strategic Management Journal*, the *Journal of Management Studies*, *Organization Studies* and *Human Relations*. He co-chaired the SMS special conference on strategy in complex settings in Glasgow in June 2013. He combines his part-time academic work with ongoing commercial, public and third-sector consultancy engagements and directorships.

KATY J. MASON is Reader in Markets, Marketing and Management, Lancaster University Management School. Katy's research focuses on how managers make and shape markets, the market devices they use to enrol others and create market boundaries. Her work looks at the materials and practices of market-makers, and specifically the representational practices managers use in working out what to do next. Through a number of engaged and collaborative research projects, her work has explored the power of market-making devices such as business models, market representations and expectations. Recent research into commissioning for the provision of UK health and social care draws on practice theory to understand how new services are imagined, disentangled from current structures of practice and reassembled in the market. Katy's work has been published in the *Journal of Management Studies*, *Industrial Marketing Management*, *Long Range Planning*, *Management Learning*, the *European Journal of Marketing* and *Journal of Marketing Management*.

ALAN MCCUSKER-THOMPSON lectures in commercial music at the University of the West of Scotland, where he is also Programme Leader for the MA Music: Innovation and Entrepreneurship. He has previously worked as a recording artist, composed music for television drama as well as working in PR, journalism, artist management and music publishing. He is a Glaswegian.

LLOYD MEREDITH co-runs Scottish DIY label Olive Grove Records, home to the likes of Jo Mango, Woodenbox and The Moth and the Mirror. In addition to this he also manages the folk-pop outfit, Randolph's Leap, and runs the Scottish music blog, Peenko.

LOUISE MITCHELL was appointed in 2011 Chief Executive of the Bristol Music Trust, an independent charitable trust set up that year to drive forward music in Bristol, and to help secure a sustainable future for Colston Hall. Previously, Louise was the first Director of Glasgow UNESCO City of Music, a position taken after being at the head of the Glasgow Royal Concert Hall for thirteen years, which included responsibility for the world-renowned Celtic Connections Festival. Previous experience includes positions with the London Philharmonic Orchestra, Barbican Centre and as Assistant Director of the Edinburgh International Festival. Louise is a Trustee of the Royal Philharmonic Society, a Fellow of the Royal Society of Arts, Vice Chair of British Association Concert Halls, and a past board member of the International Society for Performing Arts.

DAVIDE NICOLINI is Professor of Organization Studies at Warwick Business School, where he co-directs the IKON Research Centre. Prior to joining the University of Warwick he held positions at The Tavistock Institute in London and the University of Trento and Bergamo in Italy. His work has appeared in journals such as *Organisation Science*, *Organisation Studies*, the *Journal of Management Studies*, *Human Relations*, *Management Learning*, and *Social Science and Medicine*. His recent research focuses on the development of a practice-based approach to the study of organisational phenomena and its implications for the understanding of knowing, collaboration, decision-making and change in organisations. He has recently published two books: the monograph *Practice theory, work and organization: an introduction* and *How matter matters: objects, artifacts and materiality in organization studies*, co-edited with P. Carlile, H. Tsoukas and A. Langley.

DARAGH O'REILLY is a senior lecturer in creative and cultural industries at the University of Sheffield. He is the author, with Gretchen Larsen and Krzysztof Kubacki, of *Music, markets and consumption* (2013) and the editor, with Ruth Rentschler and Theresa Kirchner, of the *Routledge companion to arts marketing* (2014). His research focuses on the relationships between the arts, marketing, culture and consumption.

JILL O'SULLIVAN was born in Belfast and raised in Chicago. She currently resides in Glasgow and performs in the band Bdy_Prts with Jenny Reeve. The duo released their first single, 'IDLU', to positive reception on 3 March 2014 and are currently working on a full-length album. She also fronts three-piece band Sparrow and the Workshop, who have released three full-length albums and toured with the likes of the Brian Jonestown Massacre, the Pogues and Idlewild. She has collaborated with James Yorkston and Emma Pollock, among others, and is currently working on a storytelling project with musician and writer Sean Cumming called 'Do the Gods Speak Esperanto'.

CLIFF OSWICK is Professor of Organization Theory and Deputy Dean at Cass Business School, City University, London. His research interests focus on the application of aspects of discourse, dramaturgy, tropes, narrative and rhetoric to the study of management, organisations, organising processes, and organisational change. He has published over 130 academic articles and contributions to edited volumes. He is the European Editor for the *Journal of Organizational Change Management* and Associate Editor for the *Journal of Change Management*. He is also Co-director of the International Centre for Research on Organizational Discourse, Strategy and Change.

MARCO PANAGOPOULOS fronts the band United Fruit. United Fruit are a fast-paced and energetic alt rock band from Glasgow, Scotland, who have used their limited resources and DIY ethic to get all over the UK and Europe with goals further afield. Their music is melodic yet aggressive and catchy. The band has a relentless drive live and off the stage, which is reminiscent in their music.

JIM PRIME brings thirty years of industry experience to the University of the West of Scotland. A keyboard player and songwriter, Jim began his career in 1980 on an American tour with Altered Images, followed by a number of years – and albums – with John Martyn. During this time he was also Musical Director for Cumbernauld Theatre. His future research work focuses on bridging the gap between the secondary school music SQA higher level curriculum and higher education's level 7 curriculum, with a view to examining and improving the transition from school to university. His interests also lie in the field of musicians and wellbeing. Jim has headlined at (2011) Glastonbury, Belladrum, Tall Ship Races and Liverpool Echo Arena, and opened the Last Night of the Proms in the Park in London's Hyde Park. 2012 saw the twenty-fifth anniversary of Deacon Blue, in which he is keyboard player, and a new album and single launch, with an extensive UK tour.

JENNY REEVE is a member of Strike the Colours: four musician friends from Glasgow, united by their collective experiences and love of the music they are making together. Since they are by no means strangers to the local music scene and beyond, it could be argued that the four members of Strike the Colours have been, and continue to be, integral to the music coming out of Glasgow over the last couple of years. Indeed, Jenny Reeve (Arab Strap, Malcolm Middleton, Idlewild, Snow Patrol, The Reindeer Section, The Fruit Tree Foundation), Jonny Scott (Emma Pollock, The Phantom Band, The Unwinding Hours, Take A Worm For A Walk Week), David McAulay (Terra Diablo, composer and engineer/producer of records for Mogwai, Remember, Remember, Bill Wells, Jenna and Bethany Reid) and Graeme Smillie (Emma Pollock, Unwinding Hours, Idlewild, Sons And Daughters) all have impressive pedigrees in their own right, working with some of Scotland's most talked-about bands and musicians. Nevertheless, they still find time to come together to play music that has been championed by respected publications such as *Clash Magazine*, *Converse Music*, *The Scotsman* and *The List* and national radio DJs such as Steve Lamacq, Mark Riley, Gideon Coe and Vic Galloway.

SIMON ROSE is a professional musician and performs on baritone and alto saxophones. His research interest focuses on the process of improvisation, in which he has completed three studies. Following an MA at Middlesex University in 2008, he gained his doctorate in 2013 at Glasgow Caledonian University. For several decades he taught drama and music in London, including work with permanently excluded and special educational needs students. Studying drama at Dartington College of Arts and teacher training at Exeter University, his early career was in theatre-in-education and fringe theatre: devising theatre and touring schools, prisons, hospitals and small-scale venues. He is currently completing a book concerning the agency of improvisation. Other publications include the chapters 'Free improvisation in education' in *Investigating musical performance* (2012) and 'Improvisation as real-time composition' in *The act of musical composition* (2014). His music recordings can be found on the labels Emanem, Leo, PSI, Bruces Fingers, Not Two, Rayon and PF Mentum.

MICHAEL SAREN is Professor of Marketing at Leicester University. He previously held chairs at the universities of Stirling and Strathclyde and is honorary professor at St Andrews University. His research interests focus on the development of marketing theory, particularly regarding marketing knowledge, consumer culture and issues of creativity and sustainability. He was one of the founding editors of the journal *Marketing Theory* in 2000, and is author of *Marketing graffiti: the view from the street* (2006) and co-editor of several books including *Rethinking marketing: towards critical marketing accountings* (1999), *Critical marketing: defining the field* (2007), *The Sage handbook of marketing theory* (2010) and *Marketing pathfinder: core concepts and cases* (2014). He was made an honorary fellow and lifetime member of the UK Academy of Marketing in 2007 and was joint winner of the George Fisk award in 2012 for the best Macromarketing conference paper.

DAVID SIMS is Emeritus Professor of Organizational Behaviour at Cass Business School, City University, London, and formerly Associate Dean there. His interests are in how people learn and develop as leaders of change in different cultures and contexts, in the way in which people contribute different qualities and skills to the activity of leadership, and in the relationship between leadership, identity, the narrative processes of life, and the way in which people create narratives to justify their actions and actions to justify their narratives.

IAN SMITH came to Scotland in 1971 to join the horn section of the RSNO. He founded and directed Scottish Brass and has also guested with the London Symphony Orchestra. He became the Scotland organiser of the UK Musicians' Union in 1993 and founded the Union's specialist section for folk, roots and acoustic music. Ian was appointed Head of Music at the Scottish Arts Council in 2005 and is currently responsible for music and intellectual property development at Creative Scotland (CS). Ian oversees all international export showcasing for CS Music, including Showcase Scotland, Womex, SXSW, AWME/Australasian World Music Expo and the Cambridge, Woodford (Aus), RIFF (India) and Celtic Connections Festivals. He is also responsible for co-programming the Made in Scotland music programme at the Edinburgh International Fringe.

DUGLAS T. STEWART has been the lead singer, main writer and bandleader of the BMX Bandits since 1985. The band continues to thrive and evolve almost thirty years since its inception. BMX Bandits had a direct influence on the music scene around them, with former (and some continuing) members going on to be in Teenage Fanclub, The Soup Dragons and Belle and Sebastian. Duglas's bitter-sweet, melodious pop garnered fans and the attention of Creation Records, who signed the band in 1991. The band has toured extensively throughout Europe and Asia, with a particularly strong fan base in Japan. Duglas has written and produced for other bands, but always returns to BMX Bandits. He is an obsessive music fan and active supporter of new bands. BMX Bandits' most recent release, *BMX Bandits in Space*, was a critical success and Duglas is currently working on the new BMX Bandits album.

CHRIS STOUT has become nationally and internationally recognised as one of the most exciting and dynamic fiddle players on the traditional music scene. Whether as a solo artist, a member of Fiddlers' Bid or as a duo with long-time musical associate Catriona McKay, Chris continues to innovate within traditional and contemporary musical circles, delivering performances that continue to excite and inspire audiences all over the world.

DIMITRINKA STOYANOVA RUSSELL is Assistant Professor at Warwick Business School and Associate Researcher at the Institute for Capitalising on Creativity at St Andrews University. She has published in the area of learning and skills development, employment in the creative industries, creative careers and freelance work.

ANTONIO STRATI is Professor of Sociology of Organization at the University of Trento, Italy, Associate Researcher at PREG-CRG (Ecole Polytechnique) of Paris, France, and is an art photographer. He is the author of *Organization and aesthetics* (1999) – which also appeared in French (2004), Portuguese (2007) and Italian (2008) – and of *Theory and method in organization studies* (2000).

BEN TALBOT DUNN: Open Swimmer is the banner above songwriter Ben Talbot Dunn and those that accompany him. After seven years writing and performing in the frost of Glasgow, Ben has reappeared on our shores with a stunning album that melts the boundaries of pop. His weaving vocals dart and rest between delicate guitar lines and bashful strums that together result in truly intelligent and satisfying tunes. Predominately focused on guitar and vocals, Ben's songwriting is honest, playful and complex, using melody as much as words to tell his stories. After much success in Glasgow and several tours around the UK, Ben has finally come home with a sugar bowl of sweet soulful treats to share.

ROBYN THOMAS is Professor of Management at Cardiff Business School. Robyn's research focuses on the social and political processes of organisational change. She has published on these topics in leading international journals such as *Organization Science, Organization Studies, Organization, Public Administration* and the *British Journal of Management.* Robyn is also Editor-in-Chief of the journal *Organization.*

LORI WATSON is a leading light of the new generation of Borders fiddle players. Lori grew up in Birgham, steeped in the music and song of the Scottish Borders. Her work on Borders fiddle playing with Tom Hughes, Bob Hobkirk, Wattie Robson and Jimmy Nagle has been a driving force in the current resurgence of Borders music, along with the band Border Fiddles, whose release in 2004 was a landmark recording for Borders music. Although Lori's musical roots lie firmly in the Borders, her understanding and interpretation of Scots and worldwide traditions is undeniably resonant. A BBC Scotland Young Traditional Musician of the Year 2002 and 2003 finalist, Lori has toured extensively and broadcast on radio, television and the internet throughout Britain, Europe, Canada and the USA. Performing regularly with award-winning band Lori Watson and Rule of Three, her self-produced debut was released in 2006, followed by *Pleasure's Coin* in 2009, both on ISLE Music Scotland. Alongside performance and research work, Lori's tunes, songs, extended and experimental compositions are to the forefront of traditional music composition in Scotland. Burnsong Winner in 2007 and Celtic Colours Songhouse Writer in 2008, Lori has composed for theatre and chamber ensembles as well as her own performance groups, including the Momentum Collective. Lori is currently a lecturer, honours supervisor and performance examiner to Scottish music degree students at the Royal Conservatoire of Scotland (formerly RSAMD), fiddle tutor for Newcastle University's folk and traditional music degree and a sought-after workshop leader for all levels.

SIMON WEBB was Director of Orchestral Management at the City of Birmingham Symphony Orchestra (CBSO). He is now General Manager at the BBC Philharmonic. As a cellist he was a member of the London Philharmonic Orchestra (LPO), and he has been a board member of the LPO, Marchester Camerata and National Children's Orchestra.

RICHARD WIGLEY was born in New Zealand and trained as a bassoon player in Wellington and Boston, USA, before moving to London in 1986. As a member of the Halle Orchestra from 1988 he was an enthusiastic participant in the orchestra's community and education programme. After becoming Head of Education in 1994 he moved to become Head of Artistic Planning for the orchestra in 1999. From 2001 he was Head of Performance and Programming at the Royal Northern College of Music and was appointed General Manager of the BBC Philharmonic in 2004. In 2014 he left the BBC to form his own company, Wigley Arts Management, to help build outstanding orchestras. Currently he divides his time between the Netherlands and the UK.

SIERK YBEMA is an Associate Professor in the Department of Organization Sciences at VU University Amsterdam. His research centres on processes of politics, identity and sensemaking, with empirical settings ranging from amusement parks and the creative industries to newspaper offices and multinational corporations. He has published widely on culture and conflict, relational and temporal identity talk, managerial discourse and postalgia, intercultural communications, interorganisational relationships, and organisational change and crisis. This work has been published in such journals as *Human Relations*, the *Journal of Business Ethics*, *Organization* and *Organization Studies*.

MATTHEW YOUNG is the man behind the Song, by Toad website (www. songbytoad.com), which is a bible for many people when it comes to discovering new music. His work also evolved and Song, by Toad Records (www.songbytoadrecords.com) was born, which he now runs full-time. The label is home to the likes of Meursault (www.myspace. com/meursaulta701) and Inspector Tapehead (www.songbytoadre cords.com/artists/inspector-tapehead).

CARLO ZANOTTI works as a copywriter and continues to assist in the National Pop League Little League club nights. Despite being old enough to know better, Carlo is also partly implicated in Strangeways – a quarterly club night devoted to The Smiths and Morrissey.

Acknowledgement

The project which led to this book was funded by the ESRC, grant number RES-331–27–0065.

1   Developments in organisation theory and organising music

Nic Beech, Stephen Broad, Ann Cunliffe, Celia Duffy and Charlotte Gilmore

The intention behind this book is to bring together two fields – music-making and organisation theory – in order to explore what might be learned. Learning may proceed in various directions within and between the fields. Within fields we are concerned with learning between alternative traditions and genres. For example, the learning between punk and indie music might entail small-scale translation, whereas ideas moving between large classical orchestras and small folk bands may need considerable adaptation. Similarly, within organisation theory, insights from storytelling may integrate easily with those from metaphorical analysis, while the movement is potentially wider between complexity theory and aesthetics. Learning between fields may require a degree of imagination and creativity, and ideas originating in one field may become generative in another as connections and disconnections are identified and examined. For example, insights from leadership theory might be directly helpful in thinking about organising a festival but may also stimulate a new way of understanding how to manage the kind of portfolio of projects that many musicians – and managers – juggle. Equally, understanding the challenges of staging the first performance of a new composition might throw some light on our understanding of markets and patterns of consumer behaviour. Hence, our aspiration is to encourage learning-oriented dialogue.

We see dialogue as a process of enquiry through which self-examination is stimulated by contact with 'the other'. Such dialogue is particularly effective where the learning is less directed at the other ('my ideas can help you') and more directed towards reflexivity ('having had an encounter with you, I now think differently about my own position') in the style advocated by Shotter (2010) and Gergen et al. (2001). Because the dialogue is about learning (Hibbert and Huxham, 2011) it means that one needs to be open about things that have gone wrong as well as telling the 'success stories' – the sanitised version of reality that is often well-rehearsed (Sims, 2003). Hence, trust between storytellers and listeners/readers is paramount. Producing tales from the field in written form

1

therefore requires a 'leap of trust', in which readers are trusted to treat the material and characters of the stories with care and respect.

Dialogue is a process of finding sufficient lines of connection or translation between parties so that engagement can be productive. It is not about creating complete agreement or overlap (Bohm, 1996). In some of the literature on the creative industries there is a belief that the logic of creativity and the logic of organising are so different that they are often in conflict with each other (Caves, 2000). For example, a composer or songwriter may create a piece that involves so many musicians it is bound to make a financial loss, or managers might seek to influence musicians to produce popularist work so that audiences and revenues can be increased at the expense of artistic freedom. This implies that either the values of organising and performing are at odds with each other or there is something about the way they are practised that leads to conflict. In this book we will question this way of thinking. While some managers and musicians may inhabit oppositional world-views, we do not accept that there is a necessity for the opposition (Beech, 2011). Rather, practices of organising and performing interpenetrate and influence each other such that interconnected or hybrid practices can lead to value for a variety of stakeholders. However, achieving this is not easy and so it is useful to work through a series of empirical examples in order to develop a theoretically informed, empirically grounded perspective.

What we present below is not intended to be a classic 'theory and cases' book, in part because the cases in such books can be presented as both fairly 'neat and complete' and chosen in order to support the theory. Here, we hope that the tales from the field are brief but open – capable of interpretation from different angles and further exploration. Similarly, the theoretically oriented contributions are not written in the mode of classic theory chapters – seeking to produce a comprehensive view of a theory – but rather provide a set of 'orienting ideas' with which the reader can approach the tales from the field. Hence, these contributions are intended to provide materials for generative dialogue (Beech et al., 2010): clear but open to interpretation; informative but open to question; and theoretically informed but practically oriented.

We hope that the time is right for this dialogue. Organisation theorists have become increasingly interested in the 'creative industries'. This may be because practices that have been common in organisations in the creative industries are of particular relevance more broadly as organisations in other sectors seek to work across organisational boundaries and to be creative, focused on performance, flexibly organised and engaged with customers/service users (Bilton and Cummings, 2014). The music industry is a prime example. It involves a variety of people in composing, creating and performing. Live performance entails networks of experts enabling events in which venues, programming, marketing and sales, sound and light, among many other functions, are coordinated so that creative outcomes are achieved (Cloonan, 2011; Frith et al., 2009).

Audiences value experiences of events (such as going to concerts and festivals) for the music but also as part of lifestyle choices, and even as part of their identities. Workers (e.g. musicians, promoters, engineers) operate on several projects simultaneously (McLeod et al., 2009), often for different companies, and the musical field has many small entrepreneurial enterprises. Audience demand is affected by fashion: legitimacy is gained not only through expert opinion but also through informal reviews via social media (Gonzalez, 2010). The nature of production and consumption is not merely an economic exchange but is something incorporating aesthetics and a level of significance in people's lives and relationships. As change, innovation and flexible ways of working are central to the creative industries, there is potential for organisation theory to learn much from practices in music-making.

On the other side of the coin, making music and the way the music 'industry' is understood may be able to pick up ideas from organisation theory. The 'creative industries' are regarded as an important part of modern economies (Caves, 2000). However, the term 'industry' is often criticised as leading to false assumptions about the degree of structure in supply chains, clear product demarcation and established competition between companies. This may represent part of the story but, as Hesmondhalgh (2007) points out, the organisations involved span many areas of activity, from leisure and commercial companies dealing in a variety of media and cultural forms to micro companies and amateur activities. Hence, it is unlikely that a single way of thinking about the variety of actors will be efficacious (MacDonald et al., 2002). Pratt and Jeffcutt (2009) have drawn attention to the changing nature of competition and dynamism within creative and cultural sections of economies. They argue that these sectors are typified by the speed of change of products and by a blurring of the boundaries between competition and collaboration. Companies, venues and artists who might be competing at one moment (for example, producing alternative concerts on a particular night and thus competing for audience numbers) may also be collaborating (for example, in staging a multi-venue festival that aims to bring larger audience numbers into an area). Creative and cultural industries, and music-making in particular, are engaged in the very issues that are of primary concern in current organisation theory. These include how people can operate in uncertain and changing environments; how traditional industrial structures of competition are becoming challenged by working across organisational boundaries; how the natures of markets and marketing are being transformed by shifts in consumer behaviour; and how economic activity can be understood as a social phenomenon – something with broader and disputed meanings, identities and relationships.

We will now take a brief overview of the organisation of music, illustrated with examples from the music scene in Scotland, before discussing some relevant developments in recent organisation theory. We will then conclude this introduction with some reflections about how music-making and organisation theory may be complementary in various aspects that facilitate learning-oriented dialogue.

Organising music

When we think of how music is 'organised' we probably tend to think firstly of the observable structures that seem to govern the way music happens. These include the organisations, venues, promoters and funders that each play a role in organising the nature of the individual musical event by shaping each element; the aesthetic and commercial considerations that underpin the event; the musicians who participate and the nature of that participation; the music they play, both in outline (say, genre) and detail; the audience that chooses to attend; and the nature of the relationship between performers and audience encoded in the space in which the performance takes place and the manner in which performers and audience interact. We can sense, in general terms at least, that each of these elements is related to the others – that the process of organising is characterised by a network of interrelated considerations.

In addition, however, recent research has highlighted some of the hidden structures that may affect – and, in a slightly different sense, organise – music-making. To take just one example, Simon Frith and his colleagues (2011) have suggested that compulsory national service played an important role in the rapid growth of the guitar as the instrument of choice among young men in 1950s Britain. It was a light and portable instrument that could easily be taken on the long train journeys that were often a feature of national service, during which groups of young men were thrown together with leisure time to fill, learning from each other without formal tuition or authority figures. Similarly, Christopher Small's (1988) ethnographic analyses of well-known musical structures like the orchestra, and the application of (for example) Bourdieu's (1977) 'tools for thinking' to musical practices in a range of different contexts, also remind us of the many influencing factors that may play a more veiled role in organising musical practice.

In surveying the contemporary scene, we might try to consider both the more overt structures that shape musical practice and those that are not so obvious or easy to pin down. Most of the structuring elements mentioned above – the organisations, venues, promoters and funders – have seen some significant evolution in recent years, even if they remain more or less recognisable from previous times. So what has changed?

Audiences remain, but their nature changes

The study of patronage has always been an important way of understanding music's relationship to society, and historians of Western music traditionally trace the history of its patronage in the last 500 years as a gradual passing of responsibility from the church, via the aristocracy, to the middle classes, and finally to government and individuals. Surveying very briefly the current scene, the role of 'patronage' in its widest sense remains an important factor. Although the word carries with it connotations of 'high art', the notion of 'who pays the piper' – and why they choose to do so – is a key element that structures musical events.

Recent large-sample surveys of participation in culture and the arts (Widdop and Cutts, 2011) show that those who participate most tend to be least concerned with traditionally conceived notions of art form and genre. Rather than restrict themselves to favourite forms, the most avid consumers of art and culture increasingly tend to engage with as wide a spectrum of experiences as possible, cutting across old categories such as 'high' and popular art.

Thus, the notion that different genres of music have distinct audiences has rather less support now than it perhaps had in the past, and we can perceive significant implications in the way musical events and practices may be structured in the future as a result of this. The audiences of today and tomorrow may tend to be more stylistically promiscuous and enthusiastic to sample different musical experiences, and less concerned with the conventions and formalities of traditionally conceived musical events.

At first sight this seems to undercut the arguments of social theorists who posit consumption of the arts as the embodiment and reinforcing of a particular (and perhaps class-based) 'habitus' (Bourdieu, 1984). But it is possible that the notion of the 'promiscuous cultural consumer' is itself an identity with a strong cachet, reflecting an outlook that revels in its own confidence with diversity and accumulates its own capital. This may have the effect of eroding the conventions and practices of traditionally conceived musical events (the conventions of the orchestral concert or the jazz club, which can seem strange to the uninitiated), but it may also mean that audiences will become increasingly focused on the unique qualities of individual events, rather than on the way they enact well-worn traditions.

We might see a reflection of this trend in so-called classical music when we observe the gradual shift away from event forms rooted in a sense of continuity and genre specialism – such as the orchestral or chamber concert series, the notion of a subscription series or concert season – and note the increasing importance of discrete events and 'specials', often linked to a particular time (an anniversary, for example) or place.

Venues remain, but the way we use them changes

Venues are far from neutral in the way they shape the unfolding of musical events: the old Gewandhaus in Leipzig – in which Mendelssohn regularly conducted – had seating arranged in rows lengthways down the hall rather than crossing it, as we would now expect. Thus, concert-goers sat facing each other, with the music emerging from a performance space that was not a visual focus. Compare this with the modern concert hall or theatre, in which the orientation of each seat is planned in such a way as to maximise the sense of linear transmission from the performers on stage to the occupant of the seat: the rest of the audience – the social dimension of the experience – is clearly played down in such a formation.

The second half of the twentieth century saw a great number of large new venues constructed, often to replace Victorian halls that were considered unfit for purpose. These super-venues are still being built, but we can perceive the way they operate as signifiers of different kinds of musical experience, and in the evolving relationship between generic spaces and those that celebrate a unique identity. The Glasgow Royal Concert Hall (GRCH) illustrates an evolution of use that mirrors many other similar venues. In its opening month, October 1990, performances were given by the Scottish National Orchestra, the Band of the Royal Marines, the Berlin Philharmonic Orchestra, the Scottish Chamber Orchestra, the Bolshoi Orchestra, the Orchestra of the Age of Enlightenment, and the London Philharmonic Orchestra. The few non-classical events included a performance by the Count Basie Orchestra, a jazz evening in the smaller Strathclyde Suite, a single stand-up performance and some concerts by Runrig. This initial programming was part of the identity-forming process of the Hall, with the 'high-art' orientation of the programmes mirrored by the visual art on show (an exhibition of the 'Glasgow Boys') and even in the way the catering was promoted ('Why not entertain your guests in the ambience of the 1930s in our superbly appointed restaurant . . . or dally awhile in the sophisticated decadence of the cocktail bar?').

In October 2013, the GRCH programme still included performances by the (now) Royal Scottish National Orchestra, but these were the only orchestral events. They took their place among performances by Petula Clark, Alison Moyet, Daniel O'Donnell, The Hollies and Barbara Dickson, together with special shows such as 'Dancing Queen' and 'Bootleg Sixties', plus two performances of *The Wizard of Oz*. The comparison could be analysed from a wide range of perspectives, but focusing on the way the venue inflects the nature of the event, we might note that a large, highly formalised and mostly seated space is reshaping musical events that might previously have taken place in less formal spaces – perhaps those designed principally for dancing rather than seated appreciation. The physical formality of 'art' music, encoded in the building's design, now shapes the experience of a much wider range of genres. This changing use of space may also reflect cultural priorities and political requirements for arts venues to pay for themselves rather than relying on local government, charities and other funding bodies to help cover costs.

'Place' matters more

One of the main events in the GRCH calendar is now the Celtic Connections festival, held each January – a very diverse gathering of musical events, densely programmed with such intensity that the qualitative experience of the festival itself becomes more significant than the individual musical events that comprise it. The host city, Glasgow, is important in the 'feel' of Celtic Connections.

Other, more modest festivals – such as Aberdeenshire's Sound Festival or Llupallu (which, linguistically and metaphorically, turns Ullapull inside out) – are even more rooted in their locations. At Llupallu, it is the experience of hearing (say) Franz Ferdinand against the backdrop of Loch Broom that gives the event its particular quality: the place itself, with all its individual qualities, becomes an organising element in a way that is more thoroughgoing than a mere change of venue. Llupallu – as its name makes clear – would not be Llupallu if it were hosted somewhere else.

Of course, such festivals are not in themselves new, but their relative importance has certainly increased. In art music, this shift is reflected at various levels, with the growing importance of locationally specific festivals (e.g. St Magnus, Lammermuir, East Neuk) and of location in the working practices of artists (e.g. the rise of retreats such as Cove Park or Crear as places that offer the time and intellectual space for new work to develop). It is also reflected in the increasing standing of unique or idiosyncratic venues such as Glasgow's Fruitmarket, which is a repurposing (with minimal alteration) of the city's long-mothballed fruit market, adjacent to the City Halls and still complete with stall signs and other reminders of its former life.

That the Fruitmarket has become a significant venue for new and experimental music while the GRCH hosts less of the supposedly 'high art' performances than it did in 1990 is clearly not on account of their different capacities alone. Even with its raw acoustic, the Fruitmarket is attractive to innovating artists because it is a genuinely unique space. Somehow the paraphernalia of its old life as a marketplace is less loaded with cultural significance than the supposedly neutral space of the modern concert hall, designed to the highest acoustic specification and with a minimum of visual distraction for the listening audience. Place – and perhaps a sense of uniqueness – matters.

Genres are still significant, but they are related in new ways

Alongside the new use of venues and the rising significance of place, the use of genre as an organising concept has shifted. The new significance, for audiences, of 'genre hopping' was mentioned above, but in fact the way we use and understand the concept of genre has evolved too. In some contexts, the notion of genre continues more or less unperturbed by recent developments: the orchestral world, for example, still inhabits a fairly unified genre context of 'art' music, with occasional forays into related orchestral fields such as film music.

In other contexts, however, we see new developments. Genres, far from being 'found' categories that emerge neutrally from music itself, are being continuously created and reshaped. The creation of 'world music' in a record company sales meeting (Frootsmag, 1987) is only one famous example of a trend that we can see continuing both locally and globally. It would not be too much to say that the Celtic Connections festival – along with the Festival Interceltique in Lorient, Brittany – has been instrumental in creating a new genre of Celtic music: a genre that, within certain broad geographic and musical contexts, nonetheless embraces a fabulous variety of sounds, styles, media, performance interactions and cultural references. Along with this new genre concept comes a new way of conceptualising this music as in some way unified – as with the 'style' concept used by music historians, genre is, at root, a tool for organising and distinguishing different musics. When we create genres, we are creating new ways of organising our understanding of music, and new ways of understanding can stimulate new ideas of performance and composition so that the flow of inspiration can operate in both directions between the stage and the marketing office.

At the same time, we can see other trends that specifically eschew, or at the very least play off, the notion of genre and any concept of order. Cryptic Nights – a series of performance events 'ravishing the senses' – is an example of this. It offers events and experiences as diverse as 'Why Scotland, Why East Kilbride' (a wonderfully wacky evening of music and chemistry experiments woven around an East Kilbride Development Corporation promotional film and a fictitious gender-shifting scientist and musician) and 'The Cabinet of Curiosities' (an evening showcasing sonic curios – junk, machines and antiques, refashioned into musical instruments). While it is difficult to imagine where these events would have found an easy home in the traditional structures of art music, it is also worth noting that in creating a home for themselves through organisations like Cryptic, the artists doing this work have also created new structures – perhaps not genres, but frames or settings in which their one-off experiments can be shared and understood.

Therefore, organising music-making is a field of diverse actors, practices, influences and performances. Engaging with this field requires a degree of dynamism and flexibility in theorising, and in the next section we will outline two approaches we think are particularly appropriate to this task.

Developments in organisation theory

The ways we think about, study and act in organisations are related to our view of the world and the way we think society works: i.e. our paradigm. Some paradigms view the social world as a given reality that exists independently from the people living within it – one in which structures, systems and roles can be observed and form the basis for being an effective member of society. This is known as a 'realist' view of the world. It includes, for example, the views that managers have a position in a formal organisation structure that determines their goals, responsibilities and authority; and that people behave according to particular laws and principles. Researchers can observe these phenomena, categorise behaviour and determine a manager's source of power and whether s/he is performing the role as s/he should. By referring to these structures, categories and systems, we can identify the causal mechanisms and the factors and variables that influence effective management performance. This paradigm, known as structural-functionalism, assumes that efficiency and effectiveness occur by conforming to these external requirements and mechanisms and by behaving in a 'rational' way. Changes to an organisation or work process occur by modifying structures, systems, goals, etc.

Alternative paradigms have a different understanding of the nature of our social world. For example, researchers working from a 'subjectivist' view of the world believe that the social world is not separate from us, but that people shape and maintain social and organisational realities in their everyday interactions and conversations. This is known as the social constructionist paradigm. Analysis within this paradigm focuses on the meanings that people give to their world – how they simultaneously interpret and shape what's going on around them. Cause and effect are not that clear; neither is there one rationality, because social life is complex and open to many different interpretations by the people living it. Researchers therefore need to ask those involved in a situation what it means to them, and to look for both similar and different meanings. For example, managers interpret and enact their goals and 'roles' in different ways: some may have a great deal of influence and good relationships with employees and colleagues, while others in the same role may not. We discover this by talking to different members of the organisation and seeking to understand the way they conceive and enact their work and relationships with others.

Social constructionist researchers and managers therefore see organisations not as independent structures and systems to be measured and manipulated, but as communities of people with both shared and different ways of making sense of what's going on. While some social constructionists study the interactions and conversations between people and how these might influence strategy or teamwork, for example, others take a broader perspective to look at how language, interpretations of symbols and written documents might construct the culture of an organisation, and how that culture plays back into employees' interactions. Whichever approach is taken, it is assumed that relationships and interpretations are dynamic and change over time and place. For example, as an employee, customer or hospital patient, we can probably all identify with the old saying that 'the only thing that is constant is change', as we get different advice from different people. And what may be perceived as 'good customer service' in one organisation is interpreted differently in another. In this paradigm, therefore, language, meanings and actions are not universal and generalisable as in the structural-functionalist paradigm, but are localised to the context. It is thus important for researchers to interpret the local meaning-making and activities of people.

The paradigms outlined above are just two of many. While the former structural-functionalist paradigm still predominates, especially in North America, over the last thirty years organisation and management theory has become more pluralistic. The so called 'paradigm wars' of the 1980s and 1990s, which sprang from Burrell and Morgan's (1979) book *Sociological paradigms and organizational analysis*, raised debate about whether there should be just one paradigm for organisation studies. The debate played out in North America with exchanges between Jeffrey Pfeffer and John Van Maanen, and in Europe notably within the journal *Organization Studies* in 1991. Pfeffer (1993; 1995) claimed that diversity leads to a lack of progress and that consensus is necessary to advance knowledge because it provides the basis for greater development within the principal paradigm (i.e. structural-functionalism) and a more effective evaluation of contributions to scientific knowledge, grant allocations and publications. Van Maanen's (1995a; 1995b) counterargument was that such a high-consensus paradigm – which he termed a Pfefferdigm – is too narrow and leads to a lack of imagination and insight. For Van Maanen, pluralism was crucial: 'The goal is to learn from one another such that our ink-on-a-page theories and consequent understandings of organizations can be improved' (1995a: 140). As Chris Stout (Chapter 19, pp. 298–304), a fiddle player, composer and producer from the Shetland Islands whose diverse style of playing and composing is rooted in traditional, contemporary and classical styles, notes:

In a successful collaboration I aim to make music where you can't tell where the genre-specific boundaries are. I think when you start to consider where the elements are from, there is something that maybe hasn't been achieved in really making honest music, if it's too obvious where the styles are. And so my aim is to work with musicians regardless of genre and make an emotional connection with a musician rather than a connection through a style or other people's perceptions of what you should play like.

Chris has established a range of cross-genre collaborations with musicians from around the world and combining folk and electronica, and provides an example of how pluralism can operate very effectively in music.

Also up for debate was whether paradigms should be commensurable or should stand alone because they are incommensurable – in other words, whether we can use the standards from one paradigm to evaluate work in another. Those for incommensurability argued that the fundamental ontological (the nature of social reality) and epistemological (the nature of 'good' knowledge) assumptions underpinning each are different and so we cannot evaluate work in one paradigm by using criteria from another. Good knowledge from a structural-functionalist paradigm means identifying cause and effect and relationships between structures and systems, measuring variables, testing hypotheses and developing a theory that predicts behaviour and can be generalised across contexts. Good knowledge from a social constructionist perspective means developing rich and in-depth descriptions and explanations, and possibly different interpretations, of what's happening in a particular context. The argument for incommensurability was eloquently led by Jackson and

Carter, who saw different paradigms as a challenge to the 'intellectual imperialism' of structural-functionalism (1991: 110). They suggested that we could expand the plurality and vitality of organisation studies by establishing a way of legitimising the integrity and validity of work within each paradigm rather than across paradigms.[1]

Our foray into this debate is to make the point that although this 'war' is still unresolved, it did draw attention to the potential of diverse ways of theorising organisations and management. Indeed, back in 1999 Karl Weick applauded the turbulence and urged us to 'get over it, get on with it, and write differently' (1999: 797). Taking the pluralist line, he suggested we adopt the law of requisite variety – because we are studying complex organisations and complex behaviours, we need to think in more complex and imaginative ways. This is what we seek to do in this book. An underlying principle applied here is to allow pluralistic voices to be heard and experimented with. Each chapter is written by an expert who is deeply embedded in a community that has a particular view on organising and/or music. When writing for their own community it is normal for them to take their way of thinking for granted and to use short-cuts in technical vocabulary. But here they have sought to write for people outside their normal community, so that there is a deliberate attempt to communicate across boundaries in such a way that the boundaries might change.

There have been a number of challenges to structuralism, including the linguistic turn, the reflexive turn, the postmodern/poststructuralist turn and the practice turn. What these 'turns' represent is a challenge to the prevailing structural-functionalist way of doing scholarship based on questioning the fundamental ontological and epistemological assumptions underpinning our work. Each 'turn' questions our ability to represent – accurately – what we see in the field, and offers an alternative way of thinking about how we generate knowledge. As such, they symbolise the enactment of pluralism and an effort to move thinking and action beyond the confines of traditional fields (Gulledge and Townley, 2010). In this introductory chapter we will map two such turns – the linguistic turn and the practice turn – each having its own internal logic around which research is rigorously crafted (Cunliffe, 2011). These are relevant in the chapters that follow because they are of particular relevance to the question of how organising can be achieved in musical performance. This overarching question invites further, more detailed questions. To what extent is there a contradiction between the language and practice of organisation and creativity? Where and when should

---

[1] See Hassard's (1991) argument for commensurability, and Parker and McHugh (1991).

compromises be made? Who should be involved in the various activities? What are the consequences of adopting a pluralistic approach to analysis and practice?

The linguistic turn

The linguistic turn arose in philosophy and the social sciences because of a dissatisfaction with the realist view of the world and its associated 'scientific' epistemology. Philosophers such as Rorty (1967), Wittgenstein (1951), Foucault (1972) and Derrida (1978) questioned the relationship between language, power, knowledge and how the social world comes into being. Within organisation studies, while a number of linguistic scholars draw on these more philosophical and critical approaches, some focus purely on language and discourse (Deetz, 2003). The linguistic turn is predicated on the belief that language (talk, text, symbols) constitutes social realities, and is complex in the sense that multiple meanings occur as people use and interpret words and conversations differently in and across time and space. While it is most often associated with a social constructionist perspective, linguistic scholars do work from different paradigms and there have been a number of attempts to map the various approaches (e.g. Cunliffe, 2008; Grant et al., 1998). Probably the best known is that by Alvesson and Kärreman (2000, updated 2011), who proposed a framework based on two dimensions.

● The first dimension is big 'D' macro Discourses of talk and language systems and little 'd' micro discourses of local talk and texts. Big 'D' Discourse relates to regular ways of talking and thinking on a societal or organisational level. Such Discourses are underpinned by a set of assumptions and ideas that give cultural and social meanings to actions. They may be political (e.g. socialism), economic (e.g. capitalism), ideological (e.g. managerialism, the American Dream), disciplinary/functional (e.g. business process reengineering, transformational leadership) and so on. Little 'd' discourse relates to everyday ways of talking and writing that influence how people understand an issue and act, and how they make sense of their identity in that context. Discourses influence discourses and vice versa. However, formal Discourses (e.g. organisational vision and value statements) may differ from the everyday discourses of employees.
● The second dimension is the study of discourse and language abstracted from the context of use, and the study of how discourse constructs meanings and actions in specific contexts. The latter might examine how organisational culture or managerial identities are

discursively constructed within a particular organisation – as a lived experience – while the former might examine the broader Discourses of gender or race that play across organisations at large.

Their 2011 article updating this framework was subject to critique by others in the same journal issue (see *Human Relations*, 64(9)).

One area of research drawing on the linguistic turn relates to the social and/or co-constructed nature of organisational life. For example, Barge and Fairhurst argue that leaders 'co-create their subjectivities – personal and professional identities, relationships, communities, and cultures – in communication through linguistic and embodied performances' (2008: 228). They do so by choosing which elements of Discourse and discourse to use to connect with people. This may involve telling stories around events that help make individual and collective sense around an issue.

The linguistic turn also focuses on language use and how metaphors, framing, words and phrases can be used to construct a sense of 'reality' and persuade others. Samra-Fredericks (2003) studied how the talk-in-interaction of a group of six managers in a day-long meeting worked to shape the strategy. She examined not just the language but also how it was spoken, and the rhetorical moves used by individuals in the conversation to shape the strategic direction. Framing – using language to shape interpretations and actions – is seen as basic to managing meaning and shaping organisational culture, strategy and identities (e.g. Ybema et al., 2009; Cornelissen et al., 2011; Deetz et al., 2000; Fairhurst, 2005). For example, framing a situation as either 'a problem' or 'an opportunity' can greatly influence how people perceive and deal with the situation.

Another area of research based on poststructuralist linguistic perspectives is that relating to the D/discursive struggles that occur with society and organisations (e.g. Leclercq-Vandelannoitte, 2011). For example, Laine and Vaara examined how corporate managers in an engineering and consulting organisation use a particular Discourse around strategy (for example around 'value-added services' and 'shareholder value') to control employees' views and actions. However, middle managers and project managers resisted this Discourse by using their own form of entrepreneurial discourse such as 'strategic control from the unit' (as opposed to top management) and situated themselves as 'progressive strategic entrepreneurs', which challenged the authority and control of top management (2007: 45).

Finally, a number of researchers working within the linguistic turn explore how people construct their identities within everyday interactions and conversations (e.g. Brown and Lewis, 2011). A significant difference between studying identity from a social constructionist paradigm or from a structural-functionalist paradigm is that the former focuses on how people shape their sense of who they are and what they do in their interactions, while the latter develops generalised categories of roles and identities. Tony Watson (2009) argues from a social constructionist perspective that we need to study identity from the perspective of the whole person – that our organisational identities are just one part of who we are. This means considering how identities emerge and are shaped across time and space as we draw on both social and personal narratives of identity. For example, we find social narratives of what it means to be a manager in books, the media and education, and connect these with what we want to be like as a person. In doing so, we actively shape our identity by weaving together narratives – accounts of events and experiences organised into a sequence – into a life story.

The practice turn

The practice turn also draws on the work of a range of philosophers, including Bourdieu (1977), Foucault (1977), Garfinkel (1967), Giddens (1984) and Heidegger (1962), to contend that practices are 'embodied, materially mediated arrays of human activity centrally organised around shared practical understanding' (Schatzki, 2001: 2). As with the linguistic turn, practice theorists work in a number of disciplines across the social sciences, science and technology. Within organisation studies, practice scholars study a variety of topics, including strategy (Jarzabkowski, 2005; Vaara and Whittington, 2012), work practices (e.g. Nicolini, 2011), technology (Orlikowski, 2007), organising (Feldman and Pentland, 2003), aesthetics (Strati, 1999) and knowledge and learning (Gherardi, 2009b). Consequently, approaches to practice differ, ranging from socio-material practices and discursive practices to embedded interactions.

Several common characteristics of practices are shared within the range of practice studies.

- Practices are situated in everyday social actions and contexts, yet are different from action. Gherardi (2009a: 115) highlights the distinction between theories of action and theories of practice: the former assume that action is the result of human intentions, while the latter view practice as happening in a network of connections.
- Practices are concerned with producing and reproducing social order and organising. How this occurs is an important focus of study. In other words, practice studies identify not just what the practices are but also why they occur, what gives them legitimacy and why they may need to be changed (Geiger, 2009).
- Practices are integrative – about how work, actors, knowledge, tools, methods, etc. come together in the enactment of a practice.

Kaplan (2011), for example, studies how actors mobilise PowerPoint and related documents in their discursive practices in the enactment of strategy making. Practice theorists often assume that knowing and practising are inseparable in the sense that knowing constitutes and is constituted in practice – and vice versa (e.g. Gherardi, 2009b). Gherardi argues that rather than talking about communities of practice, where priority is often given to a pre-existing community possessing knowledge, we should study the knowing-in-practice that constitutes and is created within communities – i.e. practices of communities.

- Practices are fluid and continually created rather than fixed, and therefore practice theorists use active verbs such as organising, ordering and coordinating as opposed to nouns such as organisation or order. Jarzabkowski et al. (2012) argue that coordinating is a social accomplishment, and frame coordinating mechanisms as a dynamic social practice. They examine how actors' performances enact coordinating during an organisation's restructuring.
- Practices are recursive and interconnected at different levels in and across time and space. In his study of telemedicine in Italy, Nicolini argues that practices become durable as local individual practices become part of larger social and structural practices, which are then reproduced back at local levels. In other words, a specific practice is always immersed in a 'texture of relationships that connects it to other practices' (2011: 605). A number of practice scholars take a structuration approach to study how structural conditions and practical actions enable and constrain each other.

The aim of practice scholars is to shed light not just on practices but also on subjectivity, language and power. Feldman and Orlikowski (2011) argue that a practice lens covers:

1. empirical work that focuses on the practical activities, the routines and improvisations of people (e.g. Feldman and Pentland, 2003);
2. theoretical work that focuses on how practices are produced and changed (e.g. Simpson, 2009); and
3. a philosophical approach that addresses the ontology and epistemology of practice and how this can be used to resituate the phenomenon being studied.

For example, Sandberg and Tsoukas (2011) argue that we need to find better ways of studying how actors enact their practice, and propose a form of 'practical rationality' (as opposed to the abstraction of scientific rationality) that focuses on identifying relationships between practices and exploring the significance of temporary breakdowns in practices.

Practice theories differ significantly from the structuralist way of thinking. A classic approach is to seek to understand organisational phenomena by analysing in 'levels' – typically the individual, the group and the organisation. Explanations of behaviour are formed by analysing the motivations and abilities of individuals and their interactions in – and the dynamics of – groups and organisational forces, which enable and constrain particular behaviours. Practice theories do not see practices as being simply the behaviour of individuals. Rather, practices are collections of activities that have patterns over time and do not simply rely on individuals.

The shape and nature of a practice also relies on the available material, the historical context and significant identities. For example, a musician who was interviewed as part of the project that has led to this book explained her approach to songwriting and musical arrangement for touring. Her band played a contemporary folk style, which is now very popular, commanding big audiences and top billing at festivals. However, at an earlier career stage there was a real question of how to finance a tour. If she wrote song arrangements that would require a double bass and full acoustic drum kit, it would mean that the band had to tour in a van. This would put the costs up considerably when one considers fuel costs, ferry prices to move between countries and accommodation costs and fees for a larger band. Alternatively, arranging songs to be played by a three-piece band on fiddle, guitar/banjo and accordion meant that the whole band could fit into an estate car and hence tour much less expensively. This had the consequence that the band could play in smaller venues, and thus sell fewer tickets but still cover the costs and even make a small profit. Asked whether this meant a compromise on creativity and the nature of composition, the musician was quite clear that it helped creativity. Working out how to produce a percussive sound on non-percussive instruments, filling out the sound with more complicated vocal harmonies and emphasising variety and 'colours' of the instruments led to an exciting and distinctive style of playing.

Hence, in this form of practice, both organising and musical elements are intertwined. Commercial considerations interact with creative ones. The musicians have some open decisions, but others are constrained by socio-material reality. Nevertheless, the direction of causation is not simple or singular. The musicians have intentions that they seek to enact, but they do so within constraining factors of their socio-historical context – for example, audience sizes and normal ticket spends in the folk market. However, by practising in the way they do, they also have an impact on the nature of the market, and the very practices of producing and performing folk music. They are enacting identities of folk musicians, but also identities of commercial musicians who have careers and make a living from the music.

Thus, a practice focus enables us to seek to understand the complex web of interactions in which people and their circumstances mutually constitute each other. Of particular significance in this 'turn' is the question of how people learn and how practices can transfer from one setting to another – often changing and adapting as they do so. This latter question is pertinent to this book as we open up experiences in different settings so that the reader can participate in picking up ideas of practice and considering what might be learned from them for new practices in the future and application in other contexts.

Conclusions

The traditional structures of organisation in music and the creative industries more generally are breaking down (Bilton and Cummings, 2010) with wide-ranging consequences for performers. In the past, organisations such as orchestras may have seen their players essentially as fulfilling a well-defined role (such as orchestra leader), and valued the individual for their ability to meet the requirements of this role. Now, however, we can perceive a shift away from this essentially generic view of the person-as-role towards a greater emphasis on the unique cocktail of skills, attitudes and perspectives that each person brings.

Small chamber ensembles may always have been about individuals, but we can now see a shift in the balance for larger ensembles, and speculate about how this trend could influence even the largest of artist groupings in the future. Ensembles like RedNote are essentially focused around an artistic director and chief executive, with a pool of musicians who are drawn on according to the unique demands of the repertoire for a specific set of performances. Some of these are 'regulars', employed frequently; others will join the ensemble only rarely, when they are needed to fulfil highly specialised requirements. The ensemble becomes a group of performers rather than a collection of instruments: 'we need a bass flautist' becomes 'we need [name]'. The move is, therefore, away from the musical ensemble as a collection of role-oriented practitioners towards one in which individuals cluster around one-off artistic projects on the basis of what they, uniquely, can bring to the project – a network of practitioners focused on the needs of a specific project. This pattern is replicated in many genres such as folk and jazz, where one also sees leadership of projects by musicians as well as/instead of by managers, or those traditionally associated with organisational roles.

This change is a part of the shift in music towards the 'portfolio career' (Townley et al., 2009) in which the musician balances a number of roles and specialisms, and the significance of this evolution is evidenced in the way today's student musicians prepare themselves for a career in music. Increasingly, students seek out distinctive performance specialisms and, alongside their deep immersion in that specialism, develop parallel skills in complementary areas such as community music or promotion. Thus – perhaps paradoxically – tomorrow's musicians may be at once more specialised *and* have a wider skill base.

Shifting patterns in audiences, venues, instruments and the possibilities afforded by technology, composition and the nature of organising mean that understanding how 'the music industry' works is itself a polyphonic and dispersed task. Audiences are far from single identity groups, attached to particular venues, artists or genres. Rather, they are composed of people with quite diverse reasons for attending a performance, so that dedicated fans may sit alongside people who are simply on a night out. Musicians are self-organising and being organised in increasingly flexible ways as they pursue portfolios of activities. They may operate in a generic role as a freelancer in orchestras at the same time as leading their own projects. This may entail considerable adaptability in skills. For example, freelancing in the woodwind section of a small orchestra/band in musical theatre may require the player to be able to play several instruments, while running their own project may require them to be able to organise other players, agree contracts and devise marketing ideas.

Chia (1999) argued against the reification of 'organisation' in favour of a processual perspective on the practices of 'organising'. Fineman et al. (2010) conceptualise organising as a meaning-making process entailing embodiment, emotion, performance and identity formation. It is both a personal and a social process, as people interact with each other during their working lives, bringing with them their personal histories, anxieties and hopes for the future, all of which have an impact on what the work task in hand means for the person. We see this perspective, exemplified through the linguistic and practice turns, as being particularly fruitful for engaging with the complexity of music-making. Adopting this perspective means that the supposed opposition between art and commerce or, in our case, music and organising, is not as stark as might be imagined. The skills of organising require improvisation, not being constrained by the 'script' of a traditional role, and engaging with others in shared meaning-making. Being creative entails discipline, practice and repetition. In short, there is a basis for dialogue on the grounds of both similarities and differences between organising and music-making. We would concur with Becker et al., who argued that what is needed is the co-creation of a new conversation: one in which we avoid the old debates merely for their own sake, take risks (and hence trust others) and 'prepare for a journey into the new' (2003: 187).

Structure of the book

The rest of the book is divided into two main parts and a concluding chapter. Part I, 'Orienting ideas: perspectives from organisation theory', is a set of concise chapters that introduce key ideas from current theories, which might be of help in thinking about, and acting in, music-making. The chapters are not producing a historical overview but are rather drawing upon current thinking and seeking to make it accessible to readers from other fields. They include 'application questions', which can help with analysing empirical situations, and short illustrations of how this might be achieved. Part I is split into three sections. The first, 'Organisation and organising', emphasises social construction, practice, identity, change and creativity. The second, 'Markets and engagement between production and consumption', explores how markets may be constructed, the multiple roles of producers and consumers and the significance of networks and connections. The third section, 'Organising in complex environments', explores the break-down of traditional boundaries, complex interactions across networks and fluidity in time, role and action as actors negotiate new socio-economic realities.

Part II is entitled 'Tales of experience: organising and performing'. In this section, people working in music lay out an experience or event that has been important in the development of their practice. The stories come from diverse settings and are deliberately experiential in nature – i.e. they are stories told 'from the inside'. Therefore, they are not necessarily detached or objective: they do come from a particular stance and so are rather different from many case studies. What they provide is an insight into the immediacy of practice, the interconnectedness of different aspects of practice and meaning-making and an engagement with the emotion, embodiment and context-specificity of practice. The stories include 'key lessons' and 'discussion questions', which draw out the themes discussed and offer opportunities for further consideration. Part II is divided into two sections. The first, 'Organising playing', starts from the perspective of organising, firstly of festivals, and then proceeds to consider managing bands, organising and promoting orchestras, and lastly more diverse forms of organisation: around a university town, in a large city and the establishment of a recording label. The second section, 'Playing and organising', starts from the perspective of performance. Here performers talk through some notable experiences of playing and the implications for how things are managed. The section starts with traditional music and then moves on to indie and rock before closing with examples from the orchestral world.

The final chapter, 'Next steps in the dialogue: insights for practising and theorising', takes an inductive approach, drawing together themes that occur through the empirical chapters and posing the question: What might we learn more generally from these examples? The intention is not to produce a unifying theory: this would be inconsistent with the constructionist approach adopted here and would fail to acknowledge the diversity of the experiences and settings incorporated in the tales from the field. Therefore, we are not seeking 'one best way' or a traditional 'best practices' approach. Rather, we are interested in 'promising practices' (Delbridge et al., 2007), which are conceived as stimulation for learning rather than overly directive prescriptions. Promising practices are those providing examples that can be adapted, selected from and reinvented in new situations. Hence, in line with the dialogical approach, the themes emerging are intended to be generative of new ways of doing things rather than a source for imitation.

References

Alvesson, M. and Kärreman, D. (2000) Varieties of discourse: on the study of organizations through discourse analysis. *Human Relations*, 53(9): 1125–49.

Alvesson, M. and Kärreman, D. (2011) Decolonizing discourse: critical reflections on organizational discourse analysis. *Human Relations*, 64(9): 1121–46.

Barge, J.K. and Fairhurst, G.T. (2008) Living leadership: a systemic constructionist approach. *Leadership*, 4: 227–51.

Becker, C., Chasin, L., Chasin, R., Herzig, M. and Roth, S. (2003) From stuck debate to new conversation. In Gergen, M. and Gergen, K.J. (eds) *Social construction: a reader*, pp. 143–63. London: Sage.

Beech, N. (2011) Liminality and the practices of identity reconstruction. *Human Relations*, 64(2): 285–302.

Beech, N., MacIntosh, R. and MacLean, D. (2010) Dialogues between academics and practitioners: the role of generative dialogic encounters. *Organization Studies*, 31(9): 1341–67.

Bilton, C. and Cummings, S. (2010) *Creative strategy: reconnecting business and innovation*. London: Wiley.

Bilton, C. and Cummings, S. (2014) *Handbook of management and creativity*. Cheltenham: Edward Elgar.

Bohm, D. (1996) *On dialogue*. New York: Routledge.

Bourdieu, P. (1977) *Outline of a theory of practice*. Cambridge University Press.

Bourdieu, P. (1984) *Distinction: a social critique of the judgement of taste*, translated by Nice, R. Cambridge, MA: Harvard University Press.

Brown, A.D. and Lewis, M.A. (2011) Identities, discipline and routines. *Organization Studies*, 32(7): 871–95.

Burrell, G. and Morgan, G. (1979) *Sociological paradigms and organizational analysis*. London: Heinemann.

Caves, R.E. (2000) *Creative industries*. Cambridge, MA: Harvard University Press.

Chia, R. (1999) A rhizomic model of organizational change and transformation: perspective from a metaphysics of change. *British Journal of Management*, 10: 209–27.

Cloonan, M. (2011) Researching live music: some thoughts on policy implications. *International Journal of Cultural Policy*, 17(4): 405–20.

Cornelissen, J., Holt, R. and Zundel, M. (2011) The role of analogy and metaphor in the framing and legitimization of strategic change. *Organization Studies*, 32(12): 1701–16.

Cunliffe, A. (2008) Orientations to social constructionism: relationally-responsive social constructionism and its implications for knowledge and learning. *Management Learning*, 39: 123–39.

Cunliffe, A. (2011) Crafting qualitative research: Morgan and Smircich 30 years on. *Organizational Research Methods*, 14: 647–73.

Deetz, S. (2003) Reclaiming the legacy of the linguistic turn. *Organization*, 10(3): 421–9.

Deetz, S.A., Tracy, S.J. and Simpson, J.L. (2000) *Leading organizations through transition*. Thousand Oaks, CA: Sage.

Delbridge, R., Gratton, L., Johnson, G. and the AIM Fellows (2007) *The exceptional manager*. Oxford University Press.

Derrida, J. (1978) *Writing and difference*. London: Routledge and Kegan Paul.

Fairhurst, G.T. (2005) Reframing the art of framing: problems and prospects for leadership. *Leadership*, 1: 165–85

Feldman, M.S. and Orlikowski, W. (2011) Theorizing practice and practicing theory. *Organization Science*, 22(5): 1240–53.

Feldman, M.S. and Pentland, B.T. (2003) Reconceptualizing organizational routines as a source of flexibility and change. *Administrative Science Quarterly*, 49(1): 94–118.

Fineman, S., Gabriel, Y. and Sims, D. (2010) *Organizing and organizations*. London: Sage.

Foucault, M. (1972) *The archaeology of knowledge and the discourse on language*, translated by Sheridan Smith, A.M. New York: Pantheon Books.

Foucault, M. (1977) *Discipline and punish: the birth of the prison*, translated by Sheridan, A. London: Penguin.

Frith, S., Brennan, M., Cloonan, M. and Webster, E. (2011) *The history of live music in Britain, Volume I: 1950–1967: from dance hall to the 100 Club*. Farnham: Ashgate.

Frith, S., Cloonan, M. and Williamson, J. (2009) On music as a creative industry. In Pratt, A. and Jeffcutt, P. (eds) *Creativity, innovation and the cultural economy*, pp. 74–89. London: Routledge.

Frootsmag (1987) Minutes of meeting between the various 'world music' record companies and interested parties, Monday 29th June 1987, available at: www.frootsmag.com/content/features/world_music_history/minutes/.

Garfinkel, H. (1967) *Studies in ethnomethodology*. Englewood Cliffs, NJ: Prentice-Hall.

Geiger, D. (2009) Revisiting the concept of practice: toward an argumentative understanding of practicing. *Management Learning*, 40(2): 129–44.

Gergen, K.J., McNamee, S. and Barrett, F. (2001) Toward transformative dialogue. *International Journal of Public Administration*, 24: 697–707.

Gherardi, S. (2009a) The critical power of the 'practice lens'. *Management Learning*, 40(2): 115–28.

Gherardi, S. (2009b) Communities of practice or practices of a community? In Armstrong, S. and Fukami, C. (eds) *Handbook of management learning, education and development*, pp. 514–30. London: Sage.

Giddens, A. (1984) *The constitution of society*. Cambridge: Polity Press.

Gonzalez, L. (2010) Juicy Salif as cultish totem. In Townley, B. and Beech, N. (eds) *Managing creativity: exploring the paradox*, pp. 287–309. Cambridge University Press.

Grant, D., Keenoy, T. and Oswick, C. (1998) Organizational discourse: of diversity, dichotomy and multidisciplinarity. In Grant, D., Keenoy, T. and Oswick, C. (eds) *Discourse and organization*, pp. 1–13. London: Sage.

Gulledge, E. and Townley, B. (2010) What is a creative field? In Townley, B. and Beech, N. (eds) *Managing creativity: exploring the paradox*, pp. 321–35. Cambridge University Press.

Hassard, J. (1991) Multiple paradigms and organizational analysis: a case study. *Organization Studies*, 12(2): 275–99.

Heidegger, M. (1962) *Being and time*. Oxford: Blackwell

Hesmondhalgh, D. (2007) *The cultural industries*. London: Sage.

Hibbert, P. and Huxham, C. (2011) The carriage of tradition: knowledge and its past in network contexts. *Management Learning*, 42(1): 7–24.

Jackson, N. and Carter, P. (1991) In defence of paradigm incommensurability. *Organization Studies*, 12(1): 109–27.

Jarzabkowski, P.A. (2005) *Strategy as practice*. London: Sage.

Jarzabkowski, P.A., Lê, J.K. and Feldman, M.S. (2012) Toward a theory of coordinating: creating coordinating mechanisms in practice. *Organization Science*, 23(4) 907–27.

Kaplan, S. (2011) Strategy and PowerPoint: an inquiry into the epistemic culture and machinery of strategy making. *Organization Science*, 22(2): 320–46.

Laine, P. and Vaara, E. (2007) Struggling over subjectivity: a discursive analysis of strategic development in an engineering group. *Human Relations*, 60(1): 29–48.

Leclercq-Vandelannoitte, A. (2011) Organizations as discursive constructions: a Foucauldian approach. *Organization Studies*, 32(9): 1247–71.

MacDonald, R.R., Hargreaves, D.J. and Miell, D. (eds) (2002) *Musical identities*. Oxford University Press.

McLeod, C., O'Donohoe, S. and Townley, B. (2009) The elephant in the room: class and careers in British advertising agencies. *Human Relations*, 62(7): 1011–39.

Nicolini, D. (2011) Insights from the field of telemedicine. *Organization Science*, 22(3): 602–20.

Orlikowski, W.J. (2007) Sociomaterial practices: exploring technology at work. *Organization Studies*, 28(9): 1435–48.

Parker, M. and McHugh, G. (1991) Five texts in search of an author: a response to John Hassard's 'Multiple paradigms and organizational analysis'. *Organization Studies*, 12(3): 451–7.

Pfeffer, J. (1993) Barriers to the advance of organizational science: paradigm development as a dependent variable. *Academy of Management Review*, 18(4): 599–620.

Pfeffer, J. (1995) Mortality, reproducibility, and the persistence of styles of theory. *Organization Science*, 6(6): 680–6.

Pratt, A. and Jeffcutt, P. (2009) *Creativity, innovation and the cultural economy*. London: Routledge.

Rorty, R. (ed) (1967) *The linguistic turn: recent essays in philosophical method*. University of Chicago Press.

Samra-Fredericks, D. (2003) Strategizing as lived experience and strategists' everyday efforts to shape strategic direction. *Journal of Management Studies*, 40: 141–74.

Sandberg, J. and Tsoukas, H. (2011) Grasping the logic of practice: theorizing through practical rationality. *Academy of Management Review*, 36(2): 338–60.

Schatzki, T.R. (2001) Practice theory. In Schatzki, T.R., Knorr Cetina, K. and von Savigny, E. (eds) *The practice turn in contemporary theory*, pp. 1–14. London: Routledge.

Shotter, J. (2010) *Social construction on the edge*. Chagrin Falls, OH: Taos Institute Publications.

Simpson, B. (2009) Pragmatism, Mead and the practice turn. *Organization Studies*, 30(12): 1329–47.

Sims, D. (2003) Between the millstones: a narrative account of the vulnerability of middle managers' storying. *Human Relations*, 56(10): 1195–211.

Small, C. (1988) *Musicking: the meanings of performing and listening*. Middletown, CT: Wesleyan University Press.

Strati, A. (1999) *Organization and aesthetics*. London: Sage.

Townley, B., Beech, N. and McKinlay, A. (2009) Managing in the creative industries: managing the motley crew. *Human Relations*, 62(7): 939–62.

Vaara, E. and Whittington, R. (2012) Strategy-as-practice: taking social practices seriously. *Academy of Management Annals*, 6(1): 285–336.

Van Maanen, J. (1995a) Style as theory. *Organization Science*, 6(1): 133–43.

Van Maanen, J. (1995b) Fear and loathing in organization studies. *Organization Science*, 6(6): 687–92.

Watson, T.J. (2009) Narrative, life story and manager identity: a case study in autobiographical identity work. *Human Relations*, 62(3): 425–52.

Weick, K. (1999) Theory construction as disciplined reflexivity: tradeoffs in the 90s. *Academy of Management Review*, 24(4): 797–806.

Widdop, P. and Cutts, D. (2011) *Cultural consumption in Scotland: analysis of the Scottish Household Survey culture module*. Edinburgh: Scottish Government Social Research.

Wittgenstein, L. (1951) *Philosophical investigations*. Oxford: Blackwell.

Ybema, S., Keenoy, T., Oswick, C., Beverungen, A., Ellis, N. and Sabelis, I. (2009) Articulating identities. *Human Relations*, 63(3): 299–322.

Part I

Orienting ideas: perspectives from
organisation theory

Organisation and organising

2   Music and the aesthetic study of organisational life

Antonio Strati

When I think about music, my ears resound with celebrated motifs and profound revolutions in musical language, which I am unable entirely to detach from seeing them played – as well as hearing them. People, musical instruments, customs, stage sets, side streets and small squares alternate in playing music with corner shops and shopping centres, buses and cars, the virtual worlds of the internet, television channels, my hi-fi system at home and the smartphone with which I listen to concerts broadcast by radio as I go snowshoeing alone in the Dolomites. What is music for me, therefore, if not a phenomenon that is both aesthetic and organisational at the same time?

This awareness is the basis of the theoretical and methodological assumptions of this chapter. It is likewise – I hasten to point out – adopted in a large number of the studies and research that sociologists and social scientists have conducted on the theme of music, even if the notion of organisation may be not explicitly mentioned. For instance, Robert Faulkner and Howard Becker conclude from their research study:

> The question that we have, finally, answered is not the one we started with, but the one we learned was the right one to ask as we went on with our work: How do players combine partial knowledge to create a collective activity that is good enough for the variety of people involved in the event? (2009: 184)

Other scholars, such as Tia DeNora (2000) and Helmut Staubmann (2013), also pay attention to the wide variety of performances involved in the making of music. This is something that renders music enjoyable beyond hearing – that is, also for sight, touch, smell and, as Antoine Hennion points out, taste:

> To accentuate listening is to reintroduce into taste the act of tasting: the irreducible heterogeneity of a real event, not only the masterpiece and the listener, or a wine and a drinker, but of bodies, of devices and dispositions, of duration, an ungraspable object, an instant that passes, states that emerge. After all, outside of laboratories and schools, what else is music? (2007: 106)

Organisation scholars (Barrett, 2007; Koivunen, 2008; Meisiek and Hatch, 2008; Montuori, 2007; Sutherland, 2013), on the other hand, pay closer attention to the organisational character of the various performances involved in a musical event. The occasions when music conductors, as well as jazz musicians, cooperate with managers have become remarkable in the past two decades. In these contexts of cooperation between art and management, musicians 'introduce managers to musical concepts of rhythm, harmony, and melody to improve leadership, teamwork, management processes and even organizational design' (Meisiek and Hatch, 2008: 412). Thus emerges the dialogical relationship between music and organisational life that – I intend to argue in this chapter – however ethereal and impalpable music may be, is always a material as well as a mental one.

Organising aesthetics and social practices in music

Music is a source of pleasure or repulsion, shivers of emotion or agonies of boredom, intellectual passion or cognitive indifference. It is an expression of talent or, conversely, painful ineptitude. It stimulates aesthetic feelings and aesthetic judgements, passions, emotions, intellectual fascination and cognitive appreciation. Music is grasped by studying the social and organisational practices of its creation, performance and communication, as well as its enjoyment. These are all musical practices, even if they differ greatly from each other and must be investigated in light of their diversity. Interweaving and merging with these practices are those of the social research that studies them (Gherardi and Strati, 2012; Nicolini et al., 2003), and in particular those of aesthetic organisational research. An important question, on which I shall dwell below, is whether examination of the artistic world of music (Fubini, 1995) and musical practices has influenced the theory and method of the aesthetic study of organisational life.

I shall start, however, with the principal argument of this chapter: that the aesthetic approach to the study of organisations (Strati, 1999) gives salience to the *pathos* of music in its materiality, constituted by sounds, bodies, and non-human elements – for instance, acoustic or electronic musical instruments, the settings in which music is played and listened to, or music distribution technologies. This approach is one of the research styles adopted within the strand of organisation studies that examines the aesthetic dimension of organisations. In fact, four approaches have emerged in aesthetic organisational research – the archaeological approach, the empathic-logical approach, the aesthetic approach and the artistic approach – each of which has its own area of inquiry and research methodology (Table 1).

Table 1. *The four approaches of aesthetic organisational research*

Research approach	Researcher's style	Emphasis on	Strengths	Weaknesses
Archaeological	Guise of an archaeologist and/or a historian of art using qualitative research design and methods	The symbolism of art and aesthetics in organizational life	The aesthetic side of organizational cultures and of the symbolic management of organizations	Aesthetics are ancillary to symbolism
Empathic–logical	Empathic immersion followed by empathic and logical interpretation, and by a logical-analytical illustration of the outcomes	The *pathos* of organizational artefacts	Precognitive knowledge of organizations and the organizational control based on the *pathos* of artifacts	Aesthetics are translated into logical-analytical descriptions
Aesthetic	Empathic understanding, imaginary participant observation, aesthetic judgement, evocative process of knowing, 'open text' for communicating the outcomes	The collective everyday negotiation of organizational aesthetics	The materiality of quotidian organizational life and also of the researcher's interactions with both organizational actors and organizational scholars	Aesthetics are grounded on connoisseurship
Artistic	Hybridization of artistic creative energy and ratiocinative capacity	The creativity and playfulness of organizational interactions	The artistic performance in managing organization processes	Aesthetics are 'art-bounded'

Source: Strati (2012: 201).

The table presents these four approaches according to the chronological order in which they first arose and became established. It provides an overview of the theoretical-methodological controversies that have distinguished the approaches, their epistemological assumptions and their contributions to theory and knowledge about organisational life. The archaeological, empathic-logical and aesthetic approaches developed during the second half of the 1980s and became established during the 1990s. The artistic approach developed during the 1990s and became established at the beginning of this century.

The first three approaches originated in the symbolic study of organisations, which treats organisations as social cultures for which art and aesthetics are significant because they constitute the organisational *pathos*. The aesthetics of a workplace or an organisational song, for example, can suggest lines of inquiry to garner insights into the characteristics of the organisational culture under scrutiny. One may investigate whether those aesthetics express the values that distinguish the dominant organisational identity or whether they instead signal conflicts among organisational cultures as they negotiate power relations.

The distinctive feature of the four approaches is that they represent an entirely new and autonomous intellectual pathway within organisation studies. The 1980s and 1990s were years in which organisation theories underwent profound renewal. New strands of organisation study arose, while neglected or abandoned research topics were rediscovered. Moreover, exploration resumed of methods and epistemologies of organisational research marginalised by the dominance of the rationalist and positivist paradigm. The culturalist or linguistic turn that affected the social sciences in general also involved organisation theories. It was in this context of theoretical and methodological debate that the aesthetic study of organisations assumed a configuration autonomous from that of the organisational symbolism approach from which it had originated.

The empathic-logical approach (Gagliardi, 2006) did so by emphasising the *pathos* of the artefacts that constitute the symbolic landscapes of organisations, which exercise a form of organisational control at a precognitive level. The aesthetic approach (Strati, 1999) did so by showing the materiality of organisational life and the negotiation of organisational aesthetics as evidenced by micro practices in organisations. The archaeological approach (Berg and Kreiner, 1990) instead remained within the thematic and methodological mainstream of the symbolic study of organisations: it drew on aesthetics in order to interpret the symbolic construction of organisational life. As for the artistic approach (Guillet de Monthoux, 2004), it acquired complete form in a period distant from the culturalist and linguistic turn, though still extending its roots into the latter. The artistic approach has a number of novelties with respect to the aesthetic study of organisations because it concentrates on phenomena to do with art, and is used by artists who theorise artistic practices as legitimate ways to research organisation. The focus is on the relationship between art and management, and on how art can inspire the organising of organisational life.

I shall dwell on the last two approaches – the aesthetic and the artistic – in order to explore two crucial aspects of the relationship between music and aesthetic organisational research: materiality and performance. Discussion of these, in fact, highlights the influence exerted by the study of music on the theoretical and methodological issues debated in aesthetic organisational research.

Can you hear how it sings?

Materiality evidences the continuous expert and socially constructed activation of the perceptive faculties, as well as the sensitive-aesthetic judgement of individuals and their capacity to grasp the *pathos* of corpo-realities that are very different in character, like those of individuals and those of non-human elements. This emerges with particular clarity when one observes social and collective negotiations on organisational aesthetics – such as those ensuring that, in a given organisational context of music production, beautiful music is composed with a certain style. There thus emerge differences of aesthetic feeling at both individual and collective levels, which have developed aesthetic sensibilities distinguishing them from other groups of musicians. To be sure, these are socially constructed and culturally refined aesthetic feelings, which are based on sensory perception and on sensitive judgement – in short, on the corpo-reality of sensible knowledge. Hence, one musical composition is perceived as sublime, another as elegant and graceful, while yet another grates on the ears. Or an organisational song is so pleasant that it lingers in the mind and is hummed outside the workplace. The negotiation of their aesthetic qualities comes about subtly on the basis of not only poetic but also professional and analytical language. An example drawn from everyday life, rather than from organisational research, may give an idea of the importance of the negotiation of organisational aesthetics.

I had taken my car to a mechanic. After tinkering with the engine, he called me over and said: 'Can you hear how your Alfa Romeo's engine sings?' The mechanic's tone of voice revealed his pleasure and his desire to communicate joy, not just satisfaction that the engine was working as perfectly as he could determine before the electronic tests were performed. Put otherwise, the mechanic did not furnish me with mere information; he communicated to me an aesthetic sensation and an expert knowledge founded upon that sensation. At the same time, he began a process of negotiation on the aesthetics of his work.

All this occurred in an instant. After the mechanic had called me over and said 'the engine sings', he turned and gazed at me, as if to invite me to look and listen. I was pleased to know that the engine was working well. I almost felt proud of my Alfa Romeo. The noise emitted by the motor was clear and clean – that of a smoothly operating machine. But I was not entirely sure that I could hear it 'singing'. This is something that I shall have to train myself to hear, I thought. I also thought that in the meantime, in that situation, I had become involved in negotiation on the aesthetics of work in that organisation initiated by the mechanic's poetic language and driven by the enthusiastic tone with which he communicated it to me. What is certain is that we were both listening to the same thing, but we were not both attuned to experiencing the same aesthetic understanding, sentiment and judgement.

Hearing is a supra-individualistic thing

It was the German sociologist Georg Simmel (2009: 555) who first pointed out that hearing has the peculiar characteristic of being a supra-individualistic sense, because what happens in a shared space – for instance, an office with an open-space layout – can be perceived by all those who work in it or are present in it at a particular time. This is interesting for various reasons. The first is that we cannot prevent ourselves from hearing – or at least not easily and not always (Strati, 1999: 1–3). How, for example, can we protect ourselves against the music playing in the clothes shop we have entered, or in the mountain restaurant where we have stopped to eat? How can we do so against the ringtones of mobile phones on the train? Of course, we can follow the principle of music-trumps-music and overwhelm the unpleasant music with music of our own liking. But generally, as long as we are in that shop or restaurant or on the train, we are forced to hear the music being played.

The second reason is that, as Simmel (2009: 575) also observes, the fact that someone perceives a sound or a noise does not remove that sound or that noise from others. In this respect, in fact, hearing is in a sense anything but selfish, because when perceiving we do not appropriate something and do not prevent others from using it. On the other hand, hearing is a selfish sense because it takes without giving, and there is no reciprocity – contrary to the case of the eye, for example, which as it sees can be seen in its turn.

Third, hearing is able to create a communal social relationship whereby those involved feel that they share the same state of mind. One may compare a museum audience with a concert audience; for the determination of the hearing impression to communicate itself uniformly and in the same way to a crowd of people – a determination by no means simply external-quantitative but bound up deeply with its innermost nature – sociologically brings together a concert audience in an incomparably closer union and collective feeling than occurs with visitors to a museum (Simmel, 2009: 576).

Finally, although what we hear are momentary flows of sounds, we are able to retain them in memory with a remarkable capacity when compared with that of the other sense organs. Indeed, the most recent research in perceptual psychology and the neurosciences reports that hearing is extremely attentive to detail (Rosenblum, 2010) because we are often able to perceive both what has caused a sound and the actions that concern it without directly witnessing the event. Consider, for example, when we hear something fall in the next office: we imagine that some sheets of paper have been blown off the table by the wind, or that a cup has been knocked over; we imagine, that is, the form of the artefacts involved even before we have seen them. It is the loudness of the noise, its intelligibility, its reverberation, its sharp or muffled sound and its proximity that direct us to one hypothesis or another. We thus resort to some of the classic categories employed by experts on architectural acoustics, who are of great importance for environments devoted to producing and listening to music. These experts use instruments to measure intensity, reverberation and the other categories used to define sounds. But they also use their sense of hearing as it has been trained and refined through work, as well as all their other senses – from touch to sight – and the conscious bodily sensations that are 'more dependent on more internal bodily senses such as proprioception or kinaesthetic feelings' (Shustermann, 2008: 53).

I now leave discussion of the aspects of materiality to which the aesthetic approach gives particular salience and turn to the other theme of principal importance for the aesthetic understanding of organisational life in the world of music – that of performance, which the artistic approach conveys well.

Aesthetically managing the flow of diversified performances

The main focus of inquiry by the artistic approach to the study of organisations, in fact, is not so much the artistic product in itself as the complex set of different performances enacted during its realisation. Consider the production of operas by Richard Wagner. Works like *Parsifal*, *Tristan and Isolde* or *Ring of the Nibelung* are examined as parts of a myriad of performances that show the existence of a sort of factory – an art firm. Wagner created and ran 'one of the most influential art firms of modern times', comments Pierre Guillet de Monthoux (2004: 64). He was able to gather the funds necessary for his artistic enterprise in Bayreuth and to grasp the opportunities offered by the transformation of the art market as it increasingly catered to mass consumption and popular culture.

In an arrangement managed by theatrical agents, successful Parisian plays were packaged and sold to the provinces. Like today's franchised musicals, the deal included text, music, costume sketches and set designs. In an effort to educate the middle class to become good theatrical consumers, toy shops merchandised the shows by featuring model theatres with accompanying scripts, settings and paper dolls. As a result, provincial families making up the market for touring shows were well prepared for visits from these theatrical companies (Guillet de Monthoux, 2004: 113).

One witnesses, that is to say, a flow of different activities – or, better, diversified performances – the study of which shows how outright forms of aesthetic management are configured. These show, first of all, that music as art work is subject to constant change. A passage composed to be played on the organ can be transcribed to be played on the piano, for instance. Or it can be arranged to be performed by a rock group. These different performances also show that art firms have a multitude of desires, initiatives and users to deal with, and manage creatively by combining different social worlds – music, finance, the media and culture.

Returning to Wagner and his creative capacities as an aesthetic manager, the words of Friedrich Nietzsche – his longstanding friend – are of particular relevance to the theme of style with which I close this section. Nietzsche wrote that 'Wagner's poetic ability is shown by his thinking in visible and actual facts and not in ideas; that is to say, he thinks mythically' (1910: 172). One thus grasps Wagner's style of the musical art in his aesthetic management of his art firm. But what is meant by 'style'?

In this regard, I am persuaded by what Umberto Eco has written on the aesthetic theory of the Italian existentialist philosopher Luigi Pareyson. Towards the middle of the last century, Pareyson declared that 'art is pure formativity' (1996: 23) and that the artistic act is a particular process consisting of invention and production undertaken to give form; that is, to pursue form for its own sake. Human experience in its entirety is distinguished by 'aestheticity' and 'artisticity': it is the art of doing by giving form that constitutes a specific dimension of work experience.

Eco observes that if we take, for instance, the work of the French architect Le Corbusier, we find the entire range of the formative process, but also pure formativity. Le Corbusier either constructed housing units to deal with problems of urban planning or he constructed rooms according to a mathematical and organic model because he was driven by a moral, economic and political vision. That is to say, he was motivated by heterogeneous needs, which he nevertheless resolved into a unitary form, as if they were made to grow together into a 'style'. Eco describes this as 'a personal, unrepeatable, characteristic mode of forming; the recognisable trace that persons leave of themselves in their work and which coincides with the way in which the work is formed' (1990: 28). This form, Eco specifies, has its own autonomous life, which springs from the infinite possible interpretations to which it will be subjected by different audiences and different users. Pareyson, in fact, Marc Jimenez comments (2005: 309), reminds us that artistic creation realises the more difficult notion of sociality, in that it addresses all of us but speaks to each of us in its own specific way. This personalisation of the relationship with the work of art, continues Jimenez, is the necessary condition for its new interpretation, for a dialogue which is permanent but constantly renewed.

Concluding remarks

The four approaches of the aesthetic study of organisation are therefore very distinct from each other and sometimes also in conflict. In research practice, however, the features shared by the approaches are also very apparent, and in any case one can adopt more than one approach to conduct an empirical aesthetic study.

If one considers the National Pop League (NPL) (Chapter 18, pp. 278–84), the monthly Indie club night held in Glasgow's West End, for instance, aesthetic research on organisational life must enquire whether what it observes relates to the organisation's values system and symbolic constructs. Aesthetic feelings of the symbolic construction of NPL – feelings of such intensity that its closure after a decade of activity is preferable to the gradual stripping away of its aesthetic dimension – are evident. This is an organisational inquiry based on the archaeological approach.

If one adopts, instead, the empathic-logical approach, the aesthetic researcher questions whether the *pathos* of the artefacts, either physical or intangible, exerts deep and precognitive influences that can take the form of organisational control. As regards NPL, one thus observes the influence at a precognitive level of its *pathos* as an organisational artefact that organises music and dance for around 300 people in their self-control: even if you have to queue for forty-five minutes for a drink at the bar, 'you queue, you don't push in'.

The aesthetic approach stresses that aesthetics is a dimension to be grasped in its being-in-use – in work practices, therefore – and that the set of our sensory faculties and aesthetic judgement capable of action and able to produce the expertise constituting the stock of personal knowledge (Polanyi, 1958) often employed in routine work in organisations. In the case of NPL, the attention focuses on the work and organisational practices (Gherardi and Strati, 2012) such as the constant innovation of the playlists, as well the organising of the listening, the dancing and also of the more elementary aggregating fact, that of a social and organisational context that one likes.

Aesthetic organisational research also explores creativity, inventiveness and innovation in the management of organisational life. Mainly through the artistic approach, it investigates the flow of performances enacted in diversified social worlds that come to combine with each other, even if they sometimes do so only briefly and therefore ephemerally. This is apparent in the case of NPL: one notes the variety of performances to be creatively managed, starting from the aesthetic choices of organisational communication manifest in the badges, fanzine packs, posters and the email sent after the event to a thousand members.

Application questions

- What is the balance between materiality and aesthetics in the musical performance, and how is it achieved?
- How is hearing in the particular example both 'selfish' or individual and communicative or social?
- How is the 'flow' of practices that make up a performance influenced by aesthetic judgements?
- When researching musical performance, what advantages and disadvantages do the alternative approaches have?

References

Barrett, F.J. (2007) Creativity and improvisation in jazz and organizations: implications for organizational learning. In Minahan, S. and Wolfram Cox, J. (eds) *The aesthetic turn in management*, pp. 407–24. Farnham: Ashgate.

Berg, P.O. and Kreiner, K. (1990) Corporate architecture: turning physical settings into symbolic resources. In Gagliardi, P. (ed) *Symbols and artifacts: views of the corporate landscape*, pp. 41–67. Berlin: de Gruyter.

DeNora, T. (2000) *Music in everyday life*. Cambridge University Press.

Eco, U. (1990) *La definizione dell'arte [The definition of art]*. Milano: Mursia (first published 1968).

Faulkner, R.R. and Becker, H.S. (2009) *'Do you know…?' The jazz repertoire in action*. University of Chicago Press.

Fubini, E. (1995) *Estetica della musica [Aesthetics of music]*. Bologna: Il Mulino.

Gagliardi, P. (2006) Exploring the aesthetic side of organizational life. In Clegg, S.R., Hardy, C., Lawrence, T.B. and Nord, W.R. (eds) *The Sage handbook of organization studies*, 2nd edn, pp. 701–24. London: Sage.

Gherardi, S. and Strati, A. (2012) *Learning and knowing in practice-based studies*. Cheltenham: Edward Elgar.

Guillet de Monthoux, P. (2004) *The art firm: aesthetic management and metaphysical marketing from Wagner to Wilson*. Stanford University Press.

Hennion, A. (2007) Those things that hold us together: taste and sociology. *Cultural Sociology*, 1(1): 97–114.

Jimenez, M. (2005) *La querelle de l'art contemporain [The quarrel of contemporary art]*. Paris: Gallimard.

Koivunen, N. (2008) The recording of contemporary classical music: relational aesthetics, and some management too. *Aesthesis: International Journal of Art and Aesthetics in Management and Organizational Life*, 2(1): 52–63.

Meisiek, S. and Hatch, M.J. (2008) This is work, this is play: artful interventions and identity dynamics. In Barry, D. and Hansen, H. (eds) *The Sage handbook of new approaches in management and organization*, pp. 412–22. London: Sage.

Montuori, A. (2007) The complexity of improvisation and the improvisation of complexity: social science, art and creativity. In Minahan, S. and Wolfram Cox, J. (eds) *The aesthetic turn in management*, pp. 455–73. Farnham: Ashgate.

Nicolini, D., Gherardi, S. and Yanow, D. (eds) (2003) *Knowing in organizations: a practice-based approach*. Armonk, NY: M.E. Sharpe.

Nietzsche, F. (1910) Richard Wagner in Bayreuth. In Nietzsche, F. *Thoughts out of season*, 3rd edn, vol. IV, no. 1, translated by Ludovici, A.M. London: T.N. Foulis (first published 1876).

Pareyson, L. (1996) *Estetica. Teoria della formatività [Aesthetics. Theory of formativity]*. Milano: Bompiani (first published 1954).

Polanyi, M. (1958) *Personal knowledge: towards a post-critical philosophy*. London: Routledge & Kegan Paul.

Rosenblum, L.D. (2010) *See what I'm saying: the extraordinary powers of our five senses*. New York: Norton.

Shustermann, R. (2008) *Body consciousness: a philosophy of mindfulness and somaesthetics*. Cambridge University Press.

Simmel, G. (2009) *Soziologie. Untersuchungen über die Formen der Vergesellschaftung [Sociology. Inquiries into the Construction of Social Forms]*, vol. I–II, English translation edited by Blasi, A.J., Jacobs, A.K. and Kanjireathinkal, M. Leiden: Brill (first published 1908).

Staubmann, H. (ed) (2013) *The Rolling Stones: sociological perspectives*. Lanham, MD: Lexington Books.

Strati, A. (1999) *Organization and aesthetics*. London: Sage.

Strati, A. (2012) Do you do beautiful things? Aesthetics and art in qualitative methods of organization studies. In Gherardi, S. and Strati, A. *Learning and knowing in practice-based studies*, pp. 194–209. Cheltenham: Edward Elgar.

Sutherland, I. (2013) Arts-based methods in leadership development: affording aesthetic workplaces, reflexivity and memories with momentum. *Management Learning*, 44(1): 25–43.

3   Organising and storytelling

David Sims

The narrative turn

Over time, many different emphases have been used in trying to understand how organisational life works. In the early twentieth century most
writers saw organisations as machines that needed to be made as efficient
as possible – for example, by engineering them so that each person was
doing a small, manageable, well-defined task that they could learn to do
optimally (Taylor, 1911). This way of thinking made its contribution but
turned out to be limited, so more attention was paid to the functioning of
groups of people at work (Roethlisberger and Dickson, 1939).
Subsequently, a school brought efficiency and an understanding of the
importance of groups together in socio-technical systems (Trist and
Bamforth, 1951). Over time, many more approaches to understanding
how people work together in organisations have been brought to bear.
Like sedimentary rocks, these have added to each other and built up a
landscape of understanding rather than replacing each other.

Recently we have seen a narrative turn in many of the social sciences
(e.g. Booker, 2004; Bruner, 2002; Ellis and Flaherty, 1992; Frank, 1995;
Hutto, 2007; Josselson et al., 2007; Linde, 1993; McKee, 1999; Roberts
and Holmes, 1999; Simmons, 2001; Winslade and Monk, 2000). The
same turn can be seen in organisation studies (e.g. Boje, 2011; Brown
et al., 2005; Czarniawska, 1999; Gabriel, 2004; Kostera, 2008; Linde,
2009), and this way of understanding organisations is one that many of the
contributors to this book have found especially helpful. This chapter will
explain what we gain from focusing on narratives and stories in and of
organisations, and will illustrate its claims by looking at two of the stories
offered elsewhere in the book.

Homo narrans narratur

Christie and Orton (1988) gave us the notion that we are *homo narrans
narratur*, which expresses the core of the storytelling idea well. In contrast
to such a phrase as *homo economicus*, which suggests that the nature of the

human being is to be a rational creature maximising its own advantages, *homo narrans narratur* suggests that our nature as human beings is that we are both storytellers and stories. When we tell others about events there is always so much that we could tell them that we have to select, and we do this by finding an account that makes a story. When we recruit people to work for our organisations, we tell them a story about what they would be joining. When we see our family and they ask how our work is going, we tell them stories. When we meet colleagues at the water cooler we tell them stories about what has been happening during the day so far, and when we have to present reports to meetings, these may go better if we have thought how to tell them as stories. The natural way for people to interact is to tell and hear stories, and this may well have been the case since our ancestors did the same thing around the fire outside the cave.

In addition to this, we *are* stories. We are more or less conscious of where we are in our own stories. Careers are a deliberate and overt way of telling our lives as a story, with many of us having views on where we would like to see our story going next, and how we think we might develop the story so it turns out in the way we wish. The importance of the interview question 'where do you see yourself in five years' time?' may be that the interviewer wants to know if we have a storyline for our lives, rather than drifting. We will also have views on how we want our character to be seen by others, and therefore how we behave in front of them. How others see our character will affect the stories that are told about us.

However, people typically feel that they are not in sole control of their own stories about themselves. Some novelists have described how their characters seem to develop a life and a story of their own, and the novelists do not feel they can control this without destroying the life of the story. People sometimes talk in much the same way about the story of their lives, with a sense that they are stories, and part of the excitement of life is that we do not have total control of our own stories. We, as storytellers, find ourselves in dialogue with ourselves, as stories. If our stories are completely resistant to our own intervention we see ourselves as irresponsible; we are in the realms of the old excuse, 'this thing is bigger than both of us'. If our stories are completely under our control we risk finding them too boring to be worth living; we need to believe in a degree of autonomy for our stories from ourselves as storyteller, in order that we have a life that we find worth watching. This dilemma, built into the phrase *homo narrans narratur*, illuminates many aspects of the way that people live their lives in organisations, and thus helps us to understand organisations. The remainder of this chapter will look at some of these aspects.

The narrative approach to life

Some of the claims I have made for the importance of understanding people as storytellers and as stories may seem a little sweeping, and this may not be the same for everyone. Shakespeare presented both sides of the argument well. When, in *As You Like It*, he says:

> All the world's a stage,
> And all the men and women merely players:
> They have their exits and their entrances;
> And one man in his time plays many parts

Shakespeare is expressing a very narrative view of the human being, and taking it that we are both storytellers and stories. However, when in *Hamlet* he says:

> This above all: to thine own self be true

he might appear to be saying the opposite: that there is a single true self rather than the self being composed of many enacted roles. For many people, though, this feels quite consistent; being true to myself might mean playing many different roles, and being part of both telling and being many different stories is our way of being ourselves. For others, this would seem as though they were living out too much variety to have coherence.

This may relate quite closely to Snyder's self-monitoring scale (Snyder, 1974; Snyder and Gangestad, 2000). This is a measure of the extent to which a person feels they are in the position of the parrot sitting on their own shoulder, monitoring what they are doing (a 'high self-monitor', in Snyder's terms), or in the position of speaking from the heart without being consciously affected by the views that others will take of what they say (a 'low self-monitor'). Snyder argues that this is a personality dimension that does not correlate highly with anything else, including truthfulness. Some people are simply more prone to seeing themselves as stories, and to being conscious of choices in how they tell their stories. Being alert to this difference can have considerable practical value in organisational life: the storytellers (high self-monitors) cannot understand why the others do not put more energy into telling their stories properly, while the low self-monitors are suspicious of the deliberate self-presentation of the storytellers.

The characteristics of stories

'Story' probably works best on the 'you know one when you see one' principle. However, Boje's definition has been widely used: 'an oral or written performance involving two or more people interpreting past or

42   *David Sims*

anticipated experience' (Boje, 1991: 111). Abma (1999: 170) amplifies this by saying:

> To be able to live and understand the drama we call our lives, people give meaning to their experience by telling stories. Without stories, our lives and practices would be meaningless ... Stories imply actions toward others (claims, requests). Their aim is not primarily to describe a situation but to motivate people to act in a certain way so that a practice is continued or changed.

It could be argued that a story does not necessarily involve two or more people: we tell stories to ourselves, even if we imagine the presence of another while we are doing it. For example, after a meeting we rehearse in our minds the way we would tell the story of it, although we probably imagine a particular audience for whom we might be telling it. Sometimes in that rehearsal we find there is room for improvement, so we tell the story again, still with no one else actually present, but in a way which makes better sense to us, or that we enjoy performing more, or that casts a better light on ourselves. As Abma says, this is how we give meaning to what is going on, and we do it with one eye on the effect the story will have on other people. If we do not want our audience or potential audience to think badly of one of the characters in the story, we will choose a telling of it that does not invite this.

However, the listener may be invited to be part of the making of meaning from a story. Barthes (1970) distinguishes between 'readerly' and 'writerly' texts. A readerly text is one that is well crafted and where the meaning is clear, so the recipient is invited to respond to it as a relatively passive reader. A writerly text is usually less crafted and the meaning is less clear, so the recipient is encouraged to get involved with interpreting its meaning, possibly because the meaning is less carefully controlled by the author. If we apply the same distinction to stories, some invite the hearer to become involved in making meaning from the story, and these may be the ones that influence us most because we believe we have been involved in discovering their meaning for ourselves. Stories are often passed down through generations in a family without the hearer being told what meaning they should take from the story; feeling that you are making your own meaning binds you more effectively to a tradition.

The difference between narrative and story has been discussed at considerable length in the literature, eliciting many different ideas and many fine distinctions. Whether these distinctions are of practical value is not clear, but for the purpose of this chapter we shall take it that narrative is the stuff that stories are made from. Narratives are often seen as macro-level structures including plots and modes (epic, tragic and romantic, for example), generic characters (such as heroes and villains) and well-trodden steps (such as suspension and release or hope, disaster and reaffirmation). Stories are particular instances, told of specific events or people, and are often shaped by narrative structures that run deep within cultures. The following subsections highlight some of the aspects of stories we should pay attention to when seeking to understand their role in coordinating, organising and creating.

Stories carrying many things at once

Stories appear to be less instrumental than some other forms of communication. They carry some spare material, some decorative flourishes, which are not essential for stating what happened. They include words of style (often adverbs) and descriptions of mood, neither of which are essential for saying what happened. A story naturally brings several ideas together, giving a sense of a rounded picture of an event. Stories are naturally synthetic. When people talk of analysing stories we know that, like a living organism, the story may not survive analysis. Like a fly, if you take it to pieces you may understand many things about it, but it is now dead; it is no longer a functioning story.

Remembering in stories

One of the less modest claims for stories and narratives comes from Hardy, who says: 'We dream in narrative, daydream in narrative, remember, anticipate, hope, despair, believe, doubt, plan, revise, criticise, construct, gossip, learn, hate and love by narrative' (1968: 5). The idea that we remember in narrative is well enough accepted for it to be commonly given in advice about mnemonics: if you want to remember the sequence of the planets round the sun, create a story about them; you have a much better chance of remembering the story than a list. If we present a paper at a meeting or give a talk we may similarly choose to give the material in story form, because our audience is more likely to be able to remember it. There is some pressure on us after a meeting to rehearse a story from the meeting in our minds quickly ('daydream in narrative'), because only that way will we retain a memory of the event.

We would not wish to claim that all memory is done in narrative. Some people remember numbers without turning them into narrative; others remember melodies without a narrative. Sometimes, too, we remember snippets rather than whole ideas or stories (Sims et al., 2009). However, for most of what we need to remember in our organisations, making meaning through narrative is crucial to remembering.

Appearing in others' stories

In organisations we keep making guest appearances in other people's stories, or if we do not, we are being extremely ineffective and we might as well not be there. Edwards (2000) suggested that the meaning of life was the extent to which you could write yourself into others' stories. Not to appear in others' stories is the ultimate experience of lonely ineffectiveness. It may also be important to consider how you want to appear in those stories – with what character and effect. Are you appearing as hero, villain or fool? A major motivation for leadership is to appear as a significant actor in others' stories.

Stories for leading and misleading

In this chapter we have been talking about stories as a normal, inevitable part of how people talk to each other and work together in organisations. We have not been focusing on the negative connotations that the word can have colloquially. For example, 'telling stories or tales on someone' is a phrase from the school playground, where it meant blowing another person's cover. 'Living in a story' can be used about those who have departed to fantasy land, where they inhabit, alone, stories of their own devising. 'He is a good storyteller' can suggest someone who is spinning, who is trying to mislead others with his accounts – definitely not someone who should be trusted.

As well as telling stories to sort out in our own minds what is going on, or to give other people a picture of what we think is going on, we may also find ourselves storytelling as a virtuoso performance. Think of stories told by stand-up comedians. They skilfully hold the attention of their audience, and nothing is lost in their stories. A rapt audience, hanging on your every word, is a wonderful feeling. We tell stories for effect, and we enjoy seeing the effect we can have on other people with those stories. This may mean that we spice those stories up, that we include details which are geared more to entertainment than to description, that if we can give a comic or tragic slant to the story we will. Hence, a story may become larger than life.

Similarly, a well-told story will show particular characteristics. The characters in it will be reasonably consistent; they will display 'character' in the narrative sense of being very clearly the same person each time they appear. Some of the individual quirks and inconsistencies of everyday life may be ironed out (or inflated) in the process of developing a well-told story. In the same way, the story may be developed to have a narrative arc (McKee, 1999), in that it takes its characters from one state to another by an arc, not a straight line.

Stories are told not only about what is but also about what might be. You tell a story to show what a wonderful future your organisation has, and you persuade yourself as you tell it. Leadership may be exercised by telling stories, usually exciting and persuasive ones, and the person most powerfully led may be ourselves. It is not possible to rehearse a story without being influenced by your own storytelling.

Intertwining stories

When we form a long-term relationship with someone, our story and theirs will intertwine. This could even be used as a definition of love! In a similar way, if we have a long-term relationship with an organisation, its story and ours may become inseparable. The way my story unfolds is intertwined with the way my organisation's story unfolds, and so my commitment is to its story as well as my own. When we fire an employee or a volunteer, their response may be very personal. We have not only affected their livelihood and their career, but have also ripped them out of their entanglement in the story of the organisation, which they might have seen as being long-term and inextricable, and as the source of meaning for their own story. It may be helpful to remember this before 'letting someone go'. If we can understand their need for a story to intertwine with, we may even be able to help them to see where else they could find this.

Finding and losing the plot

There are times when we lose the plot of our own stories. We become involved in action, and the action brings its own imperatives and pressures. Our attention turns to keeping the action going – and we have completely forgotten why we started on that action in the first place. Handling crises brings its own excitement, and survival within them gives us sufficient reward, so we may not have the time or energy to challenge whether we are doing anything which takes our story or that of our organisation forward. We are busy, but we have lost the plot. Some people are never happier than when they are fully engaged in firefighting. Being the author of our own story can be hard work, and crisis handling can be a relief from it. It may also be that we learn most when we lose the plot, when we are not confident of the meaning of the stories we are involved in.

Similarly, we can get bored with our own story. We know what is going on and we think we know what is going to happen next. It is getting like a rather boring novel. To liven things up we bring new factors or people into our story. This may be one reason why people have a mid-life crisis – they are simply bored with their own story. So they do something which they know may be self-destructive and may not take their story in a direction they are happy with, but at least it is interesting. Being aware that you are doing something crazy simply to liven your story up may be enough to help you stop.

The tension of being caught between stories

One of the pressures placed on middle managers is the need to tell one set of stories upwards, to reassure the boss that all is well with their department and that s/he does not need to intervene, and another set downwards, to reassure their staff that the boss is not as mad as s/he seems and that the organisation is in safe hands. This is a significant part of the workload for some middle managers (Sims, 2003). This is demoralising, and it can be very helpful for senior people to think about the pressure they may be putting on others to tell different, conflicting stories in different directions.

Being robbed of stories

There are times when we can find no way of telling a story about our situation, so we are condemned to meaninglessness. Funkenstein (1993) has suggested that this was one of the crimes of the Holocaust. Very few survivors have been able to narrate a story about the Holocaust and their survival. Memories are too fragmented to be able to construct a sequence or pattern of events. 'The Nazis robbed them of their identity, of their capacity to construct a narrative, of investing the events of their lives with meaning and purpose' (1993: 24).

That may be the longer-term result of not being able to construct a narrative, but in the short term it can produce anger and frustration. We can find no sensible way to construct a story around the behaviour of one of our colleagues, so we dismiss them as just being wicked:

Indeed, part of the anger when anybody in these cases did describe anyone else as a bastard may have had to do with their feeling almost trapped into that definition by the target of it. Not only were they angry about particular behaviour on the part of the other person, but they were even more angry because they could not make sense of that behaviour without thinking of the person as a bastard, and this felt like failure to them. (Sims, 2005: 1,635)

To be robbed of our stories, or to be unable to find a way of telling a story that we find acceptable, is a major challenge to our sense of ourselves.

What to look for in a story

In the remainder of this chapter I shall look briefly at two of the stories from this book and illustrate a few things that might be illuminated in them by taking a narrative approach.

Lori's story

Lori's story (Chapter 19, pp. 290–7) is one of disappointment and learning. It is told at some distance from the events, and the feeling from reading it is that it discusses events that were important to her, but that she has not before had the opportunity to make sense of satisfactorily. When we tell a story it is often the teller who is affected as much as the listener, and there is a sense of her using this telling as a way of making meaning for herself of events from some way back.

The story of the composition has a narrative theme about the relationship between innovation and tradition. How do you contribute something new to a tradition without going outside that tradition? The rest of the story is about what she regards as a failed attempt to do just this – for example, by forming a patchwork of words from her fieldwork to be played through a laptop during the performance of a piece of instrumental music. At times it is difficult to follow where her story is going; this strengthens the sense that she may not have told it before. The story is told more like a succession of facts and with less narrative flow than, for example, Jenny's story (below). This may have been a mild example of Funkenstein's point about the difficulty of forming narratives about some particularly painful events, and I would be interested to know whether the opportunity to tell this story left Lori feeling happier about the events, or at least feeling closure on them.

The story is full of Lori's regrets that she had not had the confidence to intervene more in preparing the performance of her piece. 'If only I had known then what I know now' is the riff running through it. On occasions she thought, optimistically, that someone else knew how things should work and would put things right. On other occasions she was undermined (possibly) deliberately (e.g. by the piper) as part of a power-play that reminds us of a school playground. She is playing a number of different characters within the story as 'composer, performer, researcher and up-and-coming name', and maybe the complexity of being all these characters at once contributes to the difficulty she has had in building a satisfactory story for herself.

As well as having gained in confidence and experience in the eight years since the events, she talks a lot about learning from them. We tell stories about our learning; this may be partly because we think we have learned and partly because we are determined to rescue something from the wreckage. Another interesting aspect is that she tells the event's story as well as hers, discussing how the organisers have learned and the event has developed as a result of her painful experience. Her story is intertwined with the successful learning story for the event.

Jenny's story

Jenny's story (Chapter 19, pp. 310–16) is much more heroic in tone, with a number of obstacles being overcome and near disasters being averted. There is a tension and an excitement to it that come from it being told as if it is not yet certain whether the resulting triumph will happen or not. The album has not yet been released, and it is unclear whether money will be found to make this possible.

Two themes bind the story together. One is Jenny's coping with her depressive illness. Knowing about this, we realise that her character in the story faces challenges, and could be damaged by the way the story develops. The other is about Jenny's explicit wish to 'develop as an artist and band' (intertwining her story with that of her band).

The other participants in this story seem to make regular and comfortable appearances in each other's stories, so this is very much a story about community as well as about the successful struggle of Jenny. The band did not know if they would have enough money to hire the studio until just before they set off. The story about eating dinner together is a classic way of describing togetherness within a group. She mentions that she wants the finished album not only to be a product but also to show the story of its own production. The 'hard to do vocal', the snippets of recordings of the band 'messing around in the studio', the need to 'hear the room' – all of which are retained in 'knitting the album together' – all show her wish that the album should tell the story of how it was made. Will the listener be able to hear this story from the album? Who knows, but she believed that an object should tell its own story.

Jenny is a good storyteller, and unlike Lori's story, it feels as if she has rehearsed this one a few times. Her story is brought to life by details like the trip to Cardiff to get the violin repaired, taking Louie rafting on the river so that Jenny had time to write the lyrics, and the difficulty of producing in a room overheating because of the need to keep the door shut so as not to disturb the tracking next door. Such apparently extraneous, decorative flourishes are a defining characteristic of storytelling. The last potential disaster, when the mixing goes wrong, is averted, and becomes part of how Jenny plots the future story of the album towards the end of her story.

Conclusion

Thus, a storytelling approach highlights how people string events together, find a character for themselves (and others) and find a way of making sense of how to go forward. Stories tell us something about what happened, but they also tell us quite a lot about the storyteller – their way of 'framing' the world, their level of optimism/pessimism, and what they see as being important.

When using storytelling as a way of understanding (or possibly analysing) encounters or events it is worth looking out for:
- plots and how the story is structured;
- character and what sort of role is played by whom;
- the creation and recreation of memories;
- how sense is made;
- how this story is entwined with others;
- what the consequences are of a particular way of telling the story – in other words, how we might act next.

Several key lessons can be learned from the storytelling approach. We all give meaning to our lives by telling stories about them, and we craft that meaning by rehearsing the stories in front of different audiences, real and imagined. That we are all storytellers does not mean that we are not truthful, but it warns us to be aware that we may get carried away in our own or others' stories. If you cannot think why someone is behaving as they are in a meeting, think about what story they are living out, and what character they are playing in that story. Many of us want to be able to make appearances in other people's stories.

Application questions

- What does the idea that we are all both stories and storytellers mean to you?
- Can you think of an example of when your own story has become intertwined with another person's or an organisation's?
- Have you ever found yourself in a situation where you just cannot find a way of telling a story about it, or at least where there was no one you could tell the story to?
- What do we lose by taking a narrative approach to understanding what is going on in organisation?

References

Abma, T.A. (1999) Powerful stories: the role of stories in sustaining and transforming professional practice within a mental hospital. In Josselson, R. and Lieblich, A. (eds) *Making meaning of narratives:*

50   David Sims

the narrative study of lives, vol. VI, pp. 169–95. Thousand Oaks, CA: Sage.

Barthes, R. (1970) S/Z. Paris: Seuil.

Boje, D. (1991) The storytelling organization: a study of storytelling performance in an office supply firm. Administrative Science Quarterly, 36: 106–26.

Boje, D. (ed) (2011) Storytelling and the future of organizations: an antenarrative handbook. New York: Routledge.

Booker, C. (2004) The seven basic plots: why we tell stories. London: Continuum.

Brown, J.S., Denning, S., Groh, K. and Prusak, L. (2005) Storytelling in organizations: why storytelling is transforming 21st century organizations and management. Burlington, MA: Elsevier.

Bruner, J. (2002) Making stories: law, literature, life. New York: Farrar, Straus and Giroux.

Christie, J.R.R. and Orton, F. (1988) Writing a text on the life. Art History, 11(4): 543–63.

Czarniawska, B. (1999) Writing management: organization theory as a literary genre. Oxford University Press.

Edwards, L. (2000) A narrative journey to understanding self, unpublished M. Phil. dissertation, Brunel University, London.

Ellis, C. and Flaherty, M.G. (1992) Investigating subjectivity: research on lived experience. Newbury Park, CA: Sage.

Frank, A.W. (1995) The wounded storyteller: body, illness, and ethics. University of Chicago Press.

Funkenstein, A. (1993) The incomprehensible catastrophe: memory and narrative. In Josselson, R. and Lieblich, A. (eds) The narrative study of lives, vol. I, pp. 21–9. Thousand Oaks, CA: Sage.

Gabriel, Y. (ed) (2004) Myths, stories and organizations: premodern narratives for our times. Oxford University Press.

Hardy, B. (1968) Towards a poetics of fiction: an approach through narrative. Novel, 2: 5–14.

Hutto, D.D. (ed) (2007) Narrative and understanding persons. Cambridge University Press.

Josselson, R., Lieblich, A. and McAdams, D. (eds) (2007) The meaning of others: narrative studies of relationships. Washington, DC: American Psychological Association.

Kostera, M. (ed) (2008) Organizational epics and sagas: tales of organizations. Basingstoke: Palgrave Macmillan.

Linde, C. (1993) Life stories: the creation of coherence. Oxford University Press.

Linde, C. (2009) Working the past: narrative and institutional memory. Oxford University Press.

McKee, R. (1999) Story: substance, structure, style and the principles of screenwriting. London: Methuen.

Roberts, G. and Holmes, J. (eds) (1999) Healing stories: narrative in psychiatry and psychotherapy. Oxford University Press.

Roethlisberger, F.J. and Dickson, W.J. (1939) Management and the worker. New York: Wiley.

Simmons, A. (2001) *The story factor: inspiration, influence and persuasion through the art of storytelling*. New York: Basic Books.

Sims, D. (2003) Between the millstones: a narrative account of the vulnerability of middle managers' storying. *Human Relations*, 56: 1,195–211.

Sims, D. (2005) You bastard: a narrative exploration of the experience of indignation within organizations. *Organization Studies*, 26(11): 1,625–40.

Sims, D., Huxham, C. and Beech, N. (2009) On telling stories but hearing snippets: sense-taking from presentations of practice. *Organization*, 16(3): 371–88.

Snyder, M. (1974) Self-monitoring of expressive behavior. *Journal of Personality and Social Psychology*, 30: 526–37.

Snyder, M. and Gangestad, S. (2000) Self-monitoring: appraisal and reappraisal. *Psychological Bulletin*, 126(4): 530–55.

Taylor, F.W. (1911) *Principles of scientific management*. New York: Harper.

Trist, E.L. and Bamforth, K.W. (1951) Some social and psychological consequences of the Longwall method of coal-getting. *Human Relations*, 4(3): 3–38.

Winslade, J. and Monk, G. (2000) *Narrative mediation: a new approach to conflict resolution*. San Francisco, CA: Jossey-Bass.

4 Organising, music and metaphor: of connections, comparisons and correspondences

Cliff Oswick

Much of the work that connects organisations and organising with music has been explicit and literal in orientation (Prichard et al., 2007). The focus has typically been on the processes of organising in musical settings or the use of music in organisational settings. In effect, music has been the focus of analysis (i.e. the content) in some studies and the backdrop (i.e. the context) in others. Research addressing organising within musical settings has included studies of the management of orchestras (Allmendinger and Hackman, 1996; Maitlis and Lawrence, 2003), the decision-making of music producers (Mauws, 2000) and culture and conflict in the popular music industry (Negus, 1992). A number of studies have inverted the organising focus and looked at music in organisational settings by analysing the use of music in public buildings (Boutelle et al., 2001), the effect of music on waiting times (Cameron et al., 2003; North and Hargreaves, 1999) and organisational songs (Conrad, 1988; Nissley, 2002).

Beyond the considerable body of work that centres on the literal interface between music and organising, there is a far less developed literature around figurative connections. This chapter seeks to explore the non-literal relationship between the two domains and, in particular, to consider the role of metaphor.

There are three parts to this chapter. First, the dominant ways in which metaphors have been deployed in the field of organisation studies are presented and the specific applications of music-based metaphors are discussed. Second, an alternative way of conceptualising the metaphorical linkage between organising and music is developed, which also draws on one of the stories contained in this book (Lloyd's story, Chapter 18, pp. 245–50). Finally, the value of, and scope for, new metaphorical insights is explored.

Juxtaposing domains: comparison-based mappings of organising and music

Metaphors rely upon a carrying over of properties from one domain to another (Lakoff and Johnson, 1980). More specifically, they involve a process of mapping a relatively familiar or concrete object or subject (often referred to as the source or base domain) onto a less familiar or relatively abstract object or subject (typically referred to as the target domain) (Ortony, 1993; Schon, 1993). Metaphors focus upon aspects of similarity to generate insights. They work on the basis that 'subject A is, or is like, B' with 'the processes of comparison, substitution, and interaction between the images of A and B acting as generators of new meaning' (Morgan, 1980: 610).

Metaphors are most powerful when there is an optimum level similarity between a source domain and a target domain. Morgan (1980) demonstrates this point through the use of three similar metaphorical mappings – namely, boxer as man, boxer as saucepan and boxer as tiger. Arguably, if one is trying to convey the characteristics and properties of a specific boxer, describing the boxer as 'like a man' is likely to generate weak imagery because the two domains are quite simply too similar. Equally, suggesting that a boxer is 'like a saucepan' is likely to produce weak imagery because the two domains are too dissimilar. However, the idea that a boxer is 'like a tiger' has the generative capacity necessary to produce strong, evocative imagery (e.g. of the boxer being agile, ferocious, aggressive and tenacious) because the two domains have an optimum level of overlap, insofar as they occupy a space between being too similar and too dissimilar.

Metaphors have been extensively applied to the study of organisations (Grant and Oswick, 1996). The seminal contribution on organisational metaphors is Morgan's *Images of organization* (1986), in which a range of 'optimum overlap' comparisons are offered (including organisations as machines, organisations as organisms and organisations as brains). Although less common, there has been some work that has considered the application of music-based metaphors in relation to organisations and organising (see, for example, Albert and Bell, 2002; Fairfield and London, 2003; Mantere et al., 2007).

Two of the most popular metaphors utilised to understand aspects of organisations and organising have been drawn from the genres of jazz and classical music. The deployment of the jazz metaphor has largely been used to highlight the improvisational and emergent facets of organising (see, for example, Barrett, 2000; Hatch, 1998; Hatch, 1999; Hatch and Weick, 1998; Humphreys et al., 2003; Lewin, 1998; Meyer et al.,

1998). Coming from a very different direction, the figurative mapping of the performance of orchestras has generally focused on the role of 'conductor as leader' and has foregrounded the structured coordination and control of the activities of a group of disparate stakeholders (see, for example, Atik, 1994; Bathurst and Williams, 2013; Hunt et al., 2004; Koivunen and Wennes, 2011; Mintzberg, 1998; Sayles, 1964). In effect, the 'conductor as leader' metaphor has drawn attention to the predictable and controllable aspects of organising, while the 'organising as jazz' metaphor highlights the uncontrollable and spontaneous nature of organisational activities. Although adopting almost antithetical perspectives on organising, both these metaphors serve to illuminate pertinent characteristics of organising. However, it is important to remember that the metaphorical images generated are not neutral projections, insofar as the process of illuminating certain characteristics to create points of overlap or similarity ignores and marginalises aspects of the dissimilarity (Oswick, 2008). In this regard, metaphors create 'partial truths' (Morgan, 1986).

Arguably, the overriding problem with the predominant approach to metaphor use with regard to music is that it has tended to use popular and predictable metaphors (e.g. 'organising as jazz' and 'conductor as leader') in a highly conventional manner (i.e. simple one-way projections). This form of comparison-based orthodoxy is problematic in two ways. First, it is questionable whether the traditional application of metaphors in organisation theory genuinely produces new insights. If we take, for example, the 'organising as jazz' metaphor, it is fair to say that the source domain of jazz serves to highlight improvisational properties within the target domain of organising. However, in order for this metaphor to produce evocative and meaningful imagery we need to have a pre-existing understanding of the points of similarity between the two domains (i.e. some prior sense of the ways in which organising is improvisational). To restate this using the earlier example, we have to have a pre-existing understanding of the 'tiger-ish' characteristics of a boxer in order for the 'boxer as tiger' metaphor to resonate and produce vivid imagery. In this regard, the role played by highly conventionalised metaphors is primarily one of articulating or disseminating established insights rather than generating new knowledge (Keenoy et al., 2003). Following this logic, the conventional use of 'optimum overlap' comparison metaphors does not help to make an unfamiliar or abstract target domain familiar; rather, it helps to make a relatively familiar domain more familiar. If we wish to create new and innovative perspectives on organisations and organising we need to embrace more radical and less obvious metaphors, which stimulate cross-domain comparisons based upon dissonance (i.e. points of dissimilarity) rather than the current overreliance on resonance (i.e. predictable metaphors selected on the basis of relatively explicit similarities) (Oswick et al., 2002).

The second problem with the conventional use of organisational metaphors in general, and of music-instigated metaphors in particular, is that they are applied in a unidirectional fashion, insofar as they typically offer one-way projections and insights (Cornelissen, 2005). So, for example, jazz is used as a vehicle to explore organising, but organising is not used to explore jazz. By limiting the metaphorical mapping to a single flow the potential for new insights is inevitably constrained (e.g. improvisation is understood from one perspective rather than two).

Blending domains: correspondence-based mappings of organising and music

Given the limitations of conventional, comparison-based forms of metaphor use, we now turn our attention to considering the scope for an alternative form in organisation theorising, based upon correspondence (Cornelissen, 2006; Oswick and Jones, 2006). Unlike a comparison approach, which involves a process of one-way projection, a correspondence approach involves a dynamic process of interaction between domains. More specifically, the interactive juxtaposing of domains can be seen as involving a blending of characteristics and concepts. Through this process, referred to as 'conceptual blending', a new synthetic construct (i.e. a kind of virtual third domain) is produced (Fauconnier and Turner, 2002). Put simply, comparison-based mappings rely on a process of 'one-way borrowing', while correspondence-based mappings rely on a process of 'two-way blending' (Oswick et al., 2011).

In the case of the 'organising as jazz' metaphor, the application of the correspondence approach would result in a juxtaposing of the domains of jazz and organising through a back-and-forth form of generative interaction to consider points of similarity and dissimilarity in order to produce a new construct. So, for example, the blending of jazz and organising has the scope to produce new and innovating ways of thinking (e.g. perhaps the formation of new blends, such as 'structured improvisation' or 'quasi-emergent coordination'). That said, the 'organising as jazz' metaphor remains an obvious one, and the most interesting and innovative insights are far more likely to result from the blending of more disparate, and perhaps even on occasion antithetical, domains (Oswick, 2008).

A further, possibly less obvious, example of this form of engagement is provided by Albert and Bell (2002). They simultaneously utilise music theory and organisation theory to analyse what they refer to as 'point-timing questions' in order 'to understand why the FBI launched its assault upon David Koresh's compound in Waco, Texas, when it did' (Albert and Bell, 2002: 574). This work provides an excellent illustration of how the two contrasting domains of music and organising can be used to generate new insights.

A more practical example of conceptual blending can be gleaned from Lloyd's story (Chapter 18, pp. 245–50). This offers a fascinating example within which the notions of 'music as play' and 'music as work' are conceptually blended. Lloyd's account is of an enduring interest in music (expressed in the completion of a degree in music and through his blogging on music), which dynamically interacts with a desire to work within the music industry (to a certain extent realised through his involvement with an independent record label). Arguably, the interaction of contrasting domains (i.e. music as work and music as play) produces a new interesting synthetic construct (i.e. a kind of virtual third cognitive domain) around 'musical organising'. The new synthetic domain enables Lloyd to recognise and work with the subtleties of his everyday lived experience of organising activities as simultaneously constituted through 'routine organising' (as experienced within his paid 'non-music' occupation) and 'rewarding organising' (as experienced in a largely unpaid, voluntary engagement in musical work). Hence, in Lloyd's story the boundaries between music and work are somewhat blurred, but they are cognitively reconciled (i.e. conceptually blended).

Towards new insights: some concluding remarks

Rather than thinking of correspondence-based metaphors being superior to their comparison-based counterparts, it is better to see them as serving different purposes. Conventional comparison-based metaphors – such as 'boxer as tiger', 'organisation as machine' and 'conductor as leader' – are capable of generating vivid and evocative images. As such, they can be meaningfully deployed as powerful educational devices because they are valuable mechanisms for articulating and conveying existing knowledge and aiding understanding (Ortony, 1975). This form of metaphorical engagement is extremely useful in the classroom, where, for example, trying to convey the complexities of organising can be enhanced by drawing upon rich analogical referents like the jazz metaphor.

If, however, the intention is to generate genuinely new personal insights or collective insights (i.e. 'producing knowledge' as opposed to 'transferring knowledge'), correspondence-based metaphors have considerably more purchase. More specifically, embracing the notion of correspondence via conceptual blending offers substantial scope for the development of new ways of thinking about aspects of organising and aspects of music. There are numerous ways in which the correspondence approach could be enacted, but the common feature is the incorporation of a dynamic two-way interaction between aspects of organising and music in order to generate novel blended insights.

Beyond the academic example provided above (the Waco example) and the more practically embedded example discussed (Lloyd's story), there are undoubtedly many other correspondences that have the potential to produce novel and innovative insights. Indeed, there may also be considerable scope to explore correspondence-based approaches to metaphor in relation to other chapters within this book. For example, there may be scope for applying the ideas presented here by seeking to blend aspects of 'organisational consumption' and 'musical consumption' to generate novel insights into the concept of consumption. There may also be opportunities to interrogate further some of the 'tales from the field' chapters through the lens of correspondence-based metaphors.

If we set our sights beyond this volume, there are perhaps some further specific areas of inquiry where the interaction and intersection of organising and music might be particularly ripe for interrogation. For example, it may be worth exploring domain connections around aspects of pitch, timbre, tone, rhythm, tempo, harmony, noise, feedback, static, interference, resonance, genre, mood and emotion.

In conclusion, there is considerable scope for the figurative exploration of connections between music and organising. Although comparison-based metaphors are largely 'paradigm-reinforcing' devices, they nevertheless provide an effective way of transferring knowledge (i.e. acting as conduits of understanding). As a result, they are a valuable aid to learning about organisations and teaching aspects of organisation theory (and, for that matter, music). By contrast, correspondence-based mappings are potentially 'paradigm-shifting' in nature. Through the interaction between domains, and the resultant processes of blending, they facilitate the generation of new knowledge. And consequently, they aid conceptual development and research in organisation theory (and music).

Application questions

- What metaphors might be similar enough, but not too similar, to generate new insights into the example?
- How can enough dissonance be introduced to encourage innovative analysis?
- How might two-way blending be applied to produce synthetic domains?

58   Cliff Oswick

References

Albert, S. and Bell, G.G. (2002) Timing and music. *Academy of Management Review*, 27(4): 574–93.

Allmendinger, J. and Hackman, J.R. (1996) Organizations in changing environments: the case of East German symphony orchestras. *Administrative Science Quarterly*, 41: 337–69.

Atik, Y. (1994) The conductor and the orchestra: interactive aspects of the leadership process. *Leadership and Organization Development Journal*, 15(1): 22–8.

Barrett, F.J. (2000) Cultivating an aesthetic unfolding: jazz improvisation as a self-organizing system. In Linstead, S. and Höpfl, H. (eds) *The aesthetics of organization*, pp. 228–45. London: Sage.

Bathurst, R.J. and Williams, L.P. (2013) Managing musically: how acoustic space informs management practice. *Journal of Management Inquiry*, 23(1): 38–49.

Boutelle, K.N., Jeffrey, R.W., Murray, D.M. and Schmitz, M.K.H. (2001) Using signs, art work, and music to promote stair use in a public building. *American Journal of Public Health*, 91: 2,004–6.

Cameron, M.A., Baker, J., Peterson, M. and Braunsberger, K. (2003) The effects of music, wait-length evaluation, and mood on a low-cost wait experience. *Journal of Business Research*, 56: 421–30.

Conrad, C. (1988) Work songs, hegemony, and illusions of self. *Critical Studies in Mass Communication*, 5: 179–201.

Cornelissen, J.P. (2005) Beyond compare: metaphor in organization theory. *Academy of Management Review*, 30: 751–64.

Cornelissen, J.P. (2006) Metaphor in organization theory: progress and the past. *Academy of Management Review*, 31(2): 485–8.

Fairfield, K.D. and London, M.B. (2003) Tuning into the music of groups: a metaphor for team-based learning in management education. *Journal of Management Education*, 27(6): 654–72.

Fauconnier, G. and Turner, M. (2002) *The way we think: conceptual blending and the mind's hidden complexities*. New York: Basic Books.

Grant, D. and Oswick, C. (1996) Getting the measure of metaphors. In Grant, D. and Oswick, C. (eds) *Metaphor and organizations*, pp. 1–20. London: Sage.

Hatch, M.J. (1998) Jazz as a metaphor for organizing in the 21st century. *Organization Science*, 9: 556–7.

Hatch, M.J. (1999) Exploring the empty spaces of organizing: how improvisational jazz helps redescribe organizational structure. *Organization Studies*, 20: 75–100.

Hatch, M.J. and Weick, K.E. (1998) Critical resistance to the jazz metaphor. *Organization Science*, 9: 600–4.

Humphreys, M., Brown, A. and Hatch, M.J. (2003) Is ethnography jazz? *Organization*, 10: 5–31.

Hunt, J.G., Stelluto, G.E. and Hooijters, R. (2004) Toward new-wave organization creativity: beyond romance and analogy in the relationship between orchestra-conductor leadership and musical creativity. *The Leadership Quarterly*, 15(1): 145–62.

Keenoy, T., Oswick, C. and Grant, D. (2003) The edge of metaphor. *Academy of Management Review*, 28(2): 191–2.

Koivunen, N. and Wennes, G. (2011) Show us the sound! Aesthetic leadership of symphony orchestra conductors. *Leadership*, 7: 51–71.

Lakoff, G. and Johnson, M. (1980) *Metaphors we live by*. Chicago University Press.

Lewin, A.Y. (1998) Jazz improvisation as a metaphor for organization theory. *Organization Science*, 9: 539.

Maitlis, S. and Lawrence, T.B. (2003) Orchestral manoeuvres in the dark: understanding failure in organizational strategizing. *Journal of Management Studies*, 40(1): 109–39.

Mantere, S., Sillince, J.A.A. and Hämäläinen, V. (2007) Music as a metaphor for organizational change. *Journal of Organizational Change Management*, 20(3): 447–59.

Mauws, M.K. (2000) But is it art? Decision-making and discursive resources in the field of cultural production. *Journal of Applied Behavioral Science*, 36(2): 229–44.

Meyer, A., Frost, P.J. and Weick, K.E. (1998) The organization science jazz festival: improvisation as a metaphor for organizing. *Organization Science*, 9: 540–2.

Mintzberg, H. (1998) Covert leadership: notes on managing professionals. *Harvard Business Review*, November–December, 140–7.

Morgan, G. (1980) Paradigms, metaphors, and puzzle solving in organization theory. *Administrative Science Quarterly*, 25(4): 605–22.

Morgan, G. (1986) *Images of organization*. Beverly Hills, CA: Sage.

Negus, K. (1992) *Producing pop: culture and conflict in the popular music industry*. London: Edward Arnold.

Nissley, N. (2002) Tuning-in to organizational song as aesthetic discourse. *Culture and Organization*, 8: 51–68.

North, C.A. and Hargreaves, D.J. (1999) Can music move people? The effects of musical complexity on waiting time. *Environment and Behavior*, 31: 136–49.

Ortony, A. (1975) Why metaphors are necessary and not just nice. *Educational Theory*, 25: 45–53.

Ortony, A. (1993) Metaphor, language and thought. In Ortony, A. (ed) *Metaphor and thought*, 2nd edn, pp. 1–17. Cambridge University Press.

Oswick, C. (2008) Towards a critical engagement with metaphor in organizational studies. In Barry, D. and Hansen, H. (eds) *The Sage handbook of new approaches in management and organization*, pp. 300–1. London: Sage.

Oswick, C., Fleming, P. and Hanlon, G. (2011) From borrowing to blending: rethinking the processes of organizational theory building. *Academy of Management Review*, 36(2): 318–37.

Oswick, C. and Jones, P.J. (2006) Beyond correspondence: metaphor in organization theory. *Academy of Management Review*, 31(2): 483–5.

Oswick, C., Keenoy, T. and Grant, D. (2002) Metaphor and analogical reasoning in organization theory: beyond orthodoxy. *Academy of Management Review*, 27: 294–303.

Prichard, C., Korczynski, M. and Elmes, M. (2007) Music at work: an introduction. *Group and Organization Management*, 32(1): 4–21.

Sayles, L. (1964) *Managerial behavior: administration in complex organizations*. New York: McGraw-Hill.
Schon, D.A. (1993) Generative metaphor: a perspective on problem setting in social policy. In Ortony, A. (ed) *Metaphor and thought*, 2nd edn, pp. 135–61. Cambridge University Press.

5 Resisting change and changing resistance

Robyn Thomas

Introduction

Resistance is often admired and even championed within society, with individuals who resist being applauded for their willingness to 'stand up for their beliefs'. History is replete with examples of individuals and groups who have challenged tyranny and oppression, such as the resistance against the Nazis, and the civil rights and anti-apartheid movements. More recently, the Arab Spring, Occupy and the Indignados, struggles over the rights of indigenous peoples, global resistance movements such as Zapatismo, and dignity at work campaigns have all had a positive reception in the public conscience. Resisters, too, are often held up and admired by the public as celebrities and modern-day folk heroes, afforded rock star status.

The music industry too plays its own role in the celebration and lionisation of resistance. Over the history of social movements, music has inspired resistance and united people around a collective identity of outrage and grievance, as well as serving as a vital force in the emergence of new social and political movements (Eyerman and Jamison, 1998; Turino, 2008). Protest songs have championed the causes of human rights, civil rights, gay rights, women's suffrage, the anti-war movement and trade unionism. From the *nueva trova* revolutionary music of Cuba to the South African anti-apartheid anthems, and cutting across every genre from pop, folk and world to classical, the protest song has always been hugely effective in rallying people around a common cause. Music and bands have long represented alternative voices of consciousness, such as the recently much-publicised arrest, trial and imprisonment of members of the Russian feminist post-punk band Pussy Riot (Topping, 2013).

Despite our admiration for resistance on the broader stage, within the management literature – both popular and scholarly – resisters and resistance have received an enduringly negative portrayal. In the literature on the management of change, resistance by individuals and groups is singled out as the biggest impediment to achieving successful change. Recently, however, an alternative perspective has gained prominence that puts a different complexion on resistance to change, suggesting that resistance should be viewed as an important element of successful change (Ford and Ford, 2009; Ford et al., 2008; Thomas et al., 2011) and something to be encouraged.

Drawing on a power-sensitive understanding of organisations that views them as the temporary outcome of ongoing negotiations over meanings, practices and relationships, this chapter will critically examine these contrasting views on resistance and evaluate their implications for organisational change. It will conclude by showing how organisational change involves the co-construction of new meanings by organisational members as part of the everyday social construction of their realities, of which both power and resistance are an integral part.

Everybody's singing the resistance blues

With a globalising economy, a deteriorating natural environment, the ongoing global financial crisis, rapid technological development and ageing populations – not to mention the seemingly relentless consumption of new fashions for desirable management practice – managers and employees alike are called upon to embrace change, and celebrate innovation and organisational flux as normal states of affairs. Yet the track record of successful organisational change is not a good one. Despite seven decades of research devoted to the analysis of organisational change and the vast sums of money spent by organisations on change initiatives, notwithstanding the considerable promise offered by management consulting tools and techniques for transforming organisational performance through change initiatives of one form or another, the inescapable fact is that successful change remains a holy grail. The ability to realise change initiatives in organisations is fraught with problems, the majority of change programmes appear to run into difficulties and most change initiatives are almost certainly bound to fail (Ghoshal and Bartlett, 1996; Sorge and van Witteloostuijn, 2004).

Why is this the case? Why, given the money, the research, the advice and the efforts of well-meaning individuals, do most change initiatives founder? While a number of reasons are identified for the poor track record in change success, covering everything from design to implementation, by far the most popular and enduring culprit is resistance to change by individuals and groups. Popular management writing is replete with accusations of self-serving individuals who scupper change initiatives. For example, Geisler (2001) refers to the 'bottom-feeders' who resist change because of its potential to remove the 'waste' (inefficient processes) on which they 'feed' and, more succinctly, Maurer concludes: 'resistance kills change' (1996: 17). The scholarly management literature equally points to the problems of change resistance. Research from the 1940s (Coch and French, 1948) onwards has established as fact that the major impediment to successful organisational change is the resistant behaviour of individuals and groups (Armenakis and Harris, 2002; Armenakis et al., 1993; Beer and Nohria, 2000; Harvard Business School, 2005), offering explanations of why people resist and how managers can deal with such negative behaviour (Furst and Cable, 2008; Kotter and Schelsinger, 1979). This inescapable belief has endured in management thinking for as long as the topic of change management has existed.

Resistance to change is defined as the blocking of change by recipients, who express negative responses because of their fear of the unknown, poor receptiveness to change, anxieties over loss of power and status or mere habit and love of the status quo. Such resistance can be collective (whether hidden or overt and violent) or individual (low-level disturbances and anonymous forms of challenge and struggle). It can be both active (for example, sabotage, foot-dragging, theft and 'careful carelessness') and quiescent (for example, withholding information, engaging in fantasy and escape, cynicism, irony, satire and assertions of alternative versions of selfhood). However manifested, resistance to change is seen as adversarial, problematic, harmful for organisations and enacted by individuals who attempt to preserve the status quo for their own ends. This can be due to their personality (Kotter, 1995; van Dam et al., 2008) or the nature of the change itself (Tourish et al., 2004), or it can be an effect of the organisational culture within which it is introduced. Resisters are presented as 'mulish and obstinate, resisting innovations that have proved successful elsewhere' (Dobosz-Bourne and Jankowicz, 2006: 2030), as they are either too selfish or too stupid to appreciate the greater good brought about through change (Kotter and Schlesinger, 1979) or simply have a low threshold for change (Furst and Cable, 2008; Dent and Goldberg, 1999).

As a consequence of this prevailing belief about the problem of resistance, manifold solutions have been proposed to preempt, alleviate or eradicate change resistance. These range from trying to improve receptiveness to change (Armenakis et al., 1993; Oreg and Sverdlik, 2011) and various forms of communication and participation in change to sell the message (Furst and Cable, 2008; Kotter and Schlesinger, 1979), through to more coercive methods (Bennebroek Gravenhorst and In't Veld, 2004; Poole et al., 1989).

Underpinning this dominant view on change resistance is an assumption that there are two opposing camps within change. On one side is the change agent, responsible for the change vision, design and management. On the other side are the change recipients, who respond to the change often negatively, viewing it as a threat against which they are likely to kick back (Thomas and Hardy, 2011). Expressions of resistance are an indication that something is awry in the change process that should not happen and that should be avoided or eradicated through various techniques so that the change recipients are able to appreciate the ultimate benefits from the change.

The unavoidable fact, however, is that this approach to understanding change and resistance has failed to provide effective guidance for practice in achieving successful change. Moreover, this perspective fails to appreciate the many challenges to change that are born of positive intentions (Piderit, 2000). Participation by employees and other stakeholders can enhance change initiatives by challenging assumptions that are taken for granted. Consequently, an alternative view on resistance to change has gained strength over recent years, which emphasises the utility of resistance in sustaining change.

Talking resistance into existence

There are persuasive arguments to suggest that the involvement of a wide variety of stakeholders in the processes of change might lead to better change solutions. Accordingly, a position of growing strength within the change management literature argues that when such involvement reveals less complimentary feedback on a change proposal, this should not be immediately dismissed as oppositional. Such an approach moves away from the view of change as a top-down single vision to one where successful change is achieved through a dialogical mode of communication, based on the exchange of views by a wide range of stakeholders (Thomas et al., 2011). Drawing on a communicative approach to understanding change and organisations (Ford and Ford, 1995) it is argued that resistance, in the form of dialogical engagement, should be recast as a resource and something to be encouraged – even celebrated – in order to arrive at a new and shared consensus of understanding. The change agent's role, rather than preempting, controlling and eradicating resistance, should be to invite it, encourage it and harness its value (Lüscher and Lewis, 2008).

Organisations can be understood as a 'space in which meanings are ascribed to, and understandings produced of, actors, events, actions and contexts' (Brown et al., 2005: 313). Successful change involves a move in these understandings, which involves negotiation with a wide range of actors or participants. Such participation and involvement is essential in effective change management (Dobosz-Bourne and Jankowicz, 2006; Ford and Ford, 2009). When a change initiative is introduced, this takes place in an organisational setting where there are already established ongoing conversations. These provide the context into which the new change conversation is both received and understood. Change agents should not view reactions and responses to this new conversation by the change recipient merely as resistance. Rather, these 'counter-offers' (Ford et al., 2008) can be helpful suggestions on refining the change programme, which the change agent should be willing to accommodate and encourage, even if they differ from the change vision. Such change conversations (Ford and Ford, 1995) involving a wide range of participants might lead to a modifying of the change vision but in ways that result in a better informed change.

This alternative approach to resistance to change emphasises that resistance is not inevitable. When it does arise, it is more often than not something that has been created by the change agent or manager, by virtue of the way in which they have reacted negatively to a change recipient's counter offer.

There is no resistance to change existing as an independent phenomenon apart from change agent sensemaking. This does not mean that recipients don't have reactions to change, nor does it mean that their actions can't have an adverse impact on change; they can and they do. What it does mean, however, is that none of these actions/reactions are, in and of themselves, resistance, and they do not become resistance unless and until change agents assign the label resistance to them. (Ford et al., 2008: 371)

Reactions to change, which might be labelled thoughtful (Ford et al., 2008), productive (Courpasson et al., 2011) or facilitative (Thomas et al., 2011) resistance, can be crucial to its success. Under such an approach, change is viewed as an 'ongoing conversation' made up of negotiations between parties to arrive at 'mutually sensible meanings' (Dobosz-Bourne and Jankowicz, 2006: 2,030). Participating in change conversations is an essential element of change. Rather than making predetermined judgements on who is 'for' or 'against' change, based on membership of particular groups, this approach focuses attention on how different organisational members contribute to the negotiation of meaning, and in what ways (see Thomas et al., 2011).

In sum, this alternative approach suggests that resistance is an integral part of change. Resistance holds change conversations in the spotlight and keeps the change 'alive' (Kondo, 1990). Resistance, rather than being a predetermined behaviour, is something that is constructed by the change agent through the labelling of certain acts and behaviours as resistance; in doing so, the agent effectively 'talks resistance into existence'. Thoughtful resistance should be celebrated and harnessed, therefore, not overcome and eradicated.

Rethinking resistance to change

The 'celebrating resistance' (Thomas and Hardy, 2011) approach has a certain beauty to it. It opens up the idea of organisations as democratic spaces where multiple narratives are encouraged and embraced to arrive at a meeting of minds. How realistic is it to view organisations as arenas where we can all be parrhesiastes (Foucault, 2001) – that is, where different individuals and groups are able and willing to speak freely and boldly for the common good, and where everyone has a right to be heard? What seems to be missing from the explanation is the reality of organisations where relations between different individuals and groups are never power-free. Neither approach to resistance to change, as a problem or a resource, recognises the fact that organisations are systems of inequality where the interests and assumptions of management and change agents dominate. This is because both approaches are based on a unitarist view of the organisation, which discounts the experiences, interests and goals of other parties outside management, as well as assuming that everyone is motivated by the same goals. As Nord and Jermier observe:

> For managerialist writers, resistance interferes with their vision of a work force cooperating in the pursuit of organizational goals. Because these writers tend to grant a privileged position to the objectives of managers or owners, the 'resisters'' goals are of peripheral concern ... To the degree that these goals deserve to be understood at all, it is mainly to find ways to keep them from interfering with 'better' goals. (1994: 401)

With both approaches the question remains, however: who gets to decide when something is called resistance or not? And who gets to decide when someone is a resistor or a champion of change, and whether proposed alternative perspectives on a change initiative are facilitative or awkward, helpful or reactionary? In both perspectives it is the manager or change agent who is granted the privilege to decide on the nature of change, to decide also whose interests and assumptions count and which suggestions by subordinates are helpful (and worthy of accommodation) and which are not (and therefore labelled resistance) (Thomas and Hardy, 2011).

There is an inherent assumption that the change agent is always competent, well-intentioned and fundamentally doing the right thing. However, change may be motivated by many different factors beyond those espoused – for example, to boost senior managerial remuneration and to improve share value (Staw and Epstein, 2000). Furthermore, change agents may be less than receptive to radical challenges from subordinates to their change vision. There are many examples of whistleblowers whose speaking out against organisational malfeasance and scandals has resulted in their victimisation and vilification (Agocs, 1997). Challenging conceptions and institutionalised practices is rarely welcomed in organisations.

Building on the ideas of French philosopher Michel Foucault (1980, 1982) on the role of power in the creation and institutionalising of meanings, we can understand organisations as sites of ongoing negotiations, where power and resistance are part and parcel of everyday sensemaking. The focus here is on the role of power in producing meanings, and on resistance as being the harnessing of this power to produce different meanings. Power and resistance thus work in tandem to produce change. Viewing change as a combination of power and resistance has a number of implications. First, change is now conceived of as a re-articulation of existing power relations embedded in prevailing organisational meanings. Second, what constitutes power and what constitutes resistance are a matter of perspective and are difficult to separate out and isolate. This means that it is not an easy task to divide either who is 'for change' and who is 'against change' or change agents and change recipients, since the movement of meanings by participants' interactions is multilateral and iterative. Change can occur in unintended and unanticipated ways, involving shifting allegiances, views and interests.

This approach shifts the focus from questions of why and when individuals resist change to how power and resistance work together in particular ways that are constitutive of change. While one set of meanings enshrined in a change vision might be imposed, this change is much more likely to resonate and be taken on by members if they are part of this meaning constitution. New sets of meanings, new practices and new material arrangements are much more likely to become embedded in organisational members' frames of understanding if they have played a part in and informed these negotiations. Power-resistance relations lie at the heart of these negotiations.

This gives us an understanding of change and resistance that is less clear-cut than either the negative or the positive views discussed in this chapter. Rather, it suggests that change is messy, complex, unpredictable, situation-specific, multi-authored and multidimensional, and involves both power and resistance. Complicated though this picture is, surely it is better than the naïve and simplistic accounts found in the unitarist approaches, which seem wildly different from most people's experiences of organisation.

Martin John Henry: resisting and accepting change within the creative process

As noted above, thoughtful resistance should be celebrated and harnessed, and for musicians in a band such resistance is often finely balanced in terms of creative leadership and vision. For example, on reflection Martin John Henry (Chapter 19, pp. 336–42) felt that as a songwriter he was more of a dictator in terms of his creative vision. It took him years to learn how to be in a band and how to accept resistance to this power and vision, and appreciate and use the skills of those in his band. However, he then felt he had became too diplomatic, not resisting enough, and, rather, just blending in as 'one of the guys' and doing his bit. Because of Martin's lack of resistance to change, he found himself working on songs together with people with whom it did not work in terms of relationships. Looking back, he feels that working with people out of necessity and resisting change is not a sustainable way of doing things because band relationships become tense and overheated. Change happened anyway, as an attempt to make a change in the line-up was overtaken by other changes in people's work or family lives. 'Everyone was just eager to draw a line underneath it and get on with their own lives for a while.'

Moving into his solo album project, Martin had to accept change in that he was faced with a different way of working. As noted in his story, he found a big change from working in the band. Whereas there were five people in De Rosa and 'there was a bit more diplomacy required' – hence, each member perhaps resisted pursuing their own creative vision – on the solo project 'it was just me and Andy [Miller, the producer]: sometimes we are really bouncing off each other, you know, just ideas'. They were accepting resistance to each other's different ideas, enhancing the creative process. On the solo album, the music was 'pretty much half written and finished in the studio and embellished'.

On a personal note, resistance in the music business – which Martin describes as 'chaotic and unplanned' much of the time ('in fact lack of organisation is the key characteristic') – was an integral part of sustaining himself as a songwriter: it involved 'managing five or six occasional jobs in order to be able to make music when I need to make music'.

Application questions

- What is being resisted, and why?
- Is the resistance active and quiescent, and what does this tell us about the social situation?

- How does resistance contribute to the generation of a dialogue or multiple narratives?
- What might be learned from the resistance?

References

Agocs, C. (1997) Institutionalized resistance to organizational change: denial, inaction and repression. *Journal of Business Ethics*, 16: 917–31.

Armenakis, A.A. and Harris, S.G. (2002) Crafting a change message to create transformational readiness. *Journal of Organizational Change Management*, 15(2): 169–83.

Armenakis, A.A., Harris, S.G. and Mossholder, K.W. (1993) Creating readiness for organizational change. *Human Relations*, 46: 681–703.

Beer, M. and Nohria, N. (2000) Cracking the code of change. *Harvard Business Review*, (May–June): 133–41.

Bennebroek Gravenhorst, K.M. and In't Veld, R.J. (2004) Power and collaboration: methodologies for working together in change. In Boonstra, J.J. (ed) *Dynamics of organizational change and learning*, pp. 317–41. Chichester: Wiley.

Brown, A.D., Humphreys, M. and Gurney, P.M. (2005) Narrative, identity and change: a case study of Laskarina Holidays. *Journal of Organizational Change Management*, 18(4): 312–26.

Coch, L. and French, J. (1948) Overcoming resistance to change. *Human Relations*, 1: 512–32.

Courpasson, D., Dany, F. and Clegg, S. (2011) Registers at work: generating productive resistance in the workplace. *Organization Science*, 23(3): 801–19.

Dent, E.B. and Goldberg, S.G. (1999) Challenging 'resistance to change'. *Journal of Applied Behavioral Science*, 35: 25–41.

Dobosz-Bourne, D. and Jankowicz, A.D. (2006) Reframing resistance to change: experience from General Motors Poland. *International Journal of Human Resource Management*, 17: 2,021–34.

Eyerman, R. and Jamison, A. (1998) *Music and social movements: mobilizing traditions in the twentieth century*. Cambridge University Press.

Ford, J.D. and Ford, L.W. (1995) The role of conversations in producing intentional change in organizations. *Academy of Management Review*, 20(3): 541–70.

Ford, J.D. and Ford, L.W. (2009) Decoding resistance to change. *Harvard Business Review*, 87: 99–103.

Ford, J.D., Ford, L.W. and D'Amelio, A. (2008) Resistance to change: the rest of the story. *Academy of Management Review*, 33: 362–77.

Foucault, M. (1980) *Power/knowledge: selected interviews and other writings 1972–1977*, edited by Gordon, C. Brighton: Harvester Press.

Foucault, M. (1982) Afterword: the subject and power. In Dreyfus, H. and Rabinow, P. (eds) *Michel Foucault: beyond structuralism and hermeneutics*, pp. 208–66. Brighton: Harvester Press.

Foucault, M. (2001) *Fearless speech*, edited by Pearson, J. Los Angeles: Semiotext(e).

Furst, S.A. and Cable, D.M. (2008) Reducing employee resistance to organizational change: managerial influence tactics and leader-member exchange. *Journal of Applied Psychology*, 93: 453–62.

Geisler, D. (2001) Bottom-feeders: people who reject change. *Executive Excellence*, 18(12): 19.

Ghoshal, S. and Bartlett, C.A. (1996) Rebuilding behavioral context: a blueprint for corporate renewal. *MIT Sloan Management Review*, 37(2): 11–23.

Harvard Business School (2005) *Managing change to reduce resistance*. Boston, MA: Harvard Business School Press.

Kondo, D. (1990) *Crafting selves: power, gender and discourses of identity in a Japanese workplace*. University of Chicago Press.

Kotter, J. (1995) Leading change: why transformation efforts fail. *Harvard Business Review*, 73: 59–67.

Kotter, J.P. and Schlesinger, L.A. (1979) Choosing strategies for change. *Harvard Business Review*, 57: 106–14.

Lüscher, L.S. and Lewis, M.W. (2008) Organizational change and managerial sensemaking: working through paradox. *Academy of Management Journal*, 51: 221–40.

Maurer, R. (1996) *Beyond the wall of resistance: unconventional strategies that build support for change*. Austin, TX: Bard Books.

Nord, J.M. and Jermier, W.R. (1994) Overcoming resistance to resistance: insights from a study from the shadows. *Public Administration Quarterly*, Winter: 396–409.

Oreg, S. and Sverdlik, N. (2011) Ambivalence toward imposed change: the conflict between dispositional resistance to change and the orientation toward the change agent. *Journal of Applied Psychology*, 96(2): 337–49.

Piderit, S.K. (2000) Rethinking resistance and recognizing ambivalence: a multi-dimensional view of attitudes toward an organizational change. *Academy of Management Review*, 25: 783–94.

Poole, P.P., Gioia, D.A. and Gray, B. (1989) Influence modes, schema change, and organizational transformation. *Journal of Applied Behavioral Science*, 25: 271–89.

Sorge, A. and van Witteloostuijn, A. (2004) The (non)sense of organizational change: an essai about universal management hypes, sick consultancy metaphors, and healthy organization theories. *Organization Studies*, 25: 1,205–31.

Staw, B.M. and Epstein, L.D. (2000) What bandwagons bring: effects of popular management techniques on corporate performance, reputation, and CEO pay. *Administrative Science Quarterly*, 26: 501–24.

Topping, A. (2013) Pussy Riot ask Britons to flood Russia with letters of support. *Guardian*, 22 June: 23.

Tourish, D., Paulsen, N., Hobman, E. and Prashant, B. (2004) The downsides of downsizing: communication processes and information needs in the aftermath of a workforce reduction strategy. *Management Communication Quarterly*, 17(4): 485–516.

Thomas, R. and Hardy, C. (2011) Reframing resistance to organizational change. *Scandinavian Journal of Management*, 27(3): 322–31.

Thomas, R., Sargent, L. and Hardy, C. (2011) Managing organizational change: negotiating meaning and power-resistance relations. *Organization Science*, 22: 22–41.

Turino, T. (2008) *Music as social life: the politics of participation*. University of Chicago Press.

van Dam, K., Oreg, S. and Schyns, B. (2008) Daily work contexts and resistance to organisational change: the role of leader-member exchange, development climate, and change process characteristics. *Applied Psychology: an International Review*, 57(2): 313–34.

6   Identity work – organising the self, organising music

Christine Coupland

> Music constructs our sense of identity through the direct experiences it
> offers to the body, time and sociability, experiences which enable us to
> place ourselves in imaginative cultural narratives ... but what makes
> music special for identity – is that it defines space without boundaries
> (a game without frontiers).   (Frith, 1996: 124–5)

> How do I know who I am until I see what I say?   (Coupland, 2012)

Introduction to identity work

People who have an interest in identity work hold certain assumptions
about the world. These include a belief that we craft ourselves, moment by
moment, in interaction with others and our environments: an interaction
that comprises embodied, emotional and articulated practices. This is not
to suggest that we can 'be' anything, but it does suggest a belief in our
active capacity to produce a plausible self within the confines of what is
possible. I will unpick that a little. If I were to claim to be a brain surgeon
while operating a supermarket checkout I might not be believed.
However, if I were to put on a white coat and walk the corridors of a
hospital making this claim there would be a greater tendency to believe
me. Thus, how we behave in particular contexts, what we say and what we
do, all 'say' something about our 'selves' – our identities. We may have
many conscious and subconscious motivators to produce a plausible self
through identity work, but the desirable outcome remains the same – for
people to believe you – for your identity work to produce a plausible self.

Why would organisation theorists be interested in this activity? Good
question. Of course, many of them are not – just a select number of people
who have made a connection between how we organise ourselves and
what impact that has on what we do. From very early studies, carried out
by the Chicago School of sociologists, a study of identity work began to
show how people craft their 'selves' in talk (Snow and Anderson, 1987).
Scholars have considered how an interest in identity allows a study of
time, culture, language and history. In contemporary times identities,

never unified, appear as increasingly fragmented and fractured – never singular but multiply constructed across different, often intersecting and antagonistic, discourses, practices and positions. Within this apparently conflicting collection of assembled 'selves', identities are constructed within, not outside, representation and discourse (Hall, 1996: 4). And a study of their use, in both the mundane and spectacular occasion, enables us to ask questions around the resources of history, language and culture about who we can be.

More recently, scholars have been interested in how we do this identity work (Beech, 2008; Watson, 2008) and how scholars look at (or for) it in research (Alvesson et al., 2008). A number of academics have made some explicit links between language and identities, drawing on core disciplines of psychology, social psychology, sociology and anthropology, and have applied them to a study of organising (Ybema et al., 2009). 'Identity is not seen as a thing that we are, the property of an individual, but as something we do. It is a practical accomplishment, achieved and maintained through the detail of language use' (Widdicombe and Wooffitt, 1995: 133). Organisation theorists are interested in what we do because they would like to be able to (a) understand it more clearly, (b) predict it more accurately and (c) control it more precisely. (Please note that (c) is optional for some organisation theorists.)

There are several debates that surface as people attempt to study identity work. The most important one resonates around to what extent we are free to produce ourselves. That is, how much agency do we have and what are the institutional controls that prevent us from having complete agency? Institutions in this instance can include real or imagined systems of meaning around gender, class, education, etc., that offer limits to what we can be. They provide conditions of possibility within which we are able to craft ourselves. Other debates circulate around to what extent it is possible for other people to regulate or control our identity. And there are further debates around whether any agency is an illusion, whether we craft ourselves from ways of being that are largely predetermined because of powerful (hegemonic) discourses around who we 'should' be.

Before we move on to look at how this approach might be useful in order to understand practices of organising music, it is, perhaps, useful to look at examples from studies of understanding identity work practices more generally in organisations.

Organising identity work

It is not just an individual who engages in identity work: whole organisations attempt to do it too. Corporate identity claims are made up of images and words that legitimate one, or a few, preferred versions above other possible ones. They are visible in artefacts (buildings, websites, mission statements, corporate literature) as well as in organisationally espoused values. However, in a similar way to my making a claim to be a brain surgeon while scanning the frozen peas, they are made in a context of alternative meanings being available – thus, they can be contested by the receiving audience. In an earlier paper (Coupland, 2005) I demonstrated this by looking at a number of oil producers' web pages to see how they claimed to be corporately socially responsible on their corporate websites. It was at a time when there had been recent, damaging, oil spillage in Nigeria and the world had started to take notice of what the large corporations were doing in less developed countries. Thus, the context was one in which there was an alternative argument that they were not very 'responsible' at all. A great deal of identity work was done by the oil producers to counter this alternative viewpoint of the kind of organisations they were. The following extract is an example of identity work carried out on a website in the above-described context, where the corporate view is crafted for an outside audience.

To conduct business as responsible, corporate members of society, to observe the laws of the countries in which they operate, to express support for fundamental human rights in line with the legitimate role of business and to give proper regard to health, safety and the environment consistent with their commitment to contribute to sustainable development. (Extract from BP website, adapted from Coupland, 2005)

The competing ideologies of business and the environment can be seen to be woven into the text in this extract. It was ostensibly about the company's responsibility to society. However, a close exploration of the account makes visible how business concerns are positioned over societal concerns throughout the argument. In the first instance, the descriptor 'corporate members of society' appears to suggest that the organisation's first concern was a corporate one. Second, 'to observe the laws of the country in which they operate' places responsibility for perceived unethical behaviour outside the company – but within the law and therefore in accordance with the socially operable judgements pertinent to the local context of the behaviour. In addition, the term 'to express support for fundamental human rights' is interesting; it is unlikely that a company would argue for not supporting human rights. The qualifier to the statement 'in line with the legitimate role of business' positions the claim to support fundamental human rights as operable from within a business context.

Thus, the corporate argument can be seen to be slipping between business and environmental issues, selling one in terms of the other, mitigated through a claimed adherence to law. The circle of argument is retained through the act of attending to these oppositional forces, but some close reading of the text illustrates how the environment is subsumed under the more dominant rhetoric of the business case (Coupland, 2005).

On a more everyday level, we routinely and mundanely craft ourselves for public exposure. We not only use the artefacts around us to promote our preferred view – what we wear, the car we drive, where we choose to live and work – they all present a picture of our 'selves'. We may feel that we exercise some choice around some of these things – that they are within our control, at least for some of the time. But, in addition, the way we talk about ourselves, while doing our everyday interactions, is also part of our identity work and is more subtle, I would argue. Sometimes we are careful about how we construct what we say, but most of the time our concern with getting things said in a convincing way means we produce ourselves as a side-product of doing something else. This is the identity work that interests organisation scholars as we argue that everyone brings to view how they are organised through language practices of legitimation, blame, justification and accountability.

Creative identity work

So, to move our focus specifically to musicians' identity work, research suggests that there are patterns of ways of speaking that creative people draw on when being asked about their work. Recall that the assumption is, what we say 'says' something about us – even if we are talking about something as mundane as the weather. In an earlier study of musicians' talk we found that, along with descriptions of events or festivals, threaded through these stories are accounts of the self as a legitimate player, as a rightful member of a community. These patterns appear as the speaker engages in identity work around the creative self-project, the creative act and the organised creative. As organisation theorists we are interested in how each of these themes is constructed and performed in musicians' talk (Coupland et al., 2013).

There are many ways that this identity work is made visible to an intended (and sometimes unintended) audience. How musicians dress, how they behave (who they please and who they offend) and how and what they perform all carry out forms of identity work. For the purposes of this chapter, in the interest of brevity, we are focusing on how people speak about themselves, how identities are worked up and deployed in talk. Some examples of this include how, when asked to describe their involvement in a particular creative project, they pre-empt their account with descriptions of venues that they have played at. It may be that their significance is known in the main to the *cognoscente*, but there is a lightly coded set of messages around having played in certain places (big venues, elite venues, cool venues, supporting major artists, etc.). These markers are a pattern that you can see/hear in everyone's talk. It is so mundane that we miss it most of the time, but it is important, as it is identity work going on between two people as each finds out more about who the other person is. They are working up a warrant to speak. Here is a typical example exchange below:

MUSICIAN 1: I worked with Dog City, [a record label – pseudonym] ... the singer Joanna Newsome [pseudonym] ... kind of big cult appeal ... I have opened for her a few times ... are you familiar with her music?
INTERVIEWER: No, is she good?
MUSICIAN 1: American singer – yes, she is good.

(Adapted from Coupland et al., 2013)

There is a lot that can be said from this tiny extract of talk, so I will point out just a few ways in which identity is working here. First, consider how talking about working with a record label positions the musician as one with credibility. This credibility is enhanced by drawing on an association with a big name – notice, however, when the speaker's awareness that the interviewer is not one of the musician's peers is made evident as he checks if the interviewer is familiar with the singer's music. The interviewer joins in here with the musician's identity work by asking the expected question 'Is she good?' At the risk of stating the obvious, you would not mention working with someone who is particularly bad at singing – nor would you mention working with a relatively unknown artist. So the interviewer joins in the game, or work, of constructing a credible identity that legitimates and justifies his involvement with a particular project. A final observation: the musician gives a more detailed response to the interviewer's question than just 'yes' for the final comment. He adds detail that may enhance/strengthen the singer's credibility for a non-musician interviewer.

Other markers of significance, which were quite subtle, emerged during the same study. These were worked up as 'evidence' of belonging in an authentic way within an understood hierarchy of what it is to be a professional musician. I have reproduced below an extract in which the musician talks about what is important when composing music. We can make the argument that (much like oil-producing companies having to work up plausible socially responsible identities) an authentic musician identity may be tainted in some way by association with 'mainstream' popularity. Talking about emotion is key here, as it appears to function to deflect a possibility that writing for a mainstream audience in a strategic way would not be authentic.

MUSICIAN 2: For me the most important thing is to get an emotion across through a song: if that ends up, if someone in the mainstream listeners likes that song then that is fine because I know that I was not thinking about that, I was thinking about my personal connection with the emotions throughout the song.
(Adapted from Coupland et al., 2013)

It could, therefore, be argued that some of our identity work involves crafting what we are not, or what we do not do, in our creative endeavours. Thus, musicians' concerns, as creative people, appear to revolve around authenticity and belonging to a community of other people of authenticity, however diverse that community may appear to be. We can extrapolate beyond these extracts here and ask the 'So what?' question. Why would an organisation studies scholar, or someone who is interested in how music and musicians may be organised find this kind of analysis useful? There are many possible responses to that question. First, by looking at patterns of legitimate belonging we can work out who the community includes (and who it does not). We can work out aspirational belonging with a view to future collaborative work. Second, how creative people organise their 'selves' (from a range of multiple possible options) for work, or interactions about work, shows alternative ways to organise – some that work well and others less well. Finally, we can consider, by looking closely at identity work in language, how this self-organising affects the creative act – or to look at this another way, how does the creative act articulate or shape who we are?

Three themes of understanding – the creative self-project, the creative act and the organised creative – gained from studies of identity will be illustrated through an analysis of Marco's story as depicted in 'Managing a punk band' (Chapter 18, pp. 236–44) in the remainder of the chapter. This will enable speculation on how these ideas may relate to practices of organising music more generally.

Any analyst who is interested in identity work will consider what came first. What I mean by this is: how do people begin the story of 'them'? Drawing on the story of Marco taken from this volume I will demonstrate how someone, by looking at identity work, can see how our assembled 'selves' are built into fragile coherence from the discourses available in cultural and historical contexts generally and deployed specifically in interaction.

Analysts can make much of how we position ourselves as separate from or closely aligned with collectives or others. Organisers of people need to understand how we see our 'selves' as close to, or distanced from, others and who those others might be, as it will affect potentials for organising.

Thus, we are individuals who speak as individuals when asked about ourselves – or our story – but we quite quickly describe ourselves as a part of a collective for reasons sometimes unknown but often to do with the discursive business of legitimation, blame, justification and accountability. Hence, the first section of the chapter provides a description in which the crafter of the story draws on some of the legitimating techniques (venues played, bands supported, etc.) described in the earlier study of musicians' talk (Coupland et al., 2013). The 'Background' section enables the storyteller to dislocate temporally. What this does as far as identity scholars are concerned is to retrospectively make sense of who we are today. It is a story of legitimation – even, for example, if you are telling a tale of crime and a spell in prison, you are an (arguably) moral person who now knows (or is) better. Thus, retrospective telling allows us to re-story the past to create a version of us for today. Marco (or his biographer) selects this collection of descriptions of the many possible:

The band . . . had previously 'been done over' by their record label (the two friends spent the following year just listening to music).

The band is his 'first proper attempt at being in a professional band' (before this he had been just writing songs on his own).

Marco recalls a point when 'the power shifted and we became one of those bands that other bands were asking to do that [support them]'

Building friendships with other bands 'is just what you do' in order to become established.

Marco is also the band's manager and feels that networks are vital for learning how the music industry works.

These are extracts from the background story. What appears in the text is a see-saw effect of minimising what went on before followed by the 'real' effect of what is happening now. The pattern works to set up action following inaction, or organised following not or dis-organised. This operates as a description of what has happened (a history) made up from selected pieces of relevant information. The subtext, or identity work, that seems to thread through this is one of minimising being strategic. This is important to know if, for example, you were a festival organiser and you interviewed Marco for his suitability to head up a big festival involving lots of planning and coordination. At first glance you might imagine that Marco likes to drift along with the occasional realisation of arriving somewhere else almost by accident. However, as an identity scholar, I would argue instead that he is 'doing' his creative identity as a musician over and above an organised or strategic identity that may, perceivably, dissolve or challenge his authenticity as an artist. This is not to suggest that Marco consciously adopts one position over another in talk – rather, he has subconscious concerns around authenticity, and so in talk he downplays his own agency with regard to being active in organising the band. Consider his explanation of becoming a headliner rather than a supporting act: 'the power shifted', where he places agency elsewhere – nothing to do with him and his endeavours – or at least he writes his own efforts out of the story. Note how this is contradicted further down the text: 'as the band's manager he feels that networks are vital...'. With an element of identity work (self-labels as the band manager) he gives himself warrant (justification) to be strategic, knowledgeable about what is required, instrumental and highly organised. I would suggest he would make an ideal festival organiser.

Thus, we have illustrated how the creative self-project, the creative act and the organised creative are mutually constitutive when doing identity work , held in happy tension until under the academic gaze.

As we have paid some attention to the beginning of Marco's story it may be interesting to look at the end – so far, entitled 'The future...'. Most of this part of Marco's story is structured around his and the band's attitude towards signing to a label. It is well known that signing to a record label has both risks and benefits attached. Most predictably, it is a signal of esteem, belonging to the community legitimised by one of the gatekeeper groups. Less well known, perhaps, outside the musician community are the risks to artistic integrity, loss of autonomy and reputation by association with an inappropriate label. Thus, tensions are evident as this description is given by the storyteller. With regard to identity work by Marco, he constructs 'bothered but not bothered' in the following extract:

> We just have to keep on working as if we are never going to get a deal, that is really attractive to labels ... If we can show them we are a self-sustaining band that work hard in their own right, then that is much more attractive than it is to sign a band that don't know what they are doing and that they have to work really hard with to get them on the right tracks.

What I mean by 'bothered but not bothered' here is that he constructs a hard-working identity for the band (they do this anyway) – a record label would not affect this. The record label members are then positioned as wanting to sign a band and not do any work. Thus, a not-so-subtle moral positioning is carried out. It is evident that record labels hold the power of recognition (legitimation) for bands, but it is possible to undermine their right to all this power. The creative musician is, after all, the producer of the artefact that the record label wants to sell: without their labour the record labels would cease to exist. The gatekeeper identity is thus challenged as necessary but perhaps peripheral to their endeavours. The tentative relationships are constructed in the following extracts. When talking about the next move, 'signing up to an independent label', they are 'talking to a couple'. They have one label 'who are really keen, who would sign us tomorrow'. They are also talking to another label that has 'shown a little interest, and I would stress little'. But the quality of the label is relevant: 'we would only appreciate the view of a label that had produced really good artists . . . they've got good taste or taste along the lines of ours'. Though 'we might find that nobody is interested'. However, 'there is no point in jumping the gun when there may be a much more influential label that wants to work with us'.

Many things occur in these extracts that are identifiable as identity work. One of the key things is how the individual (as a member of a band) constructs his/their relationship with a larger collective – one that has the potential to organise their work for larger audiences. This relationship is constructed as tentative: 'talking to' suggests a negotiated process – not too committed but showing an interest (in both directions). This enables a speaker to demonstrate legitimacy (through the labels' interest) but agency (it is the band's choice whether the label would be right for them). These extracts, taken from a series of 'turns' in talk, are reproduced in the original order, and the final two comments appear to summarise tensions in managing this process. The identity work above, despite identifying a number of labels who are showing 'interest', suggests that it may come to nothing. Marco and the band have to make sure they have the label with the most appropriate level of influence before they decide to sign up.

What is being demonstrated here is a nuanced understanding of what is valuable. Members of bands may well feel that they would like the legitimacy of being signed to a record label, but creative artists will have a process of estimating the costs (artistic, emotional, social, cultural) attached to signing with a label that does not have 'good taste'. Thus, on a micro scale in fine detail we can see self-organising occurring as the individual or group aligns with, or rejects, other groups or collectives, despite their apparent power to increase their exposure to a public. It is not so much that there is a conflict or tension emerging as being organised and being creative are conjoined; it is that, for an independent, creative worker, artistic authenticity cannot be compromised through association with inappropriate groups, however powerful they may be.

Summary

For creative people, as with any other people, there are patterns of ways of speaking that people draw on when being asked about their work. In these patterns there are also tensions around how/who not to be; identity work takes place as speakers negotiate these tensions in their talk. We can imagine that for creative workers they may include authentic rather than inauthentic, artistic rather than material, creative rather than productive, niche rather than popular. Managing these tensions through identity work in talk can seem quite straightforward and predictable, until we encounter the logics of business. In a similar way to the example given earlier in the chapter of oil producers who told their business story as an overarching logic that subsumed their corporate, socially responsible organisation story, it seems that one set of logics has to dominate – although there may be eruptions from other logics from time to time.

For the creative worker the dominant logic appears to be artistic authenticity. For music and musical events to be organised this has to remain the dominant logic; however, this does not preclude some creative tension with other logics – of organising, for example – without which the festivals could not take place. The purpose here is not to celebrate 'authentic' as something that can be finally achieved, but rather to examine how musicians construct and manage their perceptions of authentic identities. A further purpose is to demonstrate how an exploration of authenticity-based identity work serves as a meaningful addition to studies of these artists' identities.

As we assume that what we say – the words we use – 'says' something about us, threaded through stories of events or festivals are accounts of the self as a legitimate player, as a rightful member of a community. These patterns appear as the speaker engages in identity work around the creative self-project, the creative act and the organised creative. As organisation theorists we are interested in how each of these themes is constructed and performed in musicians' talk illustrating promising practices of adaptation in creative work.

Application questions

- How do people begin their story of 'them'?
- What does what they say 'say' about them?
- With whom does the storyteller associate/dissociate?
- What identity markers are highlighted, and to what purpose?
- How are various selves/aspects of self assembled?
- What changes are/are not likely to occur?

References

Alvesson, M., Ashcraft, K.L. and Thomas, R. (2008) Identity matters: reflections on the construction of identity scholarship in organization studies. *Organization*, 15(5): 51–74.

Beech, N. (2008) On the nature of dialogic identity work. *Organization*, 15(1): 51–74.

82   *Christine Coupland*

Coupland, C. (2005) Corporate social responsibility as argument on the web. *Journal of Business Ethics*, 62: 355–66.

Coupland, C. (2012) How do I know what I mean until I see what I say? Inaugural lecture at Hull University, 20 February.

Coupland, C., Gilmour, C. and Beech, N. (2013) Composing the self: creative identity work. Paper presented to the British Academy of Management Conference, Liverpool.

Frith, S. (1996) Music and identity. In Hall, S. and du Gay, P. (eds) *Questions of cultural studies*, pp. 108–17. London: Sage.

Hall, S. (1996) Who needs 'identity'? In Hall, S. and du Gay, P. (eds) *Questions of cultural studies*, pp. 1–17. London: Sage.

Snow, D.A. and Anderson, L. (1987) Identity work among the homeless: the verbal construction and avowal of personal identities. *American Journal of Sociology*, 92(6): 1,336–71.

Watson, T.J. (2008) Managing identity: identity work, personal predicaments, structural circumstances. *Organization*, 15(1): 121–43.

Widdicombe, S. and Wooffitt, R. (1995) *The language of youth subcultures: social identity in action*. New York: Harvester Wheatsheaf.

Ybema, S., Keenoy, K., Oswick, C., Beverungen, A., Ellis, N. and Sabelis, I. (2009) Articulating identities. *Human Relations*, 62(3): 299–322.

7 Creative strategy: notes from a small label

Chris Bilton and Stephen Cummings

'Creative strategy' has two dimensions. First, it describes an attempt to apply creative thinking logic to definitions and models of strategy, on the assumption that strategy as a field is having to deal with an increasingly unpredictable economy, where innovation, talent and creative solutions are at a premium (Mann and Chan, 2011). Second, it describes an approach to strategic thinking that is adapted to the realities of working in so-called 'creative' businesses (Scase and Davis, 2000; Jeffcutt and Pratt, 2002; Florida, 2012). The first of these dimensions is more theoretical, continuing a long-standing debate about the meaning and scope of 'strategy' and 'strategic planning' (Mintzberg, 1994; Porter, 1996). The second dimension is more empirical, referring to the lived experience of those working in the creative industries[1] to ascertain what works in practice.

We believe that these two dimensions are linked, and that by analysing the creative strategies that have evolved through practical necessity in creative businesses, we can draw out some wider implications for a creative model of strategy (Bilton and Cummings, 2010; Bilton, 2007). In this chapter we are particularly concerned with the music industry, and will draw on the case study outlined in the field chapter as well as other observations on the so-called creative industries to highlight some guiding principles for encouraging effective creative strategy.

What, then, do we know about the characteristics of the music industry? And how does this challenge what we think we know about strategy? A number of authors have argued that knowledge and knowledge workers have replaced capital and access to capital as the new source of wealth in our economy (de Geus, 1997; Nonaka and Takeuchi, 1995; Stewart,

---

[1] We don't intend here to be drawn into a debate about the validity of the standard UK definition of the 'creative industries' (DCMS, 1998), other than to say that restricting this term to a prescribed list of arts, media and entertainment organisations is unnecessarily prescriptive and reflects the pragmatics of cultural policy rather than any meaningful distinction. Certainly, we have found plenty of examples of creativity outside the 'cultural sector', including sports, technology, manufacturing and services.

1997). This is borne out by the rise of global knowledge-intensive businesses like Google, Facebook and Apple, and the perceived shrinking, by comparison, of our manufacturing industries.

The music industry is part of this new 'knowledge economy', especially in the smaller independent sector. UK independent music labels are not rich in capital terms, but they are knowledge-rich. Their 'wealth' lies in their talent and their knowledge about music, as well as in their ability to recognise that knowledge and talent in others. This is the capital they draw upon, which allows them to continue to challenge the dominance of larger, better resourced major label competitors in the 'war for talent'. In the UK, the independent sector has a market share of around 25 per cent (boosted by the 'Adele effect' from a handful of successful artists); meanwhile the American Association of Independent Music claimed 32.7 per cent of the US market in 2012. This is remarkable, given that the 'big four' major labels enjoy not only greater financial resources but also cross-media partnerships, which allow them to exploit synergies with music television, film, video streaming and online media.

A second characteristic of the independent music sector is the merging of different tasks and functions in work routines and roles. In many cases, an independent record label consists of one or two people who cover everything from artists and repertoire (A&R), marketing and distribution, production and artist support, live gigs and recording through to web design and online distribution. Even in the major labels, where job descriptions are more narrowly defined, a common interest in the music and the artists means that there are considerable synergies and overlaps between functions and expertise up and down the company. The exception is the newer players such as broadband media providers and technology companies, which are increasingly influential in the music industry. These new intermediaries do not share the record labels' passionate engagement with the product, with the result that strategic decisions are likely to be more remote from any operational engagement with artists and music.

A third characteristic is closely related to this 'multitasking' culture and the collaborative nature of making music, which blurs the lines between artists, labels, intermediaries and fans (Jenkins, 2006). Creativity is increasingly co-creative, with artists and consumers working together to make or remake the product. Again, this is especially apparent in the independent sector. Independent record labels may be set up by frustrated artists initially 'self-releasing' their own material, or by enthusiastic fans helping friends to get their work out. Artists are avid consumers of music, and technology has helped to elide that relationship further, allowing samples and remixes by the artists and their fans, as well as a thriving

DIY culture of ordinary consumers and artists alike creating their own music and uploading or self-releasing this material online. Independent labels have also been at the forefront of new ways of distributing music that use technology to implicate consumers in the creative process, with bands like Radiohead, Nine Inch Nails and Trent Reznor leading the way. A more recent example of this co-creation approach, Beck's 2012 *Song Reader* project, will be considered later in this chapter.

We believe that these three emerging characteristics of the music industry, and of independent record labels in particular – the importance of knowledge as a new form of capital, the collaborative, multitasking culture of the record label and the blurring of production and consumption – are reflected in the nature of creative strategy in general. First, the importance of 'knowledge' in today's economy has not gone unremarked in the strategy literature. A recent study we were involved with confirms a growing interest in this topic in the 1990s and early 2000s (Cummings and Daellenback, 2009). The study concludes that since knowledge workers are increasingly autonomous and generally prefer to create orders rather than follow them, strategists will need to become more like politicians than commanders. Traditional business, government and military models see the organisation as a triangle, with strategy at its apex. Occasionally, an argument may be advanced for leading from the front line or 'bottom-up strategy'. Creative strategy argues for 'leading from the middle', with strategic thinking positioned at the centre of the organisational triangle, serving as a touchstone for creative and strategic thinking across all parts of the business, not as the capstone at the head of the structure. Creative strategy should not be the preserve of senior management or visionary leadership, but distributed across a knowledgeable, talented workforce that shapes the strategic vision. The role of the leader in this scenario is to provide a dexterous force at the centre of the organisation that can hold this diverse and occasionally unruly band of talents together.

Second, the need for strategic and creative thinking across every function of the organisation invites us to reconsider the scope and definition of strategy. Many books have argued for the importance of innovation or individuality in strategy, or the development of a more entrepreneurial culture, or have outlined the attributes and habits of leaders or the principles of great organisations. In *Creative strategy: reconnecting business and innovation* (Bilton and Cummings, 2010) we argue that a truly creative strategy – one that can add value to all aspects of the organisation – must strategically integrate successive processes of innovation, entrepreneurship, leadership and organisation so that each sustains the other, and the effect on the whole enterprise becomes greater than the sum of these individual parts. This integration of functions is intuitive and necessary for an independent record label, where one individual may embody all of these roles. Scaling this integrated, holistic approach up as the business grows in scale and complexity is more challenging. Along with the reliance on individual knowledge and talent and a lack of access to capital, this is a key reason that successful independent record labels choose to stay small rather than grow exponentially when they first taste success.

Third, the merging of producer and consumer in today's music industry is reflected in an emerging relationship between leaders and followers in business practice and between strategic and operational domains in the strategy literature. The pioneers of strategic management positioned strategy as something that acts upon and above the world around us, shaping it to our will and conforming the operational management of the firm to the strategic vision of the leader. Today, strategic vision and the unruly world it acts upon have become harder to separate – more co-creative in their relationship (see, for example, Nonaka and Zhu, 2012, and the emergence of the term 'open strategy', mirroring the trend towards open innovation where organisations seek to involve multiple stakeholders in strategy development). Strategy emerges as a response to operational realities, and the strategist and the strategised are coming to be regarded as more mutually dependent in a process neither entirely controls. In the creative industries, authors and producers are increasingly cast as supporting players in an evolving drama where consumers and audiences are calling the creative shots. Strategists too are increasingly in the business of supporting other people's strategies rather than originating and imposing their own plans.

Creative strategy in action: Song, by Toad

At a theoretical level, then, developments in the music industry invite us to question some of our assumptions about the position, scope and status of strategy. Creative strategy is an attempt to respond to this challenge by developing a different approach, which acknowledges the need for strategy to be more collaborative, holistic and flexible. To understand how this theoretical approach might work in practice, we turn now to the case of Song, by Toad, a Scottish independent record label launched by Matthew and his wife Kate in 2008 (Chapter 18, pp. 285–9). We analyse their development in relation to three key creative strategy themes: developing strategy as a network led from the middle of the organisation; creative strategy as a cycle that runs from innovation to organisation; and a DIY approach that formulates strategy by doing strategy.

Leading from the middle – strategy in networks

Creative work, contrary to the stereotype of the lonely artist, is highly collaborative and co-dependent. Small creative businesses are especially reliant on networks and alliances, embedded in local 'project ecologies' (Grabher, 2004) that support the germination of new ideas, and dependent on external partners up and down the value chain to gain access to finance, markets and talent. Repeatedly, Song, by Toad's Matthew is calling upon friends for favours to dig him out of a hole, suggest a venue, provide a list of contacts or another artist for a gig or simply for advice. Many of the label's formative decisions – to start writing reviews on a personal website, to help a band self-release their first album, to sign an artist – were based on friendships and favours. Many of the artists who want to work with the label today do so because they know Matthew personally and trust him.

This collaborative network is fairly typical of small creative businesses, not least because relationships and dependencies are a way of mitigating risk and improvising alternatives when things go wrong (Banks et al., 2000; Bilton, 1999b). The difficulty is that, within this web of relationships, somebody needs to pull the strings and make things happen. Fairly early in the story, Matthew realises that if the label is to succeed he is going to have to take the lead. When talent and resources are dispersed through a network, it requires some individual energy to pull these resources together. In theory, all the people Matthew works with could manage without him – they could write the songs, record the music, organise the gigs, press the CDs, commission the artwork, do the press release. But they don't. Matthew's special gift is not so much his own talent as his ability to get other people to realise and act upon their own talents and cooperate. It's notable that the label began with an impulse to help a band he liked self-release a CD. The impulse to help others achieve places Matthew in a supportive role – prompting, cajoling, encouraging and facilitating – yet a leading role in terms of impact and momentum.

There are some parallels here with the 2012 release of *Song Reader* by Beck. For this project, Beck released a book of sheet music for twenty Beck compositions, with an open invitation for people to record and interpret the songs. These versions were then uploaded to Beck's SongReader.net site. The project capitalises on the surge in consumer creativity on video sharing sites like YouTube and Vine, as well as technologies like GarageBand that allow individuals to replicate professional recording techniques. There is an intriguing clash here between the old medium of traditional printed sheet music (how music was distributed before the introduction of modern recording technologies) and the new medium of online streaming. There is also an interaction between the new rhetoric of consumer creativity and crowdsourcing, and the evolving role of the individual artist-entrepreneur, with Beck eventually releasing the album himself in more conventional form and staging concerts featuring interpretations by established professional artists. The supposed threat to individual artists posed by consumer creativity and the practice of ripping and remixing and redistributing copyrighted material is here turned to the artist's advantage. The song readers get to play, but the songwriter is still the driving creative force.

Matthew's decision to offer a guide on how to release an album via his blog follows a similar logic. In making his expertise available to others through an open-access, open-source platform, Matthew would seem to be writing himself out of a job. The reality is that enough artists will still prefer to draw on his combination of knowledge, contacts and commitment to realise their creative ambitions rather than go it alone. Even in a DIY culture of consumer creativity and user-generated content, the entrepreneurial ability to drive others to innovate and to make the most of their creative talent remains a powerful and necessary catalyst (Cummings et al., 2014).

We call this process 'leading from the middle'. Talent, expertise and knowledge are dispersed through a network, not concentrated in one person. Matthew does not claim to have all the answers, but he is the motivating force that drives those around him to act. He switches across a variety of leadership positions – promoting talent and music upwards to inform a consistent and sustainable voice for both bands and label; sussing a vision for both artists and label and ensuring their choices of venue, music and partners are consistent with that vision; mapping the terrain of the music industry and empowering artists to make their own decisions and release their own material; and linking to other promoters, associates, collaborators and artists who can contribute to what the label wants to achieve. It is this versatility that allows Matthew's label to evolve and sustain itself through a seemingly chaotic series of releases, gigs and tours (with a fair share of disasters along the way). Problems and solutions are distributed across the network. Matthew's job is to pull these energies together, not to impose his vision upon them.

From innovation to organisation: the strategy cycle

Small creative businesses are able to adopt a multitasking approach to their work and to embrace change and opportunity partly because they are focused around a small number of people and projects, governed – if at all – only by very informal, loosely coupled structures and processes. What happens when these small enterprises mature into fully fledged, sustainable businesses? What happens when small business becomes big business? When the originator of the business has to delegate work to others and manage their work rather than doing it all himself? Do the arteries harden and the youthful enthusiasms stiffen into stubborn certainties? Do the emergent strategic patterns resolve into a cage of routines and habits, locking down risk and innovation? Does the informal strategic approach of Song, by Toad have any relevance to Universal Records, a global company responsible for more than 30 per cent of global music sales in 2012? Will Song, by Toad's strategic model be sustainable if Matthew's own business is still running in ten years' time?

In *Creative strategy* we argue that creative strategy extends across innovation, entrepreneurship, leadership and organisation. These modes of creative strategy form a cycle as the business evolves, and require different capabilities. Innovation is the heart of the creative organisation – this is where ideas and insights first shape the business and continue to churn up new opportunities and solutions. Entrepreneurial drive gives the business legs, adding impetus to business innovations and taking them to market. Without that entrepreneurial energy, innovative projects fester and die. If innovation and entrepreneurship provide a beachhead for the creative enterprise, it requires a different set of abilities to establish and lead an enterprise into new territory. Leadership offers a centre of gravity to draw together the network of creative ideas and talents that drive entrepreneurship, allowing and respecting the diversity necessary for creativity while ensuring that entrepreneurs and innovators do not spin out into their own orbits. Finally, organisation provides a fertile environment within which established routines and new thinking can mutually enrich each other, offering a platform from which the creative cycle can begin again.

Song, by Toad is towards the start of this cycle. The elements of innovation and entrepreneurship in the business are obvious enough. Finding new artists and helping them develop their talent is the lifeblood of any independent label. Adding entrepreneurial drive to innovative talent, Matthew works through the messy and laborious process of releasing the CD and organising the gig. Alongside the openness to new ideas and new music is a bloody-minded determination, allowing him to trust his own judgement even when others advise him not to sign an artist. Creative thinking makes connections between contradictory attitudes and processes – in this case, Matthew's 'stubbornness' adding grit to his open-minded enthusiasm for the music. Alison Wenham, Chief Executive Officer (CEO) of the Association for Independent Music, notes that it is the independent sector's ability both to identify and invest in talent and to stand by their judgements which gives them an edge. Whereas the major labels have a hit ratio of at best one in ten, Alison argues that independent labels might improve that to a hit ratio of one success to every two or three misses. The difference reflects the independents' attention to detail and their continuing support for an artist, allowing them to convert initial failure to modest success. Admittedly, the threshold between success and failure is not set so high in commercial terms, so that personal survival and artistic success can compensate for occasional dips in sales.

Song, by Toad is moving into the next phase of the strategy cycle. Matthew's initial 'juggling' and 'doing everything' is giving way to the leadership role outlined in the previous section. Some of the work can now be entrusted to others, with Matthew coordinating and driving it forwards. The decision to commit to the label as a full-time job reflects the growing maturity of the business as well as Matthew's role within it, moving from a sole-trader or 'hobbyist' business to a network organisation.

This is where the story ends for now. The next chapter for Matthew might be the shift from owner-manager and network organisation into a business employing others. Of course, this may never happen. Business advisers, especially government-supported business development agencies, tend to push businesses to grow in order to provide employment and boost the local economy. Investors also want their assets to grow. For the business, though, growth may not always be good, triggering successive crises and disrupting relationships and processes that made the business successful in the first place. Nevertheless, it is likely that temporary associations will bed down into permanent relationships or employment, and informal partnerships become formal contracts. Matthew may need to take on staff to help him cope with the workload as the label's reputation grows and more bands ask him to sign them.

At this point, creative organisation, the fourth mode of creative strategy, becomes critical. The challenge is to maintain sufficient looseness within the organisation to allow new ideas and opportunities to emerge, while at the same time maintaining a tight enough structure to hold the different elements together. This becomes especially important for an organisation like Song, by Toad, which cannot afford to lose its entrepreneurial, innovative edge. In our experience, a consistent ethos or culture provides a loose-tight framework of this nature, which allows scope for renewal as well as a measure of continuity (Bilton and Cummings, 2011). This is where Matthew's emphasis on 'a consistent voice' is important. The ethos of Song, by Toad revolves around the personal reputation of the founder as somebody honest, trustworthy and reliable, rather than around a corporate reputation or brand. As organisations grow, there is a risk that the founder loses touch with the daily running of the enterprise or is forced to take on a new role or personality – in Matthew's terms, becoming another of those 'people in the music business who just talk and do not act'.

In *Creative strategy* we used the case of the writer Nick Hornby to exemplify the shift from innovation to entrepreneurship in the strategy cycle (Bilton and Cummings, 2010: 128–31). As well as writing novels, Hornby had diversified into a variety of collaborative projects involving screenwriting, songwriting, editing and non-fiction. One of his projects, Ministry of Stories, is a social enterprise in East London, established by Hornby with Lucy Macnab and Ben Payne in 2010 to get children and young people involved in writing and storytelling. The inspiration for this came from the American novelist Dave Eggers's 826 Valencia project in San Francisco, which works with children and teachers in the Bay area to develop writing skills and build confidence, self-respect and imagination through stories. Hornby describes Eggers as 'the most entrepreneurial person I've ever met'. As well as 826 Valencia, Eggers runs McSweeneys, a publishing house producing beautifully designed anthologies and journals, and fundraises for 826 Valencia (which has subsequently spawned branches in seven other cities including New York, Chicago, LA and Boston). He wrote the screenplay for Spike Jonze's adaptation of *Where the Wild Things Are*, writes children's books, designs album artwork, edits anthologies – while still finding time to be a highly successful and productive novelist in his own right.

As with Hornby, the diversification away from writing does not seem to have distracted Eggers from his essential identity as a writer – indeed, his literary output, combining playful subversion of literary forms and conventions with piercing honesty, seems to mirror and inform his 'extracurricular' activities as a publisher and social entrepreneur. Recent projects, combining fact with fiction in *Zeitoun* and co-writing *What next?* with a Sudanese refugee, have signalled a desire to engage with realities beyond literature, but Eggers still claims to find fiction 'more liberating and enjoyable on a daily basis' (Day, 2013). His most recent fiction works, *Hologram for a king* and *The circle*, contain a sharp satirical edge that may reflect Eggers's desire to 'tell a story that might have an impact' but also echo the impetus behind his non-profit work that 'sometimes you feel like getting out in the world and seeing if you can be useful in some more immediate or tangible way' (ibid.).

Hornby and Eggers have extended their range of activities by collaborating with teachers, musicians, film-makers and other writers, but this expansion seems if anything to have reinforced their sense of their own identity as storytellers. As Song, by Toad expands as an enterprise, Matthew's identity and ethos will remain essential to the business's continued success. The experience of writers like Hornby and Eggers suggests that changing roles and activities does not need to mean losing the essential 'voice' that encapsulates the identity of Matthew and Song, by Toad.

The cycle from innovation and entrepreneurship to leadership and organisation (and back again) is iterative. For Hornby and Eggers, successfully negotiating these transitions has given impetus to individual innovation as well as collective projects. Individual innovators and entrepreneurs can mature into leaders of organisations through a give and take between individual identity and the collective enterprise. The organisation takes its identity and direction from an individual voice, but the individual leader learns from new networks of collaboration and interaction, so the voice is continually evolving. The ethos of a creative organisation is loose enough to allow scope for new ideas and new people to come in, but tight enough to draw them together around a shared set of values, beliefs and motivations. Negotiating this balance becomes Song, by Toad's next strategic challenge.

DIY strategy: planning by doing

According to Koestler's model of bisociation (Koestler, 1964), creative thinking combines apparently contradictory frames of reference to reveal a new connection and change the way we see the world. Applying this to strategy, we argue that creative strategy requires an ability to think past familiar dualities and oppositions. One of the oldest of these oppositions is between those who plan and those who act. One school of thought argues that strategy precedes action: strategic planning provides a template for operational decisions and helps us to make sense of chaotic, turbulent events. A second school of thought argues that strategy can only emerge through action: by experimenting and responding to operational realities, a strategic pattern emerges from a stream of decisions. Henry Mintzberg is most associated with this inversion of the traditional strategy model (Mintzberg and Waters, 1985). Where conventional views of strategy promote the need for analysis and planning to precede action (Cummings and Wilson, 2003), Mintzberg's position can be summarised, if a little crudely, as 'act first, plan later'. In turn, this resonates with the newfound interest in design thinking and the consequent importance of prototyping, fast-failing or learning quickly by trial, error and adjustment (Martin, 2009). In the words of a thinker many see as Mintzberg's predecessor in this regard, Karl Weick (1983: 48; 1995: 61), 'How can I know what I think until I see what I say?' This resonates with the informal 'adhocracy' of small creative businesses, where lack of time and resources as well as unpredictable processes and markets encourage a 'just do it' mentality (Bilton, 1999a).

A creative approach to strategy would mean trying to reframe this opposition between strategic and operational decisions. Instead of separating out these processes, can managers connect them? The software industry has recently developed an 'agile methodology', which attempts to treat planning and action as simultaneous rather than placing one before the other (Shore and Warden, 2007). The core of the agile process is a daily 'scrum' meeting, in which everybody involved with a project reviews progress and defines targets for that day's work. The agile approach developed to meet the demand for rapid prototyping of new software under tight shipping deadlines, and to cope with the inevitable technical glitches that might derail a production schedule planned too far in advance. In our experience, agile methodology resonates too with artistic practice (Bilton, 2012). Here, planning too far ahead is often impractical due to the unpredictability of the artistic process. At the same time, there is constant pressure to be productive, to develop a product rather than plan a production process. Rehearsal provides a good example of agile methodology in an artistic context. Musicians and actors will launch into a song or scene without too much premeditation, review what works and what doesn't, then run it again. Rehearsal is action, but it is also a form of planning. The process is iterative and allows a steady cumulative progress through experimentation and discovery. According to many of the theatre directors and actors we have spoken to, the best performances also aspire to the conditions of rehearsal.

In 2012 we were invited to observe the Happenstance Project, an attempt to apply agile principles to organisational innovation in three visual arts organisations. As noted above, agile methodology may be intuitive to artists, but artistic organisations tend to be constrained by funders and audiences to take a more cautious, long-term approach to planning. The Happenstance Project attempted to apply agile principles to organisational processes (communication and knowledge exchange, staff meetings) by importing three pairs of technologists to work in the three arts organisations. While ostensibly the aim of the project was to discover how to embed new digital technologies into cultural organisations, the designers of Happenstance were also keen to see how far agile principles could transfer from the world of technology and software development into the different structure of a subsidised arts organisation.

The technologists were given free rein in terms of the projects they could initiate in each arts organisation. At the same time, they were placed under significant time pressure – each residency ran over two consecutive six-week 'sprints', at the end of which they were expected to discuss progress at an 'open house' event hosted by the organisation. This combination of an open-ended brief with a pressure to be productive replicated the conditions of agile software development and resulted in a similar mentality of 'act first, plan later'. Plans were formulated on the hoof, reviewed and reoriented as opportunities opened and closed and progress advanced or stalled.

In the end, the residencies were remarkably productive, producing new internal communication tools, new relationships with local designers and developers, improvements to websites and digital media presence and development of digital technology skills in each organisation. But the most significant change was perhaps cultural, as the arts organisations began to adopt some of the agile principles they observed at play among the technologists in residence. One arts manager admitted she had previously felt uncomfortable working with technology but would now feel confident to commission a new technology project or to fix simple technical problems. The arts organisations began to question their attitudes to risk and innovation, and to assume some of the 'try it and see' mentality of the technologists.

In the case of Song, by Toad, we see some of these same attitudes to 'planning by doing'. Matthew is clearly impatient with what he perceives as a tendency to substitute planning for action: to talk about a problem instead of addressing it. His own approach is more serendipitous – even the start of the label was '99 per cent by accident' – and when obstacles emerge, his attitude is 'do it anyway'. His decision-making process is pragmatic; in many cases there are no good decisions available, it's just a case of selecting the least bad option. Rather than attempting to formulate the perfect strategy, Matthew prefers to take action and live with the consequences, with no regrets: 'we can just do things, you just get on with it and you will be okay'. Despite this apparently relaxed attitude to forward planning, the label has continued to thrive, not least because of Matthew's reputation as somebody who gets things done.

In our experience it is common for people working in the so-called creative industries to claim that they do not plan, they just act. The reality is usually more complex, with underlying principles as well as experience providing a sounding board for operational decisions. Song, by Toad clearly has an ethos, based on sincerity, trust and reliability, even if Matthew prefers to define this as 'a consistent voice' rather than a strategy. This ethos allows him to be decisive in uncertain circumstances, recognising that all decisions are imperfect. Provided he sticks to his principles he can live with a few mistakes. Action and planning go together, rather than giving one mode precedence over the other.

Creative strategy takes from the artist the recognition that creativity is more often the result of co-creation and serendipity than the deliberate imposition of a singular vision. Creative strategy thus works with action, not upon or before action. For all his stubbornness, Matthew is content to work with the grain of events and circumstances rather than imposing his will upon them. He understands that his decisions and actions are dependent upon the decisions and actions of artists, promoters, CD manufacturers and venues; there is no point in trying to anticipate every possibility, or blaming himself when things don't work out. Leading from the middle, planning by doing, Song, by Toad relocates strategy as a product of diverse individuals and events converging through action. In the centre of this, Matthew's own personality and ethos provides a catalyst and touchstone, making sense of and reshaping an apparently random, unplanned series of events, decisions and actions into a forceful, coherent direction for the business.

Conclusion

This chapter has considered the experience of a Scottish independent record label in the light of our previous research and experiences in relation to the development of effective creative strategy. By leading from the middle, adapting to the needs of a business at an early stage in its life cycle and planning by doing rather than seeking perfect knowledge before the event, Song, by Toad has managed to survive and thrive on its own terms in a competitive, uncertain business. Does Song, by Toad provide a strategic template for other types of business?

An important lesson of Song, by Toad is that there is no perfect strategic recipe. Things go wrong and mistakes are made. One response to this scenario is simply to give up any attempt at planning and follow the next opportunity. Yet as we have seen, a flexible, adaptive approach to strategy is not the same thing as no strategy at all. Song, by Toad has an ethos, and action is purposeful, not random or opportunistic. Matthew is prepared to admit and accept when he has made mistakes. In the music business mistakes are inevitable. Learning from mistakes is not to say that one would have done things differently, it may simply mean acknowledging that 'there was not a good decision to make'. The inevitability of some partial failure is liberating – 'we can just do things, you just get on with it and you will be okay'.

One of the findings of the Happenstance research described in the previous section is that technology projects, following agile principles, use a fast prototyping model, adopting a mantra of 'fail fast, fail cheap'. Provided setbacks are addressed immediately and openly through the daily scrum meetings, they do not accumulate into large-scale catastrophes. By reorienting aims and adapting to problems, the projects progress through difficulties, much as Song, by Toad is able to solve problems 'on the hoof'. While this principle seems straightforward when applied to small-scale innovation projects, agile methodology has been developed primarily to deal with larger-scale software development projects, breaking down the larger objectives into smaller work units. The arts organisations involved in the Happenstance Project welcomed this approach; typically their own experience of large-scale funded projects with multiple stakeholders resulted in a mentality that 'failure is not an option'. As noted above, this fear of failure has a paralysing effect on innovation and risk-taking. An agile approach to risk and failure allows even major, high-stakes projects to proceed through experimental action and reaction, rather than through elaborate advance planning. Action and immediate reaction to problems through rolling informal progress reviews allows for an adaptive strategy, with plans and their implementation proceeding in parallel.

On the other hand, we do not offer up Song, by Toad approach as an ideal for strategy in every organisation. Clearly, the way Matthew does business is part of his personality as well as the circumstances he finds himself in. Larger, more established businesses in particular will face different challenges, and may find themselves at a different stage on the strategy cycle towards leadership and organisation rather than innovation and entrepreneurship; they would need to act differently to be authentic to their own 'personality'.

However, certain principles of creative strategy – leading from the middle, adapting to the strategy cycle, planning by doing – are useful aspects to reflect upon for any business. Effective creative strategy is a collaborative process, which is continually evolving through one's own actions and the actions and reactions of others. It invites us all to have confidence in our ability to respond calmly to crisis and error by referring back to our ethos and values, and to make our own strategic sense of our business by taking action, not talking about what we can and cannot do.

Application questions

- What stage of development is the organisation at, and what are the implications of this for how they might do strategy?
- What approach to risk-taking is adopted, and do you think it is the appropriate approach?
- What forms of collaboration, or co-creation are being undertaken?
- Is leadership being conducted 'from the middle'?

References

Banks, M., Lovatt, A., O'Connor, J. and Raffo, C. (2000) Risk and trust in the cultural industries. *Geoforum*, 31(4): 453–64.

Bilton, C. (1999a) *The new adhocracy: strategy, risk and the small creative firm*, Working Paper no. 5. Coventry: Centre for Cultural Policy Studies.

Bilton, C. (1999b) Risky business: the independent production sector in Britain's creative industries. *International Journal of Cultural Policy*, 6(1): 17–39.

Bilton, C. (2007) *Management and creativity: from creative industries to creative management*. Oxford: Blackwell.

Bilton, C. (2012) *Happenstance report*. London: NESTA.

Bilton, C. and Cummings, S. (2010) *Creative strategy: reconnecting business and innovation*. Chichester: Wiley.

Bilton, C. and Cummings, S. (2011) From bard to boardroom: how to encourage creative strategy in your organisation – creative organization. *Human Capital Review*, January, available at: www.humancapitalreview.org/content/default. asp?Article_ID=937.

Cummings, S. and Daellenbach, U. (2009) A guide to the future of strategy? The history of long range planning. *Long Range Planning*, 42(2): 234–63.

Cummings, S., Maile Petty, M. and Walker, B. (2014) Innovation is not the only thing. In Bilton, C. and Cummings, S. (eds) *Handbook of management and creativity*, pp. 97–127. Cheltenham: Edward Elgar.

Cummings, S. and Wilson, D. (eds) (2003) *Images of strategy*. Oxford: Blackwell.

Day, E. (2013) Dave Eggers: 'We tend to look everywhere but the mirror' – interview. *Observer*, 26 January, available at: www.theguardian.com/books/2 013/jan/26/dave-eggers-hologram-king-interview.

DCMS (1998) *Creative industries mapping document*. London: Department for Culture, Media and Sport.

de Geus, A. (1997) *The living company: growth, learning and longevity in business*. London: Nicholas Brealey.

Florida, R. (2012) *The rise of the creative class (revisited)*. New York: Basic Books.

Mann, L. and Chan, J. (2011) *Creativity and innovation in business and beyond*. New York: Taylor and Francis.

Grabher, G. (2004) Learning in projects, remembering in networks? Communality, sociality and connectivity in project ecologies. *European Urban and Regional Studies*, 11(2): 103–23.

Jeffcutt, P. and Pratt, A. (2002) Managing creativity in the cultural industries. *Creativity and Innovation Management*, 11(4): 225–9.

Jenkins, H. (2006) Interactive audiences? The collective intelligence of media fans. In *Fans, bloggers, gamers: exploring participatory culture*, pp. 134–52. New York University Press.

Koestler, A. (1964) *The act of creation*. London: Hutchison.

Martin, R.L. (2009) *Design of business: why design thinking is the next competitive advantage*. Boston, MA: Harvard Business School Press.

Mintzberg, H. (1994) *The rise and fall of strategic planning*. London: Prentice Hall.

Mintzberg, H. and Waters, J. (1985) Of strategies, deliberate and emergent. *Strategic Management Journal*, 6(3): 257–72.

98   Chris Bilton and Stephen Cummings

Nonaka, I. and Takeuchi, H. (1995) *The knowledge-creating company: how Japanese companies create the dynamics of innovation.* Oxford University Press.

Nonaka, I. and Zhu, Z. (2012) *Pragmatic strategy: Eastern wisdom, global success.* Cambridge University Press.

Porter, M. (1966) What is strategy? *Harvard Business Review,* 74(6): 61–78.

Scase, R. and Davis, H. (2000) *Managing creativity: the dynamics of work and organization.* Buckingham: Open University Press.

Shore, J. and Warden, S. (2007) *The art of agile development.* Sebastopol, CA: O'Reilly.

Stewart, T. (1997) *Intellectual capital: the new wealth of nations.* London: Nicholas Brealey.

Weick, K. (1983) Misconceptions about managerial productivity. *Business Horizons,* 26(4): 47–52.

Weick, K. (1995) *Sensemaking in organizations.* Thousand Oaks, CA: Sage.

Markets and engagement between production and consumption

8   Music and the making of markets

Katy J. Mason

Music is everybody's business. . .   John Lennon

In June 2013, Prime Minister David Cameron hailed the global success of British music. Big-selling albums by Adele, Emeli Sandé, One Direction and Ed Sheeran boosted UK artists' share of album sales globally to 13.3 per cent in 2012, the highest ever documented. In an interview published in *Music Week*, Cameron explained: 'We should be extremely proud of how our world-leading music industry continues to go from strength to strength, with a record share of the global market' (*MusicWeek*, 2013). The Chairman of the British Phonographic Industry, Tony Wadsworth, added:

British music continues to be a global export success story. It puts Britain on the map, culturally and economically, generating jobs both at home and abroad. We've built on a strong musical heritage to cement our position as a creative powerhouse with enormous potential for growth in the digital age. It remains important that Government supports our creative industries to give us every opportunity to compete on the world stage. (ibid.)

The importance of national and international music markets has not gone unnoticed, gaining attention from governments, policy-makers and professional bodies, artists, performers, technicians, managers and other professionals engaged in the music industry. There are always designs to intervene in ways to make the music industry prosper. Yet, in the same month as Cameron was singing the praises of the music industry, HMV, the music retailer present on the high street since 1921, was going into administration. Markets for music are changing. The introduction of new technologies such as iTunes and MP3 files and players, as well as music streaming services such as Spotify that allow the free sharing of music, have hit traditional music businesses hard. Digital music, while generating widely accessible and affordable music offerings, has also created new challenges around copyright and piracy that legislators and law enforcement agencies are yet to master, spawning a generation of young adults who assume that music should be free. Indeed, in an article in *All Things D[igital]*, Hany Nada, founding partner of GGV Capital (funders of music ventures), argues that in the future consumers won't pay for recorded music; rather, fans will pay for music experiences. Nada explains: 'When the dust finally settles between the artists, labels, and distribution companies, everyone will finally realize fans are more valuable than recorded music. As traditional monetisation models for recorded music sales slowly fade away, new monetisation methods centered on the fan will emerge' (2011). Music markets have not disappeared, but they are being remodelled, remade and reshaped by many different market actors. It is only by taking a closer look at what markets are that we stand a better chance of being able to intervene in them in ways that generate both economic and social value for our society – such observations will stand us in good stead to help music markets prosper.

In this chapter I explore the traditional marketplace as a way of unpacking how complex market systems are made. I then present some of the extant research from the marketing and management literature that generates important insights into how we might better unfold the materials and management practices that can make and shape markets, and design interventions that are likely to support a healthy music industry. Finally, I briefly draw parallels with the extraordinary and valuable observations made by Nod Knowles (Chapter 18, pp. 205–12), through his experiences of making and shaping markets for music festivals over the past twenty-five years.

What markets are

The work of the marketer is the work that connects organisations and firms with each other and with 'the market' – the customers and consumers that buy and use products and services produced by organisations. But markets are not just out there – they are the outcomes of the purposive efforts of multiple actors. It is often the connections that firms make that begin to shape and change markets. The work of the marketer is about making and shaping markets, and connecting markets and organisations. Connections Apple made with the music industry have led to changes in technologies including iTunes and MP3 files, which in turn have led to changes in the way we enjoy and consume music. In this section I begin by exploring a more traditional market, one that has remained remarkably stable in form for hundreds of years: the town market. I use this to generate insights into the markets of the future that we have not yet encountered, such as the fast-changing markets for music as musicians and managers engage with and become an important part of the digital economy.

Figure 1. Ludlow market

In 1871 Jevons stated: 'Originally a market was a public place in a town where provisions and other objects were exposed for sale...' (quoted in Marshall, 2009: e4,102). Traditional marketplaces, such as the Ludlow market in Shropshire, my home town, will be familiar to many. Such marketplaces have a dominant physical structure, often situated at the centre of a town with a square created by the buildings that frame a space where the market can be held (Figure 1). More temporary structures populate the square in the form of market stalls: metal frames support tables and white and green striped awnings protect traders from the sun and rain. The market stalls configure people's actions: walking up and down the rows, inspecting the sellers' wares, perhaps allowing buyers to contest the value of products and haggle over the price. In this way, the materiality of the market square, the stalls and the goods displayed upon them, are entangled in the practices of everyday folk as they go about their everyday business, buying and selling what – for the most part – is local produce. The market also displays social structures, in that the people who buy and sell in the market know how to act. They question sellers about their goods, try goods (for taste, for size) and, importantly, hand over an agreed amount of money in exchange for goods. Such a setting enables us partially to see and imagine the work that must be done to construct and constitute a market. The town square must be built, the stalls must be rented, the streets must be maintained, the producers must bring their goods to the market and display them, there must be an accepted currency of exchange that is agreed upon and laws against theft or copyright infringement. It takes both physical and social structures to constitute a market.

Many of the most in-depth studies of markets have been carried out in less familiar settings, where the materials and practices of market-makers are more difficult to see. For example, Knorr-Cetina and Preda's (2006) edited volume *The sociology of financial markets* and MacKenzie's (2008) *An engine, not a camera: how financial models shape markets* both describe the complexities, technologies and calculative devices that constitute the trading of financial products and services. A feature of financial markets is that they are based upon scopic systems – electronic and informational mechanisms of observing and contextualising market reality and of back-projecting this reality onto the computer screens of globally operating traders. When such a mechanism is in place, coordination and activities respond to a reflected, represented reality (Knorr-Cetina, 2006), and so the marketing practices of a traditional marketplace might be very different from those of a contemporary financial marketplace. Thus, different markets might develop alternative kinds of market and marketing practices, despite the broadly similar characteristics of markets as organising structures for the conception, production and circulation of goods for exchange.

By adopting a more anthropological and sociological approach to the study of markets, scholars foreground the social and cultural aspects of markets and market-making practices, thus recognising that markets are heterogeneous and the practices that shape them are situated through particular assemblages of actors and objects, in particular sites. This does not mean to say that markets are always as neatly geographically contained as the Ludlow market. As Jevons explained: '...the word [market] has been generalized, so as to mean any body of persons who are in intimate business relations and carry on extensive transactions in any commodity ... A great city may contain as many markets as there are important branches of trade, and these markets may or may not be localized' (quoted in Marshall, 2009: e4,102). There have been many changes since Jevons's day, with the globalisation of trade and the unimaginable changes in communications technologies that are so important in the financial markets described by Knorr-Cetina and Preda (2006). What these and other recent market studies show are deep, rich, close-up views of the complex socio-technical systems that constitute markets.[1]

---

[1] For some of the most challenging work in market studies see Araujo et al. (2010); and Zwick and Cayla (2011).

In sum, markets (in all their diverse forms) are specific arrangements of practices and material. Markets are thus configured through the performance of these practices and the configuration and use of materials through a marketisation process (Araujo et al., 2008; Kjellberg and Helgesson, 2007). However, as Çalışkan and Callon explain: 'notwithstanding variety, because of active and deliberate intervention, the markets surrounding us actually do share what Wittgenstein would have called a "family of resemblance"' (2010: 3–4). Çalışkan and Callon summarise market characteristics as follows.

1. Markets organize the conception, production and circulation of goods, as well as the voluntary transfer of some sorts of property rights attached to them. These transfers involve a monetary compensation which seals the goods' attachment to their new owners.
2. A market is an arrangement of heterogeneous constituents that deploys the following: rules and conventions; technical devices; metrological systems; logistical infrastructures; texts, discourses and narratives [...]; technical and scientific knowledge [...], as well as the competencies and skills embodied in living beings.
3. Markets delimit and construct a space of confrontation and power struggles. Multiple contradictory definitions and valuations of goods as well as agents oppose one another in markets until the terms of the transaction are peacefully determined by pricing mechanisms. (2010: 3)

As such, markets foster the production of values by organising competition between autonomous and independent actors, creating some sort of order – some sort of stability (albeit more or less temporary) in a world of constant flux. These temporary moments of stability allow us to frame and coordinate action so that we may produce, exchange and consume.

The materials and practices of market-makers

Knowing what markets can (and cannot) do affects the actions we take to shape them. When we describe a specific market – the cotton market, the recorded music market – we create a frame that rules some ideas, agents and goods in, and others out. Markets act as frames for actions. The market frame determines the parameters and boundaries that represent what the market is for (or could be for), who is part of it and the specific mechanisms through which it operates. The frame shapes what considerations, calculations and judgements managers and other market-makers make when working out what to do next. Thus, how we represent, describe and make sense of markets has a significant impact on how we act as market-makers.

The academic field of marketing has long been valued for the tools and models it has created and theorised in order to support marketing managers in describing and representing their markets and marketing strategies. For example, Ansoff's growth matrix (1965) enables managers to make sense of what they are trying to do next in their strategy for business growth: sell new products in new markets, sell existing products in existing markets, sell existing products in new markets or new products in existing markets. Each 'position' will unfold a different bundle of practices associated with growth of sales. Similarly, market segmentation tools or marketing communications models have long played an important role in the development of marketing practice (see, for example, Duncan and Moriarty, 1998; Johnson, 1971). But while the mainstream marketing literature has been excellent at conceptualising and introducing market-making models and tools, it has stopped short of exploring how these tools are used and what effects they have on shaping markets as they unfold. In contrast, the recent market studies literature concerns itself with how these tools and theories become the materials of practitioners, how they are put to work in market-making practices and how these ideas shape market-making action. In other words, the tools and models of marketing scholarship become the market-making devices of practitioners – the two worlds join, creating frames and tensions where abstract ideas are brought into confrontation with complex, situated realities of real world problems and prospects. Calculative devices are picked up and used by market-makers as they make judgements about what to do next.

However, recent studies have begun to reveal that sometimes these tools can create problems of their own. Sunderland and Denny (2011) show how a market segment model nearly thwarted their efforts to generate market research on 'entertainment' products. Using a customer list provided by the commissioning firm, which divided customers into four distinct market segments, they attempted to recruit participants. They failed to recruit 'executive manager moms' and 'buoyant boomers', as those listed as 'executive manager moms' on the customer list were men and the 'buoyant boomers' turned out to be much older than the segment label suggested – in their sixties or seventies. The actual customers did not match their segment descriptions. For Sunderland and Denny (2011: 149), therefore, the segmentation model acted as a 'conceptual cage'. The different actors (the market researchers and the commissioning firm) brought different knowledge and expertise to the segmentation model, and as the actors connected with each other using the model, new possibilities of what could be done began to unfold. They were able to achieve this despite the problems presented by their efforts to use the model. The actors continuously moved between the concrete and the abstract so that they could work out how to take the next innovative step – by contesting the model with their own interpretations of the 'real world', they transformed the abstract model into something new. Callon (1998) refers to this process as framing and overflowing, and draws on the notion of framing to show how actors disentangle agents and goods from other social worlds and practices so that discrete exchanges can be made – to buy an Adele CD we must know the musician, the technology, who owns it and what the CD is worth. Without this frame, we can't act in a way that allows us to perform a market exchange. Calculating the value of the CD is not always straightforward. For example, the CD of Adele's *21* may be worth £13.99 to me but not to you. I would buy; you would not. Enough people need to see the CD as worth £13.99 – otherwise there is no market for it. In studying marketing practices it becomes important to understand how these frames come about, how they are constructed, calculated, contested and used to make judgements about what form a market should take, how it should work, what should be traded, for what value and how.

Many marketing studies have looked at ways to better observe and understand customer needs, but far less is understood about what to do with this information and understanding once we have it. In this sense, much of the traditional marketing literature has viewed markets as groups of heterogeneous customers, rather than as complex and interconnected socio-technical systems. Stark (2009) outlines how exploring multiple, contested and reframed needs generates insights into the efforts and practices that shape orders of worth in economic life. He describes orders of worth as being framed through the moral values of social worlds. That is, orders of worth come out of prioritising and calculating economic value for the things we care about as a society. Thus, social values (what we care about) are put to work to calculate economic value (what we are prepared to pay for it). It is easy to see how such value systems may cause great tensions and disagreements. Take the emotive conversations about the role of markets in healthcare provision that so often dominate the press, as well as healthcare and management journals. Because of the rising cost of healthcare provision, our society is being asked to consider difficult questions about how we can provide the best possible healthcare from limited resources. Many commentators are deeply uncomfortable with the role of markets in healthcare provision. Others are convinced that markets hold the key to better care. The reason this debate rages is that we don't understand enough about how markets work or what happens when certain types of intervention are framed. In the end, social values have to be explored to understand how we can generate economic value for our society. These difficult questions help us begin to generate and understand orders of worth.

In his book *The sense of dissonance*, Stark (2009) also discusses the creative tensions that emerge from different and often competing orders of worth, arguing that 'rationality' – the logic followed in deliberating before reaching a conclusion – is only possible insofar as it takes place within the boundaries and through the social technologies of particular orders of worth. Boltanski and Thévenot (2006) identify multiple orders of worth that emerge through different and competing logics. They argue that an economy has a market logic, as well as a civic logic, a technological logic, an inspiration logic and so on. For them, once actors decide that the problem can be framed within one of these logics, they know how to act. The uncertainty is removed once the logic is selected. But as different actors prioritise and order logics differently (according perhaps to their expertise, knowledge or interests), such logics will inevitably be contested. Multiple logics compete and contest each other and through these con-testations reveal new possibilities of action that could not otherwise have been conceived. Competing logic creates uncertainty and thus reveals the innovative next steps. In order to make markets, we need new kinds of tools and models to frame and explore spaces for contested multiple evaluative principles in order to reveal possible entrepreneurial and market-making practices.

Business models as market-making devices

In the music industry, one of the key challenges that market-makers have faced is the contestation of multiple logics. As we have seen, there has been much in the press about the disruptive technologies that are trans-forming the music industry, such as YouTube, MP3 files and software apps that allow the easy access, sharing and illegal copying of music. The logics of emergent technologies suggest and allow us to do things that threaten existing and established revenue-generating activities such as selling CDs or music videos. This means that managers are forced to seek out new ways of generating revenues to support their activities and ventures. Yet the existing market logic would suggest that actions should be framed around creating stability rather than perhaps embracing the change that these disruptive technologies cause. Clearly, such stability has not been achievable, as demonstrated by the demise of HMV. So how do managers engaging with the music business work out what to do?

One of the ways in which managers have attempted to frame action is through the use of business models. An example of this was illustrated by the artist Adele failing to reach an agreement with Spotify to stream her award-winning album, *21*. In a magazine article about the digital music service provider, Carr explains:

108   *Katy J. Mason*

Multiple sources confirm that Adele was willing to play ball with the streaming service, as long as the content was accessible only to paying subscribers and not to its freemium users. Spotify has a freemium-to-premium model: Users can gain ad-supported access to Spotify's entire music catalog for free; to remove the ads and gain mobile access, users have to pay up as much as $10 a month. Ultimately, Spotify decided it did not want to split up its content catalog, so as to create separate music libraries for paying subscribers and freemium users. Thus, it was essentially Spotify that decided against providing streaming access to Adele's content for paying subscribers – not the other way around ... Spotify, [...] demonstrated its commitment to its freemium-to-premium business model. (2012)

According to Carr, Spotify's business models shaped its actions when working to develop its music catalogue.

Business models are generally understood to be descriptions of how business is done, conceptualised from the perspective of the business network. The business model identifies components of the business – for example, the technologies that make up the product/service offering, its delivery and management, the market offering that is made to the customer and the network architecture that configures buyers and suppliers to make the market offering possible (Mason and Spring, 2011). It is how these components are framed, brought together, contested and reframed that helps managers work out what to do next. In other words, it is how business models are put to work that enables managers to see opportunities and make judgements and calculations about what business and market practices are worth their efforts.

Over the past six years I have been researching how business models are used by market actors as market-making devices. In 'The sites and practices of business models', we analysed the development and transformation of one of the first business models in the music business – that associated with Edison's phonograph (Mason and Spring, 2011). Thomas Edison invented and patented the phonograph in 1877. It recorded sound onto a fragile tinfoil cylinder, so recording quality was poor and it could only be played back a few times. Edison had a new technology in search of an application – music recording was one possible application. The first commercial use of the phonograph was through demonstration by travelling entertainers. Edison was able to attach this new technology to an existing socio-technical system through travelling fairs and circuses. Even the poster used to advertise the phonograph performances copied the style typically used to advertise circuses at the time (Figure 2). Edison sold the phonographs to a network of entertainers, who in turn charged for attendance at demonstrations. For a short period, the entertainers made large sums of money, as did Edison through royalties and a percentage of the exhibition fees. But the novelty soon wore off with the customer.

Figure 2. Early advertising material for the 'phonograph' experience
Source: *Edison's Phonograph*. Alfred S. Seer, Engraver. Copy after:
Mathew B. Brady (photographer), c. 1878. Color woodcut poster.
National Portrait Gallery, Smithsonian Institution.

Note: This large wood-engraved poster, with a blank space over the
Brady image for inserting the specific time and place for the
demonstrations, is similar to the colour posters that promoted circuses.

Edison wanted to continue to improve his phonograph, but was short of capital. He sold the patent but retained the rights to manufacture. Some agents with leased machines were now losing money and created a new market offering by starting 'phonograph parlours', where customers could pay a nickel to listen to a tune. This became the major revenue earner. Edison was now producing more robust phonographs, and the sale of pre-recorded music took on much greater significance. As phonograph technology improved, production costs and prices declined. Consumers became used to the machines and began to operate phonographs themselves, at home: sales of machines and cylinders to private households then became the more significant market. The production of media and playback equipment became separated, as industry standards pertaining to playing speeds, and cylinder and then disc size became established. This was the business model for the next eighty or ninety years, albeit that phonographs were replaced by gramophones, and cylinders were replaced by discs.

The history of the recorded music market is rich with stories of how the various business model components travel and meet new market actors, are used to mobilise others and are contested and used to explore new opportunities. We see how technology and market offering components are distributed and developed across the business network. Each part of the business model is used by the different actors to make judgements and calculations of what is worth doing (and what is not). We see how the logics that underpin the different components are ordered and prioritised. The technology was prioritised for Edison, but for the early travelling entertainers, who were struggling to make money, the market offering component was prioritised: the creative opportunity of the phonograph parlour came out of this logic.

Recognising that different components of business models create frames that can be connected and contested helps to reveal creative opportunities and new frames for action. These affect not just the business but the business network and the market too. It is by drawing out what matters to people in their different social groups that we are able to see these differences and take advantage of them to see how markets might be imagined and shaped. We can begin to disentangle the complex interplay between innovations in business model technologies and market offerings, and network architectures. These components suggest alternative actions for making money. The connections between social values and economic value are often contested, and from such contestations there are winners and losers – paths that are followed and paths that are discarded, economic efforts that are pursued, sidelined and ignored. Particular logics become prioritised, shared and coordinated action is organised around them.

The use of business models as market-making devices requires actors to move between the abstract idea of what a business might be and the concrete practices of performing the business model in a market. Such performances reveal the limitations of the technologies, materials and practices of everyday social life, with which new products and services must become entangled if indeed they are to be made marketable. It is how managers and entrepreneurs put business models to work to understand, explore and frame actions that makes them useful market-making devices. The market studies literature has a wealth of anthropologically informed studies examining the calculative practices and judgement devices used in market-making – business models being just one (see for example, Azimont and Araujo, 2007; Geiger and Finch, 2009; Geiger et al., 2012; Mason, 2012; Rinallo and Golfetto, 2006). But there is still much to be done to understand the chains of translations between these devices, why some travel and some don't and how such devices can be used to build good markets that work for different types of social values – such as the arts, music and culture. By looking at the devices and models that shape markets we unearth interesting questions about markets that can help us in our understanding of them.

Markets for music festivals

This historic view of the market for recorded music and the materials, models and practices of market-makers has similarities with Nod Knowles's reflections on the festival business (Chapter 18, pp. 205–12). Knowles describes how the model or concept of a music festival is picked up by others wanting to organise festivals. In its situated performance each festival is unique, and social groups such as new social movements, government agencies and financiers come to contest or legitimise ways of organising and performing music and ways of enjoying and consuming music; these groups in turn influence how and from which specific activities or materials revenue is generated. What Knowles does so well is to illustrate that the market-makers are not just the managers and entrepreneurs that imagine markets but also the policy-makers, arts agencies and local activists that shape markets. The manager's job, then, is to develop markets that connect, shape and are shaped by these multiple sociotechnical worlds – and this has been Knowles's work for the past twenty-five years.

Included in Knowles's narratives are constructions of different types of festival customers. It is perhaps worth noting that the idea of constructing customers and making markets is not new. What is new is the approach by the marketing discipline to our study of markets. The in-depth, rich market studies currently being undertaken in the field of marketing and management are likely to transform our understanding of marketing practices over the coming years. As Peter Drucker so beautifully put it (1954: 37): 'because the purpose of business is to create a customer, the business enterprise has two – and only two – basic functions: marketing and innovation. Marketing and innovation produce results; all the rest are costs. Marketing is the distinguishing, unique function of the business.'

Application questions

When reading Nod Knowles's account of the changing festival market and, indeed, other tales from the field, it might be useful to ask the following.

- What do the abstract models of existing socio-technical systems (for example, the business, markets, festivals) look like?
- How are these abstract models varied in their performance in different sites, with different socio-cultural groups, at different times?
- How do (festival) models travel?
- How do they mobilise the different actors they meet?
- How are they transformed through their situated practice?
- What are the chains of translations that follow from an abstract idea or concept for a market offering (or festival) to the performed, situated practice of that market (or festival)?
- How are these (festival) models used to work out what to do next?

References

Ansoff, H.I. (1965) *Corporate strategy: an analytic approach to business policy for growth and expansion.* New York: McGraw Hill.

Araujo, L., Kjellberg, H. and Finch, J. (eds) (2010) *Reconnecting marketing to markets.* Oxford University Press.

Araujo, L., Kjellberg, H. and Spencer, R. (2008) Market practices and forms: introduction to the special issue. *Marketing Theory*, 8(1): 5–14.

Azimont, F. and Araujo, L. (2007) Category reviews as market-shaping events. *Industrial Marketing Management*, 36(7): 849–60.

Boltanski, L. and Thévenot, L. (2006) *On justification: economies of worth.* Princeton University Press.

Çalışkan, K. and Callon, M. (2010) Economization, part 2: a research programme for the study of markets. *Economy and Society*, 39(1): 1–32.

Callon, M. (ed) (1998) Introduction: the embeddedness of economic markets in economics. In *The laws of the markets*, pp. 1–57. Oxford: Basil Blackwell.

Carr, A. (2012) Why Spotify turned down Adele's '21'. *Fastcompany.com*, available at: www.fastcompany.com/1816582/why-spotify-turned-down-adeles-181 6521.

Drucker, P. (1954) *The practice of management*. New York: Harper & Row.

Duncan, T. and Moriarty, S. (1998) A communication-based marketing model for managing relationships. *Journal of Marketing*, 62(April): 1–13.

Geiger, S. and Finch, J. (2009) Industrial sales people as market actors. *Industrial Marketing Management*, 38(6): 608–17.

Geiger, S., Kjellberg, H. and Spencer, R. (2012) Shaping exchanges, building markets. *Consumption Markets and Culture*, 15(2): 133–47.

Johnson, R.M. (1971) Market segmentation: a strategic management tool. *Journal of Marketing Research*, 8(1): 13–18.

Kjellberg, H. and Helgesson, C.-F. (2007) On the nature of markets and their practices. *Marketing Theory*, 7(2): 137–62.

Knorr-Cetina, K. (2006) The market. *Theory, Culture and Society*, 23(2–3): 551–6.

Knorr-Cetina, K. and Preda, A. (eds) (2006) *The sociology of financial markets*. Oxford University Press.

MacKenzie, D. (2008) *An engine, not a camera: how financial models shape markets*. Cambridge, MA: MIT Press.

Marshall, A. (2009) *Principles of economics*, 8th edn. Orlando, FL: Signalman Publishing (first published 1890).

Mason, K. (2012) Market sensing and situated dialogic action research (with a video camera). *Management Learning*, 43(4): 405–25.

Mason, K. and Spring, M. (2011) The sites and practices of business models. *Industrial Marketing Management*, 40(6): 1032–41.

MusicWeek (2013) David Cameron applauds UK's 'world-leading music industry', 6 June, available at: www.musicweek.com/news/read/david-cameron-appl auds-uk-s-world-leading-music-industry/054948.

Nada, H. (2011) Music for nothing and the fans for free. *All Things D*, 28 October, available at: www.allthingsd.com/20111028/music-for-nothing-and-the-fans-for-free/.

Rinallo, D. and Golfetto, F. (2006) Representing markets: the shaping of fashion trends by French and Italian fabric companies. *Industrial Marketing Management*, 35(7): 856–69.

Stark, D. (2009) *The sense of dissonance: accounts of worth in economic life*. Princeton University Press.

Sunderland, P.L. and Denny, R.M. (2011) Consumer segmentation in practice: an ethnographic account of slippage. In Detlev, Z. and Cayla, J. (eds) *Inside marketing: practices, ideologies, devices*, pp. 137–61. New York: Oxford University Press.

Zwick, D. and Cayla, J. (eds) (2011) *Inside marketing: practices, ideologies, devices*. Oxford University Press.

9   Consumers and marketing

Michael Saren

> The entry of the consumer as an important figure into the world of organizations has therefore not just complicated matters ... Customers often re-enter an organization as managers or workers and, increasingly, work knowingly or unknowingly for organizations that do not employ them – they offer ideas and feedback, they discover new uses for existing products, they provide helpful suggestions to other customers.
>
> (Gabriel et al., 2013)

Gabriel et al. argue that nowadays organisations and organising cannot be understood only in terms of workers and managers or bosses and employees. The third party who must be taken into account is the consumer. Most marketing academics and managers would say that this is not new – the consumer/customer has always played a key role in the behaviour of organisations. Indeed, some argue that they have more power: 'Consumers obtain power when they can counteract companies and institutions' communication, thus influencing their credibility. Consumers complain, appropriate and transform, fight and negotiate. In all of these cases, consumers "create" circumstances to which companies can/must respond' (Cova and Dalli, 2009: 321).

'Consumer sovereignty' is the phrase often employed to represent the customer as the chooser – the one in control. This royal metaphor goes back a long way and is deeply rooted in ideas of exchange, customer service and free market choice. Indeed, the traditional 'marketing concept' proposes that the interests of customers should be the main determinant of all firms' activities. The introductory chapter of any conventional marketing text – Kotler (1972), for example – explains that the implication of the marketing concept is that all organisations' strategies and actions should be customer focused and market oriented. In the pre-Second World War days of the early profession of marketing, the market research industry developed in order to understand customers' behaviour and needs. During the 1950s and 1960s, many marketing practitioners utilised the techniques, tools and language of psychology in order to demonstrate that they possessed the means to understand 'customer' behaviour – the customer being, as per the marketing concept, the avowed central focus of the business. Psychology's behaviourist view at the time regarded the consumer as a conditioned organism, open to reconditioning (Bousch et al., 2009).

A more contemporary view of marketing is based on a positivist view of knowledge, whereby consumers are regarded as knowable entities with characteristics that can be identified and measured like natural phenomena. The rationale for all these efforts to understand customers was the need for firms to know how to satisfy the 'sovereign consumers' whom they serve. In this respect little has changed, except that the technologies of marketing have become more sophisticated, and accordingly academic theorists have developed new concepts and techniques to help marketers serve their customers.

There is an alternative to this interpretation of the customer's role in marketing, however. Several critical authors have argued that marketing should not be regarded simply as a managerial business function but should be viewed critically within the wider context of social practice (Brownlie et al., 1999; Hirschman and Holbrook, 1982). Against the backdrop of an ideological crisis in marketing management, a growing number of academics are finding it increasingly difficult to rely on traditional marketing managerial ideology to explain and provide legitimacy for their theory and practice (Marion, 2006).

Accordingly, in the following sections I examine three recent ideas that might help us understand the customer's role in marketing from both these perspectives. These are:
1. customer loyalty and engagement
2. consumer subcultures and tribes
3. consumer co-creation of value.
For each I first explain the concept from the dominant managerial position in marketing and then present a critical interpretation set against the conventional marketing view of the consumer's role.

Customer loyalty and engagement

Beyond understanding and serving customers, marketers attempt to develop loyalty on the part of customers towards the company, brand, retailer or supplier. Loyalty is not a one-dimensional concept, though. Not only are there different types and levels, there is also no agreement about what is meant by customer loyalty. The main dispute in marketing centres on whether loyalty is an attitudinal (state of mind) or a behavioural (e.g. repeat purchase) construct. And, of course, not all customers are the same, so they are found to exhibit varying degrees of loyalty. O'Malley (1998) identified four different levels.

1. No loyalty. This situation occurs when customers are not loyal to any brand or company at all; they make specific purchases because of convenience, speed, price, availability, etc.
2. Spurious loyalty. Viewed as a temporary loyalty, 'spurious' customers are often categorised as promiscuous – likely to patronise a particular outlet or brand on the basis of its promotional offers or convenience or location, and easily influenced by competing offers.
3. Latent loyalty. This occurs when a customer has a high relative attitude towards the company or brand, but this is not evident in terms of their purchase behaviour because of limiting circumstances such as inconvenient locations, peer influence or stores out of stock.
4. Sustainable loyalty. The customer displays high repeat purchase behaviour, which is associated with a strong preference for a particular store and its facilities and services.

Consumer engagement is a more recent idea in marketing, which has been developed from the well-established notion of employee engagement (Saks, 2006). Engagement is conceptually distinct from participation and involvement, according to Brodie et al. (2011), because the latter do not explicitly embody interactivity and experience. Also, in contrast with loyalty, engagement is seen as a multidimensional concept (with cognitive, emotional and behavioural dimensions), where different conditions lead to differing levels of engagement (Van Doorn et al., 2010).

Customer loyalty and engagement – or capture and control?

The counter hypothesis to the managerial view is that modern marketing techniques and the wider consumer culture may create apparent loyalty and engagement on the part of the customers, but only with the managerial intent of controlling customers' behaviour, encouraging them to consume. Far from educating and empowering consumers, marketers' advertising, packaging, product placement and sponsorship programmes are targeted at consumers, in order at best to influence, at worst to manipulate and control their purchasing behaviour. The management rhetoric may be of engagement and loyalty, but many consumers have been captured and locked in by relentless marketing efforts on the part of producers of consumer products, which are well-researched, extensive, expensive and ultimately aimed at increasing demand (Zwick and Cayla, 2011).

Research into the health effects of over-consumption shows that consumers no longer possess complete control of their desires and use of some types of product, such as food, drink and drugs (Hastings, 2012). Other examples are the many technology-based consumer products for communication, computing and entertainment that have proliferated in recent years. So much specialised knowledge is often required that consumers have neither the time nor the inclination to acquire all the necessary skills to make informed decisions about the technological requirements. Similarly, financial products such as mortgages, life insurance and savings schemes are almost impossible to discriminate between (Knights et al., 1994). Many industries with 'fast moving consumer goods', such as entertainment, fashion and clothing, are built on customers' continual dissatisfaction with the old. One marketing strategy for these firms is to attempt to make consumers dissatisfied with existing products, then to instil a desire for stimulation of the new, thus creating demand for new products. Familiarity breeds discontent. The result is potentially to create continually rising expectations as to the superiority of the new over the old, which it replaces and to which it can be directly compared by the customers.

Lots of variety and market choice also necessitate a huge amount of information gathering, as consumers try to identify, understand and evaluate the many and various options on offer. This 'tyranny of choice' (Schwartz, 2004) means that not only can consumers not choose efficiently, they also suffer confusion. Maynes explicitly blames the 'agents of marketing' – advertising, sales promotion and salespeople – and their continual construction of new needs for the creation of what he terms 'informationally imperfect consumer markets' (2003: 157).

Nor is this a recent phenomenon. Historically, marketing generated so-called technologies of governance by securing its control of market research and extending this through techniques of propaganda, persuasion and control, based on motivation research, image management, architectural spectacle and mass psychology (Goulding and Saren, 2011). Such was the extent of use of techniques such as sales manipulation, subliminal advertising and misleading product claims that even some contemporary supporters of the 'American dream' in the 1950s complained about the unethical commercial use of such techniques, and their insidious nature and effects on society. See, for example, Vance Packard's critique of the methods and effects of the advertising industry in *The hidden persuaders* (1957) and J.K. Galbraith's critical analysis of *The affluent society* (1998).

There are many marketing activities that are far from perfect. The control mechanisms work not only through direct advertising and persuasion but also through the supposed benefits that markets offer modern consumers – abundance of goods, variety of alternatives, freedom of choice. It is these mechanisms of the market that effectively disempower and captivate customers, thereby enhancing the dominating power of marketing. And despite the recent examples of attempts at resistance, there is so little hope of liberation that Kozinets asks 'Can consumers escape the market?' (2002).

Consumer subcultures and tribes

Consumer researchers have more recently begun to look at how consumers forge feelings of social solidarity and create self-selected, sometimes transitory and fragmented, (sub)cultural worlds, involving the pursuit of common consumption interests. Many of these studies adopt an anthropological focus on the material artefacts and consumption practices that underpin, support and define the existence of these subcultures, and the consumption experiences of the people involved.

Various terms have been used to describe this phenomenon, such as 'subcultures of consumption', 'consumption micro cultures', 'brand communities' and 'consumption tribes'. Much of this work is based on Maffesoli's (1996) concept of the 'neo-tribe'. Maffesoli argues that traditional bonds of community between individuals have been eroded, and that the free market ethos promotes a continual quest for personal autonomy and difference. Consumers, however, find such conditions lonely and alienating, so they form looser groupings of shared interests and engage in joint activities and rituals based on lifestyle choices and leisure pursuits.

Consumer goods are used to signify social status, as demonstrated through the choice of a particular selection of goods that classifies the consumer according to various socio-economic hierarchies – such as their wealth, knowledge, social position, taste and refinement. It is not simply the display of the material possessions themselves that is important, nor simply economic capability or the price paid. According to Bourdieu (1984), modern consumption is primarily concerned with the establishment and maintenance of 'distinction' or difference between social classes and status groups. The maintenance of difference thus not only implies a competitive relationship between consumers who perceive themselves to inhabit different groups and identities but also has the effect of 'bonding' consumers more closely within these subcultures and social communities. By seeking to align themselves with certain group norms, consumers share with the others in that group such things as their common consumption ambitions and adoption of similar behaviours and lifestyles.

Other consumer researchers looking at contemporary subcultures and tribes have studied heavy metal music fans, gay consumers, skydivers, Star Trek followers, mountain men, the rave music scene, goths, surfers and

freerunners. A number of themes emerge from these studies of different consumer subcultures or tribes.
1. Subcultures are based around product constellations, places, events and services. Businesses emerge to serve the wants and needs of participants.
2. Tribal aspects of consumption are pervasive, fostering collective identifications grounded in shared beliefs, meanings, myths, ritual practices and status hierarchies.
3. Subcultures are made up of diverse groups of people – they are not based on gender or class. Subcultures provide a platform for the display and construction of alternative consumer activity-based identities.
4. There are different levels of commitment, which reflect the individual's identity. People can escape from their 'everyday life'. For example, the subculture enables the bank manager during the week to become a biker at the weekend.

Consumer tribes are formed when members are emotionally connected by similar consumption values and usage, using the social 'linking value' of products and services to create a community and express identity. This is often the case as societies become more consumer oriented. However, tribes are different from 'brand communities', which are formed around a particular brand or product; these are explicitly commercial, whereas pure tribes are not. Brand communities are concerned about the relationship between brand and consumer, whereas tribes focus on the relationship between consumers.

Consumer subcultures and tribes – created by marketing?

The consumer tribe is a relatively new concept that has wide marketing application in advertising, innovation and branding. Some tribes that are internally formed by consumers themselves have genuine common interests and connections, shared passions and history, self-developed hierarchies. They exist independently of companies, products and brands. Such tribes are often conceived of as unmanageable, relatively autonomous consumer zones that elude and even resist organisational or managerial intervention and control (Cova et al., 2007). However, consumer tribes are becoming widely recognised in advertising and consumer research, and their application and targeting by companies has had a remarkable impact on marketing in youth and heavily branded consumer markets, like Ducati's consumer tribe 'the Ducatisti', Red Bull's 'energy tribe', Apple's 'creative tribe', Nike's 'running tribe' and Wii's 'playful tribe'. These are examples of externally formed tribes that are specifically manufactured by marketers, with artificially created interests and passions, manipulated needs and desires. This type of tribe exists because of the brand, providing significant opportunities and advantages for the company.

By encouraging, if not creating, consumer communities and networks, marketing managers can, among other things, communicate directly with lead customers, foster brand loyalty and erect powerful barriers to exit (Goulding et al., 2013). This involves finding the brand's 'true believers' and getting them to spread the word, provide charismatic leadership, create tribal culture and, most importantly, create a sense of tribal identity (Pankraz, 2009). The delineation of group options and choice parameters is set by the marketing apparatus, not the customer. And, as Zwick and Cayla (2011) point out, the visibility of marketing activities to the consumer in the marketplace contrasts with the relative obscurity of the inner workings of the marketing profession.

Marketers' traditional demographic or psychographic means of segmenting and targeting markets have become less useful because of lifestyle changes and the loosening of links between consumer behaviour and social class. Segmentation methods segregate consumers into groups according to their differences and categorise and label them accordingly. The deliberate creation of consumer tribes by marketers goes far beyond this, however, by proactively constructing, reinforcing and delineating consumers' collective group identities. One effect of this is that marketing depersonalises its consumer subjects. Marketers' attempts to create and control consumer tribes establish group identities such that groups, individuals and communities are only important insofar as they contribute to the whole. This practice is very similar to the way in which totalitarian regimes categorise people according to political, sectarian, ethnic, racial, ideological, social and lifestyle categories, which are segregated, monitored and labelled accordingly.

Consumer co-creation of value

In the twenty-first century, marketers have had to reassess their understanding and calculation of what constitutes 'value' to their customers, and how this value can be produced and delivered. According to Evert Gummesson, the true role of the customer is ignored in the 'traditional' marketing view of value, in which 'production is viewed as value creation or value added by the supplier, whereas consumption is value depletion caused by the customer. If the consumer is the focal point of marketing, however, value creation is only possible when a product or service is consumed. An unsold product has no value, and a service provider without customers cannot produce anything' (Gummesson, 1998: 246).

This idea of the consumer as co-creator of value along with the supplier has been enthusiastically adopted by many leading marketing thinkers. For Grönroos, suppliers only create resources or the means for customers to create value for themselves. 'It is only when suppliers and customers interact, they are engaged in co-creation of value' (Grönroos, 2006: 324). Notably, Lusch and Vargo make a core proposition in their 'service logic' that 'value is always uniquely and phenomenologically determined by the beneficiary' and 'the customer is always a co-creator of value' (Lusch and Vargo, 2006: 284).

Of course, this argument is not new. Many years ago, von Hippel (1978) identified customers as lead innovators for new products, and the idea of looking at the consumer as producer has been well established through the notion of the 'prosumer', whereby certain production/delivery activities are devolved by suppliers to consumers. At the basic level, for example, this occurs with the transfer of 'self-service' to the shopper from the retailer, with self-assembly and DIY functions that are passed on to consumers from manufacturing, and when some promotional activities are conducted by consumers themselves through word-of-mouth advertising and conspicuous brand labelling. More fundamentally, many service activities have to be co-created by being produced and consumed simultaneously (e.g. restaurant dining, hairdressing, legal services).

Cova and Dalli (2009: 324) propose four characteristics of 'working consumers'.

1. Consumers actually work, whether or not they are aware of being 'workers'.
2. When producing value, consumers interact with one another, and normally also with company members.
3. Consumers pursue personal purposes, such as satisfaction, pleasure, commitment and social interaction.
4. Companies often participate in the performance of these activities when consumers ask for it.

Consumer co-creation – or expropriation of value?

In terms of value creation theory, consumers are not merely recipients or even arbiters of value, but members and partners in the value production chain. What occurs is that firms 'mobilise' the consumer-labour resource as variable capital. In other words, consumers have an important and necessary role as producers, providing 'consumer capital' for firms as a factor of production in the economic system. And how exactly do firms lock in, mobilise and expropriate this consumer-labour variable capital? By marketing. It is achieved through the marketing techniques discussed above, aimed at developing brand loyalty and customer 'lock-in'. Hence the enormous amount of recent attention in marketing practice and literature to customer retention, loyalty programmes, customer relationship management and consumer lifetime value – i.e. to the firm (Saren and Tzokas, 1998).

Through these marketing mechanisms, working consumers are locked into the supply chain as a key resource just like other firms, partners, allies and collaborators in the production and supply system. Their value creation activities are appropriated by the supply network, the dominant manufacturer, retailer or service provider. In other words, these firms 'mobilise' consumers as a resource in a way that is very far removed from the traditional conceptualisation of the value creation process.

In their paper on working consumers, Cova and Dalli themselves take a critical stance. They point out that working consumers increase the value of goods and services, and companies capture this value on the market, but almost none of this is returned to consumers. Given that consumers contribute to companies' profits through the value of their co-production, they ask the following searing questions about the distribution of this value.

1. Why they do not consider the disparity in the distribution of profits arising from consumers' work?
2. Why do they not receive any 'economic' reward for their labour?
3. Why are the economic benefits of their production still in the hands of 'producing' companies?
4. If consumers produce goods and services, why do they have to purchase them? (Cova and Dalli, 2009: 326)

Furthermore, the more consumers are involved in co-production and design, the more they appear to be willing to pay for the products. In this sense, it is arguable that there is a 'double exploitation of working consumers' (Zwick et al., 2008).

Analysis of 'Managing the Zoeys': who are the consumers?

The reminiscences of band manager Martin Cloonan (Chapter 18, pp. 226–35) illustrate a lot of things about what a manager does and the music business in general. The immediate observation, or question, regarding consumers is: 'Where are they in this story?' At first sight, they don't play any major role in the story and demise of this band. Friends, partners, promoters, band members, other bands, producers, record companies and the press all play important roles, but the customers are almost completely absent from the story. Indeed, they only get a first mention – 'you gotta keep the punters happy to get their cash' – half way through the chapter. The break-up of the band comes not from poor management or lack of audience, finance, gigs or records, but because of personal tensions within the band.

With success, or in this case failure, determined by factors other than lack of customers, there appears to be no important role for the consumer. Not only does this contradict the dictum of the marketing concept that the organisation should focus primarily on customers, it renders irrelevant the existence or not of consumer loyalty or subcultures, and it may be impossible to see how they can co-create value. Indeed, if the value is fundamentally in the music and created by the artists, it is hard to identify other sources of value in the music business, except insofar as others support the musician's creative process and performance.

But there are customers in this story, although not mentioned much or labelled as such. Audiences, punters, fans and friends attended gigs and bought CDs. Money did come in, records sold, gigs sold out, and promoters, other bands and music press attended their performances. The manager explicitly identifies three important audiences for the band's output – the actual audience (fans), the music industries and other musicians. And the band cared about their audience, he says. So much so that while he always wanted to charge them more, the musicians wanted to charge them less.

So here we do have evidence of customer engagement and loyalty, but not the kind discussed in marketing texts. This represents loyalty of the band to their customers, illustrated among other ways by the band wanting to charge them less. Or perhaps, without knowing their audience members' stories, this might reflect reciprocal loyalty of their supporters and fans. Either way, this is evidence of some kind of strong engagement and loyalty. Also, it is more akin to the mainstream marketing management explanation, in which the customers freely choose to support the band, and this sort of musical engagement importantly embodies interactivity and experience through their performances.

There is little discussion of fans in the manager's account of events in his story. The term 'fans' is only mentioned once, and then somewhat reluctantly. Of course, 'fan' is also short for fanatics and fanaticism, which may be portrayed as obsessive, excessive, extremist, intolerant and incoherent. Perhaps indie bans shouldn't have fans? In marketing terms, though, fandom is surely tribal, and certainly a subculture of some sort, and it might be regarded as the highest degree of consumer loyalty. Again, here, surely building a fan base is a 'good thing' for all parties: bands, fans and mangers? If so, the critique of consumer tribes as producer-created entities to control and manipulate customers does not fit well in this case.

Finally, regarding the third marketing idea of consumer co-creation, if we take the manager's broader definition of the audience as the customer base here, the audiences of fans, friends, music industries and other musicians can be seen to contribute to the band's 'value co-creation', both in commercial and artistic terms. At a minimum they provide necessary support for the band in addition to 'consuming the product'. Indeed, we might suggest that they are part of the product, in which case their value contribution is even more significant. Again, in this case, if the audiences can be regarded as working consumers, there is no evidence of them being exploited or their value contribution being appropriated by the music producer.

Conclusion

The three marketing ideas are applicable to this case only with some significant adaptation. Perhaps the music industry is exceptional and the consumer is different, or does this reflect the poorly defined marketing concepts? Music can be heard everywhere, as Brian Eno might have put it, 'infiltrating our everyday existence'. The nature of the product is unclear. It involves more than listening to music, but if the conventional marketing dichotomy of production and consumption is to be usefully applied in the music business we need more understanding about the role of the consumer and what is consumed.

Application questions

● Who are the customers/consumers?
● What is the mix (e.g. using O'Malley's levels) of customers in the audience?
● How are consumers/customers engaged in the processes of production and communication?
● Are we part of a subculture of consumption/production – and if so, what are the implications of this for our practices? For example, might innovation in 'product' alienate our 'tribe'?
● To what extent is co-creation with consumers possible and appropriate?

References

Bourdieu, P. (1984) *Distinction: a social critique of the judgement of taste*. London: Routledge.
Boush, D.M., Friestad, M. and Wright, P. (2009) *Deception in the marketplace: the psychology of deceptive persuasion and consumer self-protection*. New York: Routledge

Brodie, R.J., Hollebeek, L.D., Juric, B. and Ilic, A. (2011) Customer engagement: conceptual domain, fundamental propositions and implications for research. *Journal of Service Research*, 14(3): 252–71.

Brownlie, D., Saren, M., Wensley, R. and Whittington, R. (1999) *Rethinking marketing: towards critical marketing accountings*. London: Sage.

Cova, B. and Dalli, D. (2009) Working consumers: the next step in marketing theory? *Marketing Theory*, 9(3): 315–39.

Cova, B., Kozinets, R.V. and Shankar, A. (2007) *Consumer tribes*. Oxford: Elsevier.

Gabriel, Y., Korczynski, M. and Rieder, K. (2013) Call for papers: organizations and their consumers: bridging work and consumption. *Organization*, 20(6): 955.

Galbraith, J.K. (1998) *The affluent society* (40th anniversary edn). New York: Houghton Mifflin.

Goulding, C. and Saren, M. (2011) One vision: marketing and totalitarianism. *Proceeding of CMS Conference*, July, Naples.

Goulding, C., Shankar, A. and Canniford, R. (2013) Learning to be tribal: facilitating the formation of consumer tribes. *European Journal of Marketing*, 47(5/6): 813–32.

Grönroos, C. (2006) Adopting a service logic for marketing. *Marketing Theory*, 6(3): 317–34.

Gummesson, E. (1998) Implementation requires a relationship marketing paradigm. *Journal of the Academy of Marketing Science*, 26(3): 242–9.

Hastings, G. (2012) *The marketing matrix*. London: Sage.

Hirschman, E.C. and Holbrook, M.B. (1982) The experiential aspects of consumption: consumer fantasies, feelings and fun. *Journal of Consumer Research*, 9, September, 132–40.

Knights, D., Sturdy, A. and Morgan, G. (1994) The consumer rules? An examination of the rhetoric and 'reality' of marketing in financial services. *European Journal of Marketing*, 28(3): 42–54.

Kotler, P. (1972) *Marketing management: analysis, planning and control*. Englewood Cliffs, NJ: Prentice-Hall.

Kozinets, R.V. (2002) Can consumers escape the market? Emancipatory illuminations from Burning Man. *Journal of Consumer Research*, 29(1): 20–38.

Lusch, R.F. and Vargo, S.L. (2006) Service-dominant logic: reactions, reflections and refinements. *Marketing Theory*, 6(3): 281–98.

Maffesoli, M. (1996) *The time of the tribes: the decline of individualism in mass society*. London: Sage.

Marion, G. (2006) Marketing ideology and criticism: legitimacy and legitimization. *Marketing Theory*, 6(2): 245–62.

Maynes, E.S. (2003) Marketing – one consumer disaster. *The Journal of Consumer Affairs*, 37(2): 196–207.

O'Malley, L. (1998) Can loyalty schemes really build loyalty? *Marketing Intelligence and Planning*, 16(1): 47–55.

Packard, V. (1957) *The hidden persuaders*. London: Longmans, Green & Co.

Pankraz, D. (2009) Youth want tribal ideas – tips on how to create a movement around your brand, available at: danpankraz.wordpress.com/2009/06/07/youth-are-tribal-tips-on-how-to-create-a-movement-around-your-brand/

Saks, A.M. (2006) Antecedents and consequences of employee engagement. *Journal of Managerial Psychology*, 21(7): 600–19.

Saren, M. and Tzokas, N. (1998) Some dangerous axioms of relationship marketing. *Journal of Strategic Marketing*, 6: 187–96.

Schwartz, B. (2004) The tyranny of choice. *Chronicle of Higher Education*, 23 January.

Van Doorn, J., Lemon, K.E., Mittal, V., Naβ, S., Pick, D., Pirner, P. and Verhoef, P.C. (2010) Customer engagement behavior: theoretical foundations and research directions. *Journal of Service Research*, 13(3): 253–66.

von Hippel, E. (1978) Users as innovators. *Technology Review*, 80(3): 30–3.

Zwick, D., Bonsu, S.K. and Darmody, A. (2008) Putting consumers to work: 'co-creation' and new marketing govern-mentality. *Journal of Consumer Culture*, 8(2): 163–96.

Zwick, D. and Cayla, J. (2011) *Inside marketing: practices, ideologies, devices*. Oxford University Press.

10   Branding and the music market

Chris Hackley

Introduction

In this chapter I will try to relate Jill and Sparrow and the Workshop's experience of engaging with markets (Chapter 19, pp. 317–25) to conventional ways of conceiving the marketing process. I will also refer occasionally to my own, slight, experience in music performing and recording. Jill and her fellow band members' ability to marshal skills of organisation, musicianship and creativity and make a living from performing original music shows formidable talent and resourcefulness. There are a great many aspiring musical artists, some of them with talent, who are unable to grasp the fundamentals of the business. Witness the thousands who audition each year for TV talent shows, hoping that a record deal will prove a springboard to stardom and bring an end to their years of toil on the pub circuit. For a few this is indeed what happens, but for most it does not, and quite a few who are a success on the shows remain unable to connect with an audience and sell product, even with prime-time TV exposure and professional management. Even without the impetus of a TV appearance, it has never been as technically easy or as affordable as today for an artist or band to record and release an EP of original material, and to build an audience though a dedicated website. The volume of material, though, along with the closed system of record plugging that limits the possibility of national radio play or critical attention for artists without major company backing, makes it very difficult indeed for new and unknown artists to generate a genuine market.

Highly trained, skilled and creative musical artists like Jill and her band would probably place themselves in a very different category from the acts that seek TV exposure on *X Factor*. The problem, in the age of the culture industry (Adorno, 1991), is that the distinction between authenticity and inauthenticity in art has become ever more difficult to disentangle. In the 1960s and 1970s bands emerged that were described pejoratively as 'manufactured'. While some ostensibly authentic bands formed spontaneously, practised, wrote, performed and built an audience through doing small gigs, there were others that seemed to roll off a production line like Model Ts. Bands like the Monkees and the Bay City Rollers were said to have held auditions, hired members on the basis of their looks rather than their musical ability, commissioned songs to be written for them, and then focused promotion and PR on 11-year-old girls as the softest market for single releases and merchandise. The distinction was never quite this straightforward, but authenticity remains a marketable quality for musicians. However, there is a much greater awareness today that no artists who want their work to be seen and heard can operate outside the world of marketing and, furthermore, that it is possible to be both authentic and commercially astute. When one considers the way that some former *X Factor* contestants have become major writing and performing artists, it seems that the distinction between authentic and inauthentic art may have been subsumed under the mass need for experiences of existential liminality, as viewers vicariously partake in that self-same struggle for authenticity (Hackley et al., 2012). Jill and her band have eschewed the glitzy realms of TV talent shows, but they have been successful, on their own terms, by embracing the commercial side of the music business.

In crude marketing terms, Jill works with her band colleagues to create product through a creative development process, and she works with partners on branding, marketing communication, performances and retail distribution. For many artists, thinking of music creation in this way gives it a misleadingly mechanistic character, when in fact the music business might be more properly conceived as a creative, cultural industry. Of course, the term 'culture industry' is a loaded one in social theory, evoking Horkheimer and Adorno's (2002) notion of a world in which autonomous art is no longer possible because the capitalist imperative absorbs and debases all creative enterprise. As I imply above, the distinction between 'serious' (for example, The Rolling Stones) and overtly commercial (say, Take That) rock and pop music is perhaps less easy to see than it once was, but for many musical artists the practice of marketing is seen as both peripheral to, and degrading of, artistic production. Nonetheless, the necessity of engaging with the market, however that engagement is conceived, is not lost on Jill. In order to continue to do what they love to do, the band has to operate as a marketing entity and negotiate the tension between producing autonomous art and making a commercial product.

Music production as marketing

I want to focus here on two particular themes in marketing: the marketing concept itself and branding. These concepts are often applied simplistically as pseudo-explanations of market processes, when in fact the processes they purport to describe are far more nuanced and contingent than conventional marketing logic allows (Hackley, 2013). The creative industries in general, and music in particular, offer specific challenges to conventional thinking in marketing. The traditional 'marketing concept' holds that commercial success arises when a market need or want is satisfied by a producer. Marketing is often conceived as the managerial process of finding a consumer need, then utilising resources to satisfy it, at a profit (Kotler, 1967). The dynamic that projects 'the offer' into the market is branding. Branding means consciously creating distinction, recognition and trust for and in the offer (Feldwick, 2002) so that the target market will seek it out, thus creating a quasi-monopoly that can command what economists call 'extra-normal profit'. A band is a brand, at least seen through the lens of marketing. Whether the brand is Heinz, Ford, The Rolling Stones or Sparrow and the Workshop, the logic of marketing is that, when you boil it down, they're all in the same need-fulfilling game.

It is plain to the casual observer, if not to some marketing writers, that marketing is far more complex than the mere satisfaction of needs and wants. Much marketing effort is devoted to creating needs, rather than satisfying them. Many marketing innovations cannot be said to have alighted on a latent need because they introduced innovations that were previously inconceivable (Hackley, 2009). For example, there was no need or want for private musical entertainment as pedestrians moved around the city, until Sony CEO Akio Morita invented the Sony Walkman. Sony's market research confirmed that there was no 'need' for the product. Morita famously ignored the research and insisted that the Walkman be put in Sony stores. It flew off the shelves. Consumers hadn't 'wanted' it when they were asked because they couldn't imagine it. When they saw it, they got it. The Walkman created a need.

In a more relevant example, Elvis Presley's music was not 'wanted' by white, middle-class America. Like the Walkman, it was inconceivable to consumers. A few entrepreneurial music producers did realise that a white man who could sing like a black man might be able to activate a huge new market for American blues and its rock variants, and so it proved. Presley is an interesting example, perhaps, since his initial success was serendipitous and his musical style unique. He went against the prevailing norms in commercial popular music, until his extraordinary breakthrough set new norms. Later in his career, though, he became a crudely marketed entertainment product, a cash generator for his notoriously cynical manager 'Colonel' Tom Parker. Presley, with help from Sam Phillips, Sun Records and backing artists like ace guitarist Scotty Moore, created a need, just by doing what came naturally. His authenticity as an artist was, and still is, celebrated, even though the latter part of his career was a characterised by creative stagnation and crude commercial opportunism.

In the creative industries it is probably intuitive that branding is more important to artists than the dubious marketing concept. Artists remain undiscovered until their audience can identify them, and identify with them (Schroeder, 2005). Many great visual artists, for example, have also been astute self-marketers, from Salvador Dalì to David Hockney and Damien Hirst. OK, perhaps some not-so-great artists too. The notion of finding out what target consumers might want in order to craft something that will satisfy them seems, on the face of it, deeply antipathetic to creative art. The hollowness of the marketing concept becomes apparent when one conceives consumers as needy not merely for functional solutions to practical problems but in a more abstract sense, in that we need novelty, excitement, inspiration and diversion, through consumption. We await the genius's vision, and then we follow. Henry Ford, Bill Gates or Steve Jobs didn't send out questionnaire surveys asking what people wanted. They created, and the market followed.

None of which really helps nascent music professionals, because they know too well that commercial success is not going to knock on their door uninvited. Many, like Jill and her bandmates, want simply to be able to make a living doing what they love to do. That is privilege enough. The case in this chapter illustrates some of the tensions within the marketing concept, as Jill and the band try to reconcile the creative integrity of being a musician and performer with the necessity of engaging with the music marketing business.

The very notion of giving consumers what they say they want, then, seems absurd in the context of creative industries. What consumers of art want, I presume, is to see something new and exciting that activates their sense of discernment. There is no way to generate consumer activation through art mechanistically – it demands cultural leadership through creativity. I argue that this is true not only of marketing in the cultural and creative industries but in other sectors too (Hackley, 2013). If one agrees with Adorno (1991) that part of the role of marketing in popular media, his 'culture industry', is to aestheticise everyday life, then it seems entirely fitting that marketing be conceived as a creative and artistic endeavour, rather than merely an as incremental and scientific one.

The commercialisation of music is undergoing radical changes. Years ago, I recorded demo tapes and sent them to A&R departments, in the deluded hope that I might be invited to a London recording studio for an audition. Miraculously, one day I was, but that's a story for another day. That was a typical approach for many musicians. More recently, I've been recording for fun with a friend who was a drummer for a highly successful rock band in the 1960s and 1970s. Today, he remains a professional musician but now has a portfolio career working with many different artists, gigging, making music for commercial applications, producing, teaching, recording and applying session tracks. Technology is central to the jobbing musician today. My friend might be sent an album of guitar tracks from Los Angeles by email; he puts the drum tracks on in his home studio and sends it back for the vocal to be added. Only a lucky few musicians find themselves in a position to earn long-term royalties from major music sales. Jill and her band are doing what they love and adapting to the commercial technologies of music as they move forward with their creative projects. Their challenge is to make their endeavour economically sustainable, and to do this they must engage with niche music markets through the new technologies of music production, marketing and branding.

Another important feature to note when assessing the fit of marketing concepts to the music business is that bands are very small businesses indeed. It is a common criticism of business school approaches to marketing that they focus disproportionately on the priorities and activities of global fast moving consumer goods sold by massive corporations, and they neglect the businesses that are defined as small to medium enterprises or SMEs. In other words, the kind of marketing taught in MBAs often has little to say to the small businesses that make up 90 per cent of the total number of commercial enterprises in the UK economy. Small businesses, such as a fish and chip shop, a local taxi firm or Sparrow and the Workshop, tend to reach markets initially through word of mouth and personal connections and by reputation, with 'marketing' coming into play once the groundwork has been done and the concern has begun to take off. What constitutes marketing, though, has changed with the rise of social media and the internet. Whether or not conventional static concepts of marketing remain salient to real small-scale businesses, if they ever were, is an open question.

Music branding

Branding is fundamental to commercial success, since commodities must be differentiated for consumers. A brand must not only be recognised but must have a distinct identity, through its visual representations and/or its values. Artistic performers, too, must find a way to be noticed, recognised and sought out. Music may be a serious form of creativity to Jill and the band, but as a band they are also part of showbusiness, and you don't have to be P.T. Barnum or Simon Cowell (Brown and Hackley, 2012) to know that image goes a long way.

Consider 'Seasick' Steve Wold, the 72-year-old country blues artist who became an overnight success as a solo performer in 2006 after a serendipitous appearance on TV's Jools Holland show, after some forty years in the music industry as a sound engineer, session musician and street busker. Seasick Steve's music, originality and craft as an artist is hard-earned, but he became successful when he adopted the stage persona of the hobo he once was. With dungarees, baseball cap, tattoos and string vest, and a selection of home-made instruments, Steve represents a music era long lost, but his musical style, his persona and his well-rehearsed hobo back story appeal to a young, contemporary audience. Steve hit on something akin to a brand in music business terms. His hobo look, raw blues sound and the plaintive themes of his songs caught the imagination of the public, not in his native USA but in the UK.

As well as understanding the importance of image and PR, Steve also embraces social media marketing. Much of his product is given away free of charge in YouTube videos and free downloads. His organisation emails fans regularly with news, selected tracks of his new albums, handwritten notes from Steve and gig dates, and the emails carry a link to his website, where fans can buy the CD. This web presence and database management leverages his market visibility, and feeds off his regular performances at major UK summer folk festivals. Steve's albums are mostly recorded at his home on a four track and released on small labels, with his sons assisting with album cover artwork, musical backing and sound engineering. Seasick Steve's persona – his brand – is the antithesis of slick marketing, but in fact he has, belatedly, shown an unlikely flair for astute market positioning and for the 'monetisation' of web presence.

The notion of branding remains problematic for artists, with its connotations of chocolate bars, hamburger chains, corny promotion and cheap and nasty production methods. In any consumer community there will be contests over authenticity and inauthenticity, and for some grassroots music fans the very fact of commercial success in itself represents an inauthentic 'sell-out'. Jill seems to allude obliquely to this when she speaks of rejecting the 'DIY community', who cannot reach audiences beyond their tiny in-crowd. By implication, Jill recognises that the refusal to engage with the business side of music is defensive, and masks a lack of creative ambition with a bogus sense of integrity. There is a line to be drawn between setting out to conform to the marketing concept by providing what a clearly defined market is known to want, as 'boybands' like One Direction unashamedly do, and trying to create something original that will draw discerning fans towards it regardless, or perhaps in spite, of their demographic characteristics. The precise nature of the difference is more nuanced than some would allow, given the dynamic of the contemporary convergence economy. Branding is a default position rather than a strategy when even the most amateurish bands can have a web presence, musical output available for download on iTunes and a logo. It is a mistake, though, to assume that the most visible aspects of branding are the most decisive. As in all things, success is a matter of attention to detail. Branding professionals would argue that popular caricatures of branding that focus on the communication issues such as logos and advertisements have mistaken the sizzle for the sausage, and that, in fact, branding represents a rational approach to fundamentals of business such as recognisability, integrity, continuity, creativity and quality. For branding professionals, the communications should be grounded firmly in an offer that has integrity.

Floppy-haired sixties foursome the Monkees were the archetype of the manufactured band, at least for my generation. They were, it was said, auditioned for looks, they had some songs written for them, they were given a ready-made TV show as a promotional vehicle, and they mimed their way through wacky music videos that delivered a carefully calculated Beatles-lite product for white American pre-teens. They then sold vinyl records by the truckload. They were seen as a bit of joke by many of their contemporaries, but members of the band spent the next fifty years arguing that, actually, they were much better performers and musicians than they were given credit for. Whatever. Today, the idea of the manufactured band is, arguably, redundant, since they all are. Marketing has fused seamlessly with music and there's no shame any more. Artists once considered culturally important, like Iggy Pop, do ads for car insurance, while some formerly frothy pop artists, such as David Bowie, are now treated reverently by critics. Horkheimer and Adorno's (2002) culture industry thesis has come to pass in the media convergence era, and high- and lowbrow, elite and popular art are flung together in a pulsating post-modern pastiche.

Sad to say, Jill and her band probably represent a shrinking music *cognoscenti*, a class of musicians and music fans who stand apart from the hit parade and the mass music market, and who prioritise an eclectic sense of musical discernment. Their fans would prefer to discover a great new band in a pub than watch *X Factor*. In fact they wouldn't watch *X Factor*. Ever.

Application questions

- Can authenticity and commerciality be combined successfully?
- What does 'success' mean in this setting?

- How is 'the offer' projected into the market?
- What does the brand draw attention to, and how well is this working for the purposes of the people involved?

References

Adorno, T.W. (1991) *The culture industry: selected essays on mass culture*, edited by Bernstein, J.M. London: Routledge.

Brown, S. and Hackley, C. (2012) The greatest showman on earth: is Simon Cowell P.T. Barnum reborn? *Journal of Historical Research in Marketing*, 4(2): 290–308.

Feldwick, P. (2002) *What is brand equity anyway?* Henley-on-Thames: World Advertising Research Centre.

Hackley, C. (2009) *Marketing: a critical introduction*. London: Sage.

Hackley, C. (2013) *Marketing in context*. London: Palgrave.

Hackley, C., Brown, S. and Hackley, R.A. (2012) The X Factor enigma: Simon Cowell and the marketization of existential liminality. *Marketing Theory*, 12(4): 451–69.

Horkheimer, M. and Adorno, T. (2002) *Dialectic of enlightenment: philosophical fragments*, edited by Schmid Noerr, G.; translated by Jephcott, E. Stanford University Press.

Kotler, P. (1967) *Marketing management: analysis, planning, implementation and control*. Englewood Cliffs, NJ: Prentice-Hall.

Schroeder, J.E. (2005) The artist and the brand. *European Journal of Marketing*, 39(11/12): 1,291–305.

11 Being 'in the room'

Alan McCusker-Thompson

The primacy of 'connections' within the music field is legendary. It could be argued that many significant business or creative connections that take place in the music industry have already been (pre)formed before two individuals meet in any given room: that they are 'in the same room' before they actually meet. This chapter looks at what it means to be 'in the room'. I am going to argue that there is a sense in which the real organising of music, the business of which is often spoken about as being informal and organic, as well as being elitist and hierarchical, takes place before an actual organised encounter occurs, and that it is this wider context that constitutes 'the room'. This chapter will consider being in the room in relation to the physical, which includes privileged physical space (backstage, aftershows, etc.) and unrelated/anonymous/public space, as well as physicality such as clothes, hair and body. It will also examine the 'socio-cultural room' and the emotional and technological context within which meanings and connections are fostered.

To be in the room one needs to recognise what 'good' or 'cool' are, what MacIntyre (2007) calls 'goods internal to the practice' – in this case, the practice being music. MacIntyre disproves the notion that *de gustibus non est disputandum* – that in matters of taste there can be no disputes. For MacIntyre, 'those who lack the relevant experience are incompetent . . . as judges of internal goods' and 'we cannot be initiated into a practice without accepting the authority of the best standards realised so far' (2007: 188–90). In essence, he is talking about recognition and respect for expertise that enable the recognition of someone who is in the room. This is different from a simple emotional commitment to a particular musical form rather than the practice of music. Tribal loyalty to a particular genre and its codes of practice, while reinforcing personal identity, is of limited value.

Let us now examine the rooms within which, I am arguing, the music industry plays itself out. These are the physical, the intellectual, the cultural, the social, the emotional and the technological. For the purpose of this chapter these non-physical, conceptual rooms will be referred to as existing within the 'socio-cultural room'. It should be emphasised that what we are talking about is actually a dynamic interplay between these variables.

The physical room

Being 'in the room' is not merely being in the room physically. Backstage passes and aftershow attendance are no guarantees of making creative or business connections. In fact, these types of event are exactly the time when understanding the secret language of music would dictate that 'buttonholing' and networking should not take place. Similarly, attendance at music business conferences is, ironically, not a good time to do business, unless you are already have prearranged meetings or are travelling with high value social capital. Meaningful relationships are more often formed in obscure 'kitchens' at privileged, intimate, socially managed parties and events.

Similarly, in relation to the physical room, the secret language of music is articulated through the physicality of individuals, whether through dress (e.g. wearing, or avoiding, iconic items of dress such as the Picasso/Warhol/Kurt Cobain Breton-striped top), hair styles or items with particular cultural associations (Ray-Ban Wayfarer shades being an obvious example). Wearing these items is no guarantee of connection if one does not understand their context, and it is easy to adopt the appearance without having the cultural 'substance'. In other words, the effective appearance is an expression of the appropriate taste, which is gained from immersion within the group. Before going on to discuss this I would like to relate a personal experience from my attendance at the music industry conference, In The City, in Manchester several years ago.

I was aware that one of the older panellists, Peter Jenner, had managed Billy Bragg and the Clash, neither of whom impressed me. He had the dress, demeanour and delivery of an 'old duffer'. Because I did not understand the cultural context, he seemed unremarkable to me. It was only later that I found out that he had a first class honours degree in economics from Cambridge, had previously managed Pink Floyd, produced classic albums by Roy Harper and organised a number of the legendary concerts in Hyde Park, including the iconic 1969 free concert by The Rolling Stones. *Mea culpa.* If you manage to get into one of the physical rooms it is often hard to tell whether you are standing next to a 'nobody' or a 'superstar' by physical appearance alone, and this is why the socio-cultural room is so important.

The socio-cultural room

Social capital is not simple to acquire. It is the result of an incremental process. As Bourdieu and Wacquart state:

Social capital is the sum of resources, actual or virtual, that accompany an individual or group by virtue of possessing durable network of more or less institutionalised relationships of mutual acquaintance and recognition. (quoted in Field, 2003: 15)

The powerplay of the contemporary music industry, despite its apparent emphasis on style over substance, is actually intellectual and not much different from the worlds of Adorno and Leavis. In *Culture and environment*, Leavis and Thompson state:

Upon the minority depends our power of profiting by the finest human experience of the past; they keep alive the subtlest ... parts of tradition. Upon them depend the ... standards that order the finer living of an age, the sense that this is worth more than that... (1933: 10)

Despite the so-called democratisation of technology, these individuals or 'mavens' or 'molecular leaders' (Gladwell, 2000: 67) still shape the workings of the music industry, and they do so as an 'intelligentsia'. This reminds us that, in MacIntyre's terms: 'those who lack the relevant experience are incompetent ... as judges of internal goods' (2007: 188–90).

The blurring of high and low culture that we associate with postmodernism defines the socio-cultural room in terms of its reach and its playfulness. Cultural literacy makes one socially articulate and allows a level of allusive communication that provides a shorthand for incrementally establishing connections and social capital. In transactional analysis terms, it enables the rapid establishment of a status quo where 'I'm OK. You're OK' (Berne, 1966: 29–40). It is how you are known that is important, rather than who you know: the extent to which your reputation generates reciprocity and trustworthiness (Putnam, quoted in Field, 2003: 32) and reputation.

The story of Duglas of the BMX Bandits (Chapter 19, pp. 352–7), gives insight into the workings of the socio-cultural room and further emphasises the importance of individualism, as it would be hard to find someone more fearlessly individual or idiosyncratic. Duglas T. Stewart of the BMX Bandits possesses an encyclopaedic knowledge of popular musical culture and has outstanding cultural and social capital. He has also worked as a music programme producer for the BBC. Duglas is incredibly rich in cultural capital, although his career in music has brought limited financial remuneration. This is a characteristic of 'indie' culture, in that musicians in this field may not have sold many records but they have been involved at the making and defining of musical history. As a result, they possess high cultural capital.

Apart from being considered by one maven of the Scottish music scene to be 'the best songwriter ever to come out of Scotland' (McPhail, 2013), Duglas received a major investment of social capital when Kurt Cobain of Nirvana said 'if I was to be in any other band, it would be the BMX Bandits'. This immediately puts Duglas's significance into a global context. His seminal influence on numerous bands that have gone on to international success and his continued influence on the music scene have also contributed not to his status but to the durability of his social capital. This has gestated over twenty-five years; it began when he and Norman Blake of Teenage Fanclub were 'making music in each other's bedrooms when they were young'. We can see a parallel with Peter Jenner here, and it also illustrates the potential difficulties of attempting to prevail in the music business when one does not understand the density of the social mechanics of the business or the depth of the emotional interconnectedness that exists between participants. There is always more to the picture than meets the eye.

The degree of emotional engagement may be particularly significant in the socio-cultural setting of music. In her book *The importance of music to girls* (2007: 171), Lavinia Greenhalgh puts forward the idea that to talk about music is to talk about the human condition; what this indicates is the idea of a profound and vital connection between music and individual identity. In 1975 Black Sabbath famously titled their greatest hits album *We Sold Our Souls For Rock & Roll*, and it is this notion of an, at times, reckless commitment to music within the music business that unifies the fantastically successful prime movers, cult heroes and inspired neophytes, whether they are business people or artists. It is a commitment that borders upon obsession, that is autonomous and that is maintained in the face of lack of financial success or artistic recognition.

This commitment informs verbal and non-verbal communication at organised events and is something that is mutually recognised and applauded by individual participants within the music business as, albeit to varying degrees, it is something that everybody who is 'in the room' shares. It is often inexactly referred to as 'passion', and this passion is the result of the aforementioned youthful transformation due to exposure to a particular musical stimulus that, in turn, resulted in autonomous study and dedication beyond social or financial reward to the practice of music. As one of Duglas's band members says: 'to be a BMX Bandit you need to be unafraid of being ridiculed or thought foolish by others'.

Changes in technology may be altering the possibilities for such communication, but technology might best be seen as an expression of the socio-cultural room, rather than something that will supplant it. Bill Gates argued that modern technology will enable 'business at the speed of thought' (1999). However, speed of exchange is not the most significant aspect of the communication that is newly enabled. As Harper states:

> Communication acts are not to be thought of as, say, a transfer of information between two machines (in the form of human bodies perhaps) but as acts that alter the moral fabric of our relationship between the senders and the receivers. (2010: 244)

Hence, moral and emotional engagement may be foundational for connections, which are subsequently based on taste, judgement and reputation.

Discourses are always changing, but with instantaneous global digital technology they are incessantly shifting, such that the significance of 'the room' may have changed without us knowing. It is increasingly possible that we as individuals don't know, to use the parlance of the 1960s, 'where it's at' – i.e. we are not in the room. The sea of potentially invisible digital feeds may appear to allow greater 'democratic' access to the receipt and sharing of much information. However, the hierarchical inclusion in and exclusion from in-groups and privileged 'back channels' are likely still to exist within these technologies, so the dimensions or shape of the room might change, while there is a degree of continuity to the enactment of the socio-cultural systems.

Key lessons on being in the room include the fact that learning how social capital is valued and gaining an insight into the rules of the in-group is an incremental process. Those seeking to be in the room should build the relationship before seeking to make the 'transaction' and should seek to understand before being understood, being aware of how things are changing.

Application questions

- What are some of the alternative routes to gaining a reputation?
- How might technological change be altering the shape of 'the room' or changing the form of connections that are made?
- What personal qualities are beneficial to building relationships and connections in the music industry?
- What could you do to improve your chances of success within the industry?

References

Berne, E. (1966) *Games people play*. London: Andre Deutsch.
Field, J. (2003) *Social capital*. London: Routledge.
Gates, B. (1999) *Business @ the speed of thought*. London: Penguin.
Gladwell, M. (2000) *The tipping point*. London: Abacus.
Greenhalgh, L. (2007) *The importance of music to girls*. London: Faber & Faber.
Harper, R. (2010) *Texture: human expression in the age of communications overload*.
    Cambridge, MA: MIT Press.
Leavis, F. and Thompson, D. (1933) *Culture and the environment*. London:
    Chatto & Windus.
MacIntyre, A. (2007) *After virtue*. London: Duckworth.
McPhail, J. (2013) Interview with the author. Glasgow, 20 June.

12   Music and marketing

Alan Bradshaw

To what extent can music legitimately retain its aesthetic authenticity in the culture industry? This chapter explores how music has been used by organisations as an instrument of social control. For example, we see studies that measure how manipulating the musical tempo determines the time and money consumers spend in a supermarket (Milliman, 1982) or analyse the ability of music in an advertisement to alter consumer affect and create a positive brand association (Kellaris and Cox, 1989). Such studies reveal a general idea of music's role in consumer culture as a stimulus in laboratory-style settings to be put to work as an instrument for organisation. This chapter reviews not just the mechanics of the laboratory that consumer culture is understood to be but also the politics and aesthetic implications of this interest in using culture as a device for manipulation. It begins with a brief exploration of the industrial uses of music during the twentieth century, alongside the attendant marketing theory, and ultimately develops an argument, drawing heavily on Adorno and Horkheimer (1997), which understands the relationship between organisation and music as one of capture and domination within a negative dialectic. Recent practices of organisational uses of music might be regarded as more ontological, as the goal is no longer to control a person's unconscious actions but to imply ways of being and forms of agency that reify people and render them commensurable with the commercial imperative. Arguably, in such a form music is reified according to a logic of the culture industry.

A cold war complex

Often, historical analyses into marketing during the twentieth century inter-war period reveal an axiomatic militaristic form. For example, early and highly influential practices of PR intersected heavily with CIA overseas interests (Tye, 2002). Advertising agencies packaged their output as part of a deliberate ideological reconstruction that emphasised the freedoms of choice in Western capitalism as rhetorical tools in the battle against communism (Schwarzkopf, 2011). At an axiomatic level, much of the idea of marketing and how particular voices came to be privileged is relatable to a history of the American Cold War effort (Tadajewski, 2006). As Holbrook reminds us (see Bradshaw and Brownlie, 2009), much of marketing's vocabulary is appropriated from the military – a 'target' market, an advertising 'campaign' – while the word 'slogan' originates from the Irish word for a battle cry. With such thoughts in mind, it is plausible to regard the history of marketing as saturated by militaristic thinking, and arguably close in spirit to the so-called 'military–industrial complex', in which the mechanisms of state and commerce combine as an infrastructure for war and profit. In such a context, as McLuhan and Fiore (1997) attest, there was a general fascination with how space could be reframed as a laboratory used to control behaviour, and how any such controlled environment could be a conditioner that creates non-perceptive somnambulists. As they argue, a thin line divides such technological innovation of exciting new consumer media and a military-led fantasy of psychological control and manipulation.

The twentieth-century use of background music as a means of providing a décor amenable to organisationally preferred modes of behaviour was hardly new. For example, military music had long been used to stimulate soldiers before battle, while the composition of court music was the businesss of many canonical composers. Within retail, the use of background music was not new: there are reports of street sellers singing about their wares dating back centuries, and by the nineteenth century the deluxe grand arcade-style shopping malls of the type analysed by Benjamin (2002) often boasted extravagant musical performances. For example, in 1904 Richard Strauss conducted the world premiere of his *Symphonia Domestica* in Wanamaker's New York shop (Schlereth, 1991). However, crucially for the modern age, in the 1920s General George Owen Squier of the US Army developed a wireless and telegraphy system – originally intended for trench warfare – which he applied commercially for the purpose of piping music into retail and labour settings, and so the Muzak corporation was born (Lanza, 1995).

Muzak arrangements typically consisted of popular numbers rearranged to mould seamlessly into the background. Heavy rhythmic parts of the arrangement were removed, as were vocals; instead, the melody line would typically played by lounge piano, guitar or saxophone. This type of music was widely produced by Seattle-based organisations like Muzak and Audio Entertainment Incorporated, whose work was extensively distributed and hence ubiquitous within consumer culture. It was also believed that such music could help boost productivity. For example, during the Second World War the BBC broadcast specially composed music into arms factories – by the end of the war, *Music While You Work* was broadcast into 9,000 factories. Central to such use of music was the discursive recourse to science that made spectacular claims about background music's impact. For example, Muzak generated musical programmes by using their so-called 'stimulus progression chart', which plotted music intensity against lapses and surges in productivity that took place at different times of day (Lanza, 1995). Corporate publications like *Effects of Muzak on industrial efficiency*, *Effects of Muzak on office personnel* and *Research findings on the physiological and psychological effects of music and Muzak* made a series of grand claims that the skilled use of music would increase metabolism; speed up breathing, typing and writing; increase muscular energy; delay fatigue; facilitate attention; and produce marked effects on blood pressure and pulse (Lanza, 1995). Meanwhile, to maintain the façade of serious science, popular hits were renamed as part of the stimulus progression chart – for example, Muzak renamed 'Funky Town' as 'S-3293 A-6'.

Apart from being indicative of the Fordist era of production, the overlap with the world of the military and government is striking. For example, Nixon piped Muzak into the White House and Pentagon, Muzak was used to keep officers attentive at US nuclear missile sites (Haden-Guest, 1973), the Polaris submarines played Muzak to their crews and Neil Armstrong and Buzz Aldrin listened to Muzak during their Apollo mission. Meanwhile, a holder of the Muzak franchise in Texas was L.B. Johnson himself, and Muzak experiments were conducted on personnel at a cordon of US nuclear missile sites in Alaska (Lanza, 1995). By the 1970s, Muzak traded with such slogans as 'The new Muzak – a system of security for the 70s' (Haden-Guest, 1973).

Marketing scholarship

Within marketing scholarship, academics seemed just as excited by the idea of music as a technology for social control. Notable seminal studies include Kotler's take on retail atmospherics, which was concerned with the science of designing space 'to produce specific emotional effects in the buyer that enhance his purchase probability' (1974: 50). Similarly, Bitner's (1992) 'servicescapes' sought to chart the relationship between environmental characteristics like the physical material but also non-tangential aspects like noise, temperature, odour and air quality with the intervening cognitive and affective consumer responses and behaviour. In both cases, interest focuses on how space may be utilised in order to generate organisationally preferred modes of behaviour and affect.

In particular, the work of Milliman came to be seminal. In two land-mark studies, Milliman demonstrated a relationship between the tempo of background music and the amount of time and money people would spend in supermarkets and restaurants (Milliman, 1982; 1986). Such studies prompted a series of enquiries in which a host of further variables were explored – for example, correlations between the familiarity of background music and temporal perception (see Yalch and Spangenberg, 1990; Kellaris and Kent, 1992), the relationship between modality and time spent (Herrington and Capella, 1994) and the suitability of the music to its context with consumer affect (MacInnis and Park, 1991; North and Hargreaves, 1997) and buying behaviour (Areni and Kim, 1993). These studies were aggregated by Oakes (2000) and also by Turley and Milliman (2000), both demonstrating a field that saw itself incrementally working towards a complete understanding of how the use of music to structure space and hence control workers and customers could eventually be mastered.

In advertising, too, we see a history of seeking to understand music as a device for control. For example, Gorn (1982) and Kellaris and Cox (1989) investigated whether music could prime people's product selections, while Park and Young (1986) explored whether music could positively condition attitudes to brands. MacInnis and Park (1991), meanwhile, found that the degree to which the music could be understood to 'fit' with the advertisement could determine the ad's likeability, and Baumgartner (1992) intervened to remind colleagues that how people might respond to music can be determined by personal associations. An excellent historical overview of the use of music in advertising is provided by Taylor (2012), who notes the transforming industry practices throughout this period. These include the use of jingles to boost the memorability of ads, the use of classical music to make products look more glamorous, the sponsoring of popular music radio programmes so that there would be a positive association and the use of music to determine affect.

The culture industry thesis

In particular, such instances of the operationalistation of music – ranging from the military-esque rise of Muzak to the Pavlov-esque body of academic experimentation – find their obvious point of theorisation in the culture industry thesis advanced by Adorno and Horkheimer (1997). Adorno and Horkheimer attest that culture exists in capitalist consumer culture as an object of mass deception, treacherously used to redirect engagement with culture towards a logic of commodification and capitalist reproduction. Such usage is treacherous because people approach culture, they argue, as an expression of and means of engaging with the enlightenment. Hence, at a very broad level, art and organisation might be expected to belong to two very different and conflicting domains. Yet 'even the aesthetic activities of political opposites are one in their enthusiastic obedience to the rhythm of the iron system' (1997: 120). For the authors, advertising became a point within the culture industry where we see such opposites becoming one. In order to facilitate such assemblage, they argue, each part of production must become akin to an industrial system – for example, this was the era of factory-like spaces for popular composition such as Tin Pan Alley, wherein we see the 'synthetic, planned method of turning out ... hit songs' (1997: 120). They argue that in such contexts the composition of music became standardised and its parts could be broken down and recycled for a series of additional uses. This was in contrast to how German philosophy had traditionally regarded culture – as something that sought to be 'higher and more pure, something untouchable which cannot be tailored according to tactical or technical considerations' (Adorno, 1991: 108). In disciplining musical production and recasting it as an object for reproduction in factory-like conditions that allow it to be broken down into parts then recycled for external purposes, such as its use in advertisements, music loses its autonomy.

Adorno emphasises that there is a basic level of antagonism that exists between culture, understood as a site of autonomy and pure humanity, and organisation, understood as a space of functional relationships. The relationship between music and organisation is necessarily, therefore, dialectical; as he puts it: 'culture suffers damage when it is planned and administered; when it is left to itself, however, everything cultural threatens not only to lose its possibility of effect, but its very existence as well' (1991: 108). However, under culture industry conditions, the relationship becomes a negative dialectic inasmuch as culture is produced as an object that is subject to domination and, as such, the degree that culture stands for any autonomy, or prospect of pure humanity, is rendered deceptive. For Adorno (1991), under threat is a matter far broader than culture: the very possibility of personal autonomy. For example, under conditions of organisational domination, everything becomes measurable by norms that are inherent to the organisation; hence, the quality of the person itself and his/her subjective dimensions are abstracted until all that remains is the person's immanence within the order of organisation: that is to say that people become reified. From such a perspective, how popular music became rearranged and represented by organisations like Muzak as an instrument to control shoppers emerges as a perfect example of culture industry.

However, just as the vocabulary that we associate with the early to mid-twentieth-century methods of control – motivational research, brainwashing, propaganda, etc. – now seems anachronistic, many of the industrial uses of music associated with that period have become transformed. Undoubtedly, the most iconic moment that marked the transition to the new order was the bankruptcy of the Muzak corporation in 2009, and its relaunch as an organisation that now channels music in its original form, rather than in a rearranged (i.e. bland) form. This general transformation has prompted a boom for musicians, who can generate an income from licensing their music to advertising agencies and other intermediaries. Accordingly, we witness the gradual disappearance of jingle-writing and rearranged music and instead observe the rise of trendhunters – cultural intermediaries whose task it is to discover the most interesting music, preferably from the far margins of popular music, which can be placed in marketing contexts (see Taylor, 2012). Holt (2002) demonstrates that this process can be quite ironic, as the sort of music most sought after is that which is 'unstained' by the corporate world and hence allows the brand to relate itself to the authenticity, truth and subjectivity to be found at the far fringes of independent music production. An example is how the music of Nick Drake and his song 'Purple Moon' became used by Volkswagen for an influential advertisement. As Volkswagen stated in their promotional releases of the time, they regarded Drake's music as conveying an 'essence' of the brand – that brand and Drake's music were 'kindred spirits' (cited in Taylor, 2012). Hence, even obscure and marginal musicians whose career might be imagined to exist outside the culture industry can become not just implicated but sought after by trendhunters in search of authenticity.

From an Adornian perspective, we might argue that the point of culture industry reification of music is completed when no further adjustment is required. In the culture industry thesis, Adorno and Horkheimer (1997) described the interchangeability of popular music as a consequence of standardised means of production, which meant that any part of a composition could easily be extracted and reapplied in a new setting. Today, such extraction is no longer necessary as the music already lends itself towards its own instrumentalisation. In tandem, Lash and Lury (2007) refer to the 'thingification' of culture, whereby an advertiser, for example, will immediately have ideas for how a piece of music can be used in an advert upon first hearing; culture now beckons to marketing for appropriation. As Taylor (2012) argues, such is the overlap between the music industry and the advertising industry that it is increasingly impossible to delineate any meaningful point of separation. In effect, when we are listening to music today, he argues, we are listening to the 'sounds of capitalism'.

This phenomenon tends to be theorised within the marketing literature as instances of musical fit. Here, music is selected for a context on the basis of its prototypicality with the object or the brand it is signifying – for example, MacInnis and Park (1991) found that the song 'You Make me Feel like a Natural Woman' fitted with an advertisement for shampoo. Accordingly, brand managers should choose a piece of music indicative of what marketers refer to as the brand's 'essence'. The purpose of music, then, is no longer to try and condition consumers according to a nexus of time perception and other forms of unconscious influence of affect, but to integrate the music into an overall coherent aesthetic and branded lifestyle that the consumer is invited to identify with and aspire to. As DeNora and Belcher (2000) suggest, the underlying logic for the use of music is that, for example, in a clothes shop: 'when you're trying something on picture yourself in a place where they are playing this kind of music'. In other words, modes of agency are now implied and sponsored by the music itself. Rather than imagine the consumer as somehow a marionette that can unconsciously be manipulated by judicious use of background music, consumers are now beckoned to ontologically identify themselves with a signifiable style implied by music as it coheres with the rest of the brand 'elements'.

Arguably, music's ability today to entangle its listeners into organisation penetrates deeper than Adorno and Horkheimer (1997) had theorised during the 1940s. The idea that consumers will identify with brands, and are therefore subjectivised rather than objectified in the process, effectively operates as a means of putting the consumer to work in performing the brand. As Arvidsson (2006) theorises, brand consumers become cast as 'immaterial labourers', whose consumption is productive of the brand value. Arvidsson argues that the relationships that consumers form on the basis of their brand identifications produce an 'ethical surplus' that converts into brand value. In this sense, we can talk of consumers' life itself being put to work. In such a context, the ability to have a quirky taste in music and overall personal aesthetic can add value to one's attractiveness to organisations, as it becomes a type of productive creativity. As Fleming (2010) demonstrates, in the so-called knowledge economy, employees are often sought who have alternative music interests and lifestyle.

Therefore, we might argue that the wheel has come full circle: while the subjective task of appropriating music and recycling it as a form of Muzak with the intention of controlling consumer behaviour disappears, the objective functional use of music for the culture industry is maintained, and is arguably far more effectively applied. That a song can be directly imported without the need for modification might be regarded by Adorno and Horkheimer (1997) as the point of total domination, capture and reification of music by the culture industry. Worse still, the fact that the music is believed to work, inasmuch as consumers are prompted to identify with the music and overall brand essence, the consumer too is reified in the process, and the more notionally 'authentic' music is sought by advertisers and used effectively, the more 'treacherous' the practice. Hence, a fluid interflow between the reified form of the music, the brand and the person all intersect in this mode of culture industry analysis. Perhaps this is the apotheosis of the culture industry as posited by Adorno and Horkheimer (1997). Such theoretical insight provides us with a powerful lens for interpreting and understanding the relationship between music and organisation today.

Implications for Hubby

Hubby (Chapter 19, pp. 305–9) presents an interesting case of an artist surviving in a harsh market. As distinct from the Cold War factory-esque analysis of music production and mass distribution depicted by Adorno and Horkheimer, Hubby proceeds on a far smaller scale and in a more humble manner. Unlike music rendered as bland as possible to disappear seamlessly into the background, Hubby's music engages with deeply personal and moving themes relating to suffering and loss that profoundly affect audiences. It is almost tempting to read Hubby's career as existing beyond the radar of commercial practice, as though his work belongs to an entirely different spectrum with no relevance to the culture industry. Yet at the same time, as has been argued, in the domain of trendhunters we find musicians such as Nick Drake targeted by advertisers, who hear in indie music an authenticity that they might wish to transfer to their brand. So too it is perfectly conceivable, if not easily predictable, that Hubby might find himself targeted by such trendhunters. The questions then posed by a musician like Hubby are: What kind of relationship can an independent musician, existing at the margins of the music industry, have with the culture industry? Can his music escape the negative dialectic? Is it too cynical and reductive to insist that such music must be explicable according to the culture industry? Or might it be that some form of escape is possible, and that through listening to such music we can in fact begin to approach the goal of music as an expression of pure humanity? Perhaps it might be argued that the double bind of the culture industry means that precisely the act of escaping the culture industry is what gives the music the aura of authenticity and autonomy but is also the same treacherous moment of recapture, as any advertising trendhunter would know well. Would it matter if Hubby's music is never played in an advertisement or sought by a trendhunter? Would it matter if he says yes or no to a trendhunter? Is the logic of trendhunting external or internal to the existence of musicians like Hubby?

Application questions

- How should we understand the relationship between music practice and the industries of culture?
- Who and what is being reified in this setting?
- To what extent, if at all, is 'thingification' acceptable?
- Can we escape the industrial ethos and find music as an expression of humanity?

References

Adorno, T. (1991) *The culture industry*. London: Routledge.

Adorno, T. and Horkheimer, M. (1997) *Dialectic of the enlightenment*. London: Verso.

Areni, C. and Kim, D. (1993) The influence of background music on shopping behaviour: classical versus top forty music in a wine store. *Advances in Consumer Research*, 20: 336–40.

Arvidsson, A. (2006) *Brands: meaning and value in media culture*. London: Routledge.

Baumgartner, H. (1992) Remembrance of things past: musical autobiographical memory and emotion. *Advances in Consumer Research*, 19: 613–20.

Benjamin, W. (2002) *The arcades project*. Boston, MA: Harvard University Press.

Bitner, M.-J. (1992) Servicescapes: the impact of physical surroundings on customers and employees. *Journal of Marketing*, 56(2): 57–71.

Bradshaw, A. and Brownlie, D. (2009) A portrait of Morris Holbrook. *Marketing Theory*, 9(3): 373–4.

DeNora, T. and Belcher, S. (2000) 'When you are trying something on, picture yourself in a place where they are playing this kind of music' – musically sponsored agency in the British clothing retail sector. *Sociological Review*, 48(1): 80–101.

Fleming, P. (2010) You are where you are not: Lacan and ideology in contemporary workplaces. In Cederström, C. and Hoedemaekers, C. (eds) *Lacan and organization*, pp. 169–86. Essex: Mayfly.

Gorn, G. (1982) The effects of music in advertising on choice behaviour: a classical conditioning approach. *Journal of Marketing*, 46(1): 94–101.

Haden-Guest, A. (1973) *The paradise program: travels through Muzak, Hilton, Coca-Cola, Texaco, Walt Disney and other world empires*. London: Morrow.

Herrington, D. and Capella, L. (1994) Practical applications of music in service settings. *Journal of Services Marketing*, 8(3): 50–65.

Holt, D. (2002) Why do brands cause trouble? A dialectical theory of consumer culture and branding. *Journal of Consumer Research*, 29(1): 70–90.

Kellaris, J. and Cox, A. (1989) The effects of background music in advertising: a reassessment. *Journal of Consumer Research*, 16(1): 113–18.

Kellaris, J. and Kent, R. (1992) The influence of music on consumers' temporal perceptions: does time fly when you're having fun? *Journal of Consumer Psychology*, 1(4): 365–74.

Kotler, P. (1974) Atmospherics as a retail tool. *Journal of Retailing*, 49(4): 48–64.

Lanza, J. (1995) *Elevator music – a surreal history of Muzak, easy-listening and other moodsong*. London: Quartet Books.

Lash, S. and Lury, C. (2007) *Global culture industry: the mediation of things*. London: Polity Press.

MacInnis, D. and Park, W. (1991) The differential role of characteristics of music in high and low involvement consumers' processing of ads. *Journal of Consumer Research*, 18(2): 161–73.

McLuhan, M. and Fiore, Q. (1997) *War and peace in the global village*. London: Wired Books.

Milliman, R. (1982) Using background music to affect the behaviour of super-market shoppers. *Journal of Marketing*, 46(3): 86–91.

Milliman, R. (1986) The influence of background music on the behaviour of restaurant patrons. *Journal of Consumer Research*, 13(2): 286–9.

North, D. and Hargreaves, D. (1997) *The social psychology of music*. Oxford University Press.

Oakes, S. (2000) The influence of the musicscape within service environments. *Journal of Services Marketing*, 14(2): 549–56.

Park, W. and Young, M. (1986) Consumer response to television commercials: the impact of involvement and background music on brand attitude formation. *Journal of Market Research*, 23(1): 11–24.

Schlereth, T. (1991) *Victorian America – transformations in everyday life: 1876–1915*. New York: Harper Perennial.

Schwarzkopf, S. (2011) The consumer as 'voter,' 'judge,' and 'jury': historical origins and political consequences of a marketing myth. *Journal of Macromarketing*, 31(1): 8–18.

Tadajewski, M. (2006) The ordering of marketing theory: the influence of McCarthyism and the Cold War. *Marketing Theory*, 6(2): 163–99.

Taylor, T. (2012) *Sounds of capitalism: advertising, music and the conquest of culture*. Chicago University Press.

Turley, L.W. and Milliman, R. (2000) Atmospheric effects on shopping behaviour: a review of the experimental evidence. *Journal of Business Research*, 49(2): 193–211.

Tye, L. (2002) *The father of spin: Edward L. Bernays and the birth of public relations*. Toledo, OH: Owl Books.

Yalch, R. and Spangenberg, E. (1990) Effects of store music on shopping behaviour. *Journal of Consumer Marketing*, 7(2): 55–63.

Organising in complex environments

13   Complexity theory

Robert MacIntosh and Donald MacLean

This chapter introduces complexity theory as an approach that challenges some of our assumptions – about both organisations and what it means to organise. Complexity theory draws on a diverse range of source literatures including physical chemistry, biology and computing science, and is increasingly being used to inform practice in management and organisation. For those interested in pursuing a more detailed review of complexity, there are introductions in the form of popular science (Waldrop, 1992) and reviews of contemporary contributions (Maguire et al., 2011), as well as introductory reviews of organisational applications of complexity theory (MacIntosh et al., 2006).

In essence, complexity thinking tends to be organised around a few key concepts. First is the observation that small events can be amplified to produce large-scale outcomes. Researching weather patterns, Lorenz (1963) coined the phrase 'the butterfly effect', which has since passed into widespread usage, to capture both sensitivity to initial conditions and the inherent unpredictability of complex systems. A key feature of such systems is that they are 'densely interconnected', such that one part of the system can influence many others in ways that are often difficult, if not impossible, to track in terms of 'cause and effect'. A second theme in complexity theory is that complex systems tend to exist in 'non-equilibrium' states. This is challenging, since so many of our organisational concepts – such as supply and demand – assume that equilibrium is the default position. Nobel prize-winner Ilya Prigogine observes that systems in highly unstable states become susceptible to tiny signals and random perturbations that would have had little impact were they still at equilibrium (Prigogine and Stengers, 1984). This introduces a third theme – namely, 'non-linearity' driven by feedback processes. Positive feedback, which is essentially an amplifying feedback, can turn these tiny changes into 'gigantic structure breaking waves' (Prigogine and Stengers, 1984: xvii). Feedback processes are therefore seen as central to the relationship between stability and change; in particular, the balance of negative (i.e. restorative or damping) and positive (i.e. amplifying) feedback influences the extent to which system-wide change occurs. A fourth theme draws attention to 'simple rules' or deep structure (Drazin and Sandelands, 1992). In complex systems, order is seen to emerge through the repeated enactment or application of simple rules. For instance, Reynolds (1987) managed to simulate the flocking behaviour of birds using only three rules.[1] Eisenhardt and Sull (2001; 2012) suggest that organisations in high-velocity environments work with simple rules – i.e. heuristics or 'rules of thumb' – to determine which products to launch, which markets to operate within, etc. The radical departure from other theoretical perspectives is that complexity theory suggests that order emerges from within a system through a process called self-organisation (Kauffman, 1993). As a shorthand summary, self-organisation – which can sometimes amount to radical new patterns emerging – occurs when the four themes set out above (a densely interconnected system, non-equilibrium conditions, non-linear feedback, a set of simple rules that are repeatedly applied) occur.

Many of the insights generated in the study of complex adaptive systems arose from studies in the natural sciences (e.g. Prigogine's work on chemical reactions), mechanical or electrical systems (e.g. Kaufmann's studies of electrical circuits) or animals (e.g. Goodwin's studies of ant behaviour; see Gordon et al. [1992]). However, a significant further complication is introduced when considering social systems. In complex adaptive social systems, issues such as voluntary behaviour, participation and reflexivity need to be incorporated (MacLean and MacIntosh, 2003).

To take one example, consider the concept of simple rules. Reynolds (1987) produced a computer simulation where each individual 'boid' (his term for a simulated bird) follows instructional statements such as 'match the velocity of other boids'. A further twist occurs when we consider the case of birds rather than boids. If one accepts that birds are not capable of formulating and following instructional rules, it is inappropriate to argue that individual birds are engaged in rule-following. A more accurate account would be to argue that the instinctive, or perhaps inherent, behaviour of individual birds can be explained via the repeated application of simple rules such as 'maintain a safe

---

[1] In 1986 Reynolds managed to produce a computer simulation that he called Boids. In the simulation each individual boid follows three simple rules: (1) steer to avoid crowding and collision, (2) align towards the average line of flight of other local boids and (3) head towards the average positional location of other boids in the flock. Using these three rules a whole flock of boids emulates the flocking behaviour of real birds. An internet search for the term 'boids' will identify several online versions of the simulation that you can experiment with.

distance from other birds'. The important thing to note here is that it is the explanation that relies on the concept of rules – not necessarily the behaviour itself. Rules may thus simply be a way of explaining behaviour that emerges from certain patterns of interaction in a way that is not fully understood.

Yet more complicated is the case of a social system where individuals are both sentient and capable of complying or contravening simple rules. It is possible to get a group of people to reproduce flocking behaviours by asking each individual to act in accordance with the set of simple rules employed in Reynolds's simulation model. Two significant issues are thrown up by this transition to human settings. First, rules can be identified, communicated and made explicit. Second, individuals are capable of making a conscious decision to enact the rules, or to misinterpret them either deliberately or inadvertently, to ignore them for some reason, or even to attempt to manipulate them.

Similar concerns arise in relation to the other concepts described above. In human systems, perception affects the extent to which individuals feel connected with others. One person's sense of instability or non-equilibrium conditions may not accord with the views of others. Intentional efforts to amplify particular behaviours, processes or outcomes may inadvertently be interpreted in ways that produce the opposite of the desired effect. Indeed, we have argued that in complex adaptive social systems all of these complexity concepts act as 'interacting gateways' (MacIntosh and MacLean, 2001: 1353) where, for example, non-linear feedback applied to a set of simple rules pushes a system to non-equilibrium conditions when interconnections reach a certain density. Each of these concepts needs to be co-present, and each is, in some ways, created by and creating the others. When these concepts operate in concert, order is produced over time, yet the potential for the spontaneous emergence of radical novelty is ever present. This is the quintessential feature of complexity.

Complexity is therefore primarily concerned with the emergence of order in so-called 'complex adaptive systems', which exist in far-from-equilibrium conditions in an irreversible medium. Such order manifests itself through emergent self-organisation, as a densely interconnected network of interacting elements selectively amplifies certain events. This propels the system away from its current state towards a new order in a way that is largely unpredictable. While the detailed form of such emergent structures cannot be predicted, the range of broad possibilities is to some extent contained within a combination of initial conditions, the set of order-generating rules and/or patterns of interconnection that are available.

Debates in the complexity literature

While there is broad agreement on these core concepts, the field of complexity theory tends to combine them differently based on two distinct views, labelled 'the edge of chaos' and 'dissipative structures'. Organisational applications of these concepts mirror the pattern that has occurred in the natural sciences, in that usage of the dissipative structures view pre-dates its edge of chaos counterpart (see Gemmill and Smith, 1985). Dissipative structures have been used to describe regional development (Allen, 1998) and organisational change (Gemmill and Smith, 1985; Leifer, 1989; MacIntosh and MacLean, 1999), as well as individual change (Gersick, 1991). The original research on dissipative structures was conducted in the fields of physics and physical chemistry (Jantsch, 1980; Prigogine and Stengers, 1984) and describes qualitative, systems-wide changes that occur episodically, in distinct phase transitions initiated by some external trigger. During these phase transitions, the system concerned imports energy and exports entropy (a measure of disorder). Since dissipative structures consume energy, they tend to stabilise again and return to equilibrium if, or when, the supply of energy stops.

Subsequent research in the field of biology (see Kauffman, 1993; Solé et al., 1993) adopted a different perspective, claiming that rather than experiencing periodic punctuations, systems can exist in a zone on the edge of chaos. The edge of chaos perspective is most frequently associated with work in so-called 'living systems' (e.g. insect colonies, organisms, the human body, neural networks, etc.). Goodwin claims that 'complex, non-linear dynamic systems with rich networks of interacting elements [have a zone which] ... lies between a region of chaotic behavior and one that is frozen, with little spontaneous activity' (1994: 169). Systems on the edge of chaos appear constantly to adapt and self-organise again and again to create configurations that ensure compatibility with the ever-changing environment. This perpetual fluidity is regarded as the norm in systems on the edge of chaos, as opposed to a periodic feature of systems that undergo dissipative transformations from one stable state to another.

It has been noted that 'the edge of chaos is a good place to be in a constantly changing world because from there you can always explore the patterns of order that are available and try them out ... you should avoid becoming stuck in one state of order which is bound to become obsolete sooner or later' (Brian Goodwin, quoted in Coveney and Highfield, 1996: 273).

Table 2 offers a comparison of the dissipative structures and edge of chaos views of change processes.

Table 2. *Comparing the edge of chaos and dissipative structures views*

	Edge of chaos	Dissipative structures
Temporal characteristics of change	Change is seen as an ongoing, evolutionary process.	Change occurs episodically.
Espoused attitude to equilibrium states	Disequilibrium is the norm and is associated with a healthy vibrant system. 'Equilibrium is the precursor to death' (Pascale, 1999: 85).	Equilibrium represents the normal state of systems; this is interrupted periodically by episodes of disequilibrium but the system will strive to return to equilibrium.
Evidence of self-organisation	Self-organising processes both create order and maintain the system's position on the edge of chaos.	Self-organising processes create order out of the far from equilibrium conditions.
Emergent properties	Emergent properties arise through the connectivity between parts of the systems and are the result of local coupling (Solé et al., 1993: 344). For a more general discussion of connectionist views see Cilliers (1998).	Order emerges through the repeated application of simple rules (Prigogine and Stengers, 1984) and, over time, the system will settle into some new configuration.
Drivers for change	The internal dynamics of the self-organising processes trigger change on an ongoing basis.	Change is triggered by the action of some external force on the system (e.g. the input of energy into the system).

While a full discussion of the relationship between these two views of complexity theory is beyond the scope of this chapter, it is perhaps worth noting that one view – dissipative structures – arose in fields of study concerned with systems of molecules and other such assemblies, while the edge of chaos view focuses mainly on living organisms or organs. The extent to which organisations are continuously fluid or episodic in their change patterns may thus boil down to whether they are primarily seen, or designed, as mechanical or living systems – i.e. whether they are fundamentally geared towards control or evolution.

Illustrating complexity in action

The conditioned emergence framework (MacIntosh and MacLean, 1999), located in the dissipative structures view of complexity, offers one way of operationalising complexity thinking in relation to organisational settings. The organisation must reconfigure its simple rules (sometimes referred to as order-generating rules or deep structure), ensure that the organisation experiences sufficient instability and make explicit efforts to encourage positive feedback (since most organisations are dominated by processes that engender negative feedback). Pascale (1999: 85) notes that 'one cannot direct a living system, only disturb it', and Stacey's extensive work in this area (e.g. 2001) centres on the assertion that for complex systems we cannot accurately predict (or control) what happens in the future. Nevertheless, the conditioned emergence framework suggests that managerial influence, if not control, can be exerted on complex adaptive social systems.

We have used this framework extensively when working with organisations to develop strategy. One such case involved working with a manufacturer of complex mechanical engineered products. The company had been performing poorly for a number of years and had experienced significant headcount reduction over a series of redundancy and restructuring exercises. We worked with the management team, and our first task was to try and explain recurrent patterns within the organisation by using the concept of simple rules. The constant pressure to reduce operating costs meant that organisational changes were seen as inextricably linked to costs. One of the rules operating within the firm was phrased as 'don't innovate unless it leads to cost reduction'. Using this one rule as an example, with the management team we seeded an alternative new framing of this rule, which was that all innovations had to result in outcomes, products or processes that were 'better, faster and cheaper'. Notably, the new rule contained echoes of the old rule in that there was still some emphasis on reducing costs, but this was set in a new context that emphasised improvement for customers and/or existing staff.

To create the conditions in which this new rule could be operationalised, we needed to work with the other main concepts set out earlier in this chapter. Over time we encouraged new processes, organisational structures and physical configurations of work spaces to create a sense of non-equilibrium conditions. Further, we encouraged new working practices, which drew individuals from different parts of the organisation into closer contact with each other, thereby increasing interconnectivity. Finally, we encouraged the explicit management of feedback processes, and in particular positive feedback, to amplify and to encourage small signals consistent with new ways of working. It would be oversimplifying a multifaceted organisational change narrative to imply that this was all that happened in the twelve months that we worked with the company, or indeed that there was a neat start and end point to the project in the reality of a continuous flow of the company's own narrative. However, the management team found it helpful to conceptualise the challenges they faced from a complexity perspective.

Complexity thinking and the analytic process

When attempting to understand any organisational setting from a complexity perspective, there are two aspects to the analytical process. The first is to apply the four core concepts set out in this chapter to the setting. Look for examples of interconnections in the setting, perhaps by looking for who or what is interacting in the situation. Assess whether the setting under consideration is relatively stable or unstable and how this appears to be changing over time. Sometimes it is easiest to begin by looking for patterns that appear to be stuck. Try to identify anything that appears to be behaving or responding in either a stagnant or, alternatively, a non-linear fashion and, perhaps most importantly of all, ask whether you could explain the dynamics of the situation by using a handful of simple rules. Having looked for instances of the four core concepts, the second stage of the analytical process is to examine the ways in which the examples you have chosen are co-producing each other.

In Simon's story (Chapter 18, pp. 251–7), many of the core concepts presented in this chapter are embedded in both the situation and in Simon's account of events. The various musicians, organised into sub-groups within the structure of the orchestra, represent one set of inter-connected elements. Guest soloists or conductors become part of the system on a temporary basis, though others like Sir Simon Rattle reappear in the story. Doubtless, at various points in the orchestra's existence it has experienced periods of instability. These are not immediately obvious in Simon's account, but a further exploration of the setting would be likely to throw up episodes of far-from-equilibrium conditions, and these are hinted at. Periods where funding crises occur may be one form of insta-bility. Another may be periods of artistic uncertainty and political unrest over the direction, nature or identity of the orchestra. Simon does men-tion the tension between being a business, being a civic organisation and having to cater to but challenge audience expectations. Each of these issues introduces uncertainty at least for periods in the organisation's story.

Non-linearity is harder to see in this particular glimpse of life within the City of Birmingham Symphony Orchestra. Perhaps by looking over time it would be possible to see non-linear changes in, for example, the number of associated organisations. The account mentions the youth orchestra, five choruses, etc. There is also reference to the fact that particular types of performance are repeated on the basis of positive outcomes – e.g. 'it has worked before, we will do it again'. A more careful analysis of the data may suggest that one such performance happened by chance, was successful and has now grown to form a regular and substantial part of the orchestra's activities. If so, this is exactly the kind of amplification of small signals that complexity thinking helps to explain.

Finally, there are some aspects of Simon's account that could be interpreted as simple rules. Some of these are formal (e.g. the service level agreements with funders). Some rules, however, are implicit, and those within the setting may not even be conscious of their operation. One such example is hidden in the explanation of the failed Christmas concert. A previously successful formula was re-enacted with disappointing results, which are partially explained by external factors (the weather was poor, etc.). The disappointing outcome led to a fundamental review of the Christmas event, which is described as going 'right back to the bare bones of what these concerts are'. Embedded in the next part of the same sentence is the observation that '(had it been more successful) we certainly would not be reconsidering it at the level we are'. Although this is an isolated example, it may be that the orchestra operates with a simple rule of 'only review failures', which is highly characteristic of organisations oriented towards negative feedback and trying to make everything just as it 'ought to be'. If by examining further examples it transpired that significant perceived failures led to reorganisations, changes in personnel or other similar outcomes, a pattern might become apparent. For a moment, assume that this rule does operate within the orchestra. If so, it may generate a particularly reactive dynamic, where strategic change is driven by external events or the perception of failure. A subtle but significant shift might occur if the rule was reframed as 'review good and bad outcomes'.

Having examined the individual concepts thus far, it would also be useful to consider the ways in which these concepts are interacting. Again, Simon's account offers insufficient data for a full analysis, but one can see how the repeated application of the 'review failures' rule could be subject to positive feedback, which (re)creates the sense of turbulence, change and instability that complexity theorists would characterise as non-equilibrium conditions.

Application questions

- Can the situation be regarded as a densely interconnected system with non-linear feedback?
- Does it appear that the system is in equilibrium or non-equilibrium?
- Can simple underlying rules be detected, or used to explain behaviour?

- Would a change in the 'order-generating rules' be advantageous? If so, for whom?
- How might the rules be reformulated?

References

Allen, P. (1998) Evolving complexity in social science. In Altman, G. and Koch, W.A. (eds) *Systems: new paradigms for the human sciences*, pp. 3–38. New York: Walter de Gruyter.

Cilliers, P. (1998) *Complexity and postmodernism*. London: Routledge.

Coveney, P. and Highfield, R. (1996) *Frontiers of complexity*. London: Faber & Faber.

Drazin, R. and Sandelands, L. (1992) Autogenesis: a perspective on the process of organizing. *Organization Science*, 3(2): 231–49.

Eisenhardt, K.M. and Sull, D.N. (2001) Strategy as simple rules. *Harvard Business Review*, 79(1): 107–16.

Gemmill, G. and Smith, C. (1985) A dissipative structure model of organization transformation. *Human Relations*, 38(8): 751–66.

Gersick, C.J.G. (1991) Revolutionary change theory: a multilevel exploration of the punctuated paradigm. *Academy of Management Review*, 32: 274–309.

Goodwin, B. (1994) *How the leopard changed its spots*. London: Phoenix Giant.

Gordon, D.M., Goodwin, B. and Trainor, L. (1992) A parallel distributed model of the behavior of ant societies. *Journal of Theoretical Biology*, 156: 293–307.

Jantsch, E. (1980) *The self-organizing universe*. New York: George Braziller.

Kauffman, S.A. (1993) *The origins of order: self organization and selection in evolution*. Oxford University Press.

Leifer, R. (1989) Understanding organizational transformation using a dissipative structures model. *Human Relations*, 42(10): 899–916.

Lorenz, E. (1963) Deterministic nonperiodic flow. *Journal of the Atmospheric Sciences*, 20(2): 235–45.

MacIntosh, R. and MacLean, D. (1999) Conditioned emergence: a dissipative structures approach to transformation. *Strategic Management Journal*, 20(4): 297–316.

MacIntosh, R. and MacLean, D. (2001) Conditioned emergence: researching change and changing research. *International Journal of Operations and Production Management*, 21(10): 1,343–57.

MacIntosh R., MacLean, D., Stacey, R. and Griffin, D. (eds) (2006) *Complexity and organization: readings and conversations*. London: Routledge.

MacLean, D. and MacIntosh, R. (2003) Complex adaptive social systems: towards a theory for practice. In Mitleton-Kelly, E. (ed) *Complex systems and evolutionary perspectives on organizations: the application of complexity theory to organizations*, pp. 149–65. Amsterdam: Elsevier Science BV.

Maguire, S., McKelvey, B. and Allen, P. (eds) (2011) *The Sage handbook of complexity and management*. London: Sage.

Pascale, R.T. (1999) Surfing the edge of chaos. *Sloan Management Review*, Spring: 83–94.

Prigogine, I. and Stengers, I. (1984) *Order out of chaos: man's new dialogue with nature*. New York: Bantam.
Reynolds, C.W. (1987) Flocks, herds, and schools: a distributed behavioral model. *Computer Graphics*, 21(4) (SIGGRAPH '87 Conference Proceedings): 25–34.
Solé, R.V., Miramontes, O. and Goodwin, B. (1993) Oscillations and chaos in ant societies. *Journal of Theoretical Biology*, 161: 343–57.
Stacey, R. (2001) *Complex responsive processes in organizations*. London: Routledge.
Sull, D.N. and Eisenhardt, K.M. (2012) Simple rules for a complex world. *Harvard Business Review*, September: 3–8.
Waldrop, W.M. (1992) *Complexity: the emerging science at the edge of order and chaos*. New York: Touchstone.

14 On leading in networks: the role of reflexive practices

Paul Hibbert

Introduction

There is a tension at the heart of the contemporary fascination with leadership in organisations and society in general. On the one hand, the cult of the charismatic, strong leader continues unabated in both contemporary academic literature and popular culture (Jan Verheul and Schaap, 2010). On the other hand, recent research has emphasised leadership that focuses less on the forceful or persuasive character of the leader and more on their mission and service to others. Ideas such as servant leadership (Mittal and Dorfman, 2012) and authentic leadership (Algera and Lips-Wiersma, 2012) are significant examples of this trend. Thus, there are divergent views about what makes (or is inherent in) a good leader, and there is similar contention about how they should lead. These divergent opinions are also present when we consider leadership in networks, but there is an additional level of complexity in such contexts. This arises because potential or presumed followers, in networks, can be quite ambivalent about leadership. For example, in their research on regional industry clusters, Sydow et al. (2011) found that there were both calls for network leadership and little real desire to be led.

In responding to the tensions and complexities alluded to above, this chapter seeks to consider the problem of leadership in networks in a different way. It focuses on leading instead of leadership, and is anchored in two particular conceptualisations. First, leading is conceptualised as a practice. By practice, I mean patterns of activity that are recognised as conveying competence within a particular community (Brown and Duguid, 2001) and are a matter of taste within a community, much as cultural preferences for food or the arts are (cf. Gherardi, 2009a). Already, this first part of the conceptualisation moves our focus from character to action, and from universal theories to localised, practical theories about leading (cf. Cunliffe, 2003).

The first conceptualisation of leading, discussed above, takes us towards a sense of how the practices of leading might differ from place to place, and from network to network. This network/place-oriented view needs to be complemented with a second conceptualisation: a time-oriented view. By this I mean the way that, even within relatively stable communities, contextual elements and interactions between people can vary over time – perhaps even moment by moment. In some cases, this possibility for variation arises from the stability of the community. The following quotation from Chris Stout's story (Chapter 19, pp. 298–304), emphasis added) illustrates this:

I think I have a style of my own because it has evolved through time and I have allowed it to be influenced by so much ... I don't feel that I need to bend my style so much now to accommodate other styles. I have never played traditional music in a purist way. I have allowed my music to be influenced by whatever musical style I have come into contact with, I have allowed it to influence my style directly, whether it be Brazilian music, jazz or classical. *I come from a place where the tradition is very, very secure, and in safe hands, so I have the confidence to reach out.*

This leads to a need to think about the practices of leading as continually adaptable, in response to greater or lesser changes in network contexts over time. For this reason, leading in networks is not just about practices, but instead it is about a particular kind: 'reflexive' practice(s). Reflexive practices capture, are adaptive and interactive. Reflexive practices account for how individuals change themselves over time – in response to changing contexts – by challenging their own frames, assumptions and ideals (Hibbert et al., 2010). But reflexive practices also emphasise the need to build on dialogue with others, and to see all those involved in such dialogue as responsible for the practices that emerge (Hibbert and Cunliffe, 2014). Thus, the reflexive practices of leading are always co-constructed in particular moments and specific milieux of interaction.

However, there are internal and external perspectives on reflexive practice. One extreme is based on the 'internal conversation' model of reflexivity (Archer, 2007) – that is, the process of questioning that entails an introspective thinking process. However, reflexivity also involves external, socially enacted processes (Adams, 2006; Hoogenboom and Ossewaarde 2005). To put it another way, reflexive practice is as much about what happens during an external conversation as it is about what happens during an internal one. From the internal perspective, reflexive practice requires being able to discern the needs of others in the context for leading action – and being aware of what is potentially wrong or injurious in our own actions – and thereby being willing to change ourselves (Hartman, 2006). From the external perspective, reflexive practice requires us to be ready to identify, advocate and support necessary changes in the systems that promote harmful values in our network contexts.

I suggest that it is important to emphasise the complementarity of the internal and external processes of reflexive practice(s) (Hibbert et al., 2010). A sole emphasis on the internal conversation leads to a clear, examined sense of ethical action but isolation from the social systems that affect the needs of others. A focus solely on the external conversation, given the turbulent and hard-to-pin-down nature of networks (Hibbert et al., 2010), leads to a lack of stability; purely focusing on social systems results in transient resolutions and leads to action that has no overall guiding purpose.

The picture of leading as situated in network contexts and time-focused – in and through reflexive practices – seems to suggest an unspecified range of plausible activity that is rather difficult to pin down. In part, this is true. But it is also true that some earlier community knowledge is always drawn upon in the construction of practice in networks (Siedlok et al., 2013), and some individual experience is always involved in interaction. Nevertheless, I do not wish to reconstruct some general theory of leadership from those elements. Rather, I want to do justice to the differences and the variety that are possible, in different network contexts. For that reason, the remainder of this chapter proceeds in three parts. First, it returns to the idea of leading and fleshes out some characteristics of how leading through reflexive practices might best be described. In the second part, the implications of this approach are considered. Then, in the final part of the chapter, brief concluding remarks are offered.

Leading through reflexive practices

I want to suggest here that leading through reflexive practices can be understood (or organised) around two particular lines of inquiry. The first is rooted in critical reflexivity (Cunliffe, 2003; 2004) and is concerned with how a reading of context might prompt an individual to consider leading. The second is rooted in self-reflexivity (Hibbert et al., 2010), and is concerned with the 'becoming' of the person to whom the possibility of leading presents itself. Each of these lines of inquiry is addressed in turn below.

Does the context present the need and possibility to lead?

A critically reflexive reading of a network context for action can help individuals to know both when there is a need for them to lead and when it might be possible. Before I explain why that is the case, it is important to say a little more about what I mean by a network context for action. Despite the practice focus in this chapter, I do not mean a gathering of a particular, professional community of practice (Lave and Wenger, 1991). Instead, by context for action I mean any situation in which member(s) of the community are involved in network activities that impinge on the interests and reputation of their community. For example, a musician working with production, marketing, sales and publicity specialists to release new material is still a part of a community-of-practice of musicians (perhaps a genre-specific community in this case). Nevertheless, how they do or do not lead in the network context may have an immediate or cumulative impact on their community of practice, through precedent or reputational effects.

Having underlined what is meant by a network context for action, I want to move on to consider how a critically reflexive (Cunliffe, 2004; Hibbert et al., 2010) reading of that context might be important. This reading involves posing such questions as:

- What theories and ideologies are influencing action in this network context, through me and through others?
- What organisational or social policies are in play in this network context?
- How do theories, ideologies and policies privilege and give voice to some of the actors in the network context, and undermine or exclude others?

An exploration of the network context in this way leads to further questions, the first being concerned with whether there is a *need* for one to undertake an act of leading. This need for leading is derived from an awareness of something to be challenged or resolved in the network context. But that still leaves a second question: Is leading a possibility in this network context, for me? A good example of this problem relates to exclusion. If the exclusion that is apparent is directed towards me, how then may I lead if I am present yet disregarded? Returning to Chris Stout's story, he shows how exclusion is avoided through creating a context – which is open, improvised and founded on communication – that creates a feeling of inclusion, even for 'non-participants':

Especially at Celtic Connections [the audience] were coming into see a 'collaboration' but I don't think they were expecting quite the level of improvisation, but because they were very clear about what was happening and they could see the communication, it was very visual, and people were just watching, and I think they felt a part of it. I felt it was really ... inclusive ... even although we are on edge at times, we never lost sight of the structure and the development of the music.

'Being on the edge' is a desirable state for leading through communication at the very smallest scale of interaction – the conversation (Cunliffe, 2009). Improvised choices of words, vigorous or quiet disagreement or even silence all have some impact on how interaction proceeds. There is perhaps a 'partial contribution' to leading in such moments. In network contexts, this partial contribution might be directed inwards or outwards. It may offer leading on internal issues such as managing unity and diversity, or it may offer leading towards external issues such as addressing confrontation and dialogue in the network/broader community context (Ospina and Saz-Carranza, 2010). But these are always partial contributions, completed in dialogue, and the relationship between leading within the network context of action and external effects on communities is not always clear. The next quotation from Chris Stout's story illustrates this kind of uncertainty about internal boundaries and external effects:

In a successful collaboration I aim to make music where you can't tell where the genre-specific boundaries are ... And so my aim is to work with musicians regardless of genre and make an emotional connection with a musician rather than a connection through a style or other people's perceptions of what you should play like.

If I lead (in this way) what do I become?

If the wider effects of moments of leading are not always clear – as alluded to above – there is also a further complication to consider. That is: when we undertake an act of leading, what is the effect on ourselves?

In general, the practices we enact are both revelatory and reconstructive (Gherardi, 2009a; 2009b; Nicolini, 2011). Practices reveal something of ourselves as we enact them – as a minimum, they exhibit something about the communities to which we belong. Practices are reconstructive because they allow for community understandings to be deployed in new contexts of action – practices are adaptable, rather than fixed routines (Siedlok et al., 2013). In particular, an act of leading places the practices of the enactor on centre stage, and – depending on the network context – can require the maximum degree of adaptation in order to influence others. This is especially the case where those in the network context for action are from very different communities of practice.

If we follow Nicolini (2011) in seeing practice as identity-forming, meaning-making and order-producing activity, then the adaptation of practice in order to lead needs to be accompanied by self-reflexivity. Specifically, the reshaping of practice in acts of leading needs to include a consideration of three effects. First, identity-forming effects – if I change my practice(s) in this way to undertake an act (or many acts) of leading, how will that affect the person that I am becoming? Furthermore, how does the person I am becoming relate to the person that I want to be? Second, meaning-making effects – where do the adaptations to my practice come from? Here, there is a link to critical reflexivity, as we need to ask ourselves which of the available ideologies, theories and policies we are drawing on (and therefore subscribing to) in order to reshape the meanings inherent in our practices. Third, how do the adapted practices I deploy in acts of leading create order, in the network context of action and in my 'home' community? To be reflexive is to be aware of our relationships and responsibilities – and the intimate connection between those two terms. This is why there is a need to consider how an act of leading, which requires an adaptation to practice, affects those relationships and responsibilities.

Taking the three questions indicated above together, we can see how demanding leading through reflexive practice is. This approach to leading does offer a route to change in network contexts. But it requires individuals to struggle and to be as aware as possible of what the internal and external effects of those changes might be. Of course, it is a counsel of perfection to expect individuals to be able to do this moment by moment. There must necessarily be times of review and repair outside of the network context of action, and perhaps some deliberate revision of practice intentions for the future in these reflective moments. Furthermore, practice is not enacted in a vacuum, and network contexts of action do not freeze while each (potential) act of leading is carefully considered, as in a game of chess. Instead, there is a need for presence in the flow of conversation, to take up and put down possibilities for leading as they arrive.

Implications: how can possibilities for leading flow?

In this final part of the chapter, the argument is focused on how – since reflexive practice should allow others as well as oneself to lead – the possibility of leading may be allowed to flow between individuals in the network context of (inter)action. As Chris Stout comments in his story: 'A good conductor will lead the orchestra but still allow them the freedom to perform'. The freedom to perform ultimately means the freedom to contribute to leading. How this flow of leading might be explored is addressed, in two parts, below. First, the inherent difficulties associated with leading through reflexive practices are considered. Second, some plausible lines of action are discussed.

Inherent difficulties: leading through reflexive practice and intractable questions

Those interested in enabling leading through reflexive practice face three difficulties. The first is that reflexive practice – since it essentially involves

and makes space for the other – suggests that individuals must be prepared
to *not* lead, and to allow others their turn in the practices of leading. Yet
there is no guarantee that everyone else in the network will necessarily take
the same view. What happens when someone offers the 'wrong' sort of
leading, and seeks to develop a permanent role for themself?

The second difficulty can occur where multiple acts of leading from the
same person are noticed, and seem to be regarded as 'successful'. In such
circumstances, individuals may continue to look to the successful actor as
a leader. This deference could compromise those who might be well
placed to undertake more helpful acts of leading themselves, in different
contexts and at particular times. What happens when reflexive practices
place an individual not temporarily, but seemingly permanently, on centre
stage?

The final difficulty follows on from the first two. In imperfect network
contexts, where the propensity for leading is not always motivated by the
interests of others and leader deference may evolve, the flow of leading
may be disrupted by the emergence of a persuasive and self-interested
leader. This can result in the development of conflict. What happens when
a reflexive practitioner feels that it is necessary to engage in conflict and
contestation? How does this affect the development of a climate that
allows leading to flow around a network?

The questions developed above are not easily answered, but in the final
part of this chapter some suggestions about working with and around
them are considered.

Working around inevitable issues

There are a number of particular aspects of reflexive practice that can
allow individuals to work with and around the problems discussed above.
These are by no means definitive principles but are rather ideas that would
benefit from further research in a range of contexts. Three particular
practices are advocated here: non-compliance, interruption and
deflection.

Non-compliance: this practice builds strongly on the principles of
critical reflexivity (Cunliffe, 2004). It involves a persistent refusal to
accept ideological concepts, theories and other systematic influences
that are clearly inequitable. This need not involve offering alternatives.
It is just a quiet and persistent refusal. However, this may only be a starting
point, as it may be necessary to take more visible action.

Interruption: sometimes compliance to dominant regimes of thought
is so deeply embedded that non-compliance can seem absurd. To put
it another way, individuals may rely so deeply and unconsciously on a

system of thought that its constraints seem to be enabling. In such cases, the relationship of belonging to such regimes of thought needs to be interrupted; it must be made visible and explored (Ricoeur, 1981). This might best be accomplished by parabolic, narrative forms of expression, which illuminate unchallenged and unhelpful assumptions in creative ways. Some of Aesop's fables and parables like 'The Good Samaritan' are obvious illustrations of this kind of interrupting narrative. I am not necessarily advocating the use of traditional narratives (although they may well have the desired interrupting effect). Instead, I am suggesting that creative, narrative forms of expression that lead others to the point of 'being struck' (Cunliffe, 2004) – of feeling the impact of a message for themselves – are more effective than attempting to explicate systematic problems in simple terms.

Deflection: this kind of practice involves a deliberate attempt to keep the possibility of leading moving, by making practice a clear 'turn' in a dialogic process (Cunliffe, 2009). Practice in dialogue always makes space for the other (or others). What I mean by this is that each act of leading (including non-compliance and interruption) must point away from the self as it invites another to pick up the conversation – and explore the possibility of taking action themself. However, this is more complex and nuanced than it may seem at first sight. It is actually quite difficult to turn the potential for action away from yourself without making it either an instance of overt leading, which reinforces your own centre-stage position, or an abandonment of the purpose you had in your act of leading. If you identify a specific individual to take the next turn in leading, then you are still leading. If you turn the opportunity for leading away from yourself in such a way that there is no obvious person to pick up the possibility, then you create a vacuum into which any (perhaps unhelpful) agenda might flow.

The three practices alluded to above are perhaps best seen as a complementary suite. There is a movement from non-compliance to signify some issue that needs to be addressed, through interruption to make it visible, to deflection to attempt to avoid being constructed as a leader, while enabling others to lead.

Conclusion

In conclusion, the task of undertaking and enabling acts of leading in networks is not straightforward, as Sydow et al. (2011) have suggested. This is particularly complex where one seeks to enable a flow of leading rather than support the development of a leader, as it is somewhat counter-cultural. Furthermore, those who take up the challenge of enabling and sharing leading through reflexive practices will seem difficult (they are non-compliant), troublesome (they interrupt the normal flow of action) and demanding (they seldom offer answers to the problems they identify, but look to others to contribute). However, I argue that is worthwhile to risk being characterised in this way. This is because reflexive practice moves individuals towards leading that is only in the interests of equity, justice and respect. It supports a concept of leadership as a desirably transient achievement; reflexive leading builds no idols and writes no eternal rules. This kind of leading is never clung to because it is a duty, and a difficult one. It does not lead to personal advantage, but instead points to others and accepts the cost of enabling them to have influence.

Application questions

- What reflexive practices of leading (rather than what leaders) can be recognised?
- Who is involved in the co-production of the practices of leading?
- What possibilities for leading does the context present? And what possibilities are proscribed?
- What are the identity-forming, meaning-making and order-producing effects of the practices of leading in the context?
- How does the dynamic 'flow of leading' proceed?

References

Adams, M. (2006) Hybridizing habitus and reflexivity: towards an understanding of contemporary identity? *Sociology*, 40: 511–28.

Algera, M. and Lips-Wiersma, M. (2012) Radical authentic leadership: co-creating the conditions under which all members of the organization can be authentic. *Leadership Quarterly*, 23(1): 118–31.

Archer, M. (2007) *Making our way through the world*. Cambridge University Press.

Brown, J. and Duguid, P. (2001) Knowledge and organization: a social practice perspective. *Organization Science*, 12(2): 198–213.

Cunliffe, A. (2003) Reflexive inquiry in organizational research: questions and possibilities. *Human Relations*, 56(8): 983–1003.

Cunliffe, A. (2004) On becoming a critically reflexive practitioner. *Journal of Management Education*, 28(4): 407–26.

Cunliffe, A. (2009) The philosopher leader: on relationalism, ethics and reflexivity – a critical perspective to teaching leadership. *Management Learning*, 40(1): 87–101.

Gherardi, S. (2009a) Practice? It's a matter of taste! *Management Learning*, 40(5): 535–50.

Gherardi, S. (2009b) Introduction: the critical power of the practice lens. *Management Learning*, 40(2): 115–28.

Hartman, E. (2006) Can we teach character? An Aristotelian answer. *Academy of Management Learning and Education*, 5: 68–81.

Hibbert, P., Coupland, C. and MacIntosh, R. (2010) Reflexivity: recursion and relationality in organizational research processes. *Qualitative Research in Organizations and Management*, 5(1): 47–62.

Hibbert, P. and Cunliffe, A. (2014) Responsible management: engaging moral reflexive practice through threshold concepts. *Journal of Business Ethics*, online early, doi: 10.1007/s10551-013-1993.

Hibbert, P., Huxham, C., Sydow, J. and Lerch, F. (2010) Barriers to process learning: authority and anomie in regional clusters. *Management Learning*, 41(4): 453–71.

Hoogenboom, M. and Ossewaarde, R. (2005) From iron cage to pigeon house: the birth of reflexive authority. *Organization Studies*, 26: 601–19.

Jan Verheul, W. and Schaap, L. (2010) Strong leaders? The challenges and pitfalls in mayoral leadership. *Public Administration*, 88(2): 439–54.

Lave, J. and Wenger, E. (1991) *Situated learning: legitimate peripheral participation.* Cambridge University Press.

Mittal, R. and Dorfman, P. (2012) Servant leadership across cultures. *Journal of World Business*, 47(4): 555–70.

Nicolini, D. (2011) Practice as the site of knowing: insights from the field of telemedicine. *Organization Science*, 22(3): 602–20.

Ospina, S. and Saz-Carranza, A. (2010) Paradox and collaboration in network management. *Administration and Society*, 42: 404–40.

Ricoeur, P. (1981) *Hermeneutics and the human sciences.* Cambridge University Press.

Siedlok, F., Hibbert, P. and Sillince, J. (2013) Careers and communities: interdisciplinary work and individual advantage. Paper presented to the Academy of Management Conference, Orlando, FL.

Sydow, J., Lerch, F., Huxham, C. and Hibbert, P. (2011) A silent cry for leadership: organizing for leading (in) clusters. *Leadership Quarterly*, 22: 328–43.

15   All of me: art, industry and identity struggles

Casper Hoedemaekers and Sierk Ybema

Introduction

Work is an area in which we spend a large part of our lives, and in which we invest a lot of our ideas about who we are in life. This might involve ideas about building a career, professional aspirations, the social relations we build in the workplace, status and so on. Who we are, what we are capable of and how we fit in are central questions posed to us when we enter an organisation, via a recruitment and selection process based on an applicant profile and a job description. As such, it should come as no surprise that identity is a major part of our working life, and that those who study work and organisation consider it important to examine (see also Coupland, Chapter 6).

But how does identity come into the work of creative and independent workers? How do identity issues affect those in the music sector, who often work autonomously? For them, there is no clearly delineated identity carved out within a formal organisational setting. At the same time, however, identity can play an especially significant role for them, since their output is often seen as an extension of the inner world of its creator(s) and a symbol of their identities, both by creators themselves and by audiences or consumers. Like any product of our professional, artistic or commercial endeavours, for a singer-songwriter making and performing music is a project of self-realisation. This is probably why a conversation about a person's artfully designed creations tends to turn into attempts to make sense of his or her self – what they find essential about themselves, how they view themselves in relation to others, how they present themselves to the outside world, how they are being seen by their 'audience' and what produces pride or doubts about their 'selves'.

In this chapter we draw close to workers' lived experience and sensemaking efforts by adopting a perspective that places identity questions centre stage. We illustrate our identity perspective on work and management by delving into the music industry and, specifically, by using examples from the case study of Ben Talbot Dunn (Chapter 19, pp. 343–51), a singer-songwriter who performs his work mainly as part of the band Open Swimmer. Analysing this singer-songwriter's identity work offers a window onto some of the recurrent dilemmas in the music industry and in people's identity work more generally. In his account, we can explore different aspects of his identity talk, different roles to which he aspires, and alternative narratives along which they are structured. In our analysis, we will look at a number of tensions that emerge from his identity accounts, which we place within the context of a Romantic ideal dominating discourse in the (independent) music industry that emphasises 'art for art's sake' and denounces commercialism. First, however, we briefly introduce our approach to identity and identity talk.

'Self' and sociality

Rather than studying identity as an objective fact or an individual's or collective's deeper essence, we explore how identities are embraced or resisted, articulated or rearticulated. Such a perspective frames identity as being constituted through the ways in which people present their 'selves' and what they say when explaining who they are to themselves and to others. It focuses on the ways in which social actors categorise themselves, individually or collectively, in the process of claiming an identity. In this way we can offer insight into, for instance, how identities are constituted and, over time, reconstituted in how people project themselves and how they are perceived.

The formation of an identity can be viewed as a constant interplay between social and self-definition. Social (re-)definitions involve, for example, professional and organisational scripts for appropriate or desirable role behaviour or disciplinary persuasions to act 'normal' or express 'appropriate' opinions. At the same time, people present their selves to an outside world, conforming to or deviating from particular prescriptions through, for instance, role embracement, rule breaking or emotional distancing. Thus, one might say identity formation is a 'dynamic interplay between internal strivings and external prescriptions, between self-presentation and labelling by others, between achievement and ascription and between regulation and resistance' (Ybema et al., 2009: 301). Identities are thus constructed somewhere 'in between' the communicator(s) and their audience(s): 'It is in the meeting of internal and external definition that identity, whether social or personal, is created' (Jenkins, 1994: 199; see also Jenkins, 2004). Seen from this viewpoint, for the individual, identity formation involves processes of negotiation between self and others, between 'inner' desires and strivings and an 'outside' world. Even in 'inner conversations', individuals adopt an image of inside-outside interplay when they speak; for example, in terms of a dialogue between internal ideas, wishes and affections ('who I want to be') and external expectations and evaluations ('who they want me to be').

Identity struggles

'One for the money, two for the show': artist or professional?

The formation of identities is a complex, multifaceted process that produces a psychologically and socially negotiated temporary outcome. For musicians and managers in the music industry, one such negotiation is between artistic and commercial identity templates. In Ben Talbot Dunn's case, a major facet of his identity work is how he tries to unite his work as a creative musician with the managerial and economic side of running a band and releasing material. Here is an excerpt that deals with some of these aspects:

Understanding this dynamic faced by many musicians in the industry – pursuing a passion while currently trying to make a living – is a reality for Ben and Open Swimmer. Ben's ultimate focus and drive is making music, but he concurrently acknowledges that some opportunities to play with his band must be considered carefully, as they can end up costing the band members money. In addition, there are some gigs that may involve investing money but represent serious opportunities for exposure amongst industry figures, and Ben insists that those gigs are always important. Therefore, it is a genuine tightrope that must be walked between pursuing a passion regardless of economic return, while at the same time making money to ensure that this same passion and dream can live on in a commercially oriented world: 'the only reason it is about the money is so that I can do it'.

We can see from this short excerpt that this is a sensitive topic, and indeed it is a tension that is often cited by artists. Is it possible to create works of art that are truly uncompromising in the context of economic market relations, under pressure to make a living? For musicians, this may lead to a meditation on whether what they are involved in is something that reflects their desire to create a personally meaningful piece of music without pre-emptively considering the audience reaction, or whether one is closer to the figure of the entertainer who exercises their musical craft for maximal audience satisfaction.

Here we see Ben's identity work play out as a struggle between an 'intrinsic' longing for an authentic self as true artist and 'extrinsic' demands to make a living as an artist. The money here, for Ben, is merely a pragmatic means towards realising an end that is fully artistic in nature. Placing such an identity narrative in a wider perspective, we could read this tension in light of a very specific idea of what musicians are supposed to do – namely, to submit themselves to art in a way in which they remain untainted by outside influences except where strictly necessary. We suggest that this can be seen as indicative of ideas about art and creativity that first emerged within the Romantic period, in which we find the idea of art and commerce as being irreconcilable. This is rooted in the Romantic notion of art for art's sake, and the idea that true art is authentic and highly personal, in that it reflects the intentions and emotions of its creator.

Viewing Ben's identity narrative as a Romantic construction shows how what he presents as 'internal' or 'external' to his identity is, in a cultural sense, more complicated and intermingled. We can thus see that the narratives that structure our individually experienced 'authentic self' are themselves socially prevalent, historically specific and evolved from earlier notions while, at the same time, the seemingly external economic demands of the musician's working life are part of the fabric of the self. It allows Ben to build an epic narrative of himself as a true artist, defending artistic authenticity against commercialism in the music industry. In the conclusion section, we will further discuss this idea of Romantic ideology as a central tenet of modern times and the contemporary music industry.

'Alone together': on individual and collective identities

Another way in which we can see an interplay of identities that are seemingly either external or internal is in the struggle between articulating 'me' and/or embracing 'we'. In the music scene, one can frequently observe tensions between, for instance, pursuing a solo career and being in a band; between an instrumental solo and collective orchestration; between being the front (wo)man and backing vocals; between being Bob Marley and/or being the Wailers. This tension is comically illustrated by the liner notes of the Judas Priest album *Killing Machine*, on which the two guitarists are both credited with 'lead guitars'. In Ben's case we can also observe a tension between individual and collective identities. Let's look at an excerpt from his case study:

Ben recalls how at the beginning, when he formed his new band, he saw it as a completely separate musical identity, entirely disconnected from his sense of a musical self as 'Ben TD'. This separateness was reinforced through the fact that, at first, Ben avoided playing his solo material with the band. However, as he once more evolved into a band member he felt more at ease using material from his solo gigs. Ben's experience in Open Swimmer vividly illustrates an oscillation between individual & collective musical identities. He clearly identifies himself as the leader of the band 'because I wrote all the music and made the album without any of the band members', but concurrently he acknowledges that it is now a band sound – a 'group of musicians as opposed to one guy'.

[...]

Ben is now comfortable with the centrality of his role in the band's identity and his established leadership of its activities. This was not always the case. Ben admits struggling at first within Open Swimmer with the issue of highlighting that it was his music that the rest of the group were just playing, even to the extent of feeling uncomfortable being the one at the front of the band singing. However, this is now something that is openly acknowledged and accepted by all band members – Ben's ownership of the group's musical outputs and the recognition of that. The band gives Ben enough separation from being a solo artist to enjoy the collectivity of making music in a group and creating that sound but, at its heart, Open Swimmer is Ben, and he is not 100 per cent aligned with the ideologies of a band and a collective essence. However, although comfortable with the one man and his band analogy, Ben does feel that there must be an element of commitment to a band identity as, psychologically, musicians don't invest in a situation where they feel it is just them supporting an individual musical pursuit. So perhaps calling them a band was more for the reassurance of those around him than any definitive alignment with a group identity.

Following our discussion of Romantic notions of the artist, we can begin to understand why it is important for Ben to portray the band as a collective agency here, even though he has composed all the material. Within popular music nowadays, the idea that those who are performing the music have engaged in a joint act of creation is a pervasive idea, since all musicians are assumed to be performing something that expresses their beliefs and convictions in some way. This can be seen as an extension of ideas from the Romantic period, in which artists are seen to convey their inner world through their art. Under these ideas, musicians are then seen not as professionals – hired guns who are making a living at their craft – but as artists who have a profound connection to the art they are representing. Ben is acutely aware that the other band members are mainly performing his songs, but he still insists on giving the band its own specific identity and thereby hiding his own role as bandleader, composer and arranger.

This reveals a fundamental understanding for Ben – people are the vehicle for him to perform the music that he is writing. The band identity is a pseudo-collective that acts not like a group but as a mechanism for Ben to continue producing, performing and enjoying the music that he alone creates. Despite Ben's insistence that the group dynamic is still appealing to him – being on the road with the band, rehearsing as a group and sharing music – it is still his music and his musical identity that is shared and at the forefront of the group's persona.

Ben here embraces his membership of Open Swimmer, and emphasises its collective representation of the music, but at the same time is ambivalent about it. He resists it, insofar that he feels that the group still fundamentally represents his music. This uneasiness can be related to the implicit social prescription that independent music is mostly a collective endeavour, and that passive membership of the group, or simply utilitarian performance of the music, is discouraged. His vacillation between collective and individual identities here can be read in this light.

'Dear boy, have a cigar. . .': the Romantic order and the music industry

We can see above that identity work of those in the music industry has recognisable reference points, expressed in identity shifts in relation to ideas of collectiveness and individuality. We can see a similar tension in the way that the more idealised aspects of creativity are reconciled with the prosaic realm of commerce. As in our little nod to Pink Floyd's cigar-offering record executive above, musicians are often disdainful of business on the surface. If we look at this short case study on Ben and his band Open Swimmer, we can see how he is also careful to preserve (and to present himself as primarily driven by) artistic ideals. His music is a collective endeavour of musicians who remain independent from business. Ben struggles with his role as a (business-like) bandleader and some of the tasks that this implies. Ben expresses hesitation at his leadership, which involves making creative decisions in a fairly autocratic manner. He is also somewhat uncomfortable with taking an instrumental approach in publicising and promoting his music, and appears to have the sense that this is at odds with his intentions as a creative musician. Here, it is useful to look at why this might be the case, which involves remembering some of the changes in the music sector and culture more generally.

The assumptions we find in Ben's account of how a band might function are historically specific, and might conceivably be quite alien to a musician from the 1950s, for example. In previous eras, and still in genres like jazz and Latin-American music, there was often a clear bandleader who would employ musicians, arrange gigs, divide fees and supply the repertoire to perform and record. This person functioned as a creative director and conductor, as well as the business manager and figurehead of the group in question. Some of these bandleaders are recognisable names and stars in their own right: Duke Ellington, Count Basie, Cab Calloway, Glenn Miller, Nelson Riddle, just to name a few. To this we can add any number of bandleaders who ran much smaller groups, in a variety of genres that comprised popular music throughout the early to mid-twentieth century.

In economic terms this was an employment model, in which musicians were hired for specific commitments on specific financial and creative terms. In musical terms this had the benefit of clearly separating what each member contributed, such as performance, arrangement, composition and so on. The relatively unambiguous nature of this model changed with the emergence of music as an element of counter-culture from the 1950s onwards. Popular music connected to an expanding teenage market and addressed itself more openly to the sentiments and sensibilities of this younger contingent; it did not eschew pushing back against societal conventions of civil obedience and propriety. With this, a different model of musical production also started to emerge. Increasingly, the idea of a band became something that reacted partly against this 'authoritarian' notion of employment and leadership, and embraced the idea of collective production and organisation. This was also a move away from a discourse of music in the service of entertainment to one of art production, driven by ideals of art for art's sake.

Within this new paradigm, creation and authorship were given an elevated status, especially when they were collective. A side effect of this was that other forms of musical labour such as arranging, production, scoring and so on were relegated to the back office, while composition took centre stage. Making music was here increasingly seen as an act of inspiration and an expression of deeply held sentiments, which de-emphasised the professional infrastructure of previous eras (even though it still pervaded the music industry). We can understand this as a resurgence of ideas that come from a much earlier period and that were suppressed over the course of the twentieth century, in which the values of the Enlightenment became dominant. Doorman (2004) argues that in contemporary ideas on art, life, politics and work we can trace a strong influence of ideas that originate in the nineteenth century and can be associated with Romanticism, a movement in art and literature that emphasised natural beauty, purity and authenticity. For Doorman, Romanticism reshaped our self-understandings, cultural production and the way in which civilisation is understood in relation to the natural world. It injected specific forms of Utopian thinking into consciousness at the time, which sought to trace origins and universal truths at the expense of the 'manufactured' civilisation of science, industry and realist art.

Doorman argues that such ideas resurged in the 1960s, when the post-war generation reacted against the societal order and political status quo prevalent at the time, and sought to assert alternative ways of living through music, art and social movements, among other things. In a similar vein, Boltanski and Chiapello (2007) have analysed the way capitalism evolved over the course of the twentieth century; they argue that the post-war generation pioneered something called 'artistic critique', which as a cultural movement sought to regain authenticity and autonomy within the lives that people lead. The counter-cultural movement in music can be seen as part of this.

Many musicians nowadays view their work as an activity that embodies a high degree of authenticity and that reflects aspects of their personality, emotions or individuality. In this way, they shape their identities within a wider narrative of what art and creative work should be, based in ideals of art for art's sake, authentic self-expression and autonomous creation. However, such ideas can sometimes sit uncomfortably alongside the very necessary entrepreneurial and organisational side of musical work. Musicians' identity work is here shaped by cultural notions of creativity and art, but also by the daily demands that are placed upon them and the diverse sets of tasks that their craft requires.

Issues such as these are something that Ben Talbot Dunn seems to grapple with. Viewed in light of historical developments in popular music and its production, this is relatively new. Ben takes on most of the hard work of running a band, as well as composing and arranging its repertoire, but finds it difficult to articulate his own role against dominant notions of what a 'band' is: individuality versus collectivity, work versus art. We can see here how identities are in a constant play between social definition and self-definition, with dominant narratives, contradictions and overlaps complicating the process. Identities are shaped not only in relation to the immediate demands of work, social relations and personal relationships but also in relation to more abstract ideals that present themselves to us through our everyday practice.

In one singer singer-songwriter's account we find that what at first sight appears as a struggle between the 'authentic self' and the pragmatic reality of economics might partly result from unknowingly attributing to his deepest, intimate self a nostalgic set of Romantic beliefs. By understanding how such wider narratives become part of how we see ourselves, we can better navigate paradoxes and tensions within how we relate to our practice and to others, and recognise how the boundary between 'inside' and 'outside' pressures is often more complex than it seems. Identity struggles shape the way in which we work, and mediate our relationship to ourselves, others and our collective endeavours.

Application questions

- How is identity talk revealed in alternative narratives?
- What tensions and struggles emerge in the identity accounts?
- Can Romantic ideologies be detected in the identity narratives presented?
- How is collective agency enabled/disabled and accounted for?

References

Boltanski, L. and Chiapello, E. (2007) *The new spirit of capitalism.* London: Verso.
Doorman, M. (2004) *De romantische orde [The romantic order].* Amsterdam: Bert Bakker.
Jenkins, R. (1994) Rethinking ethnicity: identity, categorization and power. *Ethnic and Racial Studies,* 17: 197–223.
Jenkins, R. (2004) *Social identity,* 2nd edn. London: Routledge.
Ybema, S., Keenoy, T., Oswick, C., Beverungen, A., Ellis, N. and Sabelis, I. (2009) Articulating identities. *Human Relations,* 62(3): 299–322.

16   The process of improvisation

Simon Rose and Raymond MacDonald

This chapter presents an analysis of important features of improvisation and aims to highlight how these key features could be applied in order to understand organisational processes. A major theme is that improvisation in music illustrates a social process, and better understanding of the features of improvisation can provide insights into certain aspects of social interaction.

The chapter draws from the research study 'Improvisation, music and learning: an interpretive phenomenological analysis' (Rose, 2013), in which leading musicians whose practice has been centrally concerned with improvisation were interviewed. The chapter highlights how the key themes from this study may be applicable in the range of human activity, and consequently may be relevant for understanding organisational processes. The theme titled 'Improvisation: a human capability' describes the process of improvisation through examples of human interaction as an essentially social process. The theme of 'Awareness, trust and risk' explores the finer detail of the process in the social setting. In 'Voice and improvisation', agency for autonomous action is described. 'Recognising creativity' leads to discussion of the different forms creativity may take. 'Improvisation as group composition' describes the process of improvisation's participatory character – as a collaboration system.

Improvisation: a human capability

Conceptualising improvisation as a human capability found in different spheres of human activity helps us to understand more about improvisation within distinct domains. Situating the process of improvisation in such a manner helps us understand more about organisation. The process of improvisation is found in different activities:

... this guy Phil Jackson ... he's the coach of the Lakers ... he would say this funny thing like, the team would be losing, and usually the thing is, you got somebody saying 'the team is losing take out person X and put in person Y' but his thing was 'well the team is losing, we'll let them work it out' [laughs] ... enjoy other people and

what they are doing and trust . . . you can see them working it out improvisationally –
how to do things, it was an expression of trust in their ability to work it out for
themselves. And I learnt a lot from that for improvised music. (Interviewee 1)

The basketball example points to the agency of the improvisational process
within human interactions. The point at which the team is losing becomes
an opportunity for the development of group learning: 'we'll let them work it
out'. Allowing for content and method that is not overly directed or determined by hierarchy may require a shift in understanding for organisation.
Importantly, activity utilising improvisation involves an 'expression of trust
in their ability to work it out for themselves'. The theme of trust becomes a
central one (discussed in the section on 'Awareness, trust and risk').

. . . we should be drawing larger lessons from improvisation. . . (Interviewee 1)

Adopting the stance of 'we'll let them work it out . . . enjoy other people
and what they are doing and trust . . .' opens the way for the autonomous
creative experience and interaction offered through the process of improvisation. Interviewee 1 presents musical improvisation as much more than
simply an alternative to a more traditional composed structure for players;
rather, it opens up possible relationships with 'infinite possibilities' for
exploration, as expressed in the extract below. It is the agency in improvisation that has become recognised. This is music as social practice and
can be interpreted as improvisatory interaction taking place at multiple
perceptual and inter-subjective human levels simultaneously (see
'Improvisation as group composition'), while in the process of collectively
creating music at the point of performance. For Interviewee 1, the potential of the process of improvisation goes beyond the creation of product:

So you felt good and you got a good outcome for your piece and everyone liked it,
so what, you know. I mean did you learn anything about the nature of . . . the things
that you can learn from improvised music – the nature of consciousness or the
nature of communication, things that really matter, things that you can really learn
from improvisation, that you can learn all the time. And I thought that's why they
were on stage but I guess what they really, what some of them were really on stage
for was to create a nice commodity, that they could package in some way and that
they could get a repeatable outcome from. That's a different problem, that's not
my issue – not now; maybe it was a long time ago. (Interviewee 1)

Interviewee 1 sees improvisation is an essentially social process, an opportunity to engage in collaborative creativity, and benefit from it:

. . . what we draw from the lessons in life seem to me to be the most exciting to me.
I don't know about the rest, so you may learn a lot from someone who has a
particular viewpoint that they articulate, that they play. But then that person is
maybe trying to learn too – again it hinges on the personal transformation thing,
how open are you? How vulnerable can you make yourself, how open to change,

how malleable, mutable as I think Evan [Parker] used to say . . . maybe that kind of value system is what you could use, because there are a lot of ways to go about things you know. (Interviewee 1)

What is 'most exciting' here, within the process of improvisation, is the possibilities 'we draw from the lessons' and what others, with other view-points, are simultaneously trying to learn. Interviewee 1 identifies this learning process in improvisation as being 'open to change', as a 'value system'; the value in the process of improvisation is continuous learning. The process of improvisation and the social dimension become indivisible.

Awareness, trust and risk

The lived experience of improvisation reveals how individual and group awareness is of particular importance in the process of improvisation. Improvisation requires a focus upon developing awareness in creating something new, and participants share this responsibility. This, in turn, requires continuing analysis of the structures and possibilities at play in any particular setting. For Interviewee 1 this insight was reflected in everyday musical life:

Increasingly I find the same structures are active all the time . . . you're engaged in a continual kind of analysis of what's going on, what other people are doing, what the environment is doing. (Interviewee 1)

Interviewees identified the significance of trust as an essential ingredient in the process of improvisation in music.

You have to trust the situation; you have to make it safe. (Interviewee 2)

This is echoed in drama education contexts in which improvisation has a central role. Trust is interpreted as enabling, allowing and valuing the process of improvisation to develop within different social contexts. The importance of trust can be seen as tied to the need for a willingness to risk in the process of improvising in order to create music in the act of performance:

. . . if new communication, a new experience, doesn't happen, then there is no reason to go on stage. (Interviewee 3)

Voice and improvisation

Everyone's creative – no negotiation (Interviewee 4)

Accounts of the lived experience of improvisation reveal how the process of improvisation forms a relationship with what we can refer to as 'voice': the process provides for unique self-expression. In this context we refer to voice as the process of individual creative activity within an improvising group. Moreover, conceptualising improvisation as a social process allows us to highlight the importance of individual improvisational creativity within organisation processes. For example, 'problem-solving' within a team may rely on the type of individual creativity that is present within improvising group contexts.

Improvising is a democratising process – its processes occur through autonomous action. Historical examples of improvisation's association with 'struggle' or 'the need to be heard' abound, and Interviewee 4's description of improvisation practice below illustrates this theme. Risk is implicit in the challenge to male hegemony through the formation of an all-women's improvisation ensemble in the 1970s. The theme of 'Voice and improvisation' is further illustrated in the choice of interdisciplinary performance approach challenging commonly understood performance conventions of the late 1970s. Elements of spoken word, dance, comedy and audience interaction within the music performance context were utilised as features of the improvisation process.

... you had musicians of phenomenal technique like [name removed] and [name removed] and others who didn't have such a strong technique but were amazing performers, and again that was really open and I loved the openness of that ... lots of male musicians who were big fans, but there were other men who really, really were threatened; in fact, we did the Berlin Total Music Meeting and he actually complained about us ... And it was a huge hit as well! The audience loved us but we were accused of being novelty – you have no idea of the vitriol we got. (Interviewee 4)

Recognising creativity

In order to benefit from the value the creative process of improvisation it is necessary to acknowledge potential forms of creativity. Too easily, and not necessarily knowingly, the dominant cultural orientation becomes imposed, frequently countering the benefits of engaging the diversity of creative potential. Working at recognising different kinds of creativity legitimises difference.

Inherited educational hierarchies privilege cerebral, academic activity, while activities involving making or doing have been traditionally assigned to the lower end of the hierarchy (Robinson, 2001). Improvisation may, thus, fall at the lower end of the hierarchy in some value structures. Improvisation in music is experiential and entails engagement with intuitive abilities.

If you have a road map that tells you how to get somewhere then fine, when you get there leave the map and go and do your business – why I'm going there is for some kind of relationship, whether with nature or with some people, now that's the heart business. Leave the map: we're going to do the heart to heart. That's the difference between African and European culture – see we work from the heart, European culture works from the theory – so you take theory and you apply it to everything and you clamp it down – if it don't fit then they say it ain't valid. (Oleyumi Thomas, cited in Rose, 2008)

De Certeau's (1984) reference to '... the map is not the territory ...' echoes Thomas's analogy for beginning to understand improvisation: planning is the map – improvisation becomes the territory. The process of improvisation is an open form, in which participants may engage on their own terms: a process through which subjugated knowledge may become legitimised.

Improvisation as group composition

The social process of improvisation occurs through participatory collaboration. Interviewee 4 ascribes the setting as giving rise to 'social virtuosity'. As a social process, the ability to work in what has been described elsewhere as a 'socially intelligent' manner comes to the fore. Individuals can develop a deep understanding of their own creative potential and the types of contribution that are possible within the group setting. Participants can also develop an understanding of other group members' approaches to improvisatory group work. The term 'social virtuosity' describes creativity as collaborative within the group composing, and 'social virtuosity' can be viewed as a 'marker' for improvisation activity. It is the expression of the development of skilful human interaction that can become developed through the process of improvisation.

Perhaps the most unique thing about this practice is that if it's group playing, it's a collaborative process involving often contradictory creative input of other people. Things that you wouldn't have thought of yourself, things that you may not agree with, things that will force you to operate in a way that you weren't expecting. And I find that very intrinsic to the improvising process and what makes it, when it works, almost the most interesting music you can get. (Interviewee 5)

Describing the process of improvisation as a group creativity questions the focus upon individual rather than group achievement within organisation. Sawyer (2008) describes creativity and innovation for business as a collaborative activity, and this reflects the process of improvisation found in music:

It is this thing of how to maintain your own personality, yet use it to make musical sense with the people, musical sense with the people you're working with and to accept their intentions to be as important as your own. (Interviewee 5)

This process could be regarded as being one of inter-subjectivity (Rieber and Carton, 1987), as a number of subjectivities creatively co-exist and have mutual influence on each other. Creating group music in real time requires a developed awareness of the inter-subjective possibilities and '... accept[ing] their intentions to be as important as your own'.

In processes of organisation, improvisation functions together with planning, and enables the group to cope with the emergence of new possibilities as well as problems. Through 'social virtuosity' and inter-subjective empathy it is possible to create a 'group composition', which may translate as the redefinition and solving of a problem or the development of a nascent system. In this sense, improvisation can be regarded as a self-organising system through the operation of feedback: in musical improvisation the output from a player can become the input for others, creating a musical continuum of real-time composition. This involves acceptance of the unknown outcome of the process – a necessary characteristic of improvisation.

Conclusion

As individuals and groups are technologically networked in new ways the nature of organisation becomes fundamentally challenged. The question of how organisations can successfully innovate is foregrounded, and understanding the process of improvisation may help.

The creative process of improvisation can be seen to be social and inter-subjective. In making something new, developing awareness – of the self, the other and of the emerging outcome – was seen as characteristic of improvisatory practice. Features of effective improvising which were reported by notable practitioners included trust and risk-taking, and achieving voice: the potential for autonomous expression within group contexts and creative participation in a group composition. In short, the creative process of improvisation is characterised by autonomy, participation, difference and social inclusion – characteristics that can contribute to the development of healthy organisation.

Several key lessons can be learned from an understanding of the process of improvisation. Improvisation can be conceptualised as a social process and many key features of musical improvisation can be used to understand improvisation in other contexts and in particular organisations. Improvisation is a unique form of collaborative creativity and it is universally accessible. We are all improvisers; therefore, it is crucial that we develop our understanding of the psychological and musical foundations of improvisation. Individual and group awareness is of particular importance during improvisational activities. This awareness is also crucial for effective functioning within organisations. Conceptualising improvisation as a social process highlights the importance of individual improvisational creativity within organisation processes. Understanding how organisations can successfully innovate is a crucial concern and developing our knowledge of the process of improvisation will significantly contribute to this understanding.

Application questions

• How much 'composing in the moment' is going on?
• How effectively are those involved achieving inter-subjective awareness?
• Who is being granted, and exercising, voice?

References

De Certeau, M. (1984) *The practice of everyday life*. Berkeley, CA: University of California Press.

Rieber, R.W. and Carton, A.S. (eds) (1987) *The collected works of L.S. Vygotsky*. New York: Plenum Press.

Robinson, K. (2001) *Out of our minds: learning to be creative*. Oxford: Capstone.

Rose, S.D. (2008) Articulating perspectives of free improvisation for education, unpublished master's thesis, Middlesex University.

Rose, S.D. (2013) Improvisation, music and learning: an interpretive phenomenological analysis, PhD thesis, Glasgow Caledonian University.

Sawyer, K. (2008) *Group genius: the creative power of collaboration*. New York: Basic Books.

Gail Greig and Davide Nicolini

Introduction

Singer Joni Mitchell once described the unique nature of music-making by contrasting singing with painting:

That's one thing that's always, like, been a difference between, like, the performing arts, and being a painter, you know. A painter does a painting, and he paints it, and that's it, you know. He has the joy of creating it, it hangs on a wall, and somebody buys it, and maybe somebody buys it again, or maybe nobody buys it and it sits up in a loft somewhere until he dies. But he never, you know, nobody ever, nobody ever said to Van Gogh, 'Paint a Starry Night again, man!' You know? He painted it and that was it. (Joni Mitchell, *Miles of Aisles*, 1974)

While all artistic work involves creating products, the exact nature of which is largely unknown at the outset, the objects of performance art and music are particular in that they are produced anew every time: each is a unique piece of work – a 'prototype' – that emerges from the place and time of its making. In music-making, then, the 'how it is done' cannot be untangled from its outcome. What Joni Mitchell omitted to point out, however, is that another fundamental characteristic of music-making is that such creation is a collaborative endeavour: apart from rare exceptions, the production of music involves bringing together a range of people and materials, usually in recognisable types of venue. In these circumstances, different strands of work need to be drawn together, as unfamiliar clusters – or knots (Engeström, 2008; Engeström et al., 1999) – of people and materials form and disband, in the effort to produce the final performance. When new ways of working are introduced, there is thus uncertainty both about how this will be coordinated and the music produced, rendering both the process and the product unpredictable and emergent. In this sense, music-making is a case – possibly the archetype – of an increasingly familiar form of collaborative working in temporary groupings across a range of sectors and areas of work (Engeström, 2008; Marchington et al., 2005). Studying music-making thus offers an opportunity to illuminate some of the challenges that all managers encounter, or are likely to encounter soon, in the brave new world where projects, temporary teams and virtual collaboration are becoming increasingly 'the way we do things here'.

In this chapter we explore the challenges of coordinating and organising this new form of work by examining the take-up of a new way of music-making by a well-established orchestral organisation. While our immediate goal is to shed light on a new form of music-making, our aim is to derive lessons that can be applied to a wider range of phenomena. We do so by drawing on cultural historical activity theory, an approach that we argue is particularly useful to account for and understand such work and how it may be organised. We base our discussion around an example of this work, as told through Jane's story of 'Orchestrating a flash mob' (Chapter 18, pp. 262–9). Readers may find it helpful at this point to read Jane's story and watch the example of musical work we draw upon via the web link provided in that chapter.

Organising co-configured musical work

When a musical instrument is played it produces sound, which is inherently fleeting and intangible; therefore, music-making produces perhaps the ultimate intangible artistic object (Boesch, 1997). When this is done through live musical performance, input from a range of people in a variety of roles, in addition to the musicians themselves, is needed. These people use a variety of instruments, equipment and other means in their work to produce that final intangible object: the performed musical sound. In order to succeed in this venture, each strand of work must be carefully coordinated, woven together to fabricate the final product (Weeks, 1990). This complex and sometimes painstaking work, which – in common with the music-making it seeks to coordinate and organise – is unknown at the outset, is just the type of work done by managers in many areas of work.

Although challenging, the demands of this type of work are relatively predictable within regular performance situations – for example, when orchestral music is performed in concert halls, or rock or folk music is performed at gigs in different types of public venue, from pubs to theatres. In these circumstances, those involved are all accustomed to producing a live performance in similar settings, which they achieve within a relatively short time and without too much trouble. This is their normal work, drawing on established practices carried out many times before. Although each performance is unique, there are established ways of dealing with this, in common with other areas of artistic work such as television and film (Bechky, 2006).

But increasingly, new forms of artistic work are emerging as performances become less 'staged', ostensibly, and audience members become more involved in interactive art works. This is beginning to happen in theatre (audiences becoming active participants on theatre sets as the action unfolds) and literature (stories being written by numerous people, picking the storyline up where the previous person stopped), but is less the case for music, where audience participation is both more and less evident. While music audiences participate in some forms of musical performance (e.g. singing along at a rock or folk concert, clapping in time to music, etc.), they do not tend to be involved in the actual music that is produced in that moment. This is particularly the case for classical music, where the distinction between performers and audience is well established and highly conventionalised. So involving audiences becomes an additional challenge in this musical genre. Therefore, it is perhaps no surprise to find an emergent trend towards creating ephemeral musical experiences, which rely on audience participation by interrupting the flow of day-to-day life.

An example of this type of musical experience is 'flash mob' musical events. According to the *Oxford English Dictionary*, a flash mob is 'a public gathering of complete strangers, organized via the internet or mobile phone, who perform a pointless act and then disperse again'. Flash mobs like the orchestral flash concert at the airport featured in Chapter 18 (pp. 262–9) were invented in 2003 by Bill Wasik (2006). While flash mobs are usually understood in terms of group conformity and desire to blend (Wasik, 2006; Duran, 2006) or longing for new forms of sociality (Walker, 2013), here we take the creation of such fleeting musical experiences as representative of a more general and newly emergent form of working, theorised by Victor and Boynton (1998), known as co-configuration. A key feature of co-configuration working is that customers, products or services and producers need to come together as a relational grouping for the final product of work to emerge. This frequently involves collaboration between organisations and individuals, and a good deal of coordination among different parties (Nicolini et al., 2012). In the Royal Scottish National Orchestra (RSNO) flash mob, which takes place in an airport, we see the travelling public becoming involved with members of three organised forms of work – air travel/ airport, orchestral music and theatre – as they all come together to co-configure a collective experience. Although in this case surprise and improvisation are central elements of its success, the performance is not entirely 'done in the moment'. On the contrary, this event required patient, persistent and concerted preparation, effort and co-configuring together a variety of people, things and organisations.

Theorising co-configured musical work through cultural historical activity theory

Three concepts from cultural historical activity theory (CHAT) are particularly useful to conceptualise and analyse the work of co-configuration and the co-configuration of work. These are 'activity', 'object of work/ activity' and 'contradictions'. We introduce these next and then illustrate their analytical power through discussion of the flash mob in Chapter 18 (pp. 262–9). Our tenet is that they are helpful for understanding not only the case of the RSNO flash mob but also an increasing variety of other organisational/work situations that share similar characteristics (Blackler, 1993; Engeström, 1987; 2000; 2008; Engeström et al., 1999; Nicolini, 2011; Greig et al., 2012).

Activity

The concept of activity (Leont'ev, 1974) captures the collective nature of work. In music and other forms of artistic work the final product is realised through combined collections of knowledgeable actions, enacted by people engaged in that work, using a variety of material and non-material tools to mediate their actions (Blackler, 1995; Vygotsky, 1978). For example, whether making something material like concert programmes, arranging travel for performers or performing to make the intangible sounds themselves, musical work involves a range of people through whose cumulative work the final product is made. These actions become meaningful as activity when those involved are working towards a range of mutual goals, which coalesce around what is known as the object of work (or object of activity).

Object of work or activity

The concept of the object of work (Engeström and Blackler, 2005) allows us to understand what people seek to achieve through collaborative efforts in co-configured work, and – at least to some extent – why they participate in it. Work involves engaging in purposeful, future-oriented activity to meet a range of human needs (Nicolini, 2011; Engeström, 1999). Those needs are conceptualised by those doing the work as an 'object', which may be tangible or intangible but holds the imaginings and ideas towards which people direct their efforts (Chaiklin, 2011). Thus, the object of work becomes the carrier of the purposeful goals and actions of all of those involved in the work (Axel, 1997), as people seek to transform something involving a need from one state to another (Blackler and Regan, 2009). As they work towards a shared object, those involved fulfil the objective of their work (as distinct from the object), which is manifested through the outcome of the work. In producing the outcome, those involved fulfil (to a greater or lesser degree) the range of needs they sought to meet through the collectively constructed object of work (Engeström, 1999).

Taking the object of work as its central focus, CHAT allows us to see how complex and fleeting arrangements of people and things emerge in collaborative work. By directing our attention to the ongoing construction of objects of work, we are free to be able to see the changing mix of people – and the things they use – as they work towards their mutual purpose. Therefore, we can avoid the need to classify all of those involved at the outset, or to decide which form of organising we are seeing (e.g. hierarchy, market, single organisation, etc.).

Also, since the concept of activity allows us to view the ongoing actions of whoever is involved as a collective achievement – as they work towards their mutual purposeful 'object' – CHAT allows us to conceptualise the actions of individuals and those who are involved in larger organisational units as collective. They become part of the overall, ongoing working. People may not share a view of the exact nature of the object of work, or the needs they seek to meet, but their mutual interest and motivation is sufficient to keep them involved (Blackler and Regan, 2006; Greig et al., 2012). For example, a musician may wish simultaneously to make a beautiful sound and to stir emotions in large audiences (the object) in order to establish reputation and critical esteem among other players (the objective). A music producer involved in the same performance may wish to bring highly acclaimed music to large audiences (the object) and to amass a large sum of money in the process (the objective). Both are involved in the same ongoing episode of activity, kept together by their mutual goals coalescing around a shared object of work (making music).

So although objects of work may be contested and negotiated, they hold disparate groupings together. They are partly given, drawing on established practices and ways of knowing, and partly created: new or different ways of doing things emerge as people work towards a mutual but perhaps ambiguous purpose (Miettinen and Virkkunen, 2005; Griffin and Cole, 1984). Objects are therefore dynamic, constructed through the interplay of ongoing conscious efforts of those involved, which produce insights about the intentions of those involved in frequently difficult collaborative ventures (Nardi, 1996; Blackler and Regan, 2009). These are frequently not harmonious, and give rise to tensions or contradictions between older and newer objects of work.

Tensions or contradictions

As the example in the last section illustrates, because objects bring together and organise a variety of elements – such as people with their ideas, objects with their affordances, rules and regulations and their limitations, traditions and their established ways of doing – activities are customarily characterised by issues, problems and tensions, known within CHAT as 'contradictions'. A typical example is the tension between the simultaneous aims of making beautiful music that stirs people's emotions and earning money by doing so, but contradictions can also be more mundane, such as the desire to bring music outdoors 'among people' and the problem that musical instruments do not like rain. Contradictions become especially consequential when different people involved in activity hold seemingly contradictory aims. This often happens when older, established ways of meeting previously identified needs clash with newer ways of tackling current emergent needs (Blackler and Regan, 2009). In most cases, contradictions do not split people apart – quite the opposite: they become generative of changes within the ongoing construction of the object. For example, the contradiction between playing outdoors and rain can prompt new ideas on where to play or trigger the search for new waterproof instruments. Similarly, the contrast between old ways of doing things and new needs generates invention and innovation. Contradictions are therefore potentially transformative, allowing the activity to 'expand' as people transform both the object of work and, potentially, their own actions or practices (Blackler and Regan, 2009; Engeström et al., 2003).

In sum, the concepts of activity, object and contradiction constitute a helpful perspective to theorise collaborative, co-configured forms of working, since the exact composition of those involved as work progresses is unknown at the outset, and is not restricted to the boundaries of established organisations. As work progresses towards an as yet uncertain and more or less intangible product, like a new piece of music or new way of performing that music, people and things will become involved to meet emergent needs. These may be people from within one organisation or from several, but this is not what determines their involvement. Rather, they become part of the work through their ability to contribute towards the mutual object. The inevitable contradictions that emerge from bringing together these different elements in turn become creative opportunities through which the remit of the activity is expanded and the individual and organisations involved learn new ways of doing things.

In the next paragraphs we will use these concepts to re-read the story of the flash mob at Glasgow Internationl Airport told by Jane Donald in

Chapter 18 (pp. 262–9). Our main goal is to clarify the concept of activity, object and contradiction and suggest that these and other notions from CHAT are especially useful to shed light on new and emergent forms of work and collaborations.

Reading the RSNO flash mob story through the lens of activity theory

Like so many others, the story of the RSNO flash mob starts with several characters in search of a story that could bring them together; or, less poetically, a number of organisations with separate ambitions, aspirations and goals, and a sense that joining forces with others will help, but no idea of how this may happen. In work contexts it is not unusual to hear the sentence: 'We have a lot in common: we should do something together!' Yes, but what? According to activity theory the histories that individuals and organisations carry with them set them on different paths, endow them with different interests and produce different world outlooks that often keep them apart. Collaboration requires the ability to overcome or accommodate this inherent multiplicity of views and interests. The traditional response in management studies is 'we need a plan' or 'we need a common goal' or 'we need a vision'. Activity theory suggests looking at the problem the other way around. Collaboration emerges around the identification and construction of a common object of work – something concrete that we can do together and that can hold and contain each party's different desires, expectations and goals. In fact, it is not unusual that collaborations are triggered by the emergence of a joint object of work without the need for previous planning, sharing or envisioning. The object channels pre-existing aspirations and desires and keeps them together, providing the reason and the motivation to collaborate. As the saying goes: 'Find me an object, and I will bring the world together'.

We can see this clearly in the flash mob case. Glasgow International Airport wanted to promote itself as 'Scotland's destination airport'; the RSNO wanted to enhance its profile as a national Scottish cultural organisation (something not trivial in times of potential budget cuts) and to promote the value of symphonic sound versus the thin sound we are increasingly exposed to through media and the MP3 invasion; and, finally, the orchestra was not insensitive to the promise of free or subsidised travel. Everyone sensed that forming some sort of alliance could bring mutual benefits. But what could realistically bring together organisations as different as an airport and an orchestra? Enter the idea of the flash mob. The idea is travelling from elsewhere: Jane has heard about it talking to a music colleague – she recalls hearing something about an orchestral 'flash mob' in a train station in Norway (or was it in Denmark?); the detail is irrelevant. The idea of the flash mob does not make a difference because of its innovativeness, or because of who has introduced it into the scene or where it was done before. We all live surrounded by new ideas and we hear about new things like this all the time. So the nature of the idea in itself explains little. What makes a difference in this case is that the idea of a flash mob 'captures' both the imagination and, more importantly, the interests and aspirations of the different organisations involved. The flash mob promises to tie the different expectations together by foreshadowing outcomes that will satisfy the goals and needs of all the participants. In other words, the idea of a flash mob works as an attractor that organises the different interests in play so that they can live together for a while.

From idea to activity

The problem, of course, is that at this stage the 'flash mob' is just an idea. The challenge, which is how the issue presents itself to the manager, is how to make this idea happen and how to overcome the inevitable impediments that derive from the unique histories, different ways of working, divergent goals and distinct practical constraints of the different organisations involved.

From the perspective of the manager telling the story, the task is thus how to configure a 'system' that can produce this 'something' called a flash mob (from other perspectives, the story could be told very differently). The elements are all there. The challenge is now to co-configure them.

The first step is to bring together the different subjects involved. Enrolling the orchestra is not easy. Classical musicians are by definition the custodians of a rich tradition that they contribute to keeping alive. This makes them inherently conservative, albeit for a very good reason. Will they accept playing in the lobby of an airport? Will playing in such non-artistic space diminish their standing and the value of the tradition for which they stand? Musicians also have contracts and need to be allowed to work out of hours. Will the RSNO board of directors agree? Will they find a way? Finally, the Airport Operating Committee needs to be brought on board (pun intended) and tied together with the other elements.

Every time a new subject is brought on board, the idea of a flash mob takes more shape, if nothing else, in terms of what cannot be done. As a problem space, the flash mob becomes increasingly defined and delimited. Co-configuration and definition of the object go hand in hand.

Please note that from the perspective utilised here, the work of bringing all these collective subjects together and keeping them that way is shared between the manager and the idea of the flash mob. The manager alone (without the idea of a flash mob) would be powerless and would never have been able to reconcile these disparate subjects and convince them to work together. The object of work is what provides a reason and a motivation for the collaboration; we can probably conceive the flash mob without a manager that runs it but we can hardly imagine the collaboration without the flash mob (or another comparable object).

Making the flash mob happen

As we have seen above, according to activity theory, any activity – including flash mobs – is made possible by the coming together of a number of elements. These include the subjects, which provide agency and dictate the point of view for the story; the physical and symbolic mediating instruments, which include tools, signs, ideas and words used to make the object happen; and rules, regulations, norms and conventions that enable and simultaneously constrain actions and interactions of constructing the object. Activities like the flash mob also imply a certain way of dividing work (who does what, who is responsible for whom, who has authority) and a community – that is, a set of interactions among the people involved in the activity as opposed to those who are not (but need to be taken into consideration – for example, musicians from other orchestras).

For the flash mob to happen all these elements have to be aligned together – a task of considerable difficulty as we have not one but two organisations involved. Each step towards aligning these elements is necessarily creative and generative. In order for the activity to capture the attention of the public, the right piece of music needs to be chosen. *Bolero* is the right, but not necessarily the obvious, choice (the piece is very well loved and known, particularly in the UK, but many others could have been chosen). In order to disguise the players so that the flash mob achieves its 'surprise effect' the musicians will pose as travellers (they could equally have feigned to be security staff or cleaners). At each step, the object of work – the nature of this thing called 'flash mob' – becomes increasingly defined. The traffic between the object and the activity, however, is two way. On the one hand, the collaborative activity emerges around the object – the people and the way they are organised, the rules and tools to be used (such as the airport security protocols or the use of a musical score) – and the position and identity each member will assume depends on the object of work and how it is shaped. On the other, the object 'flash mob' is also the result of the interests of the community that gathers around it (Miettinen and Virkkunen, 2005). In fact, every time a new subject is brought on board the very nature of the flash mob changes (for example, see how the nature of event changes with the arrival of Brian from the National Theatre of Scotland). The object is, in this sense, socially constructed through the negotiation of the different interests represented in the community, which in this case involves air travel and orchestral interests. It is also partly given and partly emergent; that is, both projective and objective (instantiated in and through the product and services that are the outcomes of the activity) and thus capable of 'biting back' (Engeström and Blackler, 2005). It is not the case that 'anything goes' in a flash mob, or in an airport or in a real classical orchestra. And the flash mob could have unexpected consequences, either good or bad.

Tensions, contradictions and expansion

As we have seen, the flash mob operates simultaneously as a powerful motivator that keeps energy going, an attractor that keeps interests aligned and a problem space that continually presents challenges that require invention and creation. The music has to be altered; the flash mob has to be choreographed; a new technique for rehearsing must be invented (the airport space is reproduced in theory); and marketing assistants need to pose as airline staff.

The reality of the flash mob takes shape incrementally at the intersection of all these activities and negotiations. But all is not smooth. Bringing such disparate elements together also produces tensions and contradictions, both in the existing organisations and in the new co-configuration: the new setting conflicts with the established identity of the musicians, who become anxious and nervous; the airport regulations constrain filming to ensure that no security personnel are included; the sound produced by the orchestra conflicts with the allowed decibels. Although we are not given all the details in Jane's brief account, we can imagine that these tensions produced discussions, conflicts and possibly – at times – confrontations. However, they do not constitute barriers to collaborative working. On the contrary, they constitute opportunities for innovation and what activity theorists call 'expansive' learning (Engeström, 1987). In fact, when surfaced, these contradictions require the introduction of some form of change that translates into an expansion (shift) in the object of work and in all the other elements of the activity. The constraints introduced by the fact that the flash mob takes place in a fully operating airport trigger the idea of using the digital screens to broadcast the orchestra brand. The learning is reciprocal: the airport learns to expand the use of one of its artefacts, while the orchestra manager learns how difficult it can be to have to brand a space

198   *Gail Greig and Davide Nicolini*

(using the logo) with minimal preparation. Both the flash mob and the elements are subject to this changing movement that makes them different subsequently. Humans are not immune from the expansive movement either. The musicians have to learn to play while walking rather than sitting, pulling their rolling hand luggage rather than having both hands on their instruments and following the order of play of the piece rather than in their usual positions in relation to other instrumental players. At the end of the experience they will be different musicians than when they started, with an enhanced set of capabilities. Victor, the player turned conductor, finds himself becoming a 'leader that leads from the front'. Most importantly, both organisations expand the repertoire of what is considered possible: the flash mob demonstrates that the orchestra can perform in unusual places outside the safe boundaries of an auditorium; the airport discovers that other things can take place in the concourse apart from checking in passengers. The flash mob expands the organisational capabilities, making new things possible in future.

The outcome of the flash mob itself contains generative contradictions. While the performance reaches most of its goals (the public enjoys it; the event is captured on film and circulates widely on the internet; the specialised media pick up the news and amplify the message) the musicians are not totally happy with the sound. Other lessons are learned that will in turn modify the next flash mob of this orchestra or, in all probability, how the next orchestra will do a flash mob. In sum, the contradictions stemming from the complex nature of the object constitute an inexhaustible source of change, which keeps the whole in constant motion. The shifting, contradictory and ever-changing nature of the object is not an evil to be resisted but rather a reality that needs to be reckoned with and an opportunity to be exploited.

Concluding remarks

The poet Elias Canetti once suggested that people often have a goal that is there before they can find words for it. Cultural historical activity theory suggests that this is true of most human activities. Objects of work are what bring and often hold people together, give them motive and reasons to work together, and allow them to turn tensions and conflict into generative opportunities (Nicolini et al., 2012). In other words, the mutuality performed by these objects is not a harmonious matter, having little to do with the idea of a perfect fusion of intents, goals and community sharing that underpins many other models of collaboration. Provided the pull of the object is strong enough, and its capacity to hold diverging views together is bigger than the centrifugal forces, the divergence does not result in chaos and disorder but rather in innovation and learning.

Our interpretation of the RSNO flash mob at Glasgow International Airport shows that concepts like object and contradiction are especially suited to shed light on new forms of work based on the principle of co-configuring different groups, tools, ideas and histories. However, the case also suggests lessons for management, which follow from the same principle: if the nature of work changes, so should the way it is managed.

First, when managers want to encourage people or organisations to collaborate they should ensure that the object of the joint work is sufficiently robust, appealing or engaging. No amount of team building can substitute for the need of participants to believe that the pursuit of the object of work will allow them to reach their own goals, and that this is only possible if they collaborate with others (who must also be allowed to achieve their own goals). In collaborating, either everyone wins or all lose.

Second, the idea and case discussed here indicate that while good management requires being on top of things, this does not necessarily translate into the idea that managers must try to control and plan everything. In fact, the contrary is true. Determination and focus, two characteristics often associated with effective management, must co-exist with the realisation that the object of work will inevitably change as you go along, and that contradictions will emerge at some point. Instead of viewing these as a loss of control, or a problem to be eradicated, contradictions need to be embraced. No manager achieves everything s/he initially sets out to do, and no collaboration succeeds at the expense of other participants. This means that managers need to be ready to accommodate unforeseen tensions between colleagues and areas of expertise, and between their own area of normal working and that of others. This also means that contradictions and difficulties must not be labelled as, or confused with, 'resistance to change' (see Chapter 5) and stamped out accordingly. Tensions and contradictions can constitute powerful seeds and drivers for change. Managers are advised to embrace these where possible and to look for ways that their practice might alter for the better (even though it may not look that way at the time).

Finally, our case and discussion highlight the need for those involved in managing music to distinguish between different forms of music-making, as each requires different sets of skills and managerial tools. Our discussion of the flash mob, and the way in which it differed from the RSNO's customary practice, suggests that organising music-making can be ordered along a continuum that ranges between two extremes, from more to less routine and from more to less bureaucratised. At one extreme, we can find highly structured, ordered and bureaucratised forms of organising music, such as those exemplified by large, stable orchestras. These organisations share several characteristics with other modern forms of work like offices or factories: a stable location, a set rhythm of work, a well-defined division of labour and hierarchy, stable employment relations based on technical qualifications and a distinction between (and tensions among) professional and managerial authority. At the opposite extreme, we find highly improvisational, emergent forms of music-making (see Chapter 16), from street performance to spontaneous jam sessions in cafés, restaurants or public spaces. These pre-date the creation of the modern music industry and exist in parallel. In these forms of music-making, the location is transitory, the division of labour negotiated on an ad-hoc basis, no stable employment relations exist, and participation is based on skills and capacity to contribute (rather than on technical qualifications). In between, we find intermediate forms like the flash mob, but also one-off concerts or festivals. Although in all cases the outcome of the activity is the creation of sounds for the benefit of an audience (which in extreme cases can be composed of the performers themselves), the object of the collective work, and the goals and constraints that these different forms hold together, are vastly different. Managing music will mean very different things in such diverse circumstances. What this means can be the object of further, very exciting and very relevant future research.

Application questions

- What activities, objects of activity/work and tensions/contradictions are discernable in the situation?
- How do things proceed such that objects of activity are both contested and hold together somewhat disparate groupings?
- How do contradictions function to allow the activity to expand?
- How are people enrolled into the activity?
- How is the activity co-configured (and changed) over time?
- How can leaders in the situation be sufficiently 'on top' of things without over-controlling them?

References

Axel, E. (1997) One developmental line in European activity theories. In Cole, M., Engeström, Y. and Vasquez, O. (eds) *Mind, culture and activity: seminal papers from the laboratory of comparative human cognition*, pp. 128–46. Cambridge University Press.

Bechky, B. (2006) Gaffers, gofers, and grips: role-based coordination in temporary organizations. *Organization Science*, 17(1): 3–21.

Blackler, F. (1993) Knowledge and the theory of organizations: organizations as activity systems and the reframing of management. *Journal of Management Studies*, 30(6): 863–84.

Blackler, F. (1995) Knowledge, knowledge work and organization: an overview and interpretation. *Organization Studies*, 16(6): 1021–6.

Blackler, F. and Regan, S. (2006) The conflicted object. Working paper presented at AIM/Aston Workshop: Studying Practices Empirically: University of Lancaster, March.

Blackler, F. and Regan, S. (2009) Intentionality, agency, change: practice theory and management. *Management Learning*, 40(2): 161–76.

Boesch, E. (1997) The sound of the violin. In Cole, M., Engeström, Y. and Vasquez, O. (eds) *Mind, culture and activity: seminal papers from the laboratory of comparative human cognition*, pp. 164–84. Cambridge University Press.

Chaiklin, S. (2011) The role of 'practice' in cultural-historical science. In Kontopodis, M., Wulf, C. and Fichtner, B. (eds) *Children, culture and education*, pp. 227–43. New York: Springer.

Duran, A. (2006) Flash mobs: social influence in the 21st century. *Social Influence*, 1(4): 301–15.

Engeström, Y. (1987) *Learning by expanding: an activity theoretical approach to developmental research*. Helsinki: Orienta-Konsultit.

Engeström, Y. (1999) Innovative learning in work teams: Analysing cycles of knowledge creation in work teams. In Engeström, Y., Miettinen, R. and Punamaki, R.L. (eds) *Perspectives on activity theory*, pp. 377–406. Cambridge University Press.

Engeström, Y. (2000) Activity theory as a framework for analyzing and redesigning work. *Ergonomics*, 43(7): 960–74.

Engeström, Y. (2008) *From teams to knots: activity-theoretical studies of collaboration and learning and work*. Cambridge University Press.

Engeström, Y. and Blackler, F. (2005) On the life of the object. *Organization*, 12(3): 307–30.

Engeström, Y., Engeström, R. and Kerosuo, H. (2003) The discursive construction of collaborative care. *Applied Linguistics*, 24(3): 286–315.

Engeström, Y., Engeström, R. and Vahaaho, T. (1999) When the center does not hold: the importance of knotworking. In Chaiklin, S., Hedegaard, M. and Jensen, L.J. (eds) *Activity theory and social practice: cultural-historical approaches*, pp. 345–74. Aarhus University Press.

Greig, G., Entwistle, V.A. and Beech, N. (2012) Addressing complex healthcare problems in diverse settings: insights from activity theory. *Social Science and Medicine*, 74: 305–12.

Griffin, P. and Cole, M. (1984) Current activity for the future: the zo-ped. In Damon, W. (ed) *New directions for child development*, pp. 45–64. San Francisco, CA: Jossey-Bass.

Leont'ev, A.N. (1974) The problem of activity in psychology. *Soviet Psychology*, 13(2): 4–33.

Marchington, M., Grimshaw, D., Rubery, J. and Wilmott, H. (2005) *Fragmenting work: blurring organizational boundaries and disordering hierarchies.* Oxford University Press.

Miettinen, R. and Virkkunen, J. (2005) Epistemic objects, artefacts and organizational change. *Organization,* 12(3): 437–56.

Mitchell, J. (1974) *Miles of Aisles* [vinyl LP]. Recorded live on the Court and Spark Tour in LA, 14–17 August 1974. Asylum Records.

Nardi, B.A. (1996) Studying context: a comparison of activity theory, situated action models, and distributed cognition. In Nardi, B.A. (ed) *Context and consciousness: activity theory and human–computer interaction,* pp. 69–102. Cambridge, MA: MIT Press.

Nicolini, D. (2011) Practice as the site of knowing: insights from the field of telemedicine. *Organization Science,* 22: 602–20.

Nicolini, D., Mengis, J. and Swan, J. (2012) Understanding the role of objects in cross-disciplinary collaboration. *Organization Science,* 23(3): 612–29.

Victor, B. and Boynton, A.C. (1998) *Invented here: maximising your organization's internal growth and profitability.* Boston, MA: Harvard Business School Press.

Vygotsky, L.S. (1978) *Mind in society: the development of higher psychological processes.* Cambridge, MA: Harvard University Press.

Walker, R.A. (2013) Fill/flash/memory: a history of flash mobs. *Text and Performance Quarterly,* 33(2): 115–32.

Wasik, B. (2006) My crowd: or, Phase 5, a report from the inventor of the flash mob. *Harper's Magazine,* 1870: 56–66.

Weeks, Peter A.D. (1990) Musical time as a practical accomplishment: a change in tempo. *Human Studies,* 13(4): 323–59.

Part II

Tales of experience: organising and performing

Reflections on the festival business
Nod Knowles

Background

Nod Knowles's career in music and arts management has spanned the entire spectrum of the music sector, from folk music to opera, and he has undertaken a significant number of roles within the arts sector overall, from performer to arts council policy-maker. With a long-term special interest in jazz, folk and world music (he was Director of the South West Jazz Development Agency from 1983 to 1991), Nod has also covered areas of classical music, opera and rock/pop music in significant depth as a consultant, promoter, artistic director, festival CEO, assessor, researcher and adviser. He has dealt with strategic planning and policy-making – including in music education – especially in his seven years (from 1998) as Head of Music for the Scottish Arts Council, as President of the Europe Jazz Network and in his role as CEO of Bath Festivals Ltd (2005–10). Nod has now resumed his former role as a freelance consultant, in which he has also run festivals, tours and other artistic projects, including accessing considerable project funding for many of them. In this section Nod reflects on his breadth of experience of the music festival business.

Brief history of post-war music festivals

At the outset of this set of general reflections on music festivals I should at once declare that I am not a historian, an academic or a cultural theorist.

I am a long-time arts worker, much of whose professional life has been spent in and around live music promotion – and a lot of that time has been around live music festivals. So my comments here are simply a few notions that have occurred to me as a result of my experience running or engaging with festivals – and predominantly festivals that are within, or are supported by, the public or not-for-profit sector.

In very broad terms, I think that the history of music festivals in the UK is aligned quite simply with the wider picture of changes in our social and cultural history. The festivals movement of the kind we know today starts very obviously in the dark, depleted days of the mid-1940s. First, there were plenty of motivated and experienced people wanting to get back after the hiatus of the war to the business of forming orchestras, producing operas or promoting concerts. Second, audiences had been deprived of concert-going entertainment for a large part of the war and must have been more than ready to enjoy live music again, as a distraction from the privations of those immediate pre-war years. And then, alongside the personal ambitions of promoters and audiences, there were the country's social and political aspirations, driven by the collective experience of the war to the formation of the welfare state. Although very modestly, and with a strictly limited outlook at first, the philosophy behind the welfare state prompted the introduction of state support for the arts and the formation of the Arts Council of Great Britain.

Within three years, from 1945 to 1948, a number of festivals were established that still survive today – as does their support from arts councils and local councils. The festivals of Edinburgh, Cheltenham, Bath and Aldeburgh – a capital city, two Regency towns and the adopted home of a leading British composer – were all launched with a sense of a new age: a spirit of revival and renewal. Edinburgh's vision, for example, was to 'provide a platform for the flowering of the human spirit'. Today, we think of the creation of new festivals and cultural events by public authorities – especially local towns and cities – as directly responding to the need to attract tourism, generate income and regenerate local economies. But although not expressed in such clinically instrumental terms, those early post-war festivals had pretty much the same thought.

Although they had begun with a wider arts remit – Bath, for instance, had included films for children and puppet shows in 1948 – as they grew these festivals concentrated on classical music and opera, sometimes ballet, and, in Edinburgh, also theatre. Throughout the 1950s news and reviews about their programmes and people (and in some cases their struggles to survive) dominated Britain's cultural news. Although they all seemed to be populated by organisers and audiences who had significant influence in their communities, and included public jollifications and such things as pageants in addition to classical concert programmes, there were always tensions with – and often antagonism towards the festivals from – local people, usually expressed as a perception of elitism in the programmes and audiences. The festivals – and classical music, of course – were 'not for the likes of us', so why should we be supporting them through our council taxes?

Fast forward to the 1960s and 1970s and we find that quite a lot of other towns – almost always provincial towns and mainly in England, such as Chester, Harrogate, Brighton, Chichester and many more – begin to start their own arts festivals. These are based, despite the accusation of elitism that they then generate, on the general model provided by Edinburgh and the other early festivals. Almost all of them provide a platform for classical music as a given, and almost all are founded on or seek support from their local council, as well as, in some cases, from the national or regionally based arts council agencies. The programmes – some if not all of which were artistically ambitious and introduced international artists and new work – were rarely self-financing through the box office alone. And neither was the administration that put the festivals together.

But alongside these publicly supported festivals – which looked for their inspiration to the achievements of the older 1940s cadre of festivals, inspired by the ideals of *noblesse oblige* and/or by Salzburg and Bayreuth – came a number of new and usually commercially driven events, which looked elsewhere for their inspiration. They may have been noisy, sometimes disruptive events that drew a different kind of flak from the communities where they were held, but rather than mirroring the tastes of an older-school elite they responded to the growing cultural phenomenon of popular music and to changing social attitudes. First, with the boom in traditional jazz and skiffle, hard-up noblemen opened the grounds of their stately homes – and other entrepreneurs used empty or farm land – for events such as the Beaulieu Jazz Festival, a very early starter in the late 1950s. Looking to American models such as the Newport jazz and folk festivals, and by the late 1960s the iconic hippie extravaganza, Woodstock, there began to be a growth of open-air weekend festivals, usually with campsites attached.

Developments influencing the growth of music festivals

Once again, the growth of these festivals mirrored what was happening in British society and the attitudes prevailing at the time. The festivals caught the first waves of youth culture with the generation of 'baby-boomers' distanced from the war and freed from national service. These were their audiences – informal, outwardly more liberal and easy-going – not at all the more formal, respectful patrons of the classically based festivals. And, of course, the music was everything except classical.

The growth in the record industry and the huge expansion of the music scene from skiffle and jazz and the folk revival through to blues, R&B and rock provided a rapidly increasing audience. Entrepreneurial promoters could provide these record-buyers with a weekend of immersion in live music from their favourite bands and make money – although, as always in the music business, the gap between profit and loss was very often a narrow and dangerous one.

Some of the promoters, of course, were not commercial entrepreneurs at all but enthusiasts who just wanted to get more of their favourite music – especially in the burgeoning number of folk festivals – out to a wider audience. And even the commercially savvy promoters were often initially motivated by enthusiasm for their music and the lifestyle that festivals could represent – the celebrated Somerset farmer Michael Eavis being the most obvious case in point. And 'lifestyle' was an undoubted attraction for festival-goers of all kinds, often as much as the intrinsic attractions of the music. Whether sipping champagne and picnicking on the lawn at the Glyndebourne Opera Festival, spliffing up and dancing wildly at Glastonbury or downing a pint and joining in the choruses at Cropredy Folk Festival, audiences, as ever, gravitated towards events that best suited their social attitudes and aspirations.

The growth of the festival scene has been threaded through with other factors that have influenced that growth. Technological developments – in amplification, for instance – made it possible to play live (especially in the open air) to very much larger audiences than the 500 who turned up to the first Glastonbury. Easier and quicker mobility of travel – motorways, car ownership, etc. – have allowed audiences to go further in search of their favourite places and sounds. The increased interest in 'the outdoors' encouraged people to camp out at festivals, in spite of the British weather and with a bit more help and home comforts from the range of camping equipment now available to them. The increased diversity of our own society, and our increased awareness of people and countries far beyond our own, coupled with the relative ease of international travel and mobility of artists, has made a range of musics and musicians available to enrich and extend festival programming – from the addition of international artists to any kind of specific genre of programme to the development of festivals, pioneered by WOMAD, that concentrate on presenting 'world music'. Although there has been no specific formal training for festival organisers as such, the administrative and practical organising skills and knowledge developed by a large number of people working on festivals over the years have made festival production an increasingly sophisticated and skilled business, from which a considerable number of people have been able to earn a living.

Media attention, once limited to broadsheet newspapers and those early post-war festivals, has not only been given to the news value of festivals (ever since the devastation of the Isle of Wight Festival and the ever-popular mudbath pictures of Glastonbury); the media have also increasingly taken festival programmes as content. Newspapers and magazines have found festivals valuable for feature or special edition content: Edinburgh and Glastonbury, for instance, have been particularly well served by high-profile special coverage. From its adoption of the Proms onwards, BBC Radio 3 has always taken a large part of its live recorded output of classical music from the festival circuit. And as Radio 3 has expanded its range of music styles it has followed the same pattern and taken material from jazz, folk and world music festivals, to the point of becoming the main sponsoring partner of the London Jazz Festival in recent years. Other BBC radio channels have acted similarly with music festivals suited to their programming. Television, for which live music was never the strongest suit, has nevertheless been able to use more festival broadcasts in its rock and indie output, and has become more prolific in festival coverage as channels have proliferated and needed more and more ready-made content to keep their schedules afloat.

Although a number of festivals have come and gone, since the 1980s the list and range of music festivals in the UK has continued to grow and grow. Independent, commercially viable festivals have been created to explore new markets and audiences as new styles of music have evolved. It is probably possible to find a festival in the UK (and usually quite a selection) for just about any music you might be into. And this includes my personal favourite (although I haven't broken the spell of it in my imagination by actually visiting it yet): the weekender near Leicester devoted entirely to tribute bands and appropriately named Glastonbudget.

Venues such as arts centres and concert halls have tended towards highlighting some parts of their year-round programming by turning it into a festival for a short period of time. The South Bank Centre in London, for example, created and hosts the Meltdown Festival of Contemporary Music, with a different musical celebrity as curator each year. The Glasgow Royal Concert Hall engendered the Celtic Connections festival of traditional music and the Sage Gateshead hosts its annual International Jazz Festival. These festivals are created for a variety of reasons. It may be simply to make money through an area of programming. More usually, however, it may be to strengthen areas of programming that need extra effort and focus in marketing and profile and audience development. Or the focus could be a particular interest and passion of the venue's or locality's audience, or of the venue's management. Or it may be a way to give shape and light and shade to a venue's annual programme that would otherwise be simply a series of concerts.

Bath, Cheltenham, Aldeburgh, Harrogate, Buxton, St Magnus in Orkney, Salisbury – and a slew of others, in (relatively small) towns around the UK – continue to provide a bedrock for classical music programming in Britain outside of London and a very few other major cities. They have all changed or evolved in artistic complexion as a succession of artistic directors have put their own stamp on the programmes. Bath, as just one example, developed a strong strand of contemporary jazz programming from the mid-1980s to add to the predominantly chamber-scale classical music concerts that had become its forte. Most of these festivals continue to commission and programme new work by contemporary composers and feature up-and-coming international artists. Specialist festivals with a slightly shorter history but otherwise similar pedigree – such as the Huddersfield Contemporary Music Festival or Brecon Jazz Festival – complement these long-established festivals with a focus on their specialist areas of music.

Financing of festivals

There are few festivals that haven't had to face significant political and financial challenges. Their core artistic remits were set in motion a long while ago and, with some changes of shade and emphasis, continue to be understood and followed by their staff and governing bodies. But the funders, and more particularly local politicians and residents, are often blind to the specific remit, and echo sentiments that suggest the festival is either 'not for us' or 'elitist' or 'should put on things that are more popular'. Where there is a permanent infrastructure in place to manage and produce the festival the tension is more pronounced with the local funders. When the popular perception that funds should be spent more on 'front-line services' and less on 'back office' is applied to a music festival – which may only last a fortnight or so each year, but which takes all year to fundraise, plan, market and administer – it is difficult to explain the need for a permanent festival office to a councillor with a truncated view of what constitutes value for money.

In an effort to justify the constant public pressure on value for money (although for a number of other equally, perhaps more, important reasons as well) several of the more robust festivals have extended their reach and activity far outside the festival programme period. Cheltenham, for example, expanded its annual festivals portfolio and now runs three others to add to the music festival – festivals of literature, jazz and science. Bath now promotes a festival of literature and another of children's literature, and runs a permanent box office service to serve its own festivals and other cultural promoters in the surrounding area. Brighton Festival's administration is merged with the Brighton Dome venue; Aldeburgh is attached not only to Snape Maltings Concert Hall but also to the Britten–Pears music school.

Diversification and expansion of this kind, which make festival organisations less vulnerable to financial pressures, are also a result of the aspirations of the organisations and the people who run them. Music and festival promoters are (happily) notorious for wanting to present more performances and attract more audiences – and that can be achieved year-round and in various art forms, as well as just in the music festival period. Being present in different ways throughout the year also helps any organisation maintain its profile and marketing effort and keep in touch with its otherwise once-a-year audience.

In the short term, the economic situation that will affect funded and non-funded festivals alike – through a mixture of restrictions in public funds, the absence of enough commercial sponsorship and audiences' diminishing ability to find the money to buy tickets – seems unsettling and threatening. But in the long-term view, the exponential growth of festivals and festival-going since the war is a success story for live music in Britain. And it is some comfort to us at the moment that it's a success story that has happened over a period that saw several other times of economic crisis and uncertainty, none of which seemed to stop us packing up our tents or picnic baskets and heading off to hear our favourite sounds.

Key lessons

• The exponential growth of festivals and festival-going since the war is a success story for live music in Britain.
• The creation of new festivals and cultural events directly responds to the need to attract tourism, generate income and regenerate local economies (see Chapter 8).
• Since the 1980s, independent, commercially viable festivals have been created to explore new markets and audiences as new styles of music have evolved (see Chapters 8 and 9).

Discussion questions

- From Nod's account, describe the history of the development of festivals.
- What are the political and economic challenges faced by festivals?
- If you were to create a festival, what kind of festival would it be, and why? What organisational challenges do you think you would face?

For more information, visit:
www.nodknowles.com

Organising music festivals

Louise Mitchell and Dimitrinka Stoyanova Russell

Background

Louise is a senior executive who has been involved in festival organisation and managing in music for many years. She has worked for a number of well-established festivals, including the Edinburgh International Festival and Celtic Connections. She is currently Chief Executive of the Colston Hall in Bristol. She started almost by chance, being called by a family friend to help out at an event in France as a last-minute replacement for somebody. It was then that she realised organising and management of music festivals can be a career, and she started to pursue it. Louise got involved initially at the bottom level of the organisations, observing how festivals work and learning simply through noticing, paying attention and thinking about the way things worked.

Discussing her time at the Edinburgh International Festival and Celtic Connections, Louise emphasised a few key aspects essential to anyone running a music festival: the importance of trust and of building relationships, providing space for innovation and improvisation, promoting a collaborative approach, as well as the ability to juggle various factors and interests – often ones outside the organisers' control. These were illustrated through two examples from Louise's experience – the first from her involvement in the Edinburgh International Festival and the second from her experience as Chief Executive of Celtic Connections.

Event one: finding a grand piano

Louise worked as Assistant Director for the Edinburgh International Festival and was responsible for the classical music programme for three consecutive years. Her experience on the ground required a lot of improvisation and thinking outside the box. Classical concerts and programmes are particularly difficult to organise, not least because of the number of people who need to be on stage. Also, various productions have quite different requirements, which are sometimes difficult to grasp or predict.

213

The work is, in Louise's words, often 'frighteningly close to the deadline', and solutions must be found almost instantaneously. Juggling time is only one dimension of the balancing act. Organising a festival music programme means achieving a compromise between programme coherence and availability of the musicians touring in Europe at that time. Classical music is expensive to produce and requires money and advance planning, which are rarely readily available. Being careful, persuasive and realistic is important.

The event, Louise remembers, was the show of a dance company at the Edinburgh International Festival. The organisers had not understood that the music was a piano concerto, and hence a grand instrument was needed for the production. It was only on the day of the show (which was a Sunday!) that this requirement became apparent and so, as Louise explained, 'it looked like a potential catastrophe'. Faced with the alternative of cancelling performances, Louise was determined to find a solution. But finding a grand piano in the midst of the Edinburgh International Festival was a tremendous challenge: Louise had to improvise. She went to the BBC studios and found out that they had a grand piano. Then she simply took it. Louise did not remember asking for permission; she simply announced that they would borrow it. Assertiveness and pragmatism were the way of obtaining the instrument.

Event two: crisis with the opening night at Celtic Connections

Celtic Connections is a music festival dedicated to traditional Scottish music. In addition to the array of events and concerts that transform the city of Glasgow during the festival, there is vast educational programme especially aimed at introducing children to a range of music performances.

During her time as Chief Executive at the Glasgow Royal Concert Hall and Celtic Connections, Louise had to deal with a 'big catastrophe': the first night of the festival had to be cancelled. The festival organisers had invited a performing company from Barcelona, who were supposed to put on a production with many acrobatic elements in it. The production was quite demanding technically, but the manager had not fully understood the technical aspects of the show; nor had they gone to Spain to see the production (which is customary practice). The event had, however, attracted sponsorship from a university, which had invited VIP guests to the opening. Moreover, the production was chosen because of its artistic characteristics, as the organisers wanted a 'true' opening night.

About a week before the event it became apparent that it would not be technically possible to stage the production. This presented a problem because of the reputation of the festival and the relationship with the audiences, but also because of the sponsors. They had invited a number of high-profile guests, and cancelling the first night would also have had negative impact on the sponsors' reputation. It looked like a catastrophe. But still, it had to be dealt with.

The first night was cancelled. Louise called the sponsors, with whom she had a good relationship, and explained the situation. She then discussed what the festival could do to mitigate it and agreed to organise a reception for the VIP guests. The trust between the festival and the sponsors facilitated this open conversation and the constructive discussion of remedial action. Louise tried to involve them in the solution, discussing what they thought would improve the situation.

The first night concert was also eventually 'saved' by calling on good relationships. Louise asked an artist with whom the festival had worked well in the past to step in at very short notice and perform the opening production. The audience was informed and tickets to the first night of the festival were made free. Thus, through openness and constructive discussion based on trust and good relationships, Celtic Connections managed the opening night cancellation crisis. It was far from perfect, and the intended impact of the first night was not achieved, but the impossibility of having the desired production had to be dealt with somehow, and the festival organising team did the best they could within the tight timeframe. Cancellations are an inevitable part of any festival, Louise admitted. They are just something organisers have to deal with in the best possible way. Often, the best possible alternative is not equal in terms of impact, influence and importance, but this is part and parcel of managing such situations.

Discussing the above event, Louise talked about the importance of building and maintaining good relationships. They go a long way, she stressed. She also explained that she is always trying to network, even without an immediate purpose or agenda, and always helping others if she can. Going through your career in this way, Louise reflected, you build a network of people on whom you can rely. It is important to take a long-term view and not to expect an immediate return, while also simply being a reasonable person to deal with. Related to this is the collaborative approach you need to adopt when working on festivals. Thus, managing relationships involves dealing with people both internal and external to the organisation. Louise talked about a 'no blame culture' and always backing her colleagues.

Running a music festival is like juggling: external factors (tours, orchestra schedules, weather, travel disasters and legal hurdles), artistic vision, coherence and the style of the festival are all balls that need to be kept in the air. There is an acceptance that things will go wrong: something unexpected will happen. Organisers can prepare themselves as best they can, but there will always be situations outside their control. A good team, however, will deal with these, and this is why it is important to put confidence in the team – so that they rise to the occasion in critical situations.

With the years, Louise claimed, you also develop a sense of what might go wrong. And this is where a manager's job is important – to manage by conversation, by suggesting what people might wish to check or look at, by asking the 'little steering questions': 'Have you thought about. . .?'; 'How did this work in Brazil. . .?'.

Festivals as scenes of organising

Festivals are highly pressured environments: they often run on adrenaline. Those working in them have high emotional involvement and often have to go beyond the call of duty. Therefore, it is important to let people do 'what is right for them'. Moreover, this will help people to be flexible, which is very important in this unpredictable environment.

In terms of programming and organisation, short-term turnaround is often at odds with the necessity to take a long-term vision. Planning years ahead is rarely possible at festivals. And yet, the further ahead you plan, the more creative you can be with the festival programme. In addition, there is always a risk that the choices of performer will not be a success or may be outdated by the time of the festival. And this is just part of the juggling of availability (of performers) and artistic vision (of the festival).

Constant learning and reflecting upon the work is a way to improve. Thus, Louise pointed out, getting a balance between having something that works and always questioning what you are doing is another dimension of the balance and juggling.

Key lessons

- Assertiveness, pragmatism and improvisation are important.
- Relationships, reputation and collaborative practices are absolutely essential: they build trust (see Chapters 7 and 11).
- Collaborating even without an immediate benefit pays off in the long run (see Chapter 14).
- Taking a long-term view is vital.

Discussion questions

- What are the key aspects essential to running a music festival?
- As a festival organiser, who are Louise's key stakeholders? Why is establishing good relationships with these stakeholders important?
- If you were a festival organiser and a band cancelled a sell-out concert at the last minute, how would you deal with the situation?

For more information, visit:
www.bristolmusictrust.org.uk

Organising and playing a boutique festival
Johnny Lynch and Gretchen Larsen

Introduction

Johnny Lynch owned and ran Fence Records alongside fellow musician Kenny Anderson (also known as King Creosote) in the small fishing village of Anstruther in Fife, Scotland. Johnny and Kenny founded their independent record label in 1997, recording a variety of artists who are together known as the 'Fence Collective'. Fence Records also staged an array of live events, including two annual festivals – Homegame, which took place in Anstruther, and Away Game on the Isle of Eigg: a tiny, remote island in the Scottish Inner Hebrides. The following section is Johnny's story of his experience of organising and running these two boutique festivals, which the *Guardian* described as the perfect realisation of a simple formula: 'anything-goes eclecticism fuelled by good vibes, real ale and fish and chips. It's a festival with no airs and graces.'[1]

The history of the festivals

The roots of Homegame and Away Game can be found in the foundation of Fence Records, but the inspiration for staging live events that are deeply connected with this particular community can be seen in Johnny's early attraction to the music from the area. Although born in Scotland, Johnny grew up in the United States of America, but was drawn home and chose to study at the University of St Andrews specifically because of the music he had heard coming out of there. Within a week of arriving at university he met Kenny, who he described as 'the music hub of St Andrews'. Kenny is a few years older than Johnny, and was already 'doing his own thing', which included writing and playing as King Creosote, running the local record shop Prince Records, which 'used to sell weird music', and building up the Fence Collective that was the genesis of Fence Records.

---

[1] www.guardian.co.uk/culture/2011/may/09/homegame-festival-review.

Johnny was involved in these various activities throughout his student days, playing as part of the Fence Collective and even organising a few events during his final year at university, for which he booked Fence musicians. The turning point came when, unsure of his plans following a relationship break-up, Johnny decided to take up Kenny's offer to 'come and book gigs for us full time' because he was 'just really in love with the event thing'. So after graduating in 2003, Johnny moved in with another member of the Fence Collective in Anstruther and became increasingly involved with many aspects of the Fence label.

Live events were always of great importance to Fence Records, not only in terms of making a living but also in terms of giving it a real 'presence' and promoting what Fence Records's 'thing' is. Kenny always ran Sunday socials that would start around 1pm and go on until 1am, which 'would just be members of the [Fence] Collective playing and DJ-ing, and because there were so many different members of the Collective it would kind of go on and on all day and people would be playing in each other's bands'. Johnny had a similar experience running club nights in St Andrews every Friday night, which were based around DJ sets and attracted about 200 teenagers. These experiences had been 'amazing' and 'fantastic' so, in 2004, Johnny and Kenny both thought: 'Let's do a festival, let's do this in Anstruther and let's make a proper festival out of it'. Fence Records had a new compilation coming out called *Fence Reunited*, which included King Creosote, James Yorkston, Pip Dylan, Lone Pigeon and a number of other artists from the Fence Collective. The first Homegame festival was run in an effort to promote that CD. They only had 115 tickets, which were all sold, and despite it being 'a bit of a trek getting to Anstruther', people came from as far away as London.

Homegame sold out again the following year, and continued to do so in ever-decreasing amounts of time. The most recent Homegame festivals 'sold out within five minutes' and the festival got bigger – growing from a one-day event for 115 people to a three-day event with a capacity of 450 – 'but not too much bigger'. An alternative way of satisfying their audience demand was to stage a second festival – Away Game – on the Isle of Eigg, which Kenny described as being 'equally daft as doing a festival in Anstruther. It is quite scenic; it is difficult to get to. It is just a bizarre idea.' Despite the obviously great demand for tickets, Johnny and Kenny were determined to maintain the small size and boutique, community feel of both Homegame and Away Game, which they considered was 'the kind of key'. So what were the practices that underpinned the organisation of these festivals in a way that maintained their unique feel, and that enabled the organisers, artists and festival-goers to resist the temptation and potential to grow into a much larger, yet much more commercial style of festival?

The practices of organising a festival that runs itself

Both Homegame and Away Game give the impression of, and are talked about as, being festivals that ran themselves. Johnny describes the first Away Day on the Isle of Eigg in a way that places this characteristic at the centre of the festival's success: it was 'a sort of event that organises itself and the bands who play don't expect ridiculous fees, and that is why we can make money off it'. However, these festivals were actually organised as well as being performed, so although each 'organises itself in a way, it does take a bit of work, right enough'. In the stories that Johnny tells, several important practices of organising emerge, which together provide insight into how the boutique nature of the Homegame and Away Game festivals was facilitated and maintained.

Do it yourself

Fence Records made a name for itself as a small, independent 'cottage industry record label', which emerged at a time when few labels were able to sustain operating in such a manner. Key to making this work was the collective action of all of those involved, and this is acknowledged in the name by which the artists who recorded on the Fence Records became known – the Fence Collective. It was a name that 'suited us to begin with', as the label was releasing samplers and compilations by 'different artists who lived in the area, different musicians, like Kenny's brothers and friends'. These albums were given the name of the Fence Collective so that 'everyone had their own individual identity' at the same time as a collective identity centred on Fence Records.

The adoption and popularity of the idea of the Fence Collective 'grew out of the fact that there was no one who was a gang leader' and no one artist on Fence Records was breaking out and selling lots of records. Therefore, the Collective name was 'stronger than each individual name'. Johnny acknowledges that this changed a little bit, but there was still a whole group of Fence Records people based in Anstruther who remained part of the Collective, and who were 'at the heart of our festival'. For example, the artist HMS Pinafore and her parents are based in Anstruther and helped out with the catering, and 'they look after all the acts when they come through'. They did this without remuneration, because they wanted to be part of making the festival happen.

This sense of community and collective action extended beyond the 'official' organisers of the Homegame and Away Game festivals. Festival-goers were part of the community and became known to each other over time – not only the 'hardcore of people who go to every one' but also those who did not attend for a couple of years. Johnny believes that this was because 'there is no ... line between the artists and the bands ... and that allows people to go back'. The boundaries between musicians and audiences that are often so tangible and impassable at larger, more commercially driven festivals were broken down and blurred at Homegame and Away Game. It seems that this was because the festivals were embedded within their host communities, and everyone felt they had a role in making the festival what it was. It was also because of the small size of the festivals, as described by Kenny:

You would walk around the town on the day of the Homegame and you would see people coming towards you and you would think: 'They are not locals, do you think they are at Homegame?' And you would kind of look at each other and you would be, all right. Then you would see people the first time walking about the street, then you would go to the gigs, then you would see those people at the gigs. Then afterwards walking around town you would see them again, this time you would say hello. And then you would bump into them again at a gig and you would be like, all right, where are you from, then you would slowly chat to people.

Kenny suggests that this is what a festival should be – for and about people, and their sense of belonging and community.

Community networks

The community that effectively organised and performed the Homegame and Away Game festivals was fairly egalitarian, resulting in a complex network of 'stakeholders', whose roles, relationships and responsibilities were not immediately apparent. For example, fans and friends acted as stewards, gaining a free ticket as thanks for performing this role. However, there was a sense of cooperation and co-dependency that held the network together and ensured the long-term sustainability of the festival. The absence of a traditional hierarchy of artists, organisers and audiences enabled people to become 'friends' across these different roles, transforming the festivals into social events, which 'works as a sustainable business, because people trust it and they kind of know it, love it and they have a connection with it'. Johnny comments that 500 loyal fans were going to be enough to ensure the Homegame and Away Game festivals run for 'a long time'. Because the fans were part of the wider festival community, they understood the importance of their support and felt that it was valued. Kenny explains:

Our fans know if they don't support us they lose live events that they want to come to. I think they realise how kind of fragile it all is and not every Fence fan will buy whatever we put out, but I think they know if they don't, and they don't support us, then the thing that they really want to be at is not going to exist: well, it cannot.

The complexity of the community network is evident in Kenny's description of the relationship between Fence Records and the label Domino, and the interplay between the recorded and live performances of the two labels' artists:

So every band has gone from Fence on to Domino. There has been myself [King Creosote], James Yorkston, Ewan and now Francois and the Atlas Mountains. Domino are delighted that there is a Fence tie right there: it works for them. They can take a new band like Francois, get them to play at Homegame. Francois supported me and Jon Hopkins on our last tour, and that is all because of the Fence connection. So they [Domino artists] will often play in front of 700 folk in Glasgow, 300 plus in Manchester and 1,100 in London, like no band starting out with a record deal with Domino would ever get to play in front of an audience of that size. Not only that, but it is a Fence audience and that is Fence people who are at those gigs and they know about Francois and the Atlas Mountains because Fence have put out one of their albums. So it was a Fence gig and folk absolutely loved it, and that is a massive leapfrog for any band.

A strong ethos

A very strong ethos of intimacy, creativity and commitment underpinned and drove the organisation and performance of both the Homegame and Away Game festivals. The driving force behind maintaining the small size and boutique nature of the two festivals was the aim of developing a sense of intimacy among the festival community. This was achieved in various ways. For example, gigs were staged in 'different little pubs and little hall venues and little back rooms around [Anstruther]'. These were all intimate settings, which enabled the audiences, artists and organisers to connect with one another so that they all experienced their favourite music 'up close and personal and not just in a big vacuous gig'. The intimacy of these small gigs enhanced the sense of community at the festival, through the insightful scheduling of gigs across different venues. There is one hall in the village that accommodated all the festival community and this was used for gigs to bring everyone together, usually for the first part of the evening. During the day, 'weird, little small shows' were staged, during which people had an intimate experience. Then there was 'a thing from 6 until 10 at night where everyone comes together. It is one hall, and we watch the big show' as a festival community. Following this, people were 'split into small venues again, so you have to walk around the town in the dark and you have to discover all these wee rooms and stuff where all the music is going on'. Intimacy was also achieved by subverting the normal headliner/venue size relationship that exists throughout the live music industry. At Homegame, festival-goers coud see the headliner of the festival in the smallest of venues, 'interacting with the audience, giving them an intimate experience that they would never get anywhere else'.

Creativity was central to the ethos of the festivals. In order to ensure the sustainability of the festivals, the organisers believed that they had 'to be creative because we are swimming against the tide in terms of value and what people are willing to spend on the very thing that we create'. It was no longer enough simply to stage a gig for which audiences pay to go and 'see three bands perform, two of which you have never heard of, and one of which you have maybe heard one of their singles on the radio'. The festival community expected more than that and, in order to deliver, the Homegame and Away Game festivals were 'not your normal festival'. Experiences were actively created by, for example, 'giving someone a 7-inch at the end of the night or holding it in a weird venue or having it, like in a place where the power is not going to work'. These experiences connected the members of the festival community and gave them something different from the standard, mainstream festivals.

In return, members of the festival community were expected to be committed and to put in the effort to attend, participate and support Homegame and Away Game. In order to purchase one of the limited tickets, potential festival-goers had to 'make an effort to find them in the right shops, as they are not in HMV, and they are not in Virgin Megastores or whatever'. Then, once they had a ticket, they 'have to make an effort to get to Anstruther'. All members of the festival community worked hard in order to create the experience of the festival that they were seeking.

Sustainability

The nature and strength of this ethos was central to ensuring the sustainability – and thus the longevity – of the Homegame and Away Game festivals. The organisers' vision of the future was never one of ever-increasing economic profits but one of maintaining the boutique nature of their festivals. Thus, growth was achieved by staging more events, rather than increasing the size of the audiences at any one of the festivals. The decision to stage Away Game on the Isle of Eigg was made because it was a small community and they didn't have to:

... go through all the loopholes that bigger festivals do, because it is quite a contained thing. But you can charge for it. People want to pay money to be in a place where they can experience the music. And we are not making ridiculous amounts of money out of it but we are paying everyone decently and no one feels ripped off by it.

Tickets for the previous Away Game were £90 and included not only entry but also the ferry to the island and camping. This is more than reasonable in comparison to standard festival ticket prices in the United Kingdom, and is evidence that the goal was not to make excessive amounts of money but to stage events that were manageable and also congruent with the ethos of Fence Records and the Homegame and Away Game festivals.

This is not to say that Johnny and Kenny never toyed with the idea of increasing the size of the festivals and making more money. At one point they were approached to do something on a much bigger scale, starting with an audience of 1,000 and increasing anywhere up to 10,000, with the support of an additional event manager. They initially thought 'this could be quite cool; we could make a bit of money out of this', but later realised that they would have to surrender much of their control over and involvement in the event. Control, in this case, was not over the minutiae of organisation but of the ethos, atmosphere and experience of the event. In the end, they decided that increasing the size of any of the festivals would run the risk of a loss of their 'personality', which was the unique selling point 'not only with our audience, but with the other artists that want to be part of our Collective, and other artists who want to play a set'.

The latter Away Game and Homegame festivals continued to be organised and performed according to these practices:

People have just kind of done things that have made sense, made it kind of unique and they have kept it small, they have understood what the value of it is. The value is that you cannot see everything, you cannot get everybody, you cannot turn up without a ticket and you will not get a ticket unless you go online. If you keep it small you let people feel that they are part of it without making it [about] having enough money to come.

Key lessons

- Organisation is as important in running a successful and artistically driven boutique festival as it is for a large-scale commercial festival. Although the festival gave the impression of being improvised, organic and self-managing, a high degree of careful organisation and specific practices went into ensuring this image was maintained (see Chapter 17).
- There was an absence of the traditional roles and hierarchies commonly found in organisations. The boundaries of 'promoter', 'artist' and 'audience' were broken down, blurred and challenged, with many participants taking on multiple roles and performing a range of tasks throughout the running of both festivals (see Chapters 6 and 15).

- A complex relationship existed between the egalitarian nature of the community that organised and performed Homegame and Away Game and the central, quasi-figurehead role that Johnny and Kenny played in ensuring the special nature and character of these festivals. This led to some tensions in considering the future of these festivals, as both Johnny and Kenny felt the need to maintain control of the festival organisation in order for that sense of intimacy and egalitarianism to be sustained (see Chapter 5).
- Creativity was a vitally important characteristic, not only of the performance at Homegame and Away Game but also in the practices of organising those performances.

Discussion questions

- What were the main organising practices that contributed to the creation of the boutique nature and experience of Homegame and Away Game?
- Compare Homegame and Away Game to a large, commercially driven music festival of your choice. What are the main differences between the two festivals in:
  - the structure of the organisation and the key roles within that structure;
  - the strategic objective of the organisation;
  - the practices of artist selection?
- Examine the way in which the notion of community both infused and manifested itself in the practices of organising Homegame and Away Game.
- Consider and discuss Johnny and Kenny's response to the opportunity to organise a larger-scale festival. What does this reveal about the relationship between organising and performing at music festivals? How would you have responded to the same opportunity, and why?

For more information, visit:
www.fencerecords.com

Managing the Zoeys: some reminiscences
Martin Cloonan

I used to be a band manager, but I'm all right now. Here's a wee story...

Introduction to the band

Zoey Van Goey were a band that formed in Glasgow in 2006 and stopped making music together in 2012. The band started as a three-piece of Matt Brennan (drums), Michael John McCarthy (guitar) and Kim Moore (vocals, keyboards and viola); they were joined in 2010 by bassist Adam Scott.[1] The band self-released their first album, *The Cage Was Unlocked All Along*, on the Left In The Dark label (formed by myself and a partner) in 2009, with Scotland's leading independent label, Chemikal Underground, later re-releasing the album. Their second album, *Propeller Versus Wings*, was released in 2011. Highlights of the band's live career included support slots on Belle and Sebastian's European tour in 2011 and appearances at festivals such as T in The Park and Rock Ness. They also provided many Glaswegians with numerous memorable nights. But enough about them; what about their manager?

Becoming a manager

I am an academic and have researched aspects of the music industries for over twenty years. I'm not a musician, but work in a music department and my research has brought me into contact with various people in the music industries, especially within Scotland. For various reasons I am, in the local parlance, a well kent face.

In 2006 I knew both Matt and Michael John and was vaguely intrigued by what they were up to musically. Although she had attended the institution I worked in (including, as I recall, at least one of my lectures) I didn't know Kim and probably first saw her on stage. In their early

[1] All the band members are actually multi-instrumentalists and I have simply listed their main band instrument here.

days the band was called the Lost Marbles, but there was already a band with that name so a change was needed. I'll spare readers the details of trying to pick a name. Let's just say it was a protracted process.

Anyway, in the autumn of 2006 I was just about to go on a research trip to Australia when Michael John (I think) invited me to be their manager. I wasn't keen, as I am always busy and didn't want yet another thing to do. However, I was intrigued and agreed that if they didn't find anyone in the six weeks I was away then I'd think about it. I don't actually think that they tried *that* hard to find anyone else, and I recall getting numerous emails asking me for advice while I was away. Offers were coming in and bullshit being spouted and 'could I just advise' on this and that. More often than once this involved me asking someone else.[2] By the time I arrived back in Scotland I was the de facto manager. So what did that mean?

What a manager does

Any working band above a certain level undertakes a number of activities around live, recorded and broadcast work, with varying levels of complication and recompense. Income streams are likely to be multiple (if minuscule) and bands often need (or think they need) a person to have a handle on all this while they get on with making music. Enter the manager – someone who has to understand everything, advise and try to implement some sort of strategy. This last can be difficult when the band is more often responding to requests than it is planning its own destiny. In our case, strategy consisted of making plans at our monthly meetings. These were minuted and included action points for all: more civil service than rock 'n' roll.

The move to appoint a manager is also a statement. It says 'we're serious: this is not just pissing about'. Indeed, for many musicians a key part of the 'not-pissing-about'-ness is that someone else is investing in them. Someone else is taking it seriously enough to invest their time (audience), their social capital (reviewers), their time and reputation (manager) or actual hard cash (in this case, the manager again, although sometimes with help).[3] For me, part of what it meant was that some people in the Scottish music industries – within which I was already an active researcher – suddenly had a grudging respect for me. By taking on

---

[2] In particular I would ask John Williamson, then manager of Belle and Sebastian and someone I am honoured to call a friend. I owe John more than I can ever repay and it's good to be able to acknowledge that here.

[3] Time for another tribute. Thanks very much to Sarah O'Neill, who put up half the cash for the first album. She did get her money back, plus an A for the MBA essay she did on the album as a commercial project.

the role of artist manager I had seemingly come out of my ivory tower and was getting my hands dirty. I still spoke rubbish but, hey, now it was band-managerial rubbish.

In essence, I became a manager to do some friends a favour and because I thought it might be interesting. I had originally hoped to help take the band to a level where the work involved in managing them would become so much that I couldn't cope and then I could hand them over to a 'proper' manager – i.e. someone who made a living out of it, had better contacts than me and had the time to do it. I never took money from the band, and in my guiltier moments I wonder whether, if I had been on 20 per cent, I might have hustled more. But the band always knew that I was more a safe pair of hands than an entrepreneurial go-getter. There are limits to my bullshit, and when dealing with business folk I generally tried to convey the excitement I had for the band. And I promised never to bother them about another band again. Just this one. Honest.

But I did have a vision – of sorts. This primarily consisted of asking the band what they wanted to do, to which they generally replied 'take it as far as we can'. In the end this was not Wembley, but it was a 2,800-seater cinema in Paris[4] and two highly regarded albums. Plus, when they split the band actually had money in the bank. This is at least a score draw. Actually, a sneaky 1–0 win, I think (scorer: Cloonan, 90' +5).

What I did *not* have was an artistic vision. That was not my job. I never wanted to get involved in artistic decisions and made that clear to the band. I'm not sure that they shared my aesthetics, in any case. For some bizarre reason they felt that the world didn't need another version of the Fall. The nearest we came to an argument about artistic direction was about an early track that I thought should be a single and they thought was too 'poppy' and not representative of the sort of band they had become. I still think that was the wrong decision, and had 'Lick A 99' been released as a single we could all have been living on desert islands from the royalties. But what can you do?

So, take it as far as we can. Play some gigs? Sure. Make a record? Love to. OK, how? I'll deal with each in turn. But first, let's talk money.

Business

Money does indeed make the world go round. Trust me, I'm a Marxist: I know. At the start, bands generally need more money than they actually have simply to function. In addition to the endless hours learning to play and

---

[4] See www.en.wikipedia.org/wiki/Le_Grand_Rex.

then writing and rehearsing, musicians must buy instruments, maintain them and in all probability pay for rehearsal space. They'll pay to get to gigs and then probably for drinks at the venue (bar takings being the main reason that a lot of gigs are put on). So, while I put in some cash and a great deal of time, I was always keenly aware that the real investment came from the band. A lot of crap is talked about entrepreneurs in the music industries taking risks. OK, some do. But they also spend a lot of time making sure that the real risk is taken by the musicians. Record companies work on a model of lending the band money, hoping they will pay it back via sales, and putting lots of conditions into contracts about what will happen. Meanwhile, promoters also try and ensure that musicians take the most risk via such scandals as 'pay to play'. Talking of which . . .

Gigging and growing

Getting gigs in Glasgow is not hard. In fact, the city probably has an oversupply of venues. On the other hand, getting paid for playing a gig is somewhat harder. Initially, bands will be lucky to get a free beer; many will accept piss-poor conditions as they need the experience of playing live and they need to develop as a live act and, hopefully, gain a following. The next stage may well be various forms of ticket deals, whereby promoters will allow bands onto the lower rungs of a bill in return for the band selling tickets for a show. So, a ticket may be £6, the band will be charged £3 and told that they can keep the difference of how many tickets they sell. Of course, if they don't sell enough they won't be invited back. And at prestigious venues many bands will simply give those tickets away to fans and pay the promoter the twenty or thirty times £3 themselves, as they want the prestige of (and possible publicity that comes from) having played venue X. All this means that what should be a chance to earn money through the undertaking of work can often turn out to be yet another expense. Believe me, there are more ways than one of paying to play.

So, what can you do? Well, you can't keep on losing money. Well, you can, but . . . So you begin to think of other ways to monetise the live thing. Hey, we're getting an audience now: let's try to get some of their money. Surely they'll buy a badge? Cheap to make and can make us a few quid. How about we turn those home recordings we've done into saleable CDs? Same principle as badges, but more lucrative. Maybe even t-shirts. . .[5]

With Zoey Van Goey, some of this hard-nosed commercialism didn't sit well with their image as cute indie kids, and there were certainly

---

[5] I wanted Zoey Van Goey yo-yos, but was persuaded otherwise.

reservations around things like signing autographs and what to charge for various things. But you gotta pay for rehearsal spaces, travel to gigs, instruments, etc., and you gotta keep the punters happy in order to get their cash. Art and commerce are not opposed – they just sometimes take a while to get into bed with one another.

Once gigging, the next thing is to get reviews so that more people notice the band. While the press write reviews and need to be courted, there are three important audiences for their output – the actual audience (can we now say fan base?), the music industries and other musicians. Audiences will hopefully come, people in the industries will invite you to play gigs or make records and other musicians might do the same. Zoey Van Goey were good, very good, and so the offers came. When they did, I would email all the band members, make a recommendation, all would vote and the majority prevailed. Not many disputes here, but one problem is reconciling the band's desire (and need) to play with the fact that playing too often will diminish an audience. No one wants to see the same band every night. So I'd spend a lot of time thinking about – and then pointing out – the consequences of the band's decisions. But it was their art and their money. I was merely the custodian.

Records

So, now we're[6] a gigging band, which is gathering a local following that is now beginning to expand beyond our friends. We also have a Myspace site (how ancient is that?) and are struggling to keep up with friend requests. Some songs are becoming crowd favourites, and we're in a position where we can put on our own gigs, headline, get others to support, pay them and actually still make money. Then we get approached to make records. So, we pay for studio time, do a deal with a local label (Say Dirty) to put out a single and play legendary Glasgow venue Nice – Sleazy to launch it. The single is called 'Foxtrot Vandals'. We do vinyl, with a lovely cover, and it sells. The venue is sold out. I'm on the door and have to turn people away. I'm torn because I want their £5 to put in to the band's (non-existent) coffers, but hey, I'm now managing a band that sells out a well-known venue. Cool.

We've also got to know Stuart Murdoch of Belle and Sebastian, who agrees to produce the single. Not only a great pair of ears, but a good publicity coup. The band like the former; I'm rather more struck by the latter.

---

[6] I always struggled when referring to the band: was it 'us' or 'them'? Of course I never played, but I did feel part of the team.

We get asked to do a second single, split with two local labels (Say Dirty and Lucky Number Nine). This one is called 'Sweethearts in Disguise'. This time, the launch is a sell-out show at the 300-capacity venue Stereo. I do deals with both singles that mean they are limited licences and the rights soon return to the band. Not quite complete control, but not a bad compromise.

Next the album. Now this will cost money, especially with recording coming in at about £400 a day. Luckily, the Scottish Arts Council has a recording budget. We apply for three grand to do the album. Turned down. Apply again, get it. We then set a budget for the album, based on a friend and me each lending the band an additional £1,500. I wince at some of the expenses (artwork and publicity) but the band makes the decisions. They have to pay us back and I know where they live. We arrange for 1,300 albums to be made (1,000 to sell and 300 for reviews and assorted publicity). We also arrange for them to be delivered to my flat. They turn up a day early while I'm at work. Only Kim and Matt can get to my flat on time to meet the delivery guy, who then refuses to help them carry the multiple boxes of CDs up the two flights of stairs to my flat. Doesn't he realise these people are delicate artists? But, hey, we have an album. It's called *The Cage Was Unlocked All Along* and is released on Left In The Dark Records, which I co-own with my co-lender, Sarah O'Neill. So now I manage a band and have a label. Can things get any cooler? Maybe. . .

So we do another launch. By now I'm pulling in more favours from friends in the biz. We need good supports and ask Jo Mango and Emma Pollock – both with international reputations – to support the album launch. They agree. By now, Jamie Savage and Graeme Smillie, both from Emma's band, are also part of the Zoey Van Goey live band. The album launch consists of playing the album in order and I will never forget the cheers after the band finished playing the first track. This truly was special.

By now we're at the stage where the friends coming along are part of a bigger crowd and I spend a lot of time apologising for not being able to spend more time talking to my friends who are there. 'Sorry, the band need drinks', 'Sorry need to get on the merch table', 'Sorry, the support act needs something'. Sorry, sorry, sorry. But no need for a 'sorry' to the band. We've made an album, launched it and made over £1,000 at the launch. Lovely.

Touring

But we'll need that money, as we're getting the chance to lose it by touring. By far the least pleasant part of my job was dealing with promoters. Will the band play a gig 300 miles away for £50? Fuck off! Actually, come back because we might if we can also get dates nearby on the day before or after and we can factor in some merch sales. And sleep on friends' floors. Call it £75 and we may be there. By far the best gigs for money, other than our own shows, were festivals where the PRS[7] forms got filled in, meaning that – in theory and in due course – as songwriters each member of the band got paid for playing their own songs. Never got my 20 per cent, mind...

In fact, via careful budgeting we normally broke even on touring, even in the latter days when the band added to costs by employing a sound person to travel with them. Towards the end I even booked a series of shows over a weekend, where we would have been paid enough money to fund recording the next album. However, the band fell out and the shows didn't happen. So more lost cash. But I'm jumping ahead.

Signing

The success of the album launch convinces Scotland's leading independent label, Chemikal Underground, to get involved. We agree a licensing deal and the album is re-released. Hey, we're on a proper label. For the manager this means more people to deal with. But while they need to get a return for their investment (mainly of time) the Chemikal folk are the salt of the earth. People of genuine integrity. Please go out and buy their records. Now.

Assuming that you've now bought that record, we can continue...

We make a second album. As with the first one, it's recorded and produced by the god-like Paul Savage, co-owner of Chem 19 studios and Chemikal Underground Records. This time, we launch at a 500-capacity venue (Glasgow's Classic Grand) and pretty much sell it out, helped by the fact that we manage to get the awesome Malcolm Middleton to support us. Plus a fifty-piece choir. Obviously. This album is called *Propeller Versus Wings*, and is again played in order at the launch – to a very enthusiastic crowd. By now Adam has joined and added a new dimension to the sound and personality of the band. I take pride in the fact that I recommended him. Of course, a new member also gives me the manager something else to worry about. Not that there is a shortage...

Europe

By now the band is pretty well known and local scenesters are coming to our gigs. An early one of these is Stuart Murdoch. So when Belle and

---

[7] PRS is the Performing Right Society, which collects royalties due to songwriters for the use of their songs in live shows. At larger gigs this money amounts to 3 per cent of the ticket price, although this is not always honoured.

Sebastian announce a European tour, we're asked if we can do some of the dates. We end up playing Cologne, Rotterdam, Brussels and Paris. This last is in a large cinema and is a definite highlight for the band and a few close friends who travelled over. But not the manager, as he's made the mistake of arranging to teach in Finland at the same time as the European tour and so misses it. What a fool.

Meanwhile, the second album is a harder sell than the first. A band is only new once, and while it gets good reviews, maintaining press and radio interest is getting harder. But the gig offers are still coming in and the music is great. We're still winning.

Mixing it up

By now we're tiring of the Zoeys plus two supports type of show and want to try something different. There is also talk of a remix album. So why not do a remix album and then launch it with a special gig with our own specially designed stage? And one support. And get filmed by a professional crew for a video single? Sounds good. So we do that. The gig is back at Stereo and doesn't quite sell out. But the band are fantastic. They introduce a dance routine somewhat à la Talking Heads and bring the house down. Glasgow still loves them.

More shows follow. New songs for the next album are being written and we are also solvent. The recordings are licensed and the rights will soon revert to us. Gig offers are still flooding in. What could possibly go wrong?

Ending

Well, tensions emerge within the band about what the next album will be like. People begin to pull in different directions for the first time, and a few days away to write new material for the third album brings some serious disagreements. This happens while I'm away and I get an urgent phone call to send emails cancelling gigs for 'personal reasons'. I'm impressed by how understanding people are that we are pulling shows at such short notice.

We have a couple of meetings and I try to stitch things back together. But I fail and the band splits. We only tell close friends, many of whom had been fantastically supportive. Rumours spread, but we stay officially tight lipped. No one quite knows what to do. I swear even more than usual.

But it's over and so is my stint as a manager. It was a favour that went on for a while. I didn't really want to be a Svengali, and I promised people in 'the biz' that if they if they would give the Zoeys a listen I would never ask them to listen to another band again. So I won't (probably).

I still love all the members of the band. And I smile and cry a lot to their music. I always knew that these were the days we'd look back on and tried desperately to enjoy it while it lasted. It was often fucking hard work, especially for them. But making moments of rare beauty often are. Other than missing the Paris show, *je ne regrette rien*.

Of course, I still wonder if I should have seen the warning signs earlier and tried harder to keep it going, but I'm not sure that I could have done. The people who split the band in 2012 were very different from those who formed it in 2006. They'd grown up, got different friends (and, sometimes, partners). They had clearer senses of what they wanted to do and, perhaps more importantly, what they didn't want. I still feel a little numbed by the split, but can see why it happened. *C'est la vie.*

What can a poor manager boy do when he's not good enough to sing in a rock 'n' roll band?

Now some reflections...

Managing a band puts you at the centre of everything. You are the one person who knows everything that is going on in and around the band. Or you should do. You gain unique insights and get to argue with all sorts of people about all sorts of things. Mainly money. I certainly don't miss having to argue with promoters about fees. But I do miss being able to put on our own shows, get great people in to play and even make a few quid. Check the video of 'Sackville Sun' on YouTube and see how much people loved the band. And they did make two great albums. Being a footnote in all that does elicit a warm glow.

There are too few academic accounts of music management, and the managers most people have heard of tend to be mythical figures. As ever, it's important not to believe the hype. The managers I admire have the total confidence of their artists and have earned it. Ideally, the artists should get on with the art and let the manager take care of business. Of course, life isn't quite that simple and artists do need to care enough about the business to make informed decisions. Zoey Van Goey were pretty hands on, and we did argue about what they should get for their music. As I loved them, I always wanted to charge more; they cared about the audience and wanted to charge less. Ultimately, they made the decisions. That's fair enough. It's their music, not mine.

While there are not many academic accounts of artist management, there are 'how to' guides that will offer advice. So here's mine. You *have* to love the band's music, and it certainly helps if you love the people too. Put their interest first at all times. Try to get them to agree what to do and don't hang around. Try not to let others down and apologise if you do. Get agreements in writing, and don't be afraid to tell people who deserve to be told to fuck off to do so, even if you don't use those words. Make great art, but realise that you live in a market economy, so try to get a good sense of your market value, then increase it. (Don't ask me how.)

So I did (and do) love the band. I'd like to thank them very much for asking me to get involved. It was hard work, but worth it for the music and associated good times. I mentioned a few things that we did, but also missed a few. So I didn't mention the videos (go to YouTube). Or the theatre show (called *Dolls*). Or wandering drunkenly round the Hague while fans hailed us in the street. Or being backstage with Paul Simon's son. Or the other big festivals we played. Or why we hate Bloc Party. Or the radio sessions. Or the film soundtrack. Or lots of other things. Damn. Typical manager – just can't keep up.

Key lessons

- Merchandise is important for sustaining bands: 'art and commerce are not opposed – they just sometimes take a while to get into bed with one another' (see Chapters 10 and 12).
- There is a need to invest both finance and time when starting a band.
- When a band appoints a manager it is significant: 'we're serious, this is not just pissing about'.
- Bands need experience of playing live to develop as a live act, and there are stages of developing relationships with venues (see Chapter 17).

Discussion questions

- Do artists need managers?
- What are the most important characteristics of a good manager?
- What is success? (For example, in which senses were Zoey Van Goey successful?)
- Why should I manage your band/you?

For more information, visit:
www.gla.ac.uk/schools/cca/staff/martincloonan

Managing a punk band

Marco Panagopoulos and Shiona Chillas

Introduction

United Fruit, formed in 2008 by the founding members Iskandar Stewart (vox/guitar) and Stuart Galbraith (guitar), were joined by Marco Panagopoulos (bass) and Ross Jenkins (drums). The band have taken the traditional format of guitars, bass and drums in a thunderous direction ever since. To date, United Fruit have supported numerous contemporary bands on tour, including Maps & Atlases, Die! Die! Die!, Future Of The Left, Monotonix and Desalvo. The band's debut EP *Mistress, Reptile Mistress!* was met by rapturous reviews from the music press, including *The List*. Well-received appearances at a variety of festivals, including GoNorth and Wickerman, also earned them further enthusiastic column inches. United Fruit tracks have been aired on a variety of radio stations around Europe, including BBC Radio 1. United Fruit's debut album *Fault Lines*, released in May 2011, marked a step forward in their songwriting skills, while maintaining a raw energy, balancing melody with mayhem and delivering a 'payload of pop sensibility within a sonic assault'.

This section tells Marco's story of learning to engage with the music industry.

Background

Iskandar and Stuart had previously 'been done over' by their record label. The two friends spent the following year just listening to music and writing songs until they felt ready to start another band. Marco contacted the band through an advert on Myspace, although he knew Iskandar through a mutual friend, and was welcomed as the band's bass player. Marco says that United Fruit was his 'first proper attempt at being in a professional band'; before joining United Fruit he had just been writing songs on his own and getting to grips with the creative side of making music. At first, the band took things gradually, practising and working on their music. They felt ready to introduce themselves to the 'circuit' once they had a set of seven or eight songs, and the first year was spent 'basically trying to figure out how to get people to the concerts'. They did this through making connections with bands who were already established in the Glasgow music scene, building friendships with these bands, and by touring. Marco recalls that a point came where 'the power shifted and we became one of those bands that other bands were asking to do that'. He feels that building friendships with other bands 'is just what you do' in order to become established. The network of bands in Glasgow is just 'like-minded individuals who all like the same kind of music and a bit of banter'. Marco is also the band's manager and feels that networks are vital for learning how the music industry works. United Fruit have made a conscious decision to take the DIY route, keeping control of their music but encountering some problems along the way. In common with other stories in this volume, grappling with the creative and business elements of the music industry involves determination, hard work and a steep learning curve.

Funding the album

Once the band had tinkered with their songs to the point that they felt ready to release their music, the next stage was to source funding for an album. The band met with a representative from a record label which, although very interested in United Fruit's music, 'had bigger bands that they were going to prioritise more than us', and so advised the band to release the album themselves. Marco's view is that bands think that they should sign to a big label 'because those guys know what they are doing, they are throwing money at you'. However, that type of relationship is non-existent, he says, because there is not much money in recording any more. The music industry is 'not as black and white as it used to be', and Marco feels there is more opportunity for aspiring bands and more competition. The growth in downloaded music means 'more people are listening to you and you get bigger audiences at your shows'.

In order to fund their musical endeavours, the band filled out an application form from a major Scottish arts funder and spent considerable time ensuring they had the information required. Marco recalled that the form was very complicated and that they had to 'account for every penny that we were asking for'. They had to supply information on the instruments to be used and a detailed plan for how the money would be spent. Their application was successful, and yet there were constraints on the £3,000 grant: the money was to cover 'mastering, mixing and manufacturing' of a CD, so the band were told that they could not use the grant money for instruments or a vinyl album. At the same time, the band felt that self-releasing was the 'right thing'; they did not want to sign with a record label who 'were not going to put any amount of effort into us'. The band created their own label – United Fruit Records – to release the album, which, Marco says, is a relatively simple process that involves registering the name to obtain release codes to distribute the record online.

Marco recalls sitting at a meeting with his bandmates thinking 'I am going to have to do a lot of work for this'; this was of some concern, given that he had two other jobs. He feels he was the only one who had the motivation to 'really get stuck into all the boring aspects of the band'. Although he recognised that the music was a priority, and that all creative decisions were made by the band collectively, he also wanted to be able to make a living from being in the band. He knew that, having just been on an expensive tour, the album had to go well or 'it will be the end of the band'. It is a standing joke among bands that 'there's always got to be one responsible person because no one else can be bothered doing it'. Marco recognises that his bandmates trust his opinion when it comes to making responsible decisions, but acknowledges that he has had to 'learn so much', particularly about all the background work alongside the creative process.

Making the album

The album was recorded in three weeks 'in a relatively small studio' for financial reasons. The associated time pressure was hard for the band, but they needed to keep money for other aspects of making the record. The band did not have a producer; instead, they relied on an experienced sound engineer, recommended by a music industry insider. The sound engineer 'knew how to record and knew how to get good sounds from the instruments'. Although United Fruit share decisions on the creative process, Marco is in charge of the finances, so he knew that they had to set aside a certain amount of money and set deadlines for recording.

Marco recalls that 'a lot of the finalisation of the songs came during the recording'. The process of recording was very different from playing live, and recording helped the band to 'take a step back' and actually listen to the way the songs were structured. At first, the band had wanted to make the album 'properly live and raw', but during the recording process they realised that they actually had to 'cut corners'. The process of recording became one of trying to perfect parts of songs 'through performances and routines'. For example, the band used 'click tracks' to keep time on some of the tracks; this process means that the bass player and drummer play a tempo all the way through the track. Although the band worked hard during the recording, they found the process 'quite tough', particularly in terms of finding perspective on their songs. They only had ten songs and ended up 'ditching one for various reasons', with consequent pressure to perfect the remaining songs. If they had not had time and money pressures, Marco says, the band would 'probably have spent a lot more time and written a lot more songs – we would probably have been a lot more happy with the album'. Even though 'you put so much effort in changing how it sounds', you 'just get fed up with changing it'. Without the help of a producer who has 'recorded loads and loads of bands and knows how recording should be going', the band found it particularly difficult to judge their own work. They had a strong idea of what they wanted the sound to be like, and had to compromise slightly following the advice of the sound engineer. Maintaining the integrity of their music is crucial for United Fruit; however, Marco reflects on the difficulties of being objective about their music. When 'it is only the four of us who call the shots', he says, 'it would be really good to have someone to tell us if we are on the right track or starting to lose it a little bit'.

Mixing and mastering

The lack of professional production in the recording raised issues for United Fruit. The band opened a dialogue with a producer based in Ireland, who involved one of their sound engineers in mixing the album. This was an exciting development for the band, as they felt that it would help them to forge links with a label who would 'give us a bit of money to tour and write and record albums'. They sent some material to the label by email and were told that 'they really liked the song but production was an issue'. Dialogue with the producer began by sending tracks backwards and forwards by email – a long process in comparison to doing the production 'in real time', which is the way the band had previously operated. After the sound engineer understood the general idea of how the band wanted to sound, the mixing process began. Once the mixing was done, the next stage was to move on to the mastering aspect. Marco emphasises that 'mastering is a very fine art' and brings out all the fine intricacies of the music. He likens the mastering of a song to 'taking a human being, an average, healthy human being and then mastering it makes that healthy human being go on steroids, makes it complete'. Mastering is important because it means that the music sounds good on any player and irons out variations in volume levels across album tracks. While Marco understood the advantages of mastering, he reflected that 'unfortunately we did not really consider it [mastering] when we were recording'. This caused all sorts of problems.

The mixer had 'manipulated the music, pressing lots of compressors and limiters' so that he could 'boost the overall volume'. What he had done, Marco says, was to 'manipulate the mixes so that all the mastering aspects were already done', although he did not necessarily have the correct equipment or expertise to master the record. That was the reason the band thought the music was so good when it came back from the mixer. When the expert masterer came into the process, he pointed out that there was nothing he could do: 'it is way too loud'. He had all the correct equipment and twenty years of expertise, and United Fruit were keen to have their record mastered by him, particularly because he had charged an 'incredibly reasonable price for the level of skills that he has'. The band then had to go back to the mixer to ask him to remove 'all those limiters and all those things you have put on because we need just the mix'. When he did as requested it changed the mix so that the band felt 'it did not sound good any more'. The band had to liaise between mixer and masterer to try to 'get this perfect thing out'. At the time Marco was also working full time and booking a European tour, and felt excessively pressurised to have a record to sell on tour. The remixing took another five different drafts of the record. Subsequently, the band began working with another mixing engineer and now that they 'know the score, we can check him out and so that won't happen again'.

Artwork for the album

Once the difficulties with mastering and mixing were resolved, the next stage in the process was manufacturing the CD, which again caused problems. The band 'really wanted our product to be fresh and original', but 'the reality was that we spent so much money on the recording, mixing and mastering that we couldn't do that' and it had to be 'just a normal CD that you would see anywhere'. Creating and formatting the artwork for the CD posed further problems, and involved considerable research to find out what was needed and how to go about getting the artwork together. The band enlisted help from graphic artists they knew, who were keen to be involved but found it difficult to work within the tight timescale. Eventually, Iskandar and a close friend of the band took on the role of creating and designing the artwork. The manufacturer 'basically had to tell us what we had to do', which meant that they spent time working on 'getting the artwork ready, getting stuff formatted to specific sizes, making sure artwork photoshopped into correct size and still looked good'. Marco recalls that it was so easy to make mistakes: even after a meticulous process of going over the work, the manufacturers still found errors and the artwork and text had to be edited time and time again.

Touring

In his role as manager, Marco arranges all the band's live performances, and from the very beginning United Fruit have been keen to increase their audience. Marco feels that 'the more you play, the more people might hear about you, be impressed by you'. Alongside the technical problems associated with producing the album themselves, Marco was also involved in setting up a tour to promote the album. Organising the tour was sheer hard work, and Marco recollects 'just plugging and plugging, there are literally thousands of emails'. The impending tour dates added pressure: the original release date had to be met; if not, Marco felt the 'tour would be ruined because there would be no CDs'. He was also aware that if he cancelled, the band would be blacklisted by venues and that people would 'lose interest' in the band. United Fruit have now been on four tours and visited France, Belgium and the Netherlands. It is clear that Marco has learned a lot about organising tours, and the process has become successively easier to plan and manage. Although it is hard work to get into a venue the first time – 'when no one knew who we were' – after a successful show, 'the next time you make friends, you see people, you legitimise yourself'. Gradually, the band have moved from subsidising tours themselves to making a small profit on the last tour. Marco admits the band have to be resourceful in financing their touring: they are fortunate to have a friend who owns a fleet of vans and so they 'get mates' rates'. Previously they enlisted friends to help with driving and selling merchandise, but this time 'we haven't had anyone'. Marco feels it is difficult to continually ask friends to go away with the band for three weeks 'but we can't pay you', and recognises that being with the band as a helper 'is pretty boring'. The latest tour was great, he reflects, 'we were all helping each other out – it was exhausting but it makes us feel good about ourselves, we are working harder than a lot of people'. In comparing United Fruit to more established bands Marco notes that on tour 'we are the roadies, we are the merchandise sellers, we are the musicians, we do it all ourselves'. Reflecting on the tour, where he did all the driving, he recalls that he was ill when he came back, and says: 'I didn't really have time to eat'. He says that 'he hates to sound corporate' but understands that 'money is an imperative – if we don't have an income, we are going to end up splitting up'. Making a small profit on the latest tour has been a key milestone for the band, much of it through merchandise such as t-shirts and posters, as well as 'getting more people into shows' and 'trying to drive economically'. The band are proud that they have become self-sustaining, making enough to fund their activities so that the other jobs they do maintain their lives rather than subsidising the band.

The future...

The motif of hard work runs through Marco's account of the life of United Fruit – for them, hard work is something that they feel will distinguish them from other bands and make them attractive to the music industry. He says:

We just have to keep on working as if we are never going to get a deal – that is really attractive to labels ... If we can show them we are a self-sustaining band that work hard in their own right, then that is much more attractive than it is to sign a band that don't know what they are doing and that they have to work really hard with to get them on the right tracks.

The benefits to the band, though, are clear. A label would help the band get bigger audiences, invest money in producing CDs and perhaps even fund vinyl records, a resurgent development in the music industry. Marco thinks that 'CDs are dying' and predicts that the future will be online release or vinyl, 'just because it's more of a physical product'. He adds that there are good technical reasons for a return to vinyl: recording on vinyl adds to the overall sound and is more true to the original recording. However, it comes at a price: although United Fruit are continually asked for vinyl records, they cannot afford the 'extortionate' manufacturing cost of producing them.

United Fruit's aim is to 'move up a level', perhaps signing up to an independent label, and they are 'talking to a couple'. The band have reached the point in their career where they need an independent view of their music and also some help with negotiating the music industry. Marco is fairly strategic about the move – the band have gathered enough knowledge about the industry to capitalise on their growing popularity. While they have one label 'who are really keen, who would sign us tomorrow', they intend to send out their latest demo with their new songs and a press pack with 'all our previous conquests' to a wide range of labels, in order to evaluate interest in the band. The band have recorded nine tracks and are planning to record another four and then 'pick the best from the bunch'. They are also talking to another label that has 'shown a little interest, and I would stress little'. Despite forming a strategy to market the band, United Fruit have clear criteria for the kind of label that would be acceptable. United Fruit would have to respect a prospective label's roster of bands:

We would only appreciate the view of a label that had produced really good artists, produced records that we love. They gave those records the thumbs up, so they know what they are talking about, they've got good taste, or taste along the lines of ours anyway.

Another advantage of being with a label is that 'a lot of people will listen to bands on a certain label because they know they are associated with consistently good material'. There is an element of esteem associated with the label each band is signed to, so that these days 'instead of getting you loads of money, being signed to a label is more like a seal of approval'. However, Marco also recognises that signing to a label with 'a stacked roster' is a risk, and another factor in the decision that will be taken collectively. It seems that United Fruit have benefited and learned from their experiences – Marco is candid about the next step in the band's career. On the one hand, he says, 'we might find that nobody is interested'; however, 'there is no point in jumping the gun when there may be a much more influential label that wants to work with us'. On reflection, Marco feels the band have come on 'leaps and bounds' since they formed – they have learned a lot, and are still a 'total unit', operating as a collective with a strong emphasis on delivering the music they love.

Key lessons

- Marco enacts several different identities during the making of the album, each of which affects the finished product. Marco is a mix of musician, performer, researcher, manager, administrator and strategist. Some of these identities conflict – for example, being musician/manager and strategist (see Chapters 6 and 15).
- Marco's reflexive account of the story illustrates that he has learned from his experiences (see Chapters 3 and 14).
- Organisational practices involved in making an album are crucial (in this case, knowing what each expert in the process does, coordinating supporting activities such as gigs and establishing relationships with record labels) (see Chapter 17).
- Managing relationships informs the career trajectory of the band. Decisions around which label to sign with have advantages and drawbacks that will affect the artistic and commercial future of the band (see Chapters 7 and 8).

Discussion questions

- Reflect on, and discuss, how commercial and artistic considerations have affected United Fruit.
- What and how has Marco learned during his time with the band?

244   *Marco Panagopoulos and Shiona Chillas*

- List and discuss the relative importance of the different people involved in making an album.
- What would your advice be to United Fruit, and why?

For more information, visit:
www.soundcloud.com/unitedfruit
www.unitedfruit.co.uk.

Blogging, running a label and band management
Lloyd Meredith and Shiona Chillas

Introduction

Lloyd Meredith from Glasgow music blog, Peenko, co-founded Olive Grove Records, an innovative independent Scottish DIY label, with Halina Rifai, the founder of Glasgow PodcART. The two decided to join forces to create an independent label that is essentially an organic platform for chosen artists to release their material. Any profits made are given straight to the artists, and Olive Grove's aim is to network with independent people to provide something a bit different for artists. The label currently supports seven artists: Esperi, Randolph's Leap, The Moth and the Mirror, The Son(s), Pensioner, State Broadcaster and Jo Mango. Lloyd has recently moved into band management with Randolph's Leap, and he also runs gigs and organises festivals to showcase Scottish bands.

This section tells a story of the different aspects of Lloyd's involvement with the music industry.

Peenko – the blogger

Lloyd started his music blog in 2008. His 'back story' is that he has a degree in music and always wanted to work in the industry, 'but essentially it never came to anything' and so he ended up working in an office job, harbouring a 'desire to do something in music'. The blog came about as a result of 'being fed up going to the pub and telling my friends what bands were on and they ignored me'. He set up the blog using Google Blogger, really because 'it was simple to use'. Initially, Lloyd says that he just wrote about music that he liked; however, as he progressed, the blog became solely about Scottish bands. For the first year he wrote for himself, and is now 'up to about 400 [hits] which is pretty good'. Publicity was not necessary for the blog. Lloyd feels that 'people searching for bands will eventually come to you'. When he started the blog he had a clear strategy, noting that 'I don't have the skills or heart to review' – instead he would feature bands that he liked, interview them for the blog and leave the reader to decide whether they liked the music. His minor concession to a critic's role is to say at the end of each year which music he most likes.

As Lloyd got to know more people and started writing more he entered 'a whole different world', talking to other people through the blog, meeting other bloggers and bands at gigs he was covering. Lloyd feels that there is a real community in the Scottish music industry, and this sense of community is a recurring theme in Lloyd's tale. He also acknowledges the facilitating role of the internet in his engagement with the music industry – when he started he was 'mysterious', and yet now 'everybody knows me'. For Lloyd, blogging is a way of reaching out to like-minded people, getting to know them online, talking via the blog and then meeting them in 'real life' and becoming friends. He also thinks Twitter is 'the best thing we have got'. Lloyd has an organised approach:

I will post an interview on a Monday, I will record a session and post that, then another interview, and another interview on a Thursday and on a Friday I will spend most of my spare time looking for free stuff on the internet, so someone will post a free download and it will go up on the fan page. On Saturday I will do a cover version and then Sunday I end up doing a news post.

Lloyd says that he now prefers to find music to write about rather than to be sent it by bands, largely because 'if you don't like it, it is very hard to do a blog'. As the blog has become more popular and established, and Lloyd has begun to pursue other interests in the music industry, he has enlisted other people to work on the blog. Lloyd's role in the blog has changed from being sole contributor towards 'managing people to write reviews'. He gives these contributors 'free rein' to write. They 'drift in, drift out', he says, but if they are not reviewing they don't get paid, so there is 'usually one of them there' at gigs. Although he is not as hands-on with the blog, Lloyd still goes to a number of gigs, 'probably one a week'. Incorporating more people on the blog has allowed it to develop and it now also features podcasts. The second theme running through Lloyd's tale is the love of music, which encourages bloggers to invest the time and effort to be involved in something they are passionate about.

Olive Grove Records – the label

Halina and Lloyd became friends via their respective blogs; one day 'she phoned me out of the blue' and invited him to put together a label with her. Lloyd sees Olive Grove as giving their bands a platform perhaps to sign with a bigger label, by providing the organisational skills to boost their music. Both Lloyd and Halina were well connected and drew on their contacts for information on setting up the label. Two months before they started the label, Lloyd researched a feature for the blog entitled 'About Scottish DIY labels', in which he asked people for advice on starting a label. The feature produced some concrete information on, for example, how to source CDs, but more importantly for Lloyd, it opened up a whole new network of contacts in the DIY music industry. Lloyd feels that there is little competition among DIY labels 'because we are all in the same boat and we have not got any money', so that small labels are happy to share information, experiences and contacts. The size and nature of the Scottish music industry facilitates word-of-mouth communication, and reputation becomes a commodity in the market. As with the blog, the ethos of Olive Grove Records is to support local bands, not for any financial return. Indeed, both Lloyd and Halina have invested money in bands that the label supports – money that they do not expect to be reimbursed. From its inception, the ethos has been to cover costs and return any profits to the band who made the music. Lloyd feels that 'going in thinking that you are going to make money out of it is a recipe for disaster at the moment'. The label is run from Lloyd and Halina's homes, and both feel that they are very much 'learning as we go'.

Essentially, the way the label works is that the band will pay for everything and the label 'does everything for them' – it is just a step up from self-release, Lloyd says. All the bands Olive Grove represent come from 'a pre-existing relationship' with Lloyd and/or Halina, either through reviewing a single or through meeting the band at gigs. Each band has its own needs, but typically the label would organise distribution of the music on iTunes and getting physical copies of CDs into record stores; they also operate a press agency. The leap from making music to releasing an album and getting the music to the market is difficult to take, and most bands 'don't know what to do'. The precise nature of help from the label seems to vary, sometimes because bands simply do not have the time to devote to the 'other stuff', or because 'they are not interested'. Conversely, others 'work their backsides off' and are 'savvy about what needs to be done'. These bands might arrange all the recording themselves and come to the label with the finished product, so they are really just looking for help to put it 'out there'. Organising mastering of the recording, artwork and making CD packages has become almost second nature to Lloyd – things that he admits he 'had no idea about' before he had to do it on behalf of Olive Grove bands. He recalls handmaking CD packages for Randolph's Leap, the label's first signing. Lloyd says that he works well with bands who don't really know what they are doing – he has built up so many contacts that he can pull in favours, right, left and centre. The small label scene seems to work on favours given and received: at the beginning Lloyd felt that he was getting back a lot of the favours he had done for people over the years.

Although some of the bands that Olive Grove work with will organise their own tours, for example, Lloyd has learned that an album release needs at least three months' lead-in time. All the organisational work starts after the music has been recorded: promo CDs take two to three weeks, the album itself takes about four weeks to press. In between, the artwork has to be organised, reviewed and finalised and an album launch and tour arranged. Although some of the bands Olive Grove represent don't tour, many play live as often as they can, to sell more albums and to 'keep themselves in people's memories'.

The promo albums are sent to the print press (who, where and when also has to be decided), and press photos are taken. To promote the record with radio and bloggers, the band need to work out a single or a sequence of singles and, of course, send free downloads to bloggers for review. The label releases via Bandcamp links to the bands' websites, where purchasers can download the music. Some bands are quite happy for Olive Grove to get on with releasing the work that needs to be done, others 'want to know what is going on, they want updates on how their actual sales are going' but they 'know they can trust us'. Olive Grove has settled into a pattern of releasing two albums each year, and although 'loads of great bands will approach us, I have to say I just don't have the time right now'. Given the vibrant music scene, Lloyd says he doesn't want to 'make a million promises and not deliver'. He has had to remove his email address from the website to cut down on the incoming traffic; however, he also admits to checking his phone 'every hour just to keep up to date'.

Recently, Lloyd has begun to manage Randolph's Leap, who are an eight-piece band, and he says that he 'sort of manages' some of the other bands on the label. Randolph's Leap are becoming more successful, and along with organising a festival and booking travel and accommodation for the band, Lloyd is also involved in liaising with the press.

Organising gigs

In a related but separate activity, Lloyd also puts on gigs to showcase bands, whether or not they are represented by Olive Grove. He does this with another blogger he knows. They always put on 'bands that we like, were friendly with – we learned our trade that way'. As with Lloyd's other ventures, this facet of the music industry has been a learning experience. Some gigs are fine because 'all you have to do is make sure you tell the bands what time to turn up'. Others can be a 'pain in the arse' if, for example, the venue does not have its own PA, which in turn means that

Lloyd, 'has to source all the bits and pieces, going there twice in a day, just to pick up equipment' and 'at the end of the day I'm not making any money from it'. Lloyd has learned from bitter experience that some venues will charge extortionate costs and be less than honest about the receipts taken at the door, and on occasion he has had to subsidise a gig, even though it has been really busy. Organising gigs entails significant forward planning, and Lloyd has learned a lot about the process; he now knows the different charges venues levy and their equipment, and has made contacts with venue bookers, which makes arranging gigs a lot easier. Arranging a gig also means getting tickets and posters printed and, as Lloyd says, 'me walking around on a Saturday morning putting posters up' – something that he is trying to avoid in the future.

Reflections

Lloyd comes across as a really personable, committed and enthusiastic person. Given that he works from 9am to 5pm in an office job that he admits is 'not exciting' and has a small child, his reach and involvement in and around the music industry is astounding. Everything Lloyd says and does is underpinned by a strong sense of 'giving', and he describes his involvement in the music industry as an 'all-consuming hobby'. Essentially, Lloyd spends all his free time working – he reflects that he 'has deadlines in my head, reminders on my phone, calendars' and notes he is always 'supposed to be doing this, supposed to be doing that'. He has five email addresses, all for different facets of his life. Everything he does is working towards a goal on behalf of a band. Olive Grove Records is Lloyd's 'outlet to explore what I want to do'. When asked what he gives up for his involvement in the music industry, Lloyd admits that 'he doesn't see friends as much as he used to'. In among the clearly altruistic ethos of Olive Grove, there lies an extremely well-organised, well-connected hub of contacts and information on the Scottish music industry. Lloyd is well respected – for example, he is now asked to sit on the panel with music journalists at a festival that he used to cover for the blog. Lloyd hints that he is trying to build up a brand name with Olive Grove and 'is always plotting at the back of my head' – just for now, though, he is content to keep 'learning as we go'.

Key lessons

- There are many supporting roles in the music industry: Lloyd fulfils a number of important roles, presenting music through the blog, organising gigs and managing bands. The accumulated knowledge Lloyd brings is invaluable for bands, particularly at early stages in their careers (see Chapter 13).

• Lloyd's account illustrates the importance of networking in learning to negotiate the music industry.

• Lloyd gives a different perspective on the commercial and artistic: he does the 'day job' in order to fund what he loves to do – in this case, not making music but helping others to make their music and make it known (see Chapter 4).

Discussion questions

• Discuss Lloyd's different roles in the music industry – what skills are required in each and how does Lloyd manage the different roles?

• Discuss the place of blogging in the music industry – how influential do you think bloggers are and should be?

• Why do you think Lloyd does what he does? Would you describe Lloyd as a music industry entrepreneur? Can you be an entrepreneur without monetary reward?

For more information, visit:
www.peenko.co.uk
www.olivegroverecords.com

The organising and artistic demands of orchestral performances

Simon Webb and Martin Dowling

Introduction

In this section we review the links between the 'organising' and 'artistic' requirements of the performances undertaken by one of the UK's principal orchestras, the City of Birmingham Symphony Orchestra (CBSO). Our account is derived from the narrative provided by Simon Webb, who joined the CBSO in 2008 as Director of Orchestral Management, a post that carries responsibility for all the CBSO's choral, educational and orchestral activity. Simon left the CBSO in 2014 to become the General Manager of the BBC Philharmonic.

Before considering the organising and artistic aspects, we first provide some context by reviewing the CBSO's organisational characteristics and principal activities.

Context

The CBSO was founded in 1920 as a civic institution funded by the local council. Today, Birmingham City Council is still a major source of funding for the orchestra, providing some £1.4 million, or 14 per cent, of the orchestra's £10 million income. Other primary sources of income include the Arts Council of Great Britain (£2 million) and ticket sales, which – at approximately £2 million per annum – provide the highest ticket sale income of any orchestra in the country. Other income comes from trusts, sponsors and individual donors, and the remaining income from engagements and touring.

The CBSO comprises a series of performing ensembles, with the ninety musicians of the orchestra at its heart. In addition to the main orchestra there is a youth orchestra and five choruses (all unpaid): three symphonic choruses (the CBSO Chorus, CBSO Youth Chorus and CBSO Children's Chorus) and two community choruses (the SO Vocal and CBSO Young Voices). All three symphonic choruses are in regular demand, performing with the CBSO and other orchestras in the UK and beyond.

The orchestra performs some 130 concerts a year and plays regularly in the city of Birmingham, as well as regionally, nationally and internationally. The orchestral programme ranges from the core classical and formal repertoire to contemporary music and 'lighter' concerts such as film nights, Strictly Come Dancing and tribute nights. The CBSO also undertakes substantial community outreach activity under its 'Learning and Participation Programme'.

The CBSO is a company limited by guarantee and registered as a charity with the Charity Commission. A board of trustees oversees the running of the CBSO, while its CEO and a small management team deal with strategic matters and day-to-day operational activities. The musicians of the orchestra are all full-time employees, whose terms and conditions of employment are determined through negotiation with the Musicians' Union. Outside of their contractual duties musicians can do freelance work, some of which is undertaken for the CBSO, such as certain aspects of the Learning and Participation Programme. The CBSO will negotiate contracts as appropriate for guest conductors, soloists and freelance musicians brought in to cover special instrument requirements, staff illness, etc.

Organising and artistic aspects

The CBSO's CEO, working closely with the music director and the principal guest conductor, has the final decision over programming. However, making such decisions arises from due consideration of the perspectives of a variety of stakeholders and after the assessment of many artistic, educational, commercial and organisational factors. Let's explore some of these.

Observing the 'service level agreements' with principal funders, such as Birmingham City Council and the Arts Council England, provides an important backdrop to programming decisions relating, for instance, to choices concerning traditional and contemporary works, new commissions, the nature of outreach work and so on. Simon argued: '... the service level agreements state what we deliver on ... [they] are based on what we say we are setting out to do, so it is a symbiotic relationship in terms of what our remit is'. Similar requirements may come from trusts, sponsors and donors who financially support the orchestra.

Programmes of complex or less familiar works may require more rehearsal time, thus eating into the contracted hours of the musicians, while 'lighter' or more popular works may enable repeat performances with less rehearsal time involved. Here, Simon emphasised:

... we make no distinction in terms of the quality of what we are doing, but we do make a distinction in terms of the audience that we are reaching. And so we will try to balance the mainstream classical – for example, a Mahler cycle or other mainstream symphonic composers that we are all familiar with. We balance that with a generous sprinkling of contemporary work, which might be new commissions but more often is UK premieres or work that does not get done a great deal ...

The musical tastes of the music director, principal guest conductor, associate conductors and invited guest conductors in relation to the standard repertoire, contemporary works, commissions and UK premieres have an obvious input.

The preferences of the orchestra's musicians also have to be taken into account. These preferences can relate to factors such as player evaluations of potential guest conductors; preferences for 'heavy' or 'lighter' works; performance schedules and the volume of work they perceive; music that will enable them to keep up their professional skills:

We have to give our musicians sufficient really meaty repertoire to keep them interested, but also we have to give them the lighter stuff which does not have so much rehearsal but keeps them on their toes. Also the schedule – we cannot schedule oppressively. The scheduling is quite carefully managed through contract, the number of days, number of hours and all that kind of thing ... [Also,] the general rule is that they will give the same level of commitment whatever they are playing and they will play to the same level. We are very strict about not making a distinction in terms of the commitment to the performance or the attitude that is taken.

The musicians' views of every concert taken by guest conductors are sought:

... quite a high proportion [of the players complete conductor assessments] – probably about half will do it every time. These are then discussed; every six weeks we meet with the player representatives and that forms part of that meeting. We are given all the feedback and we discuss it at that forum and so sometimes we come across someone and we will say, 'we have to see them again', and sometimes, 'we must never see them again'. ...

The audience profile and preferences are an obvious requirement to assess. Catering for the 'bread and butter' likes of audiences and recognising things they don't like have to be balanced with the educational/informing role of the orchestra. Timing of performances is another issue: early afternoon matinees are becoming more popular than the traditional evening performances. Winter schedules can be disrupted by the weather and unwillingness of audiences to travel. Simon commented: 'Our remit is to serve the region and nationally as well, and it is important that we don't just cater for people who like to hear Beethoven or Bach, so we respond to the audience and we do that through audience surveys; we do that through analysing box office data we have and developing strong customer relation management'.

Programmes that require expensive soloists and additional freelance musicians often have significant cost implications (the local area does not have many freelance musicians, meaning that additional travel/expense costs have to be paid for musicians coming from the traditional supplier cities of London, Manchester, Cardiff and Glasgow). Profiling of past concerts and cost–benefit analyses are undertaken to assess popularity and risk:

> We have a spreadsheet, which we try to contain to being printable on one side of A4, but it is increasingly challenging as we add columns, which is effectively adding factors, and with every concert we do, we analyse the contribution it makes to the bottom line. So we have a formula for the cost of everything we do. So, taking all that into account we look to see what contribution every piece of work makes and that does inform our programming . . . You try to balance the artistic programme but you do respond to ticket sales, absolutely.

The Artistic Forum – a senior group involving trustees, CBSO senior management, players and conductors – analyses and discusses every concert, looks at the marketing figures, balances competing perspectives (e.g. the players did not like a particular guest conductor but he brought in a huge audience) and so on. This year-on-year information provides lots of input when considering future programming possibilities:

> We have a specific discussion about every concert, which is then analysed. You have the marketing figures, which are also analysed by board subcommittees in real detail, and all of that feeds through and it is not just within the last year, it is year on year as well, so you get the patterns emerging over time. All of that informs all of the programming choices. Sometimes, it is 'well this conductor was not popular with the orchestra, but they brought in a huge audience'. Or 'this repertoire failed to bring the audience in but it is artistically really important that we do it' . . . It is making sure you have got the right apparatus to make the decisions, so when you are challenged on the decisions, as frequently you are, you are able to go back and say, 'well the reason we made that decision was that it pulled in this evidence and this is the decision we made'. So, all of it is tracked and it is now so habitual across the organisation that it is not high maintenance to do this but it is a really important part of our operation.

Such inputs are all 'mediated' by the CEO, who has the ultimate authority to make programming decisions. A balance of information from all sides has to inform his decision-making, but he must not be seen as 'blowing this way and that':

> . . . the artistic vision is very much owned by the Chief Executive. He is very keen to listen to the range of opinions that feed into that and I think that this is the crucial part of it: it is not in any way a dictation, it is absolutely he will feed on that and

quite often, you know, he will find himself making a decision which, on a personal level, he might disagree with but he can hear the volume of opinion, whether it is numerical through ticket sales or musical through people . . . they are not balanced directly against each other, they are all part of the same equation . . . it is not so much apples and pears it is just making sure that all the factors are considered in totality rather than setting them against each other. . .

Consideration of the various factors that enter into programme decision-making can be seen through Simon's account of two recent events – one of which went well, the other not so well. Looking at these events, Simon's perspective is to think that although an event went well, how could it have gone better; if an event did not go so well, what were the good things?

The event that went well was a programme of *St Matthew Passion*, conducted by Sir Simon Rattle. It went well because:

. . . there was very clearly a sense of what we were wanting to do with that concert. It was very high profile artistic work; it was welcoming Sir Simon Rattle back, having not been here for four or five years; we were able to repeat it, so for the same rehearsal costs we were able to get twice the box office . . . It was everything that the CBSO was about, in that it was celebrating the development of talents that had been nurtured by us, as well as very high-quality performance . . . It pushed our musicians really to the limit, so it was challenging for them . . . crucially, also, it was mapped out very clearly in advance how we were going to do it . . . It being that well planned and that well delivered meant that it all fell into place really well . . . it was a huge success [and] very exciting. I think the key to that was knowing what we were setting out to do, and putting all the pieces in place well in advance and everyone pulling in the same direction. It was classic management stuff but that was what happened.

Turning to the event that did not go so well, a series of Christmas concerts one year recently, Simon began by saying that these five concerts – performed over three or four days – usually worked really well, generally sold out and brought in 'a whole load of income'. This particular year they were not successful. There were a number of reasons:

. . . we had not looked back at the concerts for a long time and said, why are they so successful, what are we setting out to do, what is it that we should be holding on to here which is making them a success? We had kind of sat back on it and thought, well let's just do it again, it works and then suddenly it doesn't. There were a lot of factors which were beyond our control, which I think is always a reason why things didn't go so well; the weather militated against us [and] we lost a lot of audience through bad weather, but we cannot do anything about that. Also, we were just not clear enough on what we were doing: they had become a little bit of a muddle, there was some sing-along stuff for the audience but there was not quite enough of it to make people think they were going to go and sing lots of carols. The presenter we had was not as popular as we had anticipated, so he did not draw in the punters. In previous years, we have had much more high-profile presenters, so we missed a trick there. There were other details on the way which we had not seen coming, including a contractual dispute over a new commission in the few days leading up to the concerts, which meant that we got a bit distracted from other details and ended up not having clean rehearsal halls for the chorus to warm up in, for example. So we ended up with a less festive atmosphere around the concerts and also not the usual number of people coming in, so economically they were a bit of a disappointment. Artistically, they did not go as well as in previous years, and in morale terms it was just not a very satisfactory outcome.

For both events, Simon reflected on the key learning points. For *St Matthew Passion*:

... the amount of administrative time, operational time it takes to put something like that on, and how much of a distraction it can be from other activities, and to make sure we are properly staffed to deliver it. I think we did it well and we managed it but we had to put all of our energies into that one project for a couple of weeks. For the Christmas concerts, similarly, making sure that we are properly equipped to make the decisions about how they are going to be programmed, don't fall back on the kind of slightly passive, 'well it has worked before, we will do it again'. What was good about it was that actually the performers on stage all pulled together: they said, 'Look, there have been problems this year but let's make it as good as we possibly can', and actually, you know, people trudging through the snow for hours to get there on time, making a huge effort to come in. The best thing that has come out of it is the insistence from all of us that we go right back to the bare bones of what these concerts are and replan them differently for next year. [Had it been more success-ful] we certainly would not be reconsidering it at the level we are – we would be much more relaxed about it, so that would not have been a good thing.

When considering the link between the organising and the creative side of things, Simon commented:

I think only that the two are inseparable: there is no single part of the operation that you could consider either as artistic or operational or whatever the tag we give to it. If at any time we are tempted to look at one part of the operation without considering the others we force ourselves to bring other aspects in to the discus-sion. The danger of having one part of the organisation thinking artistically, one part thinking financially and one part operationally is that things just start to unravel; what we have done over a number of years here is to make sure that that conversation is right at the heart of everything. Whenever somebody is making a very strong economic point we would always bring in the artistic balances and vice versa, and that is how you make the strong decisions.

Key lessons

- There is a need for managers to take account of the various stakeholders they have to deal with, and how their often competing but also com-plementary interests, expectations and perspectives have to be man-aged (see 2_vjt'} pt>Chapters 7 and 13).

- In running artistic/creative organisations, a participative and inclusive style of management is important.
- Artistic/creative organisations need to balance the 'practical' as well as the 'creative' needs of their employees (see Chapters 1 and 5).
- Artistic/creative organisations also need to balance their 'practical', 'hard-headed' business objectives as well as their 'creative' objectives (see Chapter 2).
- Reflection and learning from things that go well and those that do not go so well is important (see Chapter 14).

Discussion questions

- List the range of duties involved in Simon's role. What competencies does he need to undertake his role?
- Managing and leading organisations is often characterised by paradox, ambiguity and contradiction. To what extent does Simon's story reflect these characteristics?
- Show how a 'participative and inclusive' management style is achieved in the CBSO.
- What sort of objectives does the CBSO have? How are they achieved?
- What core competencies does the CBSO exhibit?
- How might both artistic/creative and business demands be met? Are the two types of demand ultimately in conflict? If so, why? If not, why not?
- What lessons would you draw from Simon's analysis of the two episodes that went well/not so well?

For more information, visit:
www.cbso.co.uk/

Leadership in the BBC Philharmonic

Richard Wigley and Elizabeth Gulledge

Introduction

Until 2014 Richard Wigley managed the BBC Philharmonic Orchestra, which gives public concerts in Manchester and across the north of England. Most of the live concerts are recorded and serve as the seventy to eighty broadcasts provided for Radio 3 annually. In addition, the BBC Philharmonic annually goes on two international tours, performs at the BBC Proms and produces commercial recordings under special contract to Chandos. Alongside this broad range of activities they run an extensive learning programme focused on the city of Salford, which sponsors the orchestra.

Decision-making at the BBC Philharmonic

The BBC Philharmonic is run by a relatively uncomplicated decision-making process. The primary stakeholder and funder is the BBC, in the form of Radio 3; other stakeholders include Salford City Council, local authority promoters, BBC colleagues and other orchestras. The significant decision-making falls within the general manager's remit, and tends to be around artistic, financial or managerial issues.

Programming

Richard worked collaboratively with Senior Producer Mike George to make decisions about repertoire programming. There was plenty of consultation with conductors – predominantly the chief conductor, principal guest conductor, composer/conductor, a conductor laureate, two conductors emeritus and other regular conductors. An initial brainstorm around thematic ideas was common prior to securing the detailed programmes. Richard and Mike were aware of each conductor's strengths and tended to include a mix of styles based on the conductors' expertise. Ultimately, the general manager would informally sign off all the artistic plans, although not all of them were generated by him (for example, programming might follow a specific request from Radio 3 colleagues).

The BBC Philharmonic aims to collaborate with other orchestras in Manchester and the north. For example, the orchestra recently undertook a complete cycle of Mahler symphonies with the other Manchester orchestra, the Halle. This included a joint performance with both orchestras.

In addition to playing new, neglected and large-scale repertoire it is important, on occasion, to aim for a full house for the orchestra's well-being and for commercial reasons. The orchestra uses a system of one to four stars to categorise its concerts. Four-star concerts are the ones expected to gather big audiences and one-star concerts tend to be the difficult repertoire. The orchestra plans to open and close its season with a four-star concert, then manage the programmes between to sustain the audience's interest. The BBC Philharmonic audience tends to be knowledgeable and often comes for high-brow repertoire. It is vital to gauge how challenged they want to be. Critical review is important feedback; some critics are very sympathetic to the BBC Philharmonic's style, while others are less so.

One example of a concert deemed successful was the Mahler *Symphony No 10* project. This was in the planning for five years. It is a notoriously difficult piece, but by the time the BBC Philharmonic played it at the BBC Proms it was at a high performance level. Integrated into this plan was a recording for Chandos Records. Another example would be the joint projects with the Halle. These involved a great deal of collaborative thinking, particularly in a joint concert of two orchestras.

The tension between artistic success and financial success is different for the BBC Philharmonic in comparison to most orchestras. Although the orchestra does not experience the same box office income requirements that an independent orchestra might, commercial pressure is not entirely absent. The BBC covers the basic cost of the orchestra; however, for an international tour, say, the orchestra needs to generate the income to cover any additional travel costs, etc.

Managing musicians

Musicians who work with the BBC tend to have a willingness to commit to the relationship with the Corporation, and staff turnover is therefore very low. A typical BBC Philharmonic employee is incredibly talented and creative, and strongly believes in the organisation.

An extreme example of the challenges in managing musicians was the 2011 tour of Japan. Half way through a wonderful tour, an earthquake and tsunami hit. When Fukushima nuclear power plant suffered major problems and threatened to blow up, the orchestra was in rehearsal in Yokohama. Many musicians were understandably concerned about safety and, given the uncertainty in the situation, wanted to return home immediately. The decision was taken to cancel the tour, but arranging travel home was far from easy, as there was a significant increase in demand for diminished travel services. The orchestra's management were able to get all the flights organised and new hotels booked within twenty-four hours, but during this time some musicians felt they had not been dealt with sufficiently urgently. There was one group within the orchestra that expressed dissatisfaction to a high level among themselves, and although they did not represent the whole orchestra, the level of anxiety was considerable. Managing the interactions so that people felt they were being taken seriously, at the same time as seeking to allay fears and cope with the practicalities and stresses of changing bookings, was a notable challenge. It entailed improvisation and a high degree of emotional resilience.

Although things had worked out in the short term, this kind of shock to the system can have a lasting effect. It required careful management over a number of months. Richard was able to resurrect the tour and have it rescheduled two years later. During this process he simultaneously dealt with conducting issues and personality issues, as well as learning something about crisis management.

Hiring and retaining musicians is a challenging part of managerial work. In some settings, being able to replace players who leave is a crucial dynamic. However, the other side of that coin – particularly in an orchestra where players want to stay – is managing the hopes and expectations of those who have long careers in one orchestra. For example, highly skilled players who may have joined the orchestra twenty years ago still receive the same equivalent amount of pay. While there was little Richard could do to change the level of pay, he made it a priority to ensure that musicians were challenged by the repertoire chosen and felt they were an integral part of experimenting with new ways of performing classical music. Seeking to keep a certain amount of change and challenge and to provide some intrinsic motivation, along with (non-financial) recognition of contribution, was thus very important in this context.

Overall, in terms of managing human relations and leadership, Richard felt the orchestra did not need a charismatic management leader as much as they expected someone they could trust to be reliable and to operate successfully within the BBC. He saw his primary role as creating an environment in which great music happened. This often required him to put himself in the firing line when he made programming decisions and when trying to meet both the emotional and organisational needs of his musicians.

In 2014 Richard left the BBC to form his own company, Wigley Arts Management, to help build outstanding orchestras. He currently divides his time between the Netherlands and the UK.

Key lessons

- Collaborative artistic leadership around thematic ideas is necessary, alongside a requirement to balance the artistic and commercial needs of the orchestra (see Chapters 3 and 9).
- The players need trust in the orchestral leadership to operate reliably within the organisation, rather than charismatic leadership (see Chapters 5 and 15).
- It is important that the management understands and knows the audience in order to keep the right balance within the orchestral repertoire (see Chapters 8, 9 and 10).

Discussion questions

- What were the key aspects to Richard's job as the orchestral general manager?
- Reflect on the disaster that occurred when the orchestra was in Japan. What organisational challenges did that pose for Richard? Would you have done anything differently?
- What are the key aspects of managing the relationship between the orchestra and the BBC?

Orchestrating a flash mob: reach and reputation

Jane Donald and Gail Greig

Introduction

Jane Donald is Director of External Relations at the Royal Scottish National Orchestra (RSNO). Her professional career has been spent working in marketing and PR for arts organisations, including Glasgow Concert Halls, the Celtic Connections festival and the Theatre Royal in Glasgow. Jane has experience of organising a range of musical events to maximise audience reach and engagement, reflecting the social remit of the publicly funded national arts organisations in which she has spent most of her working life. One such initiative involved the RSNO and a performance of an orchestral 'flash mob', undertaken in collaboration with colleagues at Glasgow International Airport. This section tells the story of how the flash mob came to be, and what happened when the orchestra visited the airport.

Marketing the RSNO

The RSNO is one of five Scottish nationally funded arts organisations, with a cultural remit including raising the profile of Scotland among international audiences and bringing music to as wide a range of Scottish people as possible. It is a complex organisation, with the seventy-nine musicians who constitute its heart in the form of the orchestra playing on stage. Organising a performing orchestra requires significant work, which is the responsibility of a range of people with a variety of roles. These include the RSNO board, the chief executive, the music director, concert and programme planning, learning and engagement, marketing, communications development and finance, as well as a host of other technical and support roles.

Each year, the RSNO gives a variety of performances of different types of classical music, from popular favourites to less well-known critically acclaimed pieces, and music that enables young people and hard-to-reach audiences engage with the classical genre. Organising events to showcase particular musical styles to the relevant audiences is central to performing this wide-ranging repertoire. Raising and maintaining the RSNO's profile as a national Scottish cultural organisation is an important part of ensuring that classical music reaches the range of possible audiences, both at home and abroad. This challenging responsibility is central to the work of the RSNO's marketing and development team, who need to achieve maximum effect with minimum budget. Therefore, opportunities to support the RSNO remit through publicity and sponsorship, in partnership with other suitable organisations, are most welcome.

The following sets out how collaboration with Glasgow International Airport, around a mutual desire to raise Scotland's cultural profile and to represent the country on the international stage, resulted in some unusual marketing and international publicity for the RSNO in its efforts to bring classical music to a wide-ranging audience.

Publicity through collaboration

The RSNO had professional contact with the PR manager at Glasgow International Airport. He was running an initiative to promote the airport as 'Scotland's destination airport' by showcasing Scottish culture to enhance the experience of passengers spending time at the airport. The initiative would take the form of a festival and was entitled 'Best of Scotland'. As Scotland's national classical music organisation, he wanted the RSNO to contribute to the event. In return, the RSNO could expect free advertising and publicity at the airport (worth a considerable amount, given the RSNO's small marketing budget). This seemed like a good reciprocal collaborative opportunity, so thoughts turned to what the orchestra might do at the airport.

Ideas – orchestral music in public places: the flash mob

An airport is not the typical setting for orchestral music: spaces are designated for particular functions, some are more accessible than others, and everyone is trying to go somewhere else. So how to present classical orchestral music in this setting? Run-of-the-mill suggestions in situations where space is limited are to provide soloists or small groups of players, much like a chamber orchestra. As they discussed this, the RSNO team realised it would be important to present a symphonic sound, as this is what marks the RSNO out from other performing classical music forms. So, how might the collective orchestral sound be produced in a constrained place like an airport? And which pieces of music would be suitable? Classical music pieces are often quite long, but air travel involves relatively limited time and a range of required travel tasks. The team started to talk about the possibility of creating an orchestral flash mob. According to *Brewer's Dictionary of Modern Phrase and Fable* (2009), a flash mob is 'a phenomenon of the early twenty-first century consisting of a crowd that suddenly assembles in a place, engages briefly in a coordinated and apparently gratuitous activity (e.g. a pillow fight) and then as suddenly disperses'. This sounded like the perfect solution: a (seemingly) spontaneous, short, live, collective performance for no apparent reason, apart from bringing pleasure – could the RSNO perform a flash mob at the airport?

Planning a flash mob

The logistics of organising the flash mob were challenging. The first step was to articulate plans internally: not an inconsiderable task. Players would need their instruments, many of which are large and difficult to conceal. Some – like cellos – feature spikes to rest upon. This presented a headache in the sharp-resistant security culture of a modern airport. Even a conductor's baton was problematic from this perspective.

Of course, in addition to players and instruments, the right piece of music was needed. Choosing music to perform is a serious issue for an orchestra: it needs to suit the occasion and audience; not damage the orchestra's reputation among the classical music fraternity and fans; and be capable of being tailored to the time slot (perhaps not as originally written), thus requiring the services of the orchestral librarian to produce a suitable score for the players/instruments/time available.

These challenges required the involvement of colleagues on the RSNO board (including the player directors – two members of the orchestra who are elected to represent the players on the board, of which no one in management is a director member) in programming, concert planning and the library. After much discussion, agreement to perform a flash mob was reached by the board and the necessary number of players by doing this on a 'contracted day', so that players were not committed to work other than for the RSNO on that day, and the costs were already incurred by the RSNO. Player directors appreciated the idea of the free advertising at the airport, as they understood the possibility of reaching a wider audience than their core supporters, together with possible assistance with other costs through associated airlines.

Securing airport 'buy-in'

While the approach to the RSNO came from the airport PR manager, the broader agreement of the Airport Operating Committee was needed. This involved addressing issues that were of no consequence to the orchestra but were significant for the various organisations involved at the airport. For example, the decibel level of the music needed to be measured for check-in staff health and safety, and normal everyday objects like the conductor's baton and the cello spike presented serious security issues for the airport. In addition, although seeking to enhance the passenger experience at the airport, there was an imperative not to disrupt the already complex process of air travel: passenger flows at different times of day had to be identified to decide when and where the flash mob could be performed.

These challenges – obvious to airport staff – contrasted directly with those for the orchestra. For example, passenger flows and player contracted days had to be aligned to agree when and where to stage the flash mob. This required careful, patient attention to detail by both RSNO and airport personnel to address contrasting challenges sufficiently so that the Airport Operating Committee could agree to the flash mob.

Organising the flash mob

After securing RSNO and airport agreement, the next obvious question was: How do you do a flash mob? No one involved had any experience of this sort of ostensibly impromptu performance, but the communications manager at the RSNO had a contact at the National Theatre of Scotland (NTS), who was experienced at flash mobs: ' He was great because . . . he just knew – he had a whole event plan of things that we had not thought about'. He explained that successful 'mobs' formed suddenly, performed and then melted away, so performers had to be in situ before the performance. A narrative of 'The RSNO Goes On Tour' was established, providing 'cover' for being at the airport.

Now attention turned to more practical, central details. First, music: if flash mobs begin small, build quickly, reach a peak and then melt away quickly, appropriate music was needed. They settled upon Ravel's *Bolero*, which was ideal – even though it was a 'popular classic', seen by some as potentially damaging to the RSNO's reputation. Starting with one player (drum), the music gradually builds to involve many more players – giving the full orchestral sound – and then fades again as it ends. *Bolero* therefore allowed for a shorter period of loudness than some pieces (in accordance with airport needs), and the orchestra's librarian was able to provide a short score of about five minutes (although the airport stipulated no more than four minutes).

Second, choreography: clearly the players would be performing in a way that was quite different from how they normally played, since they would not be seated, nor in normal concert dress nor necessarily with a musical score. Knowing where to be and how to do this was crucial – this required choreography and rehearsal to perform 'The RSNO Goes On Tour'. The NTS expert and members of the RSNO team gathered at the airport at night to work out the logistics for staging the performance, then using their measurements to mark out the RSNO hall to rehearse 'staging' the flash mob with participating players.

Performing the flash mob required players, other RSNO people and airport personnel either to do things that were entirely new to them or to do familiar things in unfamiliar ways. For example, two marketing assistants from the airport marketing team played airline staff at 'assigned Madrid flight' check-in desks. Those responsible for putting flights on the departures noticeboard had to include a 'fake' Madrid flight with other actual flights and agree this with others at the airport. Hiding places for large instruments had to be found in advance, so they could just be brought out as the players needed them. This meant that the NTS expert – who knew nothing about the musical aspect – needed a running order of which instruments were needed when, in order to choreograph this (somewhat unusual, for him) performance. Players practised playing music while walking (not sitting), pulling their rolling hand luggage with them (rather than having both hands on their instruments) in the check-in hall (not concert platform), dressed in normal clothes (not evening dress), not in their usual positions in relation to one another's instruments (but in the order of play of the piece).

Rehearsing the music back at the RSNO performance space initially made the sound level seem louder than the airport's agreed decibel level (what would the acoustics be at the airport on the day?). Victor – the 'conductor' – was also a player. He worked with Richard (RSNO Planning Department) and Charlie (RSNO Concert Manager – responsible for stage managing normal concerts/performances, who had also been a player) to provide the NTS expert with the musical detail he needed to choreograph and direct what would be something of a theatrical performance. Well-respected among the players, Victor and Charlie understood the challenges and could persuade players to perform in such unfamiliar ways, while an outsider would probably not have been so successful.

Those from the RSNO became anxious, but there was a sense that they were 'all in this together', and when one person flagged, another provided positive support. In particular the players were nervous, since this was totally out of their comfort zone of performing orchestral music in usual settings. The NTS expert had advised them to be very confident and exaggerated in what they were doing to make the necessary impact on the day, and Victor helped greatly with this: he led from the front by being entirely positive, conducting in an exaggerated way as advised, and predicting everyone would love it.

If executing the flash mob was challenging for the RSNO, their need to make the performance as widely available as possible through social media and the internet was particularly problematic for the Airport Operating Committee. The performance was being professionally filmed from four vantage points. This presented a serious problem for the airport, in case security personnel were inadvertently captured by any of the four cameras. Initially, the Airport Operating Committee refused permission for filming, but the airport PR manager reassured them by providing camera angles, and similar. Players' luggage had brown card labels bearing the RSNO logo, Facebook and Twitter addresses to enable members of the public to feel they were 'in on the secret' as the flash mob got underway. This enabled the event to be not only filmed but also posted on YouTube and managed via social media – both notoriously difficult for orchestral performances.

In addition to filming the flash mob, the agreed free advertising at the airport came – unexpectedly, at the last minute – in the form of 'reciprocal branding'. At the height of the flash mob preparations at the airport, the airport PR manager told Jane: 'I can get you just about every digital screen in the airport for the day, but we're on a tight timescale – you'll have to send me everything by Monday!' Airport screens are often well above eye level, so the RSNO needed simple but high-impact visuals with few details. Given the (very) short timescale, Jane opted for the RSNO logo, colours and a somewhat contrived but simple image to make the most of this high-profile advertising opportunity throughout the airport complex; it would be almost impossible for travelling passengers to miss. This was captured on the flash mob film and actually remained in place for three weeks, thereby providing the RSNO with the opportunity to reach a wide, diverse group of people travelling through the international airport.

On the day – the performance

The tour bus arrives at the airport with forty-five players with their (smaller) instruments, who go to 'check in' for their 'Madrid flight' dressed normally for travel. They form two queues in front of the two designated check-in desks (in the order that they will play/according to the size of their instruments – some of the larger but still portable ones at the back). 'The conductor' checks in first, and is asked: 'Do you have any sharp objects in your hand luggage?' He takes out his conductor's baton and the performance begins. A single drummer plays the opening bars of Ravel's *Bolero*. The music builds as players emerge, some materialising with their large, less portable instruments as if from nowhere, and crowds begin to gather as they realise something is happening. For four to five minutes, Glasgow International Airport is transformed by orchestral music. People stop to pay attention – some bemused, others' expressions turning from incredulous to happy. People take out their smartphones or cameras to record the scene, to share or play back later. Just as Victor predicted, the audience response is overwhelmingly positive: 'It was amazing, and there were little kids who just went, "It was the nicest thing". I felt so proud.'

(Share the experience – watch the flash mob at: www.youtube.com/watch?v=btnnBn5UMZ4)

After the event – reviews and outcomes

The filming captured the event well, and although Jane had hoped it could be uploaded to YouTube immediately, the digital format meant that the film-maker needed the afternoon to prepare the upload to the web. Meantime, passengers posted their own films of the event and commented on it, and shared it via Twitter. This was an exciting development for the RSNO marketing and communications team: 'My colleague, who does our social media – getting social media to do anything big for an orchestra is always hard – she was so excited, she texted me: "We are trending in Glasgow!"'.

The story was covered on Classic FM radio and in various newspapers, although timing could have been better in terms of cultural news – it was competing with the Edinburgh Festival. Nonetheless, the novelty of the event captured people's imaginations: 'Robert [RSNO Communications Manager] put as the strapline on the press release: "RSNO get out of their concert zone", and in some ways it was a really great pun, because that is exactly what we were doing – we were asking them to get into a situation that was unfamiliar.'

As a flash mob, the event was a success. The performance was very well received and was, and continues to be, viewed by many over the internet. The airport was also happy with it: 'they would have us back every week!' For the RSNO, there were mixed outcomes. In terms of reaching a wide and diverse audience the flash mob was extremely successful, as the social media presence and reaction demonstrated. This helped the RSNO in one key performance area, given their status as a nationally funded cultural organisation. They were also praised by their funder for working with another nationally funded cultural organisation through their collaboration with the NTS – Robert's link with the expert from the NTS served them well beyond the performance of the flash mob. But in terms of reputation, the picture was mixed. Bringing classical music to a wider audience and working with others was good for their reputation to some extent, but in musical terms there were some challenges about the sound quality. The choice of music was a matter of some debate, and although the players did a marvellous job, the sound quality on the day was not of the usual concert standard. Acoustics, player placement in relation to one another (and one another's instruments), the physical nature of the performance and background noise all combined to make the sound quality less than perfect. This was a point of learning among the RSNO, for whom sound is so important and usually tightly controlled. So while the film was a huge success, the soundtrack received mixed reviews internally.

Nevertheless, as a whole, the flash mob was a highly successful means of bringing orchestral music to people in an unusual and frequently stressful setting. It appeared to enhance the quality of their experience on that day. People said it made them feel emotional and happy – as evidenced by their expressions. Music performed in these ways seems to elicit such reaction, and the number of classical music flash mobs has increased since the RSNO was brave enough to step 'out of their concert zone' to bring such pleasure to so many, working with colleagues to orchestrate a flash mob at the airport.

Key lessons

- Collaboration on several fronts is one way of moving outside the norms of performance (see Chapters 2 and 14).
- The interplay between cultural and commercial activities can be worked to the advantage of both (see Chapters 10 and 12).
- The overlap of established practices, and the tensions between them, can be a source of innovation (see Chapter 17).

Discussion questions

- How can risk-taking and innovation be enabled in musical settings?
- How might some of the dangers with risk-taking be ameliorated?
- What lessons might be learned from this example about the connections and planning needed for 'apparently spontaneous' performances?

For more information, visit:
www.rsno.org.uk

Developing a university's musical culture: a partnership approach

Michael Downes

My background

I took up the newly created position of Director of Music at the University of St Andrews in September 2008, having previously been part-time Director of Music at Fitzwilliam College, Cambridge. My professional musical experience had previously been divided between academic work and performance. After a first degree in English, I took an MPhil in Musicology (both at Cambridge); the change of discipline was motivated in part by the amount of time I had spent during my first degree participating in music, mainly as cellist and conductor. My doctorate at Sussex was on the music and ideas of Debussy, while my musicological work since then has included a book on Jonathan Harvey, one of Britain's leading composers until his death in 2012 (published by Ashgate, 2009). Alongside my academic work I have worked professionally as a conductor, directing numerous amateur choirs and orchestras in the south-east of England and organising and conducting my own London-based professional contemporary music group, the Bergamo Ensemble. Much of this work was freelance and thus often difficult to coordinate: I was excited by the opportunity St Andrews offered to develop my performance, administrative and academic abilities within a single position.

Developing music in St Andrews

St Andrews is a small university town in rural Scotland. There is a rich tradition of amateur music in the town, but the university has not had a music degree since the late 1980s, meaning that its musical life has at times been lacking in investment and leadership. In order to catalyse an enhancement to both quality and quantity of music-making a number of initiatives have been taken, and this section focuses on two of them: the residency by the Scottish Chamber Orchestra (SCO) and the establishment of St Andrews Opera.

The SCO residency

The SCO has been a regular visitor to St Andrews for many years, presenting a five-concert series each season in the Younger Hall, the 1,000-seater auditorium where the university's Music Centre is based. It is remarkable that such a small town should be so regularly visited by one of the world's finest chamber orchestras: only Edinburgh and Glasgow have more SCO concerts; Aberdeen (population 225,000) receives five per season – the same number as St Andrews. The orchestra has built up a loyal following from audiences both within the town and further afield.

Until 2009 the orchestra's relationship with the university was restricted to the commercial transaction of hiring the venue: its players had not been invited to become involved in the university's musical life. In 2009 I approached the orchestra's Chief Executive, Roy McEwan, to ask him whether he would be willing to consider developing the relationship into a residency. This approach was partly influenced by having been involved in the Britten Sinfonia's successful residency at Cambridge University, but that is an exceptional case: very few British universities, and no other universities in Scotland, have a professional orchestra in residence. Roy McEwan was immediately enthusiastic, and discussions advanced quickly, with Lucy Lowe, the then Director of SCO Connect (the orchestra's education department) also heavily involved. The residency was launched at the first St Andrews concert of the SCO's 2009–10 season.

It was intended from the start to offer a framework for flexible cooperation between the two organisations: certain elements were explicitly articulated, but with scope left for new ideas to be developed creatively as the relationship developed. Among the first new initiatives was a series of pre-performance talks and interviews, already a regular and valued part of the orchestra's schedule in Edinburgh and Glasgow. Audiences in the town appreciated the chance to hear from players, conductors and composers, particularly the newly appointed Principal Conductor, Robin Ticciati, who was one of the first interviewees and who gave some fascinating and wide-ranging insights into his work with the SCO and his plans for its future. This very simple initiative helped to humanise the orchestra for its St Andrews audiences, allowing them to get to know some of the personalities involved, and also established the orchestra's St Andrews programme as equal in status to those elsewhere.

Two other key aspects of the residency – chamber concerts and education work – were also in place from the very start. In October 2009 the orchestra's recently appointed Principal Horn, Alec Frank-Gemmill, gave a lunchtime concert followed by a masterclass for both university students and schoolchildren who took part in a Music Centre brass group. Over the following two years many SCO players visited the university to take part in the series of weekly Wednesday lunchtime concerts and to give master-classes and coaching – mainly to students, but also on occasion to musicians from the wider community. The appearances of SCO players as 'star guests' in the lunchtime series were certainly appreciated, but we began to feel that it was a waste to confine players of this calibre to the 40-minute programme that the lunchtime slot allowed. In October 2011 we launched a new series of SCO early evening concerts at 5.30pm, allowing players to plan more ambitious programmes of 60–70 minutes. Though it has taken a little while to establish audience awareness of this unusual slot (for St Andrews), the concerts have been very well received: audiences have enjoyed the chance to hear rarely performed repertoire and unusual combinations of instruments, with particularly memorable recitals given by the orchestra's two double basses and two clarinets. Masterclasses have remained a central part of the residency and have now been given by members of every section.

In 2011 a three-way collaboration was mounted between the orchestra, the university and StANZA, the prestigious poetry festival held every March in St Andrews. To mark the centenary of the Gaelic poet Sorley MacLean, featured in that year's festival, composers under thirty from all over the country were invited to take part in a competition to set a MacLean text. The successful compositions, judged by a panel including Sally Beamish, were performed by soprano Lesley-Jane Rogers, three SCO players – flautist Alison Mitchell, violist Jane Atkins and guest harpist Sharron Griffiths – and the St Andrews Chamber Orchestra in a concert in the town's Byre Theatre, broadcast by BBC Radio nan Gàidheal, the Gaelic-speaking station. This project provided a great opportunity both for the composers and for student performers, who had the exceptional experience to work alongside SCO principals. The strong relationship that the residency had already fostered between the orchestra and the university greatly facilitated what would otherwise have been a very complex project to organise. It also helped the festival to add a musical dimension to its programme, linking in with the SCO concert the same week, which also had a strong literary element.

Perhaps the most unusual and ambitious project so far initiated through the residency, however, is StAFCO – the St Andrews and Fife Community Orchestra – which was launched in October 2010 with a special weekend workshop, and which has since rehearsed weekly under the direction of Gillian Craig, a St Andrews musician with long experience of community music-making. This project offers a unique example of a university and a professional orchestra collaborating to provide an opportunity for amateur musicians, some of whom have only been learning for a couple of years, and some of whom are returning to music after a long gap. It has proved immensely popular, with membership growing every year and now numbering about seventy, and with many players travelling very long distances to take part. The relationship with the SCO is crucial to the project: StAFCO's members rehearse extracts from music the SCO is performing that season, attend SCO performances as a group, receive sectional coaching from SCO members, work with SCO soloists (cellists Su-a Lee and Donald Gillan recently shared the four movements of Elgar's *Cello Concerto* in a project stretching over two seasons) and enjoy the opportunity to play alongside SCO performers. The complementarity between the contribution of the university (venue, administrative infrastructure, links with local teachers and the other activities of the Music Centre) and that of the orchestra (world-class soloists and coaches, creative expertise of SCO Connect, the inspiration offered by attending its concerts) allows an exceptional opportunity to be offered to local amateur musicians for a very modest financial outlay on their part.

The success of the residency has come in large part from the development of a network of relationships between individuals in the two organisations, which has enabled the collaboration to evolve more elaborately than might first have been envisaged. For example, SCO players have been invited by instrumental teachers to coach chamber groups; I and other university staff have become involved in SCO education work in Edinburgh as well as St Andrews; our students have benefited from opportunities for voluntary work with the orchestra; and we are hoping to offer a joint internship next year. The residency costs nothing to either side – although, of course, players are remunerated for the extra work that they do as a result of it – but it brings great benefits to both parties. Players appreciate the opportunities for professional development that work in the university offers; the orchestra reports healthy audience numbers in St Andrews, consolidated by the range of extra activities that it now mounts in the town; and audiences are now willing to attend 'difficult' programmes containing contemporary music, whereas before the residency the orchestra avoided programming such repertoire in St Andrews due to a perception of conservative tastes. The musical life of the university, meanwhile, is immeasurably enriched by the commitment, expertise and creativity of SCO Connect, now directed by Lucy Forde, and by the frequent engagement with musicians of the highest calibre that the residency brings.

St Andrews Opera

When I arrived at St Andrews I was keen to establish an opera company: this is an area of particular interest to me, and at Cambridge I had successfully established Fitzwilliam Chamber Opera, the only college-based opera company. Coincidentally, plans were already afoot at St Andrews to perform Purcell's *Dido and Aeneas*; we combined this with Monteverdi's rarely performed *Il Ballo delle Ingrate* to form an attractive but manageable double bill for early 2009. The production was put together on a very low budget and directed by Jane Pettegree, who taught in the university's School of English. Finding enough time for rehearsals was difficult within the congested weekly timetable that the student singers already had, and there were difficulties finding the necessary expertise in lighting, costume design and choreography, but these problems were surmounted to produce excellent performances. It was particularly notable that the 100 tickets available for each of the three nights in the church hall where we performed sold extremely quickly, by comparison with those for other ventures; there was clearly an interest in the area in attending live opera that went beyond personal contacts of the performers.

The auditions for the production had unearthed a talented pool of singers, with particular strengths (unusual for a university group) among the men. The presence of three outstanding baritones encouraged me to programme Britten's *Rape of Lucretia* as the project for 2010. Though this would be a considerably greater challenge both musically and in its subject matter, I was confident that it could succeed if the necessary links could be made. We agreed that we needed a professional director from outside the university: I approached Alex Reedijk, General Director of Scottish Opera, who suggested Kally Lloyd-Jones, the company's movement director. Kally was seeking to move into opera direction alongside her very successful career as dancer and choreographer, and proved an inspired choice. Crucial to her approach was that she treated the students as though they were professionals: though she was sympathetic to the demands the piece posed, she made no concessions in her expectations.

Other vital elements in the production's success were its timing – such a demanding enterprise could not have been mounted during term-time, so we moved it to the post-exam period, giving students three uninterrupted weeks to rehearse – and the involvement of other professionals: orchestra, an excellent lighting designer (Daniel Murfin) and the staff of the town's 200-seat Byre Theatre. The Royal Scottish Academy of Music and Drama (now the Royal Conservatoire of Scotland), an institution with which the university already had strong links, also helped by recommending advanced student singers for two of the roles. A generous contribution to what was an expensive project was made by a private supporter of music in the town, who recognised its transformative potential for the students involved. Audience numbers were again encouraging: although it did not sell out (perhaps not surprising, given that many students were not in town and the piece's reputation for being 'difficult'), it nevertheless attracted many people beyond the immediate contacts of the performers, suggesting that opera-lovers in Scotland were willing to take a chance on an unknown company in order to hear a rarely performed piece.

Subsequent projects have furthered the company's reputation for ambition, high standards and exploring repertoire that is rarely performed, at least in Scotland. The double bill of John Eccles's *Judgment of Paris* and Lennox Berkeley's *A Dinner Engagement* in 2011 was followed in 2012 by a production of Tchaikovsky's *Eugene Onegin* in a reduced orchestration, also directed by Kally Lloyd-Jones. The latter was a co-production with Bloomsbury Opera, based at Goodenough College in London, where Kally also had strong links, with the roles divided between the two groups. This created a range of new contacts for the company and its members, and provided the St Andrews singers with the valuable opportunity of singing in London. On the negative side, however, there was considerable extra expenditure on transport and accommodation, and the splitting of the roles meant that fewer St Andrews singers had the chance to perform.

The St Andrews performances in the Byre Theatre were again very well supported, but sadly the theatre itself had gone into liquidation by the time of the company's 2013 production, Handel's *Acis and Galatea*. Jane Pettegree, again directing, reached an ingenious solution to the problem of performing the piece in a venue that was not a fully equipped theatre, by commissioning the artist Jean Duncan to create images that would be projected on a screen behind the performers, slowly rotating and shifting as the drama developed. We put together an excellent period-instrument orchestra for this production, drawing on London-based contacts of Lucy Russell, the university's Honorary Professor of Violin, who led the group. This decision was of great educational benefit to the singers, none of whom had worked with period instruments or considered baroque style in any detail before, and contributed hugely to the excellent reception of the production. Two performances in the Younger Hall were followed by one in Perth Concert Hall, one of Scotland's leading classical music venues. This attracted an audience which, though modest compared with more commercial ventures, greatly surpassed the venue's expectations.

As in the Byre Theatre, it seemed clear that many audience members had attended because they wanted to experience live opera, rather than because they knew cast members; the fact that the singers were students did not hinder their enjoyment, because of the high standard of performance and the professional approach to the production. The company returned to Perth Concert Hall for its 2014 production of Britten's *Albert Herring*, and also gave a performance in the new Beacon Arts

Centre in Greenock. This spreading of its activities produces a double benefit: it brings valuable experience to the performers, while also offering live opera to a wider public across Scotland, a country where this is in short supply, despite Scottish Opera's excellent touring programme. We are already planning a 2015 production of Gluck's *Iphigénie en Tauride*, in a new English version to be produced by students in the School of Modern Languages as part of a module in translation. This will be guided by the academic and singer Julia Prest and the university's distinguished Honorary Professor of Singing, Brian Bannatyne-Scott, who has been heavily involved in coaching for recent productions. It will bring interesting new academic dimensions to the project and will further integrate the company into the university's work.

Though many universities in the UK have student opera companies, what we are offering is somewhat different, because of the professional way in which the project is organised, the opportunity it brings to sing in varied venues and the links with professional practitioners it brings to our students. The exceptional nature of the opportunity is becoming recognised by prospective applicants to the university: several talented singers in recent years have applied to St Andrews specifically because of its strength in opera. If this trend continues it will lead to a virtuous circle, whereby still more ambitious projects can be mounted. Together with other opportunities for singers, particularly St Salvator's Chapel Choir, St Andrews Opera makes the university an increasingly attractive choice for students wishing to become professional singers. Because singers generally mature relatively late, it is common for them to gain a degree in another discipline before specialising in music, and so the lack of a full music degree in St Andrews is less of a disincentive than it would be for instrumentalists. While giving opportunities to student singers, St Andrews Opera also enhances the offering of live opera available to Scottish audiences, thereby helping to fulfil the wider community remit of the Music Centre.

Conclusion

All the projects mentioned above have scope for further development, and the fact that talented musicians are now making a positive choice to come to St Andrews because of the opportunities on offer brings optimism that the rapid increase in the quality and ambition of the university's performances can be maintained. This aspiration would, of course, be shared by any university director of music. But perhaps the particular lesson of this story is that through creative engagement with outside organisations and professionals, the perceived disadvantages of St Andrews – the small size of the university and town, its geographical isolation, and above all its lack of a music degree – can be negated and even turned into strengths. It is these very features that permit a freedom and flexibility of interaction that would be more difficult in larger, more impersonal towns and institutions, or ones in which the requirements of an academic degree necessarily impose certain patterns of activity.

Key lessons

• Addressing public perceptions and creating a belief that high standards are possible even within the perceived limitations of the context is a vital pre-requisite to mounting ambitious projects (see Chapters 3 and 13).
• Identifying partners within the music profession who have an equal interest in developing the provision on offer can stimulate creative and rewarding collaborations (see Chapter 2).
• Exposing student performers to professional working methods and levels of expectation can produce exceptional results that are of interest to audiences beyond the university context (see Chapters 4 and 8).

Discussion questions

• How can the qualities that characterise the best amateur music-making (enthusiasm, flexibility, willingness to dedicate large amounts of time without remuneration) be best combined with professional working practices?
• Can the working relationships described in this story – which concerns a small university in a small town – be effectively transferred to a larger and more complex organisation?
• How can a project characterised by constant expansion and increase in levels of ambition be made sustainable, given necessary limitations on resources such as staff time and administrative infrastructure within the institution that supports it?

For more information, visit:
www.st-andrews.ac.uk/music/
www.sco.org.uk/education-project/orchestra-residence-university-of-st-andrews
www.st-andrews.ac.uk/music/perform/singers/opera/

Organising the National Pop League events

John Hunt, Carlo Zanotti and Charlotte Gilmore

It's hard to emphasize just how important NPL [National Pop League] has been to Glasgow's West End scene for almost this entire decade. As [John] Hunt [organiser and DJ] says non-boastfully, the club regularly welcomes members of Belle and Sebastian, Franz Ferdinand, Camera Obscura, Teenage Fanclub and The Pastels through its doors, yet an atmosphere of friendly inclusion to all prevails. His [John's] biggest pride in NPL has been inspiring others to form similar nights around the city. (*The List*, 17 July 2008)

John Hunt and the National Pop League

John Hunt works in finance. He is also a songwriter, playing guitar and singing with his band Butcher Boy. For seven years John was also the organiser, promoter and DJ for the National Pop League (NPL), a monthly indie club night at the Woodside Social Club in the West End area of Glasgow. The first NPL was in November 2001 and the last was in July 2008 – the 80th edition of NPL (each had its own number). In an interview at the time of the 80th NPL, John noted in a national magazine interview that: 'The Woodside's such a strange place, there's no air conditioning, and it's so hot that, at about one o'clock in the morning, it almost starts to feel like a dream. I'm glad I can look back on every single one in that way, rather than with any glass shards of reality in there' (*The List*, 17 July 2008). The decision to close NPL was informed by concerns for the future of the Woodside. It was sited in a residential area, and its owners were known to have had developers looking at the building. Additionally, new government legislation regarding door staff had had a subtle effect on the mood of the place. At the time John noted: 'I'm glad I made the decision to finish NPL while it's still really special . . . I would just hate to let it tail off' (*The List*, 17 July 2008). The following is the story of NPL.

The beginnings of NPL

You know sometimes you hear people say their entire life had been leading up to this one point – that this was the kind of sum total of everything that they had ever lived for. I think for John the inception of the National Pop League was maybe that point. (Carlo, ticket seller at NPL)

John started NPL because of his passion for music: 'I really love music, and for that reason ... it was a kind of different nightclub because it was people who were really passionate about music and that was the be all and end all of it.' For John, putting on the monthly NPL nights became an obsession. He liked the regularity of it, of having something specific to do that you have to work towards: 'It stops you wallowing in things, making sure that you do something creative constantly ... to have created something and to have some sort of reward for your effort.'

At that time, in the early 2000s in Glasgow, I think I am right in saying, there was not really anywhere you could go and have any chance of hearing something like say Orange Juice or The Darling Buds. There was really nowhere that served that kind of 'proper' indie scene, separate from the really big hitters like Oasis. I think NPL proved that gap existed – and quickly helped fill it. (Carlo)

A club called Offbeat in Sheffield, where John went to university, inspired the idea of NPL. Offbeat played indie pop music and it had an 'inclusive atmosphere'. After university John came back to Glasgow and tried to find a club like Offbeat, but he couldn't, so he began NPL. John was 'indefatigable' in terms of the amount of work he put into NPL:

to the point where I got kind of obsessed ... so I would say every single month, we have to do this and we have to build it, I knew that if we did not do it, if we did not work really hard then it was not going to succeed, so I had a couple of friends who were keen to help with it at the start but what was important was I really wanted it to be an inclusive kind of club and to be really welcoming and not to be snobbish. What I wanted to do was to have it in a social club environment, so it was quite welcoming, it was quite, well I guess a bit down at the heel, and people felt comfortable ... it was really important that people were comfortable there, so I found a venue like that.

To John the venue of the NPL night was important to create the right kind of atmosphere, and the Woodside Social Club was the perfect venue.

The Woodside Social Club

That is what it [NPL] was about, it was about music and it was about dancing.

According to Carlo, John 'meticulously worked out' finding the 'right kind of venue':

An easy option would have been for John to have hired a city centre club, but that would have contradicted the kind of club I think he wanted to create. Most people I know dislike the city centre on a weekend night. It's busy and boozy – as was NPL – however, in the centre there's often a tension that suggests something unpleasant will happen at any given point. As far as I understand it, it was exactly that kind of tension John wanted NPL to exist outside of. The Woodside Social Club – where the Boys' Brigade was founded in 1883 – was perfect.

The Woodside 'was not very dowdy, but it was not terribly fabulous. It had that kind of bashed charm.' The venue was on North Woodside Road, just off Great Western Road in Glasgow, with seating for around 150 people, and capacity for around 300 people in total. When the nights began, the ticket price was £2 and by the end it was £4. In keeping the ticket price low John was aware that he could have lost money 'because I had costs and we did not know if anyone was going to come'.

The fanzine packs

Inside the little plastic packs there was always a sweet, always a badge and always a fanzine. Sometimes we would try to marry up whatever was going on at the time – for example, Halloween, Christmas or Wimbledon – with what went onto the badge. So on the great day of the smoking ban we had a badge that emulated the classic 'No Smoking' sign. I still have most of the packs, and the sweets are in varying states of decomposition (Carlo).

After finding the Woodside, John started working, in the summer of 2001, towards the first NPL. This 'inaugural meeting' happened on 9 November 2001. John's idea from the very start was to have fanzines to give to people as they came into the club: 'to let people know what it was all about and why we were doing it'. These individually numbered fanzines became another creative outlet for John. He would handwrite a master copy and then run off 100 copies of it every month, and design an accompanying badge that, alongside a sweet, were packaged up and presented to the first 100 people through the door. John explained his motivation for the fanzine: 'I love writing, so I wanted to do something . . . it was like a manifesto, about how a particular song would make me feel, how much I loved it and why I was so happy to share it with other people, and there was such a positive response to that.' The fanzine always had a cartoon from Charles Schulz's *Peanuts* series in it, because John is a massive *Peanuts* fan, and there would always be some song lyrics. The amount of work put into preparing these individual fanzines was enormous: 'I would make these up for every one that I did and I would give it out to everyone that came, and I am really glad that I did it, but I look back at it now and I cannot believe how much work it was.'

The playlists

I had internal rules: I would not repeat songs from one month to the next.

John also spent a lot of time getting the playlist right: 'it was always meticulously planned right down to the last minute what we were going to play'. Each track had to 'fit' together and each month the playlist would be entirely different:

What I loved was being able to getting each track to fit and I would spend twelve hours doing the playlist and getting it to fit coherently as a journey. Just things that you would not think about, playing Shirley Ellis and playing soul records and then fitting them beside The Smiths and how do you do it. If you listen to something like 'Accept Yourself', which is just a Motown beat, you would play a Motown record beside it and suddenly it works. You get this really diverse music but you try to knit it into a whole and I think that was as important as anything else with it.

'On the posters, John came up with this sort of three-line whip: "postpunk, c.86, indiepop". That one line perfectly communicated what people could expect to hear. And just to absolutely make sure, below the line was a roll-call of typical bands and artists' (Carlo). John played the records on CD format for the whole night, so:

In a lot of ways I did not enjoy it too much because I was worried about things going wrong: CDs could still go wrong and skip and that was an absolute nightmare. I would have a ritual of cleaning the CD players before I did every single night and ... every single month I never ever once took it for granted that people were going to come.

The only chat John gave over the course of the night would be 'either something like a wallet has been found or just before the third last song he would say: "Last three songs of the night coming up, thanks very much for coming, next Pop League is August whatever, hope to see you there". There was no chat.'

Postering Saturdays

When I did the National Pop League every month without fail I went around Glasgow putting up posters, making sure that I did it every month ... two Saturdays before the National Pop League it was postering Saturday.

In addition to the playlist and fanzine packs, John also spent time designing posters and distributing them across Glasgow. On the posters there would be a list of the types of band who would be played on the night, and there would always be an image on them. 'It was different every month and another cool thing was that there was always a little headline that was different for every one as well.'

NPL people

You would get people from various bands, like various members of Belle and Sebastian would come down . . . it was a loyal following . . . it is funny looking back on it because it grew itself really and it became quite a special place for people.

NPL sold out most nights and it soon built up a loyal following:

you would just go and sit and you could speak to your friends and have a drink if you wanted, it was a social club feel which was what was important . . . I feel proud of it in a lot of ways because a lot of people met other people there and people have got married that have met there . . . I feel really proud about it because of that.

The people who went were looking for something a bit more genteel, 'and where there is virtually no chance of a fight and where you won't get laughed at if you dance on your own'.

The bar queues

It was just one quite small bar and lots and lots of people.

The bar queues at NPL were notorious: sometimes people would queue for forty-five minutes for a drink. However, on the whole people used to queue politely for drinks: 'when you go to the National Pop League you queue, you don't push in, that is the kind of people that were coming to it'. John had attempted to sort this issue by instigating a can bar in order to aid a quick transaction, 'but it never got off the ground, I don't think they (the staff at the Woodside Social Club) went for it, for whatever reason. That would certainly be a complaint you would hear quite often; that, and "Do you have a cloakroom?", which we didn't.'

Piece written after event

Hunt distributes a little personal email reminiscence after every club, harking back to a culture of fanzines and limited-release vinyl rarities (*The List*, 17 July 2008).

After each NPL night John would write an email to the NPL mailing list. The messages sought to capture the essence of the previous night and often his feelings towards particular songs: 'I might have been walking about town and listening to a particular song that had moved me in a certain way, and that is what the night was about, that kind of experience.' For John, these pieces were a way of creating a dialogue with the NPL attendees:

you have got 1,000 people on your mailing list and it is funny because you think about it and sometimes you worry about what you are saying . . . you think '1,000 people going to read this . . .' but the way I started thinking about it was that I was

writing this for one person, so you invite a dialogue ... you would get quite a lot
back from what you'd send out.

The smoking ban

The Woodside Social Club had quite a narrow entryway. With people
arriving, or making their way to the toilets, the area would quickly become
congested. The ban on smoking in enclosed public places (2006) contributed further to this congestion.

You would have all your smokers trying to go out and it would create a kind of
collision and also it is a residential area ... so there were concerns about people
making noise after midnight ... people kind of gathering outside or meandering up
and down the street whilst they are smoking so that became slightly problematic.

To overcome this problem John established a pass system where only
three people could go out at any one time.

Bouncers

I used to just have a couple of friends who would come, they did tae kwon do, they
used to come and stand on the door, just for security, but after that [legislation]
you had to have official door staff: for every 100 people you had to have one
member of door staff and the venue started getting in these guys on the door ...
and that really rankled with me, I guess that was just the beginning of the end
because I thought I don't want to do this now.

In the last six to twelve months of the night, new government legislation
regarding bouncers also contributed to the decision to close NPL. John
felt that the presence of bouncers on the door searching bags did not fit
with the NPL ethos:

The NPL tried to separate itself from the less pleasant facets of going out and the
age we live in, but the bouncers were old school and used to chucking folk out,
fights and things like that, and we had people going to the place who were really not
going to start a fight, so it was slightly out of step.

This was when John started seriously thinking about winding the NPL
nights down. He did not really want to, but then he 'did not want it to
fizzle out, I wanted to go out on a real high when it was still as popular as it
had ever been and I feel really glad that I did it then'. John captured these
sentiments and his feelings about the ending of NPL, in his last email to
the NPL mailing list:

There are a number of mundane reasons for ending the Pop League now. I really
can't see the Woodside being open for much longer ... if it makes it to the end of

this year I will be very surprised. It's being run into the ground. The new door staff don't help – even though I have nothing to do with them, I feel personally responsible for their actions. I also, simply, am finding it increasingly hard work to put together something I feel entirely happy with – I worry about the playlists being repetitive, about songs skipping, making a mess of the night...

...The terrible thing is, I know that I could quite easily put together a night every month and be done with it. I could cheat; could lift old playlists, line up forty songs from midnight till two that I know would keep the dance floor busy and put my feet up. But if I don't have a struggle with it, if I don't feel as if I have moulded every detail of the night carefully, then I don't feel as if I've done it justice. What is at the heart of the Pop League is perhaps what is most important in the world to me; to be anything other than devoted to it makes a mockery of that.

What John was alluding to in the last line of his email was that he was afraid of running out of steam and of not being able to give everything he could to NPL. The 'bind' that John found himself in was that he would no longer be able to pay tribute to all of the things he loved so much: 'but then I realised these songs would stay mine anyway, and they'd always be in me'.

The spirit of NPL lives on through John's occasional 'Little League' club nights in Glasgow.

The building once housing the Woodside Social Club has been developed into luxury flats.

Key lessons

- Organisational aesthetics and personal communication construct a clear identity, and in so doing creating a loyal organisational following (see Chapters 7 and 15).
- Commitment and meticulous organisation are required to create and sustain a regular club night event.
- External factors such as government legislation have an impact on event organisation (see Chapter 13).

Discussion questions

- What organisational tasks did John undertake for each club night, and why?
- What are the 'internal rules' John talks about?
- If you ran a club night, what would be your internal rules? And what choices of aesthetic organisational communication would you create?

Starting a record label: Song, by Toad

Matthew Young and Dimitrinka Stoyanova Russell

Background

Song, by Toad is a small independent record label based in Scotland, which is run by Matthew Young. Starting the label was not planned. Matthew describes it as '99 per cent by accident'. Nor did it happen overnight. Matthew had a strong interest in music, but also a day job in a design engineering studio. Because of his interest in music, he started writing about it on the internet. His initial drive was the design of the site: he was using it as a place to put his own portfolio in search of design commissions and he also liked 'playing' with the design of the website. A friend then suggested he might write reviews on it, and so Matthew started sharing information and views on music on his blogging site. There was also a more personal element to this: his family was away at the time and he wanted to keep them informed about his tastes, likes, excitements. He started to enjoy writing more and more. By 2006 his blogging traffic became quite busy, and his blog became popular and gained good standing within the music community.

The record label grew out of this blog. By 2007 Matthew had managed to establish a reputation for being able to spot new interesting bands such as Twilight Sad, Frightened Rabbit, Broken Records and Sparrow and the Workshop. A number of bands got record deals, in part, as a result of his reviews and publicity.

Starting the label

One of these upcoming bands, Broken Records, was the stimulus for the establishment of the record label. There were many bands Matthew liked that he suspected others might not know about. So he thought that he might help them to self-release or to release demo CDs to bloggers and music journalists and reviewers. In August 2007 Broken Records were playing in Leith and, in the euphoria of the gig, Matthew and his partner Kate promised that they would release an album for the band if they did not get signed elsewhere. Everyone was very enthusiastic. At least until the following morning, when Matthew and Kate realised they had made a promise they did not quite know how to fulfil!

The next few months passed in continuous discussions about how they could make the release. The main questions Matthew considered were how big an investment to make, whether to pay for PR, and whether or not to release online. Over the course of the following year (2008) Matthew and Kate continued to think and discuss, and finally decided to do the release on their own label; thus, the label 'Song, by Toad' was launched in July.

After Broken Records, the next album to be released was by Meursault. In the following few years Matthew was juggling a number of things: he was writing the blog, running the record label and continuing to work full time. The label was doing well. They had four or five releases and Meursault's second album created a lot of buzz. Matthew was really busy and getting increasingly very tired. He remembers he and his wife had a summer holiday, during which he slept for nearly twenty-two hours continuously. Being on the verge of complete exhaustion, Matthew decided to take a risk on the success of Song, by Toad and handed in his notice to quit his day job.

Releasing albums

It is standard that the label makes 'a run of 300' copies which, if sold, cover the expenses for the production and provide a few hundred pounds for the band and the label. Most of the songs released by the label have made revenue of a few thousand pounds, but only a few have broken even when costs are taken into account. The label sells in Avalanche Records, a small independent record store in Edinburgh. Most of the albums are CDs, although a few have been vinyl. The label can only afford to have one or the other. One of the exceptions was Meursault's second album, which they produced both as vinyl and as CD.

Learning from experience

Matthew had 1,000 copies of Meursault's second album hand-printed. The inserts were folded – a small element in all of them had to be coloured by hand – and all 1,000 copies were posted in order to be at the venue in time for the album's launch party. Then, unfortunately, or perhaps fortunately, Matthew realised that they had put the wrong CD in all 1,000 sleeves, which now contained the demo instead of the final version of the album. Something needed to be done. Matthew quickly had another

1,000 CDs handmade and posted them to Edinburgh, where the album launch party was going to be. But the courier company (for some unknown reason) took them to Berwick instead of Edinburgh. It was the day of the release. Matthew considered personally going to Berwick to collect the copies but then decided to 'stick to his guns with the courier company'. He argued with them, insisting it was their responsibility to get the CDs to Edinburgh, until they hired a third party who drove them up for the launch. The CDs arrived only half an hour before the doors opened, so Matthew and his colleagues had thirty minutes to replace the demo CDs with the new copies.

Matthew remembers being at his day job that day and having to make a large number of phone calls from the office, introducing himself as 'Matthew Young from Toad Records', and arguing with the courier company in the middle of an office of people working on engineering projects. Matthew found it embarrassing.

Having been through the stress of the CD release on the day of the launch, Matthew now does everything in advance. The company gets the promo copies well ahead of the release – about a month in advance. Then they start the manufacturing process, the final artwork and sending it to print. Matthew himself does the final layout and much of the artwork for many of the releases. As a result, more recent album launches have run 'with military precision'.

The true nightmare...

There was one project, however, which was a 'hellish nightmare' of 'epic proportions'. The musician was someone Matthew liked on first hearing. His blog readers thought the opposite. But Mathew persevered. The artist was already in conversations with a big label, but nine months later Mathew received an email from the musician asking him whether he was interested in releasing his album. The release of the album went well. But the 'disaster' came when Matthew tried to get the artist on tour.

Booking the venues proved problematic. For example, they had just booked a venue in Edinburgh and had the posters printed when the venue closed down, which meant they had to put a halt on the publicity around the gig. Moreover, it was approaching December and many venues were already booked. Finding an alternative was stressful. They eventually managed to secure a venue in Edinburgh, but then the one in Glasgow closed. Matthew had to have the posters printed very quickly and posted, only to start realising that the concerts were clashing with many other events, especially those around the Christmas season.

But that was not all. On the week of the shows, the support act dropped out. Matthew started frantically phoning around to find a replacement, which he did, only for the weather to turn against him. On the night of the Aberdeen date there was a major snowfall: the audience was significantly reduced, meaning that Toad Records ended up losing a considerable sum of money. Matthew's philosophy is that sometimes things happen and one has to accept this. Making the best decision at the time with the information available and not regretting it is how issues are to be solved. Matthew also admits that he did not want to give up. He calls it 'stubbornness'. He thinks this is the message a record label should be sending to their artists: not giving up but getting through difficulties. As he says: 'we can just do things, you just get on with it and you will be okay'. This was the principle he built the record label on.

Many people want to have their songs released by Toad Records because they know him personally and trust him. The bands know that they will be paid immediately and treated well. They also know that the company will put in serious effort to promote them. Matthew gets annoyed by people in the music business who just talk and do not act, especially with so many good bands coming out all the time. For Matthew, the most important thing is endurance: persevering and continuing to do the business in the way he thinks is fair and right, not being guided only by the number of albums sold. According to him, coming across as honest and frank – a consistent voice – is far more important than having a targeted brand building exercise.

Having been asked a number of times how one can self-release or what is needed to release an album, Matthew prepared a file with a check list, which is publicly available on his blog.

Key lessons

- Developing a good reputation and networking within the music industry is important (see Chapters 7 and 11).
- When developing a DIY label, the nature of organising is 'learning as you go' (see Chapter 16).
- DIY labels have an artistic led approach as opposed to a commercially led approach (see Chapter 2).

Discussion questions

- Reflect on Matthew's experiences of starting his record label: what were the main organisational issues he experienced?

- Describe how you would go about setting up a label. How would you attract artists? What would you consider when organising tours and gigs?
- What constitutes a 'good' blog?

For more information, visit:
www.songbytoad.com

Traditional music and the network

Lori Watson and Charlotte Gilmore

Background

Lori Watson is a Scottish traditional music specialist with a portfolio of projects including performance, composition, youth music and research. She is a BBC Scotland Young Traditional Musician of the Year 2002 and 2003 finalist, has toured extensively and broadcast on radio, television and the internet. Lori performs regularly with her award-winning band, Lori Watson and Rule of Three, and her self-produced debut album was released in 2006, followed by *Pleasure's Coin* in 2009.

In 2006 Lori composed a piece of music that was performed as part of the Distil Showcase. Distil is a professional development programme set up in 2002 for professional traditional musicians. The Showcase began as a route for the musicians to continue to develop their ideas and to provide the first major public platform for these developing composers. Each year, musicians submit their compositions, ideas and proposals to the Distil Showcase; between seven and twelve are selected for the live event. The selected pieces are then rehearsed and played by a professional music ensemble for an audience at a well-known concert venue.

This is Lori's story of, and reflections on, her first experience of the Distil Showcase – a live performance in which she felt there were 'lots of levels of non-success'.

The composition

Lori's tunes, songs, extended and experimental compositions explore issues surrounding the question of innovation and creativity in a contemporary Scottish context. These issues are also the basis for Lori's PhD studies, which she was undertaking at the Royal Conservatoire of Scotland (now successfully completed). This story explores Lori's combination of composition, organising a major performance and application of ideas derived from research. Her research considers a musical and verbal dialogue in the traditional music world in Scotland between convention and innovation, which exists within and between the practitioners. Some musicians believe innovation is a threat to the preservation of tradition: it is seen as damaging the perceived integrity of the traditions. But others, including Lori, view creativity as integral to tradition: 'You know I want to be creative and I want to put my own stamp on things, express myself, or even learn more about who I am by interacting in my own way with things.'

For her Distil composition Lori explored her feelings of becoming a traditional musician. Musically, at the time of Distil Lori was becoming 'experimental' and 'adventurous'; 'I was just finding my feet creatively'. She was beginning to enjoy more of a contemporary sound, involving some forms of improvisation and melodies that were unconventional. Lori developed these ideas within her Distil composition; she felt that it would appeal to a Distil folk audience because 'they are more adventurous than the concert-going kind of fiddle playing audiences'. Lori wanted to challenge the audience to engage with their preconceptions of traditional music.

Lori's composition was a twelve-minute piece called 'Inheritance Converse'. The piece was written for an ensemble of fiddle, Border pipes, percussion, accordion and cello. The composition opened up 'with a kind of session feel'; she wanted to start off with something easily recognisable, but that would 'very quickly degrade or just fall apart … shatter into something quite uncomfortable and unrecognisable'. The session and dance themes were mixed with the voices of traditional musicians she had interviewed and recorded for the purposes of her research. These audio clips were then used to create a 'backdrop conversation' to the musical composition. The clips were the snippets of her fieldwork conversations with contemporary and traditional singers and musicians. The research conversations explored these musicians' perceptions of contemporary traditional music and its future. Lori chose particular pieces of recordings that 'jumped out' at her – for example, one older musician remarking: 'all these young musicians sound the same to me'. By using these audio clips Lori sought to create a 'conversation' with the audience, to question their own relationship with traditional music – for example, how they view it and what it might mean to them, or how they view the treatment of it.

Lori felt that she made the 'classic mistake of trying to be too clever' by putting too many concepts into one composition. In retrospect, Lori felt that she was asking a lot of the audience to pick up all the ideas that she was trying to express; she was asking a lot of the musicians to try to communicate all her ideas; and she was asking a lot of herself to try to encapsulate all these different ideas in one composition. As Lori was becoming more experimental with her music, 'Inheritance Converse' provided her with the opportunity to 'throw all these ideas away' so that she could have 'more creative freedom' in order for her to develop and learn as an artist. After the Distil experience, Lori learned to trust and value her 'split-second decisions that you don't notice you're making', rather than follow other musicians' preconceived notions of music.

The event organisation

There were some organisational aspects of the event that made Lori's experience difficult and contributed to her piece not going as well as it should have. The composers were inexperienced and the event organisers were also inexperienced; thus, both were both developing new skills, and in a sense 'everyone was learning on the job'. The composers were developing new composition skills by writing new music, and the players were 'trying to keep up' performing the 'new and weird music'. In musician terms, 'everything was happening at the cutting edge'; therefore, in organisation terms, there was a 'large margin for error', particularly as they had hired musicians based on the general instrumental needs of the composers rather than hiring specific musicians for each of the pieces. While all her ensemble musicians were very good, Lori's players would have been different if she had a free choice of the musicians for 'Inheritance Converse'. She had not anticipated that some of the musicians would find her composition challenging – for example, they had 'not dealt with syncopation', a feature of her piece and widely used in contemporary traditional music. In fact, Lori had been worried that her music was not going to be challenging enough for the musicians: 'another rooky mistake'.

The ensemble had not played together prior to the Distil Showcase. There were two rehearsals before the live performance in the concert venue: the first was two weeks prior to the event, and the other was on the day of the Showcase. The first rehearsal took place in a country hotel room, which had a very different environment and acoustic from the live concert space. Distil's musical director came to help Lori direct her rehearsal.

The musicians had rehearsed Lori's composition individually but had not played it together. Lori regrets not being confident enough to direct her piece musically in the hotel rehearsal; she was intimidated because the ensemble musicians were older and well-respected professionals. Crucially, Lori did not have the confidence to tell them to leave out or change the sections of the composition they were struggling with – in particular the piper, who could not play one section of his piece. Lori's position with the piper had been undermined when he brought to her attention some small mistakes on his section of the score, and so she did not want to make their relationship more uncomfortable by being directive. In any case, throughout the rehearsal process it remained unclear to Lori whether she had the final say on the musical direction of her composition. Nevertheless, she would have appreciated the authority of the Distil musical director's backing at some point in front of the musicians. On reflection, with the benefit of eight years of experience, Lori notes that she would not care 'how old or experienced [the musicians are]': she would now take ownership of the direction because if her name was on the piece her reputation would be at stake. 'I think communicating my artistic vision is paramount here: reputation wouldn't matter if the music sounded the way I intended.'

Lori was worried after these rehearsals, but at the same time she was excited: 'it was exciting to hear it in any other form apart from my head . . . that was really exciting . . . but I was frustrated and worried because it had not gotten to where I felt it should be by then'. In particular, at this stage Lori had not prepared the musicians enough for the audio backdrop, which in retrospect is what she thinks must have felt like 'a strange interruption' to them during the live performance. This backdrop was an improvisation of the research voice recordings coordinated by an electro-acoustic musician, Alastair. Lori reflected that, had there been enough rehearsal time, the musicians should have spent more time working with Alastair to acclimatise to playing 'against' the 'weird noises coming out of the laptop'.

Lori also regrets that she did not collaborate with Alastair on the improvisation. The actual process was quite linear, and so the piece did not benefit from their combined expertise. Rather, Lori gave the composition to Alastair, and he came back with some changes to the piece, and Lori rewrote some sections. However, a more collaborative approach would have allowed her to communicate her ideas more effectively to him. At the same time, it would also have allowed her to integrate more of Alastair's knowledge and experience into the set-up of the piece.

294   *Lori Watson and Charlotte Gilmore*

The second rehearsal on the day of the performance was in a practice room in the concert venue. The composers and musicians had to bring some of their own equipment to set up, which ate into their three-hour rehearsal time. Because of the set-up time, the actual playing time was just less than two hours. Lori's piece was just one of ten that the ensemble were rehearsing prior to the performance, and so 'it felt rushed'. There were technical issues throughout the set-up of the performance: the computer kept crashing throughout the pre-performance rehearsal. By the time it came to do the live performance Lori knew that she was asking a 'huge amount of the musicians, I was really asking them to stick their neck out and do something that was quite scary for all of them'. In hindsight, Lori would now 'write a five-minute piece on one idea to keep it more contained'. However, the Distil organisers had not stipulated any guidelines (there was a time limit of twelve or fifteen minutes) for composers, which meant that for the live performance of their pieces the musicians had to make sacrifices, because the organisational set-up was not able to deal with the variety of requirements made by the compositions. In this sense, Lori was not helped by the organisational set-up of the event, particularly in terms of the musicians' choice of rehearsal time and spaces. In addition, Lori was not made aware prior to the event that the organisers had designed an acoustic programme, which did not work for Lori's piece. Given the event's technical constraints, 'we ended up with kind of a half-way house': an inadequate PA system, which was set up on the day of the performance.

The organisers have learned from their shortcomings and the event has changed and runs far more smoothly than in Lori's first year: 'I cannot say a bad word about the project, I think it is fantastic.' The organisers now choose musicians who are currently working in ensembles, and not disparate individuals brought together specifically for the event. The composers are also given more of a framework and starting point in terms of the technical specification and ensemble they are writing for.

The performance

On the night of the Showcase there were 250 people in the audience. The atmosphere in the concert venue was 'really formal'. At the beginning of the performance the computer crashed, so everyone had to wait for it to reboot. To 'save the atmosphere a little bit' in the concert hall and because the first section had a session atmosphere, Lori went on stage with a tray of drinks for the musicians, which she had waiting by the stage as a thank you for after the performance. Everyone was sitting in silence so Lori going on stage broke the tensions a little; it made the musicians and audience laugh 'a little'.

Once the piece began, Lori, who was sitting in the third row from the front could 'feel the atmosphere from behind . . . I could feel confusion'. In the context of the other 'polite acoustic' compositions, her piece was 'a bit like a barrage to the senses'. This is what excited Lori about the piece; however, the audience did not have the time to 'tune in' and 'get acclimatised' to the new level of sound and so they were missing the 'clues' to the piece – that is, the details in the audio 'conversation' about traditional music. Other than the computer crashing at the start, the electronic section was as Lori had intended it to be, but the audience and reviewers 'did not get it'. In the discussion about the piece afterwards, audience members thought that the problem had been with the electronic piece element rather than with the musicians' band (although the electro-acoustic person was also a musician).

The ensemble had not had enough of a sound check. The individual musicians were amplified for the electro-acoustic desk rather than for the hall. Once the performance began it became evident that there was an imbalance between the volume of instruments and the electro-acoustic set-up. The pipes were too loud, and this was a problem when the piper 'messed up' the section he had found difficult in rehearsal: 'he thought he could manage it but he was taking a big risk on my piece'. From this point the piece began to fall apart, because the rest of the ensemble, who had been taking their lead from the pipes (it being the loudest instrument), lost their places in the score. Although the Distil musical director was conducting at the front, being traditional musicians 'nobody paid attention to him'. In the end, the piece was 'saved a little' by the fiddle player, who shouted one of the marker numbers in a section of the score; this allowed the other musicians to find where she was in the piece and enabled them to come back together for the last section.

The aftermath

Immediately after the piece finished Lori sat with her head in her hands. She was frustrated that all she could do was sit there, watching her piece fall apart. Lori was unsure of the audience reaction and feeling bad for the musicians: 'I was frustrated, hysterical and just full of tension and release . . . but I had to be really polite'. Lori was sitting next to one of the other composers, who turned 'with a really enthusiastic face' to ask her what she thought of the performance. In Lori's mind it had been a 'complete disaster', so that was 'absolutely the worst thing' anyone could have said to her. Lori recalled: '. . . it was such an intense moment when you can hear blood thumping in your head . . . I am not violent but in my head I think I might have punched her in the face'.

Lori was getting herself 'really tangled up worrying what other people thought I was feeling'. She wanted to thank the musicians but she was not able to look any of them in the eye. And at the drinks reception after the performance, Lori was 'on autopilot, drank a lot of wine', brushed off comments and suppressed her emotions. Members of the press and audience were coming up to her tentatively, not sure whether she was upset about it or not. Lori felt that she had let the audience down, even though she appreciated that her experience of the performance had been different to theirs.

Being in the audience meant that Lori felt she was 'not in control of her remit', which she found was difficult because of her emotional and ideo-logical investment. The whole experience 'scared' Lori because she felt out of her depth from start to finish: '. . . at the time I was just beating myself up thinking about it . . . I was expecting far more of myself and not being forgiving about . . . Now I see all the mistakes . . . accept responsi-bility for it . . . it was my first attempt, so I am ok about it'. However, it has taken a long time for Lori to listen to and reflect on the music 'and really not cringe so much that I cannot hear it'.

Lori cringed throughout her telling of Distil Showcase tale: 'I remem-ber how bad it felt at the time and so remembering that . . . re-enacting the flinches, I think'. For some time Lori could not bear to reflect on the performance experience and she could not move on to other creative composition projects. She wishes that she had realised the effect the performance had had on her at the time: 'I still have not really reflected on it . . . I have been wading around in this stuff for far too long without having any conclusion or closure'. After the Distil experience Lori did not compose a piece of music for a year and a half. During this time she gigged and wrote songs for her album, but she could not move forward with her traditional composition. Lori has now moved on to other projects: 'I've kind of buried it and not been able to extract what I should have from it: I think I have to go back and do that . . . that is probably the final stage . . . that is what is holding me up from putting an end to everything'.

Key lessons

• Know your audience(s): when communicating innovative practice and ideas, as a composer and musician you need to know the 'repertoire' (and tastes) of your audience (in this case, both performers and concert-goers) (see Chapters 10 and 12).

- Lori had to enact different identities during her Distil experience, and these affected her interactions with the musicians, organisers and audience and her own experience of the performance. Lori is a mix of composer, performer, researcher and up-and-coming name. Some of these identities interact to make things more difficult – for example, being a composer and up-and-coming/not yet fully established (see Chapters 6 and 15).
- Lori's reflexive account of the story illustrates that she has sought to draw lessons from the event to apply to her current practice (see Chapter 3).
- The organisational practices of the Distil event contributed to Lori's problems as a composer and organiser of the performance of her music (see Chapter 17).

Discussion questions

- Using the YouTube clip of Lori's performance and the Distil event, reflect on and discuss the aim of the event and different pieces of music performed. Do you think it is possible both to preserve the tradition and to be innovative with the music?
- List, explain and discuss some of the problems faced by Lori as a composer and Lori as a performance manager. How do these identities and sets of problems differ? How could Lori have dealt with these problems differently?
- Consider and discuss how the Distil organisers contributed to Lori's problems as manager and composer. If you were organising such events, what would be the key lessons you would bear in mind?
- Examine Lori's reaction to the 'Inheritance Converse' performance. What do you feel this reveals about composing and performing, and the relationship between the two?

For more information, visit:
  ruleofthreemusic.com
  boreasband.com
  islemusicscotland.com

Multiple simultaneous projects in traditional and electronica and orchestral music

Chris Stout and Charlotte Gilmore

When I was younger I spent too much time searching for a music world in which I belonged and felt accepted: now I have a self-belief that what I am doing is enough so that I don't have to seek the acceptance of one particular genre of music or another, whether it be folk music or classical or jazz. I just make my music and present it to people, and those who want to listen to it are happy with what it is rather than trying to pigeonhole it.

Background

Chris Stout is a dynamic and charismatic fiddle player, composer and producer from the Shetland Islands. His diverse styles of playing and composing are rooted in traditional, contemporary and classical styles. Chris's ambition to collaborate and discover music from around the world has taken him to countless countries such as Brazil, Japan, Jordan, Algeria and Norway. As well as working in traditional line-ups, Chris has composed for and performed with the BBC Scottish Symphony Orchestra, the Royal Scottish National Orchestra (RSNO) and the Singapore Chinese Orchestra. He continues to innovate within traditional and contemporary musical circles as a solo artist, a member of Fiddlers' Bid, a leader of his own quintet and the True North Orchestra, or one half of his duo with long-time musical associate Catriona McKay.

In 2011 Chris released *Chris Stout's Brazilian Theory Live*. This was a live recording of an ambitious collaborative performance between Brazilian and Scottish musicians, which took to the stage in Glasgow during the Celtic Connections festival. The concert was described in a UK national newspaper as 'a gloriously exuberant and at times emotionally glowing collaboration'. The following is his story of this collaboration, in which he contrasts the improvisational nature of this performance with composing a new piece of work called 'Tingaholm' for the RSNO, which was premiered in Shetland in March 2012 as part of their Out and About tours.

Chris's diverse collaborations

In a successful collaboration I aim to make music where you can't tell where the genre-specific boundaries are. I think when you start to consider where the elements are, there is something that maybe hasn't been achieved in really making honest music, if it's too obvious where the styles are. And so my aim is to work with musicians regardless of genre and make an emotional connection with a musician rather than a connection through a style or other people's perceptions of what you should play like.

Chris talked about playing in an 'open' rather than 'pure' way when collaborating, so that there are not 'two styles of music, which are struggling to come out of their own pure worlds'. He believes that for a collaboration to work certain compromises have to be made, and a musician has to be realistic about which elements of the music can work together and which don't. Chris gave an example of a highland bagpipe tune played in its most pure form over an African drumbeat: the piece is never going to sound like anything other than a Highland pipe tune played over an African drumbeat. If the musicians are relaxed in the styles of both genres of music, then there is a chance of making something new that people can relate to a little bit, and either accept or not, but at least it works as a musical piece.

I think I have a style of my own because it has evolved through time and I have allowed it to be influenced by so much ... I don't feel that I need to bend my style so much now to accommodate other styles. I have never played traditional music in a purist way. I have allowed my music to be influenced by whatever musical style I have come into contact with; I have allowed it to influence my style directly, whether it be Brazilian music, jazz or classical. I come from a place where the tradition is very, very secure, and in safe hands, so I have the confidence to reach out.

For Chris, improvisation is about going beyond what he knows, about searching to create different sounds:

The success of real improvisation is difficult to define: it can vary so much. If you are really improvising you shouldn't just be regurgitating what you already know. I can't say that I always achieve this ultimate freedom; sometimes you do rely on things you know to make a success of it, but I aspire to that freedom.

For example:

In the performance of the Brazilian collaboration there were genuine moments of improvisation, where the musicians and the audience were BOTH experiencing something new ... it's nice to turn round to your colleagues with an element of surprise at what has just happened, as well as an audience perhaps responding to it, you know: 'Oh, I didn't expect that'. It's a good feeling, rather than everything being rehearsed and organised, like a presentation to an audience, to entertain them, it's quite a good feeling to be able to step away from that for moments, and just make yourself vulnerable and then create something brand new, and that kind of energy and excitement and freshness can't be practised: it's something that can just happen. When it's successful you know that you've just created something on the spot, which is really good, and it's great for an audience to be with you there – they become a part of the whole experience. So it's not just a 'we'll entertain you' sort of thing. It's important where they are, how many people there are, how they feel, how they make you feel, you know, so everything becomes really important. I really enjoy that aspect of music, and respond to it a lot: it's not always easy, but as a musician I am very aware of that, rather than going into a rehearsal studio and making sure that everything is going to be perfect, just doing the same. It's exciting. Don't get me wrong – it's not like every single gig I don't know what's going on, you have to know what you are doing. I just like to leave five per cent or ten per cent of a gig to chance so that I feel excited by it, or excitement and nerves, and I want to keep performing so that I never feel like Groundhog Day, because every night is different. I think a lot of musicians would be the same.

However, that being said, Chris still felt that there was need to:

deliver structured music to people so they have very clear points of reference that they can hold on to. It has to be structured so that people don't just feel lost in that sound: they still have to feel that they are being drawn through music. Even if it is internal, the audience cannot just feel like they don't know what is going to happen, or if they don't know what is going to happen, the musicians need to support and give them the confidence that it will become structured at some point so they can relax. An hour and a half of unstructured music can be pretty hardcore you know ... you can leave a performance feeling a bit twisted. If it is that kind of concert then fine, but it is pretty niche.

Brazilian Theory

The album *Brazilian Theory* is a live recording of a performance at the 2010 Celtic Connections Folk Festival. Chris collaborated with regular musical partner and harpist Catriona McKay, together with Brazilian guitarist Carlinhos Antunes and Swiss-born violinist/saxophonist Thomas Rohrer to perform some of the music originally explored in São Paulo in 2003 with Orquestra Scotland Brasil. In 2010 Chris reformed this group of musicians because he had a desire to explore in more detail the collaborative potential between his own traditional fiddle roots and Thomas's traditional rabeca, the Brazilian equivalent. Chris's main collaborator in the group was Thomas, who – according to Chris – is a 'very evolved' musician:

He has immersed himself in the world of free improvisation, and his music has been a great inspiration to me ... When you get two melody instruments then you can create chords or just create sound effects which work for each other, it does not have to be about playing notes, it can just be about creating sound. Sound without melody can also have a huge impact.

With Catriona McKay on the harp, Ian Stephenson on guitar and melodeon, Rui Barossi and Neil Harland on double bass and Martin O'Neill on bodhran, the musicians performed at Glasgow's City Hall for a concert featuring music composed by Stout, Antunes and Rohrer. The band had a couple of days' rehearsal just to play together, but a lot of the *Brazilian Theory* concert was improvised. It was the first time that Chris had put a performance together where there were so many players capable of improvising. 'There were moments where suddenly it would just go BANG and we were free to grow and grow in the music, where if you make it, it is so special, but if it falls on its backside, it would be terrible!' Chris talked about the art of improvisation as being:

... when you all grow as a group together, live on stage, you show that the situation is as important as the music you are making; the audience are involved in that – your relationship in the concert for the last hour has helped that improvisation because you are all happy and you can just pour yourselves out. You are also all in tune with each other as well, and you know what the audience wants to hear.

Especially at Celtic Connections, [the audience] were coming into see a 'collaboration' but I don't think they were expecting quite the level of improvisation, but because they were very clear about what was happening and they could see the communication, it was very visual, and people were just watching, and I think they felt a part of it. I felt it was really ... inclusive ... even although we are on edge at times – we never lost sight of the structure and the development of the music.

Leadership

A key factor in the 'art of improvisation' was the trusting relationships between the musicians, but not all the musicians within the group knew each other. Chris had chosen musicians he thought might respond to each other: the collaboration was made up of two sets of musicians that he had worked with before. Therefore, Chris took on the role as leader and was the linchpin in building the trust between the players: 'everyone knew that their common link was me and they all trusted me'. For Chris, having a leader is not essential but it can be an important factor in achieving a performance of a high musical standard: 'It is good to have a leader's vision and to create a framework within which the musicians have plenty of room to manoeuvre.'

'Tingaholm'

Chris was commissioned to compose a new piece called 'Tingaholm' for the RSNO, which was premiered in Shetland in March 2012 as part of their Out and About tours. Chris contrasted leading the improvisation with the *Brazilian Theory* project to leading the RSNO:

The situation is very different . . . we have small workshop sessions with some of the musicians and there will be a big one coming up with the whole string section where I have got to stand up and say, right guys, I want you to play like this, which you can imagine is quite stressful. I know once I do it I will feel stronger and able to put myself forward for other jobs like that again. I have to do it but I am not looking forward to it. It is scary.

For Chris, the RSNO workshop rehearsals were 'scary' because 'it is like standing up in front of amazing musicians who are highly trained and telling them how to play'. This situation was made more difficult because Chris's objective with his composition was to allow the orchestral players access to a way of playing that they were perhaps unfamiliar with: 'I wanted the composition to allow the musicians to experience a little bit of freedom of expression'.

Managing the workshops

Managing the workshops was a careful process. Chris shared techniques that were probably more familiar to traditional musicians with the orchestral musicians, but at the same time he was careful never to move too far away from the field of music in which these musicians were highly developed. In addition, Chris knew a number of the 'fiddle players'; because they were Scottish these players were familiar with his music – they understood what he does, in terms of mixing genres of music. However, some of the players came 'from another background', and were not familiar with Chris's music and techniques. Therefore, he had to also be careful not to 'divide the orchestra . . . because it is important that all these musicians still feel like they belong to the same group', so Chris didn't want to spend his time pointing out the players' differences.

Indeed, Chris talked about how writing the piece was the 'easy bit and getting it performed now is difficult'. As a composer, for him the piece was not about the crossover of genres; rather, it was about 'writing music that I like to listen to and that can be played by a group of musicians . . . at the moment it is all my life consists of'. One of the difficulties with the piece for Chris was that 'every note matters'. He was also not used to composing alone, being used to collaborating with other musicians:

Many conventional classical composers wouldn't collaborate – they compose and the musicians play it, whereas in other musical worlds they are used to composing and playing together. I think that is changing slowly, for the better. I think that the development of classical music has probably been stifled to a degree because it has always been about ... the composer is everything, he is god, the musicians will just follow him.

Chris doesn't feel 'that the creativity gap that between the musicians and the composer is a healthy one'.

Chris also noted the importance of getting the right conductor for his piece: 'he has not to over-conduct the music – he has to allow it to be free'. Chris needed the conductor to help him to articulate his words to the orchestra, and 'if he is open and we get on as people, we will be able to be successful'. Within this context, Chris described what he values in a good conductor: 'A good conductor is a great thing, and will realise the thoughts of the composer and draw the best out of the orchestra. A good conductor will lead the orchestra but still allow them the freedom to perform.'

Originally, the RSNO had asked Chris to write himself into the composition, which Chris felt would have made the job of being able to communicate with the string players much easier, 'because it easy for them to watch, or just follow, or just emulate'. However, he was not able to be at the performance due to other gig commitments, so he did not write a part for himself. While it was difficult for Chris to give over the control of his piece to the conductor, the fact that he was not playing in it helped him to overcome this. In addition, he knew that in order for the piece to be played by other orchestras, 'he needed to be more open'.

'Tingaholm': reviews and parliamentary motions

Latterly, in a review in the *Guardian* (6 March 2012), Kate Molleson described the RSNO live performance of Chris's composition:

Local fiddler Chris Stout was commissioned to write a piece for the occasion, and to include in it a tune that each team could arrange for a kind of inter-island playoff. Those versions had turned out brilliantly varied and imaginative; the full version, called 'Tingaholm' after Shetland's ancient Norse gathering point, was premiered in Lerwick.

As always, Stout's tunes are haunting, underpinned with earthy drones and ferocious, foot-stomping rhythms. He treats his violins like a band of Shetland fiddlers hurtling through a lopsided fugue, and fragments his melodies into rhythmic motives with shifting accents à la Stravinsky. There's a touch of Reich, too, in his ostinatos that loop until fadeout. Some of these tripped the orchestra – probably a mix of the score needing fine-tuning and the orchestra being under-rehearsed. There's great material here, though; I'd love to hear a repeat performance before long.

In addition, in the Scottish Parliament MSP Tavish Scott tabled a motion congratulating Shetland Arts and the RSNO on their successful partnership. Part of the motion read: 'Parliament congratulates Shetland Arts and the Royal Scottish National Orchestra for their collaborative Out and About in Shetland tour, involving 24 separate musical, cultural and educational events between 1 and 5 March 2012 and including The Sunday Symphony, featuring the premiere of Fair Isle-born Chris Stout's new RSNO-commissioned "Tingaholm", conducted by David Danzmayr.'

Key lessons

- As leader of a creative collaboration it is important to build trust between players, and to have a clear vision (see Chapter 14).
- The leadership styles in improvisation and as a composer have important differences.

Discussion questions

- What are the main differences between Chris's work on the Brazilian project and his work with the RSNO?
- What were the management issues faced by Chris when composing for and working with the RSNO?
- Reflect on Chris's experience of the 'art of improvisation': what are its key features?

For more information, visit:
www.chrisstout.co.uk

Storytelling and performance

R.M. Hubbert and Elizabeth Gulledge

Introduction

Hubby, an indie musician, discussed his experiences in a band and as a solo artist. Two key issues emerged in the account of his career trajectory. The first relates to the many roles played early in his career as manager, promoter and organiser in the industry. The second speaks to the process of becoming a musician and creating songs as a solo artist. Of particular note is how personal loss shaped his creative work. These formative experiences influenced his development as an artist.

Experiences in a band

I had a desire to become a musician relatively early. I saw a Buzzcocks video and got a hold of a guitar and started playing. I started my own band at age 17 and was doing a European tour by 18. The experience of playing on a European tour was eye-opening. I became aware that the life of a musician would include contrasting experiences. There are two types of live venues in Europe. There are 'squats', which are incredibly well organised. They provide free childcare and include the local community. However, a lot of these venues are a bit scabby and scary. The others are plush government-run venues that are clean and upscale. Musicians tend to receive proper food and accommodation at these places. As an 18-year-old this shaped how I understood what being a musician involved and how musicians are perceived and treated. I found it odd that the various experiences were so different.

Early on as a musician I found my way into organisational and managerial roles. I fell into this work haphazardly as a musician in bands. For example, once my band and I showed up at Thirteenth Note, a small but well-known venue, for a gig. I met a guy who put bands on on Tuesday night for free. We took part in this but nobody was showing up except the other bands. We found we were just listening to each other. The guy finally gave up doing this, and my friend and I volunteered to help out of

305

passion for live music and the desire to keep such an event running. I began seeking out ways to get young new bands in venues in Glasgow. My friend started to book bands and I ran the sound. Through this experience I developed a network of musicians and other industry contacts as I continued to experiment with ways to get new bands into venues.

'Riot Girl' was a women's empowerment movement growing at the time. This provided an example of how to get a following for new indie bands. Several women's punk bands would get together and play one night a week and they promoted it as a women's empowerment event. A community of followers and supporters began to show up on these nights and bands were able to get more attention as part of a collective than they would have done individually. This issue-based way of organising events revealed to me how important it was to build a community to attract audience members and book bands. I became actively involved in efforts to create a community of support for young punk bands in search of venues to play live. This also inspired my interest in joining the Glasgow Music Collective, which was a group dedicated to putting on hardcore shows to promote punk music in every major city in the world. This got the attention of industry magazines, and a group of kids began to follow and support the trend. An international network emerged through the collective, which enabled my own band and others to tap into as a way to find venues and connect to a community of fans.

Around this time, my first band decided to release a live record. I spoke with older musicians who had experience and they pointed me in the right direction. I found a Czechoslovakian pressing plant and they were able to do 500 7-inches for £250, which is relatively cheap. Many other bands had their own 7-inch pressed, but everyone ended up with an excess in supply just lying around in boxes. No one knew what to do with them. Several of us decided to set up a label and figure out how to distribute the large supply of 7-inches we had all made. We set up a distribution deal with Southern Records and helped other bands by offering to let them release their record through us. We didn't take any money – we just wanted to help others deal with the same issues we faced.

Several years later I produced and manufactured CDs entirely on my own. I experimented with ways to record the records for a band and minimise the financial and ecological impact. I bought a CD-duplicating machine that burns and then prints the cover. We designed the sleeves and had them made out of recycled card. We made the CDs in lesser numbers to reduce the financial pressure. We made them as we went along and it cost us very little to make each CD, as opposed to making a bigger number and then having a surplus. We found this to be a really good way to release a CD.

Through this process I learned to press, import and put records into shops. I learned to create the right form of artwork and developed knowledge about tax implications. At the time, it was exciting that we could make 300 records and they would all be bought in stores within three weeks. This was before the web but it was great because lots of people were releasing records and relatively large numbers of people bought them.

A friend and I also gained experience organising tours for our band but this always presented numerous challenges. Touring with a band is always difficult because booking is tricky. On one tour we only ended up doing about ten shows over the course of five weeks. We were stuck in Poland with no money for petrol and no shows to do. It created a disjuncture in the band and I did not talk to the others for about ten years after that. We had a really bad time, and I got home and had a major breakdown: it was horrendous. I just stopped touring after that.

Touring is very expensive. Bands will get paid well but they have to pay for everyone on the tour, including all the travel costs, the hire of the lighting rig, the sleeper bus, etc. After everyone is paid there is little money left. It is a bit of a fallacy that musicians make lots of money from touring. Instead, it is the merchandise that generates profits. I grossed about £10,000 from a major support slot over thirty shows. In the wake of these challenging experiences in a band I decided to direct my creative energies towards work as a solo musician. The understanding of the inner workings of the industry gave me the confidence to launch out on my own.

Experiences as a solo musician

My work as a solo musician following my 'band years' would prove to be profoundly shaped by experiences from my youth. At a young age my father was diagnosed with cancer and passed away. Two years later I lost my mother. I suffered from depression for about twenty-plus years and I struggled to cope or communicate what was going on in my head. I finally realised I needed to try to document the experience by writing a piece of music each month on my own. I set up a website and gave myself the rule that after I had written a piece of music it had to be online within twenty-four hours. As a result I was forced to share my work. I wanted do something honest. I ended up writing nine songs and people began to listen to them online.

An old friend found my music online and asked me to play live. When I first went out to play I found that I could talk openly to complete strangers. I could explain what happened on each of the pieces of music with honesty. I kept writing music and found the experience of performing and telling stories cathartic. Storytelling became a significant part of my creative output and performance. Stories were the main reason I played music at all. When I play I talk about what the songs are about and share a story that connects to each one. I decided I would continue with this, even if only ten people showed up to a gig. I have found that in general people are very open to my work.

Music writing and performance that incorporated storytelling became a form of therapy for me. I also managed to find this through the experience of touring on my own. When I go out and do my own tours it is generally just me. I enjoy it because it forces me to go and talk to people. Usually, when you are in a band you are with each other most of the time. When you are by yourself you are obliged to talk to the other musicians and promoters. The social aspect of touring alone helped my mental health.

I find touring on my own enriching, especially due to the extent to which people connect with the music. However, I experience a tension between tending to people's need to share their stories with me and the financial pressures that come after performing at gigs. From an economic standpoint I must sell records and t-shirts. It is very difficult to ask people to stop telling me about their personal loss because I desperately need to sign records and sell merchandise. As a touring musician I faced the challenging task of both being a musician and working as a t-shirt sales-man. My time as solo musician was critical for my creative and personal development; however, this would not have been possible without the time I spent in bands at the start of my career.

The roles I played organising albums and tours for my own bands and others helped me develop the knowledge I needed to become a solo artist. I had an in-depth understanding of how bands organised a DIY (do it yourself) label. While a solo artist, the idea of an open-source record label was new and I decided to experiment with how to use it. In this process you buy software and use it to change any piece of music and then redistribute it. This was cutting edge at the time, because it was based on the idea that ideas are not proprietary.

The organisation Creative Commons, initiated in the early 2000s, worked on the basis of a new understanding of copyright. 'Copyleft' is based on the presumption that the creator of music or a film can do whatever they want once they have paid and have rights to it. Traditional notions of copyright grant restrictive rights as to what can be done with the creative output. For example, the Creative Commons Licence allows anyone to do whatever they want with a piece of music as long as no money is made. This encourages people to share and use artists' work for non-profit purposes. I worked with this idea and set up a label to experiment with this new approach to copyright.

In addition to working with the music through open software, I wanted to tie an album to a handbound book. I wanted to create a beautiful, physical object for people to buy. The book included explanations and context that surrounded each song on the album. I learned the process of Coptic binding, which is an ancient form of book binding that does not require a press. I used covers made out of recycled glass. I made 105 books in total. They were beautiful and handmade and sold quickly. This helped pay for the record.

As a solo musician I developed the ability to perform, book and handle all my own affairs. I spend 95 per cent of time writing the music, giving interviews, replying to emails, setting up shows, talking to printers, talking to press agents and the activities that labels would normally do for you. Twenty years as a solo musician allowed me to develop creatively, cope with personal tragedy and experiment with ways to get my work out there and generate income. Now I feel I have found a balance as a musician. I find work with other musicians – whether in a band or as a solo musician – an important part of my life as an artist. I recently put out an album, *Thirteen Lost & Found*, that involved collaboration with musicians who are part of a unique community in Scotland. Despite being produced without a big budget, it received the Scottish Album of the Year award. It came as a great surprise, but confirmed that people connect with music that expresses authentic emotion.

Key lessons

- Networking and community are important within the music-making industry (see Chapter 8).
- Expressing the self through music has a therapeutic nature (see Chapter 15).
- Being a self-releasing musician has a 'learning as you go' nature (see Chapter 16).

Discussion questions

- What are the organisational and managerial roles that Hubby talks about?
- What kind of label would you set up, and why?
- What are the difficulties of touring as a DIY musician?

For more information, visit:
www.rmhubbert.com

Creating and making an album

Jenny Reeve and Charlotte Gilmore

Background

Jenny Reeve formed her band Strike the Colours in 2006; they have released one EP and two albums. Strike the Colours are four musician friends from Glasgow: Jenny Reeve (vocals, guitar and violin), David McAulay (guitar and sound engineer), Graeme Smillie (bass guitar and piano) and Jonny Scott (drums). Prior to forming the band they had been integral members of the Glasgow indie music scene for many years, collaborating with many of Scotland's currently most respected indie bands and musicians – for example, Arab Strap, Idlewild, Snow Patrol, Emma Pollock and Mogwai. Together as Strike the Colours they create music that has been championed by respected publications such as *Clash Magazine* and *Converse Music*, and BBC Radio 6 Music DJs such as Steve Lamacq and Mark Riley.

Band history

In 2005 Jenny began composing songs in response to the dissatisfaction she felt with her then band, 'whose music did not have room' for her folk-inspired compositions. Together with her friend, musician and sound engineer David McAulay, Jenny began to demo her songs. They created the 'sound-scapes' and 'intricate guitar hooks' behind Jenny's vocal melodies. They officially formed Strike the Colours with the addition of bassist Gareth Russell and drummer Denis Sheridan.

In 2007 the band released these recordings on an EP titled *The Face That Sunk A Thousand Ships*. With the release of the EP and some live performances, the band's profile quickly rose among the national media and public audiences. In early 2008 they recruited a new drummer, Jonny Scott. In the same year, the band began the process of writing their first major album: 'a more considered and orchestrated affair than the DIY efforts of the first EP'. In September 2009, a full-length album – *Seven Roads* – was released, which was acclaimed by the UK national press.

Following the album's release, the band played a number of BBC Radio live sessions and toured the UK.

In spring 2010, Strike the Colours began work on their second album, with bassist Graeme Smillie replacing Gareth Russell in the band's line-up. Over the year the band formed a new sound, influenced by P.J. Harvey and Radiohead. Early in 2011, the band thought up a 'a pie-in-the-sky plan', setting themselves the challenge of recording the album entirely live at the Monnow Valley studios in Wales. With an 'unrivalled live-room', this residential studio provided the band with 'perfect acoustics' and an environment to develop their ideas. The band asked Paul Savage, who had produced their first album, to produce their second. Through Paul's contacts the band got a 'really good deal' to hire the studios to record and mix the album over twelve days.

As a young unsigned band it was 'a huge thing for a band like us to go down to studios like this'. They didn't have enough money to pay the studio until a few days before leaving for Wales. Jenny recalled: 'we put all the money we had in the world into making it . . . it was a bit hair-raising'. As a gigging live band, every month there was a steady stream of money (albeit small amounts) going into a 'band fund' – for example, from gig fees, back-dated PRS, and record and online sales. They also successfully applied for funding of £1,000 from a musicians' charity to help them cover the shortfall in recording, subsistence and travel costs: 'we were close to the wire . . . we had £60 left when we came home [from Wales]'.

The following is Jenny's story of the making of album number two: 'one of the most important experiences of my life so far musically and person-ally'. The album documents Jenny's struggles with depression, which she was diagnosed with two months prior to recording the album.

The band experience

The band were residents in the on-site accommodation and they had 24-hour access to the studio. Despite being a round-the-clock studio, the producer 'was really good about keeping his hours because there is only so much listening somebody can do before getting exhausted'. If the band started late then they would finish late, but generally they began recording and mixing around 10am or 11am and finished about 9pm.

As residents, when the band finished for the day they cooked and ate dinner together and relaxed. For Jenny, it was this aspect of the process that made recording the album 'effortless'. The residential studio was set in an 'idyllic' remote countryside location, and being away from Glasgow and cut off in this remote location with no mobile phone reception freed Jenny from 'her everyday worries and stresses', such as being accessible to people from her 'everyday jobs'. The continuity of the band's daily routine living, working and eating together gave Jenny a sense of 'finally being supported and reassured'. This 'kinship' and the studio location added to the band's experience, and contributed to the recording process. The guest vocalist Louie also added 'loads' to the record, as did Paul's singer-songwriter wife Emma, who came to visit and was persuaded to do some harmonies: 'it is just nice to have friends like that contributing'.

For Jenny, it was important that the finished album reflected and captured the stories and experience around making the record – for example, including a 'hard-to-do' vocal, which was eventually recorded when Jenny was 'wasted at 3am'; and the recordings that were just 'thrown down', such as Louie's last vocal, tracked while sorting out his washing five minutes before leaving for his train. There were also the unique moments such as Jenny and Emma singing harmonies on one microphone – the so-called 'steak dinner ... because we looked so romantic the producer thought that he should take a wee candlelit steak dinner into the tracking room ... we're campaigning to make it a technical term'.

The segue sections were also an important part of capturing the experience and sound of the studio. These were snippets of recordings of the band 'messing about in the studio': Jenny singing into a guitar, Louie and Jonny jamming, lots of people shouting, clinking glasses, flip flops used as percussion instruments. All these live snippets of recording will be important when knitting the album together: 'when you really hear the room and the recording, that is for me what is going to make the record sound like a record, rather than a bunch of songs put together in a certain order'.

The tracking experience

This album was a particularly personal one for Jenny, who had been diagnosed with depression two months before recording, so a lot of the album was about that. Jenny had been putting off writing the most difficult lyrics until she had to: 'even when we were down there I was still writing'. In the past, Jenny had got 'too focused on particular ideas to let go of them', so before going down to the studio Paul had made Jenny aware that he was going to put pressure on her. She knew before going to Wales that 'doing the vocals was going to be an issue'.

Added pressure to the writing and recording process in Wales came early in the first week, when Jenny's violin broke. One of the studio engineers drove Jenny to the nearest violin shop in Cardiff for it to be fixed overnight; this involved a two-hour return car journey. The day the violin was to be collected guest vocalist Louie was due to arrive to record his pieces, but Jenny hadn't finished his lyrics. So in the car on the way to collect the violin, Jenny was thinking of lyric ideas and singing them into Jonny's iPhone (he had gone with her to be a 'calming influence'). By the time they got back to the studio Jenny was ready to record her lyrics, until Paul told her they 'sounded like a Snow Patrol song'. Louie arrived, so the 'boys' took him down to raft on the river while Jenny worked on new lyrics with Paul. Every day the 'boys' went rafting on the nearby river to give Jenny time and space to work with Paul to rewrite and track her vocals. Paul told Jenny to just:

Sing whatever comes into your head ... [so] I just had to ... just the first thing I sang, I was like 'that's a bit rubbish' but Paul was like '...no ... do it again', so I sang again, and he said 'I think that's your melody...' I was just having to come up with stuff off the top of my head.

By the time the rest of the band came back off the river to the studio Jenny had completed the vocal, 'but my God that was tough'.

Jenny's purpose in working with Paul and hiring the studio in Wales was to 'develop as an artist and band'. She was willing to take the pressure and stress of being pushed into an 'uncomfortable place' personally and professionally to move forward as a band, '... otherwise there would be no point in booking studios in Wales and taking the guys down there ... there has to be an element of risk ... it comes back to the thing that there is no point making the same album twice ... he was pressurising me.' At points during the tracking of her vocals Jenny lost the perspective because she was so 'tired' and 'strung out'. Jenny had got a 'bee in her bonnet', about singing out of tune, 'like really, really badly and it was driving Paul crazy'. Her classical musical training meant that she was 'conditioned' to have everything always 'immaculately' in tune. However, Jenny preferred to take Paul's advice because she respects and trusts him as a producer. 'He is the producer, and that is why we have him there. If there is anything that I don't fully agree with then I will say so but I trust him. I prefer to go "of course – that makes sense to me".'

The internal struggles and stress that Jenny was experiencing and putting on herself and the band led to her having 'a bit of a meltdown'. 'Paul was like, "take a break" ... I was able to go up to my room and had a good cry ... I thought, "I cannot do it, it is rubbish" and then I thought, "Well, I don't really have an alternative".' Paul was concerned that Jenny's anxiety was compromising her vocal performance, so he often had to 'entertain' Jenny's 'neuroticism' to let her redo vocals – retakes that were never used.

Finishing touches

The band had still to finalise the plans for releasing the album, but 'we will not hang about too much: obviously, money is an issue'. The album was made without the band being signed to a label, and there were various reasons for this. 'It is a weird time to be releasing music just now – nobody has any money, people are not buying records anymore but in a way it is quite a good time to be doing it DIY, if you have got the time and patience to dedicate towards doing it.' For example, the last time the band had released a single the cover sleeves had been done by hand by Jenny and her friends:

I did all the artwork by hand, I made all the sleeves by hand, wrote it, did the stuff in the background, so I had to get all my friends to help me. By the end of it, they were like 'I hate you', covered in bits of paper and glue, but I think it was kind of worth it.

Jenny had had trouble in the past with the artwork for her 'main records': 'the trouble we had with the main records, the formatting of that, was I got somebody to help me, who charged me a lot of money and got it wrong, so it was sent away to the manufacturers and it came back and it was wrong, it was way too dark, the contrast was too high'. So Jenny sent them back and:

they ran off another 1,000 copies, sent them back up to me, I got them back and they were practically black and white. I was, 'I cannot believe you have got this wrong again', so I wrote to the guy about what was wrong and [said]: 'I am not going to attempt to get you to fix it because I just think you are incapable of doing it'. I was really horrible but I had to be. That is one thing: I am not good at being that person, but sometimes you have to be.

From Jenny's previous experience of releasing albums she was aware of the general process the band needed to go through and the options open to her in order to release and market the new record; she also has industry contacts to help her. In terms of self-releasing, the band could initially release a 'teaser' download-only single to get a bit of media coverage, 'just to let people know we're imminent … we've got an imminent album release'. Jenny has a PR friend who specialises in music promotion, and who 'is well connected and will help the band get in front of people'. Media such as online press, the regional press and using a radio plugger had been successful for Jenny before, but they needed more coverage in the UK national press. One thing she felt might help with this exposure is the fact that the record is more upbeat, louder (than previous albums) and 'it is a lot more radio friendly, so I would hope it would get more exposure radio-wise'. BBC Radio 6 Music DJ Mark Riley had always supported the band, giving them live sessions and radio play. Jenny recounted her favourite Mark Riley story: 'I had given Mark a copy of the first album before we had any of the artwork ... and he had his shoes off and he said, "I will put it in my shoe so that I don't forget it".'

For Jenny, December and January were generally quiet months, so she was hoping to push on with doing the design brief for the album cover and thinking about which labels to approach with the rest of the band. She wanted to do this before the rest of her year began, which with gigging is 'pretty full-on, struggling for work, just constantly pushing things forward' with her band and working on other music collaborations: 'It is a really happy band but it's nice to have some extra-curricular stuff'.

Key lessons

- Some roles and practices in the team were directly about the musical product and others – for example, rafting and driving to Cardiff – were about creating the environment for Jenny to compose and contribute her performances to the creation of the album. These experiences are reflected within the makeup of the album (see Chapters 15 and 17).
- There were different forms of leadership: both Paul and Jenny were involved in creative leadership, and Jenny took the leader role within the organisation of the album-making – for example, organising the studio in Wales. There was also 'swapping of the leadership baton' as the situation required, including musical, producing, interpersonal and inspirational aspects of leadership (see Chapter 14).
- The friendship and security created during the band's time in Wales, particularly for Jenny, enabled her to create and record her vocals during a time of anxiety – for example, recording vocals with Jonny in the car (see Chapters 3, 4 and 11).

Discussion questions

- What were the main organising practices that contributed to the making of the album?
- Discuss the management practices that enabled the artists to overcome their difficulties when making and mixing the album. How may these difficulties have contributed to the creative process?
- Discuss the different forms of materiality and time (the location, equipment, what happened to the equipment and how people reacted) involved in making the album. How did the material and socio-material practices affect the creative process?

- What forms of leadership did Jenny and Paul perform? How did the leadership role each played change over time? How did these roles help the band overcome the difficulties involved when making the album?

For more information, visit:
www.strikethecolours.com

Relationships between music, management, agents and labels
Jill O'Sullivan and Shiona Chillas

The Band – Sparrow and the Workshop

Sparrow and the Workshop are a three-piece band based in Glasgow, consisting of Jill O'Sullivan (vocals, acoustic guitar), Nick Packer (guitar, bass, basstard) and Gregor Donaldson (drums, vocals). They are known for their use of harmonies, bastardised instruments and FX pedals. They formed in early 2008 in Glasgow and soon after began playing gigs throughout the city. The band's debut album, *Crystals Fall*, was released in 2010 to critical acclaim. In late April 2011 the band released their second album, *Spitting Daggers*. Both albums attracted radio play from BBC6 Music, BBC Radio Scotland, Radio4 (Austria), XFM and Kerrang Radio, and Sparrow have performed extensive radio sessions, including for Lauren Laverne, Marc Riley, Rob da Bank @ Maida Vale, Janice Long and Vic Galloway. In addition to completing two UK headline tours and one European headline tour, Sparrow have also supported many bands on tour, including Brian Jonestown Massacre, the Pogues, Idlewild, Broken Records and British Sea Power, and have supported the Lemonheads and Thee Oh Sees. Sparrow completed their third album, *Murderopolis*, in late 2012, and also engage in a number of side projects with other musicians.

The following is Jill's story of how the band are organised, the division of labour and the experience of writing and playing music together.

The band's history

Jill has a background in classical music and played the violin as child. Her parents were 'really into folk music and country music', and from an early age would take her to blues festivals, jazz festivals and free festivals in Chicago. She was given a guitar for her eighteenth birthday, and from then on: 'that was it – I like this because I can write songs on it'. Jill started playing in bands at the age of 19 and wrote her first song at 23. Chicago then became really stifling and so Jill took jobs to save enough money to

317

take a master's degree in London. Jill described her experience of London as 'lonely and alienating', and she moved to Glasgow with her boyfriend, which gave her 'breathing space and you kind of need that when you are trying to be creative'. Completely by chance she moved into a flat with the band's drummer, Gregor; they formed a band and then Nick joined. From then on, the three band members were 'just lashed together'. There was an immediate trust between the members, which the band have worked on and consolidated over time. The three moved into a different flat and lived together 'for moments of creativity' and also for financial reasons, so that they could afford to work less. Jill and Nick have been a couple for six years and now live in the flat together; Gregor moved out a few years ago to live with his girlfriend.

From the beginning of the band's relationship Nick and Jill had no connections in Glasgow, but Gregor had been in many bands and knew of some local places to play, and the band began to be offered support slots at small venues. They were noticed by promoters in Glasgow and then in Edinburgh, particularly an influential blogger (Matthew Young; see Chapter 18, pp. 285–9), who was the first person to get in touch with the band and is someone who is committed to helping new bands in Scotland. By the band's fourth or fifth gig in Glasgow, offers to play were rolling in. Jill describes the music community in Glasgow as 'very encouraging and generous' to new bands. Success in playing live music led to Sparrow being taken up by an independent label. First the band put out two EPs; the label suggested they combine the EPs, add another three songs and then make an album, which they made on a budget of £1,000. The second album was a more difficult experience: the band were now contractually bound to make an album, with a specified release date. Although they were writing songs anyway, the band were under some pressure to compile their material more quickly under slightly more stressful circumstances. After the second album there was an amicable split between Sparrow and their label and the band financed the third album themselves.

Working and living in a band

The pressing need to make money is ever present in Jill's story. The costs of making music are high, in terms of time, effort and hard cash. For Jill, making music is not about profit: 'it's just about breaking even'. There is so much involved in producing an album: printing, choosing singles, artwork and merchandise, all of which is expensive and time consuming. The band are committed to making music, yet the creative process is constrained, as Jill comments: 'writing songs is not hard work but it takes a lot of time'. During their time together the band have all had other jobs to make a living and finance their music. Jill has worked in various jobs and at present works in a café with other musicians, where there is an implicit understanding that you will go away on tour, and where cover can be arranged.

The band work well together and have loosely defined roles in making their music and in the associated activities of the band, each member contributing according to their skills and interests. Gregor has often done the driving on tour and contributed merchandising ideas such as posters for gigs, fake tattoos and flower pot shots. Nick is the 'tech boy', recording and mixing demos. He also does all the admin for the band's tours, giving festival promoters advance material and specs for the sets. Jill's role is to keep on top of emails, deal with press crews and maintain social networking sites and fan interaction. Jill is very aware that the background work is important to the band, particularly during the making and promoting of the second album when the band members 'made a sacrifice by quitting our jobs', putting added pressure to 'make it work'. She describes the 'business' of working in a band as hard work, saying: 'I wake up, I check my mail, I call my manager, I email our agents, we email the PR guy for our label: these are constant things'. Jill differentiates between the ordered business of making music and the disordered creative process, saying that bands need to have 'a democracy organisation wise' and 'musically there needs to be a bit of anarchy'.

The creative process

The creative part of the band's life is also organised and split among members. The band work hard to create freedom from a prescriptive 'verse/chorus/verse/chorus' song structure, and generally practise once or twice a week for three hours. The guiding principle for Jill's songs is to get an emotion across through a song; she says that commercial considerations do not enter her mind while she is writing. In describing the creative process, Jill says she does 'the basics' – the skeleton melodies and the lyrics. The boys then 'put the flesh on the bones' and the three band members work on the arrangement. Everybody has their own creative input: as the drummer, Gregor often sets the pace of the songs and Nick has a tendency towards developing melodic bass lines that both accompany the rhythm and weave in and out of it. Sometimes Jill will begin with a melody and find lyrics that 'match the mood and the melody', the band will work on it and produce a song. In other songs she will fiddle around with her guitar, 'doodling', and call the guys in to add their input. Sometimes, she says, the melody comes first and sometimes the lyrics.

She feels, or would like to feel, the creative process has to be 'like spontaneous combustion', yet she also knows that songs have to be worked at. Not all of her ideas materialise in songs and she keeps melodies on a Dictaphone – only when Jill, Nick and Gregor agree does a song come into being. Jill says she instinctively knows when a song is right 'because it gets stuck in my head, you get a rush and if I play my initial idea, and both Nick and Gregor's eyes light up, then it is right'.

Reflecting on the creative process, Jill sees that her attitude towards writing has changed over time. When she was younger, she felt she had to be in a certain mood to write songs. In 2009 she was invited to spend time with other songwriters and realised that everyone has different approaches to writing. After that experience, she now knows that 'if you sit down and start playing around, then something will come out'. Being forced to write with others made her realise 'you can channel a mood' – just pick up a guitar and get lost in it. Writing itself has become a source of happiness and she enjoys the process, regardless of her mood. Jill's confidence has grown over time, and while she has been told in the past that she is not confident enough speaking to people, she finds writing songs fulfilling and says: 'it's the only thing I feel confident about'. Although she still has doubts about her abilities, she feels now that doubt 'pushes my music forward', and says she feels free when she is writing, making music and working with people that she trusts. These feelings have led to other projects and collaborations writing songs and making music.

Band relationships

While the band have somewhat defined roles in the creative process, making music requires sensitivity and can create tensions in relationships within and outside the band. Jill remembers times when she has been working with her bandmates and has not liked the direction of the music. Arguments can flare and there are times when the band do not necessarily get along. Managing creative disagreements is connected to choosing the right time to address differences: 'when everyone is in a good mood', then the band can discuss how they sound and how they might change parts of the song. Sometimes it is better to say nothing in emotionally charged situations and wait for people to calm down. Jill says that the band are all so passionate about their music, and although there are times when the creative process is really emotional and difficult, they have learned to combat that aspect of band life by achieving a 'tender balance' of not offending each other, but equally getting on with things and making the best music possible. Arguments are healthy for the band, and working, living and touring together means that personal differences can be blown out of proportion, yet the shared love of their music and mutual trust overrides the rare clashes. When two of the band members are having a creative discussion, the third member seems to take the role of mediator, making suggestions and smoothing out entrenched positions with 'a bit of diplomacy'. In particular, the second album was made under a strict timeline from the label and the three band members felt the pressure, so that working together became 'a bit strained'. The pressures of suddenly becoming a 'buzz band' and the accompanying raised expectations from the label affected the band. These pressures are symptomatic of the contradiction in the music industry between making art and making money.

Jill is candid in her explanation of the different and sometimes competing interests at play in the music industry, and reveals the complexities in relationships that are influenced by a musician's attitude to music and attendant pressures. Musicians, she says, can join the DIY community, where people shun the commercial but often end up 'never getting out of their bedroom' and 'playing to the same ten people all day'. If a band wants to make connections with listeners outside of 'their bedroom', they have some options. They can self-release – some choose physical only, press some vinyl and a handful of CDs – and/or make the music available online, producing digital releases available on Bandcamp or other online outlets, and attempt to let the music do the talking, which Jill thinks may be becoming more common. The downside is that bands may not be taken seriously by the wider music-listening public. Jill thinks that some listeners perceive bands as more legitimate if they are connected to a label. Sales may also be limited, and the music press and bloggers may not hear and publicise the band's music.

To get music 'out there', a more traditional strategy is to sign with a label; this is what Sparrow and the Workshop did for the first two albums. In entering a contract with the label, Jill realised that the band had to grapple with the business side of the industry. They quickly went from having no expectations and just making music to having a 'weight of expectations', feeling pressure to comply with market forces outside their control. The contract basically includes releasing and promoting the album; the band's agent is responsible for organising a tour to promote the album. The label has to try to satisfy the demands of the industry by selling albums, which in turn has effects on the creativity of musicians. Business decisions begin to conflict with making music in, for example, choosing which track on the album will be put out as a single. The band might want a certain song because they love it, but a radio plugger might choose a different song, either because it is shorter or follows the prescription for a single of verse/chorus/verse/chorus, or because it is more commercial. The band are very clear that they would resist any attempt to alter their music and Jill emphasises that Sparrow retained complete creative control of their songs and the decisions regarding writing, arrangement, production and so on. Music is deeply personal to Sparrow, and Jill feels it reflects the personalities of band members. Jill's view is that there are tensions between labels, who are 'too interested in numbers' and the band, who are interested 'in the art form'. Losing control over decisions related to their work, Jill says, used to 'freak her out', but over time she has learned to 'zoom out' and think of the bigger picture. Whichever single is chosen for radio play, it is still their song and people will hear it. In the past, Jill has wondered whether it is arrogant to want to do well, to want to reach people and get the music 'out there'. Looking back, she says, it would be silly not to have tried to make a living from music and she will be able to say that she made an album that she loved, that people heard and loved.

The joy of figuring out arrangements and capturing emotion in a song is evident in Jill's story. She returns to the difficulties of turning art into a product and sees the dilemma in terms of having to become business savvy if you want to get your music beyond your bedroom walls. The experience of touring and dealing with the music business and relationships outside the band has taught her to take control, but only where necessary. She sees relationships based on trust as being crucial for the band – otherwise, there is too much 'zooming in' and conflict over really specific 'stupid things like how many t-shirts to print to take on tour'.

The third album – going it alone

After two years of touring with the second album, and the new experiences connected with negotiating the music industry, Jill felt that the band had become 'burnt out'. They were tired and jaded by their experiences, prompting a split with their label that, although amicable, meant that the band were back in Glasgow with a clean slate and lots of free time. Jill felt that the split with the label was good for the band: they were exhausted from touring and wanted to come back and get to know Glasgow again, and 'get to know ourselves'. Without the pressures of touring, Jill and the band found a new vigour for making music and started writing songs again 'for fun'. They had lots of material and decided to think about making another album with a different approach. Once they had recorded the album, they reconnected with Matthew Young of Song, by Toad – the blogger turned label-manager who had encouraged them in earlier years. The band felt the blogger 'was on their wavelength' and 'in it for the right reasons', in that he liked their music and liked them, and – importantly – they had a mutual trust relationship. As Jill said:

> They [Song, by Toad] give us a lot of support actually because they are independent, it is like: 'Oh right, your first album, it was okay, but we are going to stick with you for the second and let you kind of get your fans and blah, blah, blah, whatever' – that is business talk, but it has been really good.

The band members had all taken other work to make a living and had to figure out a way of funding the album. They applied for funding from a large Scottish funding body, feeling confident enough to book studio time in advance. Unfortunately, the funding application was rejected; this was a hard blow to the band – particularly Gregor, who has lived and worked in Glasgow all his life. Jill felt the band put so much time into the application and that they were not asking for too much, just funding to produce the album. She recognises that they may have become victims of a larger political strategy involving cuts in funding for the arts. This was a particularly hard time for the band but, quoting an old saying, Jill stated: 'what doesn't kill you makes you stronger'. Ultimately, they funded the recording of the album using a bit of money left over from touring and publishing, money raised at a fundraising gig and personal contributions from band members. Sparrow also received financial support from their publisher, who happened to be the label they were previously signed with. Jill says: 'despite not being our label any more they are still supportive and did not want us to fall on our faces. We weren't contractually due the publishing money until release of the album, so they did us a massive favour.' Jill feels that the band were lucky to have support from their fans, from the studio who allowed payment by instalments and from their publishers. Although the third album will entail a lot of work for the band, the experience has been very positive. Jill is proud of the album, in part because the band have funded the recording of it entirely themselves. She describes it as a 'culmination of everything we have done as a band', yet recognises that without luck and support 'we wouldn't have been able to make the album'.

Playing live and touring – mixed emotions

Playing live and interactions with audiences are unpredictable, producing different experiences for the band. There are technical issues around the monitors, which can mean that band members cannot hear each other, or times when guitar strings break, there is noisy feedback or groundloop. However, Jill recognises that the most important element in playing live is the audience reaction. The best gigs are 'when you feel you are not just doing it, that you are actually engaging, when people come up to you after and say that they got something out of that, they felt good'. Jill says the best compliment she can get is inspiring people to go home and write music, because that is exactly how she feels when she loves a gig. Conversely, the band have had audiences who have been chatting throughout the gig and 'totally disengaged'. From her perspective, Jill also tells of gigs where she has been more or less going through the motions, her hands moving, her mouth moving, but she is thinking of something else entirely.

Having fans has been a strange development for the band. They know they love to make music for themselves, but Jill finds it strange to think that 'people like me'. She recognises that she shouldn't feel that way, but would like to think that she's connecting to people through the band's music. Touring is part of the business of being in a band. It is vital to promote the album, and over the years Sparrow have developed strong relationships with a number of venues in Scotland. Despite the exhaustion and occasional boredom involved in touring, where 'if you are not driving, you are just sitting and staring at the road', Jill says she loves being on the road, visiting different countries and observing subtle differences in culture and in audience reactions. Touring is a unique experience, and the band have learned practical and emotional lessons from being together on the road. In the past they might have driven themselves to save money; now they realise that it is worth spending some extra money to employ a driver and give their legs and minds a rest before the next gig.

Key lessons

- Organising in a band: it is important to understand and allocate roles in the creative process and deal with the music industry according to abilities and preferences (in this case, the band understand each other's strengths and allocate the workload democratically) (see Chapter 4).
- Managing relationships: band members must learn to be sensitive to the feelings of other members, dealing with different interests and learning which aspects of work are important to control (zooming in and zooming out) (see Chapters 3 and 5).
- Addressing the art/commerce contradiction: the band needs to decide which strategy to use, understanding the effects and implications personally and musically (see Chapters 1 and 9).

Discussion questions

• What roles are adopted by band members, and why? Discuss where conflicts may arise between band members and how they are resolved. Is Jill a leader – how does she achieve her goals?
• Compare and contrast the different experiences of signing with a label and self-funding an album. Which do you think worked for Sparrow – why might this be?
• Reflect on how learning to 'zoom in and zoom out' has helped Jill. Discuss other circumstances where these different perspectives might apply.

For more information, visit:
www.sparrowandtheworkshop.co.uk

Dead or American: reasons to be fearless

Chris Cusack

Introduction

It's a steep learning curve as a young musician. Especially today. The music industry is in bad shape financially, as well as in a seemingly perpetual state of flux, hastened by the incessant march of technology (and in particular the advent of broadband and the internet's resultant impact on sales revenue and publicity).

The old guard: the major labels and print media outlets – who used to call the shots regarding taste-making and market shares – are struggling to hold on to their positions of superiority. Every year they watch their sales decline as piracy and general apathy become endemic in their audience. Teams of employees, formerly engaged in the kind of narcotic-fuelled hijinks related by the likes of Hunter S. Thompson, now find themselves chained behind a computer desk, desperately tracking what new thing is trending on the blogosphere. A task akin to snatching fireflies out of the air. Sometimes they get lucky but, more often than not, things move so fast that by the time they grab on to something, public attention has shifted.

So instead – and after a period of operational upheaval – rather than chase them, these companies again attempt to dictate these trends, affording them more control and risking less speculative investment. To that end they are now buying into the online media – the same way they did with the print media for the previous four decades, blurring the lines between advertising, film, TV, radio, gossip columns and hard news. Paying to place their next new break-out act under your nose, albeit in a much more subtle, surreptitious way than before, taking care not to shatter the illusion of free will. After all, we discerning consumers would like to think it is us deciding what we want to hear, rather than acknowledge that we are perhaps still at the mercy of what the common financial interests of major publishing houses, record labels and management firms allow us to 'discover'.

Thus, in a shrinking pond, these huge financial beasts war for food and territory, thrashing around in panic, baring their teeth in ever more ruthless ways. Sending musicians on tour for years at a time to the point of physical and mental breakdown. Dropping acts after one album. Creating hideously unfair contracts via which to trap all but the most fortunate or cautious individuals. Loading the dice ever more in their favour at the expense of smaller labels and independent operations, as the financial risk becomes too great to allow any revenue to land outside their realm of influence. The media are monopolised. Promotional methods grow ever more unscrupulous across the spectrum. Nobody who doesn't play the game gets famous.

Amidst this grizzly, morally dubious fight for survival are the musicians. People with a skill and a message and a need to give voice to their art. Often little more than naïve recruits caught in an intensifying crossfire. Faced with the choice of: 'get into one of these big trenches and do what we tell you or you're out there, exposed, effectively dead. And to make sure of that, we're going to shoot at you too.'

This is a bleak outlook, granted. But for those people attempting to exist outside the pseudo-creative indenture of the musical mainstream it is also an exhaustingly mundane reality.

The reality – welcome to the cruel world

Like so many young musicians, my career ambitions began in earnest in school, spurred on by my 'discovery' of bands and artists who reflected my deeper beliefs. Alienated by the fashionable misogyny and stupidity of Guns N' Roses et al., people like Nirvana, Smashing Pumpkins and Bad Religion spoke to the part of me that knew the politics of our age was riddled with hypocrisy and injustice. Watching these acts succeed seemed to say that apparently it was possible to create art on a big scale and also represent something other than vanity, egotism and commerce.

Whether or not that is true is entirely debatable. All of these acts, at that time, operated from the base of a major record label. They accepted all of the considerable benefits their status afforded, yet simultaneously rebelled against the system that put them so inescapably in the public eye. In all likelihood, the executives at those record companies were perfectly happy for the bands to posture and pontificate on the perceived evils of contemporary culture since, with tens of millions of sales racked up, it was clearly not having any detrimental effect on said industry.

As that realisation downed, the weight of the words that had previously served as encouragement began to evaporate. Indeed, Kurt Cobain's suicide in 1994 was attributed, among many other factors, to his internal conflict about 'selling out' his ideals and propping up the very industry and prejudices he despised. Can you really bring down the machine from within or are you merely paying lip service to the rebellious spirit of youth, spewing forth benign sound bites, exploiting the faith and idealism of a naïve audience for notoriety and the financial rewards it generates?

When this contradiction became too apparent to ignore, I realised that my path had to be even further away from the sickening superficiality and duplicity of MTV and its ilk. As a member of Dead or American, I strove to exist completely apart from these mechanisms. To record, tour, release, perform, create and flourish free from the corrupting influence of big business.

In fairness, as mentioned previously, this was a steep learning curve. We started out assuming everyone was involved in music for the same reasons as us. Surely promoters, DJs, fellow musicians and all these people backstage at concerts were there out of a genuine love for the art form, we thought. Clearly, with hindsight, that was a blissfully ignorant time in our existence. One scenario that illustrates the rude awakening to follow was the thrill of being invited to play at the infamous King Tut's in Glasgow for the first time: the kind of accolade that impresses even the most musically ignorant Scottish family member. What should have been a landmark moment was tempered by the troubling revelation that, despite being obliged to sell an allocation of tickets and dutifully doing so, we had to watch the other bands – who had attracted substantially fewer people – eat a meal we were not offered, before we were sent on stage first as people had only begun to arrive. It was a loss of innocence. A disillusioning foray into how the contemporary musical environment operates. We were bottom of the food chain. There to plump out the crowd, make the bar some cash and then get out of the road as quickly as possible.

Making sense of the scene – which way is up?

In our attempts to get our bearings within the wider context of this alien musical environment we were trying to comprehend, another scenario from this epoch springs to mind. From an early date we had collectively rejected the idea of performing as part of that trite clichéd rite of passage, the 'Battle of the Bands', for the primary reason that bands surely shouldn't 'battle'. Why were we competing with other musicians? Why would one prosper to the detriment of others? On that note, we were disillusioned by our invitation to participate in what we understood was a showcase for young acts chosen to appear at the T in the Park festival. In fact, this was not a showcase but a series of 'heats', with a couple of bands selected by a panel of judges, the most unconventional acts largely being shunned due to the inherently esoteric nature of their style. Effectively, this was a streamlining of those groups attaining the highest profile, and thus a narrowing of which made it to the public's attention. Those acts that made the cut were slick, competent, but also broadly centrist bands. It raised serious doubts for us. Was a truly great heavy metal band or a masterful, inspired experimental jazz band less likely to prosper than a mediocre pop band? As far as we could tell from our experiences, absolutely. Sadly, this conclusion has never been convincingly contradicted since.

From an early stage it is important that any band agrees on its objectives. The members should have at least some understanding of what constitutes success in their own minds. For many people lucky enough to achieve unexpected success, they quickly realise that the brutal schedules and compulsory compromises it entails are not what they envisioned when they first set out and begin to have serious doubts. When the reluctance of one or two individuals then jeopardises the contract of a full band, tensions can arise, friendships crumble, relationships be destroyed and huge financial problems ensue, often ending in legal action.

Bands need to know each other's limitations. It is unlikely that a drummer with three young children and a good career will want to sacrifice that for eight months of touring with only the possibility of financial success at the end. Likewise, if a strong-willed frontman presses for more and more exposure in mainstream media, but an independently minded backing band find themselves being placed alongside corporate logos with which they are uncomfortable, cracks can quickly appear. It is thus vital for musicians to speak openly with all participants about where they see this going, especially if labels start to call. Defaulting on a publishing contract is no fun, and if you find your meticulously crafted art playing over a washing powder commercial – from which you receive not a penny – you will wish that these conversations had taken place sooner.

Getting momentum – push-starting the van

Becoming a fully autonomous musical unit required a great deal of research. Dead or American learned as we went, booking concerts in a foreign language, formatting the liner notes for CD manufacture, knowing what we should and shouldn't expect from promoters. It was trial and error. One of the best ways to acquire this knowledge without so many of the errors is to draw on the experiences of others. Read as much as possible about and by musicians and record labels whose practices you admire. They will furnish you with many cautionary tales, as well as many valuable tips for progressing. It is also worth noting that DIY musicians tend to be much easier to contact directly, due to their handling of their own correspondence, so try getting in touch if you find yourself looking for answers to a troubling issue. Via our own imprint, Predestination Records – and later in my work with Bloc+Music – I spent as much time offering advice to musicians who wrote to us as I ever did listening to and releasing albums.

At the very early stages of any musical career it can be tremendously advantageous to capitalise on the interest that a new act may achieve. People will want to hear this new band. Magazines may well want to write about it as part of a 'newcomer' article. If a plan is in place, this momentum can easily be maintained. Being well rehearsed is invaluable. Having good recordings at the ready certainly helps, as does a run of concerts and some sort of plan regarding future releases. Speaking from experience, Dead or American stumbled into being a band, not deciding on our next step soon enough, and thus finding it considerably harder to capture the public attention and keep it. While it is still possible to get to the same level, there are definitely some extra stress-lines on our brows that might not be there had we spent a bit longer at the development/planning stage instead of racing into our first live appearance then finding ourselves in a confused void immediately afterwards.

Touring – strife on the open road

One particularly abrupt and poignant lesson came during our first foray outside Scotland to Bradford in 2001, shortly after the notorious race riots that had gripped that city. With shop fronts still sporting smashed glass, we arrived in darkness on the back of an arduous, snowy, five-hour drive. The atmosphere in the city was predictably tense and carrying thousands of pounds' worth of musical equipment into the building past gangs of surly-looking boys seemed even more inadvisable than usual.

Not long before our departure for this one-off gig we had learned that we needed to provide our own PA. Somehow this had not been made apparent in our previous contact with the venue. These days such a set-up seems ridiculous – more akin to a wedding or covers band – and would be an early warning sign of a venue deserving a wide berth, but in those embryonic stages we simply took it as par for the course and hired a small PA system at our own expense.

The gig itself turned out to be a complete waste of time. This was not a dedicated venue, just a pub looking to attract some custom on the vague basis of live entertainment, without investing any real energy in researching or publicising the concert. What little audience did attend (including a bored-looking dog on a string) didn't seem to connect with our array of original alternative rock material and, at the end of the evening, money was rudely slapped onto the bar top in front of us and no pleasantries were exchanged. It had become quite apparent, quite quickly, that discriminating between good and bad venues – factoring in musical suitability, clientele, operational procedures, etc. – was an important part of smooth running on the road. We set off back north, through more winter weather, money gone on petrol and expenses, to arrive home at 5am tired, disgruntled, but collectively wiser.

Such early lessons taken on board, later touring further afield proved much more successful. Booking with as much advance notice as possible was crucial. The further ahead, the more likely we were to get a venue that fitted with our planned route and the more likely we were to get a show with a reputable promoter, generally meaning better organisation, payment and attendance. Certainly there were hiccups along the way, but the more we booked, the more we built up a dossier of reliable contacts, many of whom also worked as booking agents for other touring acts. A common way of currying favour was therefore to offer our services in assisting those acts with concerts in Scotland in return for their assistance elsewhere.

This phenomenon, commonly known as the 'gig swap', is an indispensable weapon in any young DIY band or promoter's arsenal. It enables them to identify suitable venues and audiences more easily and, via cooperation, helps to ensure their acts are playing to receptive audiences. It is also relatively self-regulatory, insofar as any bands or promoters not seen to be upholding their end of the deal soon fall out of favour and are thus cut out of the wider reciprocal loop.

In this spirit, having had the good fortune to play alongside a number of excellent European acts in our native land, the members of Dead or American began to set our sights on continental locations and opportunities. Given the numerous logistical barriers – language, transportation, distance, cultural factors – it did prove quite a challenge, but many of the same conventions applied. Mainland Europe was full of musicians looking for help finding shows in the UK; by assisting them, we secured an expanding network of continental peers who in turn assisted us with our arrangements. Indeed, some thirteen years after my first touring experiences, my current band, Hey Enemy, despite being based in central Scotland, tours in Europe far more regularly than the UK due to the greater number of opportunities and comparatively better terms we receive over there.

That is not to say there was not considerable legwork to be done. A scatter-gun approach, involving easily 500 speculative emails to European venues, might only yield a dozen productive responses. A far more effective method was to target collectives and bands specifically. Investigate their previous output and events. Ask their honest advice and proceed in a less haphazard fashion, more efficiently deploying our energies. It should go without saying that European tours also required the same consideration for advance notice that any such venture should – if not more – to allow for affordable travel arrangements.

Good treatment and audiences aside, European touring is clearly not without its potential pitfalls. In 2008, despite a fair level of experience, Dead or American fell foul of some quite dreadful luck when a run of dates in Germany and eastern Europe turned into a reluctant holiday in Prague. Having performed to good effect in Chemnitz the night before, we were racing to reach our Prague concert late one Sunday night when dashboard lights started bursting into life, followed by a billowing cloud of steam from underneath our van bonnet. Grinding to a halt at the side of the autobahn, where lorries race past at close to 100mph, we realised that something was seriously wrong. After a few panicked calls to a mechanically savvy parent back in the UK, we managed to patch things together long enough to limp the last few miles into the city. We barely made it to the venue, where we then split into two groups: one minding the stricken vehicle and the other loading into the venue. Unfortunately, it transpired that the concert had been cancelled without our being informed (the thoughtful barman allowed us to bring in all our equipment and set it up before informing us of this). Had it not been for a stroke of luck – an owner of a local rehearsal room overhearing our anxious conversation at the bar and offering us a place to stay – we would have been stranded without much money or any accommodation. Sadly, as the terminal state of our engine failure became apparent over the next few days, we were forced to cancel a few, and then finally all, of our remaining tour dates. Something that is extremely undesirable for any independent band or promoter, as it has a financial impact on the venues, wastes a lot of hard work and – crucially – taints the reputation of the band and their booking agent. Many contrite apologies were required to salvage the good relationship with the DIY bookers who had put their faith in us. It served to underline the importance of contingency planning. Before touring we now try to predict every reasonable hurdle that could present itself and have a plan in place. This can include bringing spare equipment, furnishing ourselves with travel insurance and keeping funds aside for emergency situations.

The cast of characters – a Svengali under every rock

Despite the overall annual depletion in musical revenue, it seems there is an ever-expanding array of individuals trying to insert themselves into the musical process as time goes on. In addition to the usual managers, tour bookers, publicists and their legions, the internet boom in particular has led to a flurry of self-styled entrepreneurs offering myriad services to further the reach of your music. Especially at the early stages. For a small subscription you can earn an extra 50,000 Soundcloud listens or Facebook likes and impress any potential suitors. Or perhaps you can afford to pay them to email American college radio stations on your behalf. Or maybe you just need advice on your next haircut. Whatever the service, the influx of emails offering to part young bands from their money has increased exponentially in the last decade. The amusing caricature of the pony-tailed, smooth-talking Svengali in the suit wandering into a rehearsal room and promising to make you the biggest band in the world might be something of an exaggeration, but these characters abound within the industry, albeit in much subtler guises.

Certainly, as a musician, exposure is crucial. Especially in the modern environment, where hard touring does not necessarily reap the breakthrough into mainstream success it once seemed to. However, as DIY aficionado Steve Albini shrewdly observed: 'publicity generates publicity, not money'. Those companies and individuals offering to get your music into the public arena or onto the desks of influential people might well do so. For a price. That does not mean that those influential people will ever even open that envelope, let alone follow up the lead. Especially given that thousands of other bands have exactly the same idea. Thus, the net effect is for money to drain from the least profitable sector of the industry into the pockets of middlemen, while young bands find themselves even more burdened with debts.

Management, too, can be a valuable asset, especially if things begin to pick up for an artist or group and they need to coordinate their efforts to maximise efficiency. However, management can also be an unnecessary expense. Too often it is practised by enthusiastic amateurs, not to mention over-zealous parents. In the early stages of any musical career it can form a superfluous layer of bureaucracy between promoters and musicians, often even serving to deter working with some individuals if they have a difficult or unprofessional reputation.

Most managers work on a form of commission, usually hovering between the 10 and 20 per cent marks, and this is another slice of pie going to someone other than the band. While the merits of management (done well) are undeniable, it is crucial for any young act to critically assess whether they already have the skills to fulfil these duties and thus maintain more control – and revenue – for themselves. At least up to a certain level. Some of the most successful DIY acts – including Albini's group Shellac and Washington DC legends Fugazi – continue to manage the bulk of their own affairs to this day, even down to dictating door prices at their concerts so nobody is being ripped off. Management structure is not 'one size fits all', and it is imperative that musicians objectively appraise the pros and cons of any arrangement rather than seeing it as a badge of professionalism and validity.

The case for – reasons to be fearless

The DIY approach is a uniquely rewarding approach to modern music. Your achievements are your own. While most signed acts rely on the money of corporations to buy their way onto front pages – and are thus at the mercy of these corporations when the funding dries up – the DIY act can take pride in knowing its coverage is based largely on merit and hard work.

That said, it is an extremely demanding course to take. It requires motivation, the suppression of ego and the realisation that one's fate is largely in one's own hands. If you seek mainstream recognition, more often than not the DIY route will not yield it, except for the lucky few. However, the relationships forged within this scene – genuine respect from and shared admiration for one's fellow independent acts across the globe – is a profoundly satisfying phenomenon. Unlike the fickle hand of market-driven commercial success, these relationships outlive the fleeting gaze of fashion and trends. Long after the latest novelty haircut drifts from the cover of *NME*, the individuals who forged memories and experiences together as part of any DIY or underground scene will share that bond and sense of accomplishment.

Involvement with large record labels and multinational media corporations necessitates certain unavoidable sacrifices, not least in terms of ethical credibility and the way in which those companies benefiting from your art institutionally suppress the mass of your unsigned peers. While the rewards for success in that environment can be considerable, the vast majority of those choosing such a route never succeed, at least not financially. It is thus an entirely admirable thing to set your sights on a sustainable, ethical mode of conduct like DIY that does not impinge on the opportunities of fellow musicians. It might not get you on any billboards, but it affords you a level of control – and self-respect – few signed acts can hope to muster in the long term.

Key lessons

- Decide on the values of the band early on, and stick to those values (see Chapters 5 and 12).
- Work out how to become part of a collaborative network through reciprocal cooperative behaviour (see Chapters 4 and 11).

• Plan and learn from the experiences of others in advance (see Chapter 7).

Discussion questions

• What are the most significant activities that are needed when starting out on the DIY route?
• What lessons might be derived from DIY for the (self)management of bands more generally?
• How can networking be achieved from a modest resource base?

Experiencing a creative journey

Martin John Henry and Daragh O'Reilly

Introduction

Martin John Henry is a songwriter and musician from Bellshill in Scotland – a place which features strongly in his work. This section tells the story of the different musical projects he has worked on, and the issues of collaboration and leadership that have emerged in the course of the work. He is the founder and frontman of Scottish independent rock band De Rosa, formed in 2001. The band released its first single on the Gargleblast Records label in 2004, with its first album, *Mend*, seeing the light in 2006 on the Chemikal Underground label. There followed a period of touring in the UK and Europe during 2006 and 2007. The second studio album, *Prevention*, was released in 2009, with cover artwork by Alasdair Gray, the well-known novelist and artist. After further touring, the band announced it was breaking up, but then reformed in 2012. During this hiatus, Martin made his first solo album, *The Other Half of Everything*, also released on Gargleblast. De Rosa describes itself as a 'Scottish musical collective'. The members are currently working on a new album.

"0>Early collaboration

Martin started a band with friends from school. In the early days – between 2000 and 2004 – it felt, looking back, like a time of complete chaos and turmoil. It was a question of 'just grabbing people who would help out', getting involved with people quite closely, people that he did not know well personally at all. He found himself working with these people on songs and realising that maybe it was not working in terms of relationships. In retrospect, working with people out of necessity without considering the social aspect was not a sustainable way of doing things.

Music was a lonely pursuit for many years. As a songwriter, he had a particular vision of the band and how it should work. At that point, he felt he was more of a dictator. It took him years to learn how to be in a band

and how to appreciate and use the skills of other people. He had to learn the right way to talk to people he was working with. By the time De Rosa was started properly, Martin had had the chance to work with good musicians and to grasp how 'amazing' it can be when you can get the right group of people together.

Andy Miller of Glasgow label Chemikal Underground heard De Rosa rehearsing, which led to the band recording their first studio demo. Martin was keen to get a well-recorded demo. Miller worked with them, and this mentoring relationship and collaboration helped to develop the band. Miller wanted De Rosa to be the band that started the independent Gargleblast Records label he co-founded with Shaun Tallamy. Miller, Martin and Shaun became good friends as a result of this collaboration.

The demo was duly sent out and attracted the interest of Chemikal Underground, who licensed the work from Gargleblast. This led to the band's first single coming out in 2004. It received good airplay, with iconic figures such as John Peel and Steve Lamacq picking it up. The album, *Mend*, followed in 2006. Its eleven tracks are infused with a strong sense of place and emotion, and range from the pensive lyrics of 'New Lanark' to the story of the Hattonrigg mining disaster.

Line-up changes

Like most bands, De Rosa has had its share of line-up changes. On the first album, *Mend*, the band was a three-piece, 'with a couple of orbiting musicians coming in and out'. After the first album it was more about 'tweaking the line-up' and getting new members – becoming more professional. By 2007–2008 when they were recording *Prevention*, the second studio album (again produced by Andy Miller), the band became a four-piece, which was 'pretty solid' and remained together until the band split in 2009. They toured with Mogwai and Arabstrap, and did a couple of European tours on their own.

Martin feels envious of those bands that are 'four guys at school and it just works'. He never had that, and instead was involved in a long process of finding the ideal line-up. He was at the core of De Rosa, and over the years many efforts were made to get a line-up that worked. There were many friends and other musicians who came and went. 'There must have been about fifteen different people in that band over the years.' He feels that the story is so complex that he would need to sit down and write it all out. The ultimate challenge in the De Rosa experience was 'making the band and keeping the band together'. There were relationship issues within the band, as well as members having commitments outside the band. For the last couple of years before they split in 2009, he feels, they had 'a great line-up', but only after it 'took years to get there'. By the time the second album emerged, the sound was changing from indie rock to a blend of folk rock with electronics and keyboards. The band became a five-piece. This gave Martin the line-up he wanted, and people he could trust and rely on to take ideas and 'be nice to them'. He felt sure that as a unit, as a whole, they were really creative; he had the confidence to do the songs.

The *Prevention* tour in 2009 took a long time and drained a lot of energy out of the band members. They were all working as well as playing in the band, so they were taking time off work and phoning in sick. By the end of the tour they were 'shattered'; they split up, after having an argument, on the last night of that tour. In Martin's view, being a band, one can end up working closely with other people one would not be close to otherwise. Things became tense and overheated. An attempt was made to make a change in the line-up, but that was overtaken by other changes in people's work or family lives. 'Everyone was just eager to draw a line underneath it and get on with their own lives for a while.' They had spent five years' work on the band by this time.

In the midst of all the line-up changes, there have been some constants in Martin's musical projects – some relationships that have stood the test of time and remained with him in different ways within the music business.

Collaborative process

The band felt somehow like a group based on friendship, since Martin knew Chris Connick, the guitarist, from school, and two other members (the Woodside brothers: James and Neil) were from the same town. It 'just felt right'. When Andrew Bush joined during the recording of the second album Martin felt that things 'took a step up in terms of the songs: there was just an extra flourish to them'. They were all excited about recording *Prevention*. The band members were all working or studying at the time, so the recording had to take place at weekends and holidays. The *Prevention* recording sessions were not as much fun as the *Mend* sessions or as Martin's solo album. However, Martin was very happy with how the music turned out. It was done 'in one go'. Martin had written most of the parts on *Mend*. On the second album, everyone got to write their own parts for the first time. With five musicians all writing their own parts with Martin's lyrics and chords: 'it was very different sounds, and a really different album, it was much more melodic and kind of gentle'. There was never much disagreement about musical direction – maybe a few small differences in musical taste, but one good thing about the band was that the members had different musical tastes.

Working solo

In the gap between De Rosa breaking up and reforming (2009–2012), Martin worked on his solo album, *The Other Half of Everything*, whose eleven tracks offer a wide variety of musical and lyrical textures. Running through the poetic, personal, enigmatic lyrics on the album is a theme of space, place, maps, contours and navigation. The spaces in question have to do with both physical and emotional geography. In 'New Maps', for example, he sings in his strong Lanarkshire accent: 'Fill my heart, fill my lungs/With a map of where I'm from . . . Take my heart, take my lungs/As a map of where I'm from'.

This solo album was a project that faced him with a different way of working. The collaboration with a group of other musicians was no longer there. Martin found it a big change from working in the band. Whereas there were five people in De Rosa and 'there was a bit more diplomacy required', on the solo project 'it was just me and Andy [Miller, once again the producer]: sometimes we are really bouncing off each other, you know, just ideas'. On the solo album, the music was 'pretty much half written and finished in the studio and embellished'. With De Rosa, the recording process was more important in shaping the music.

Whereas, as the songwriter, he used to see the songwriting as his job and other than that did not do much for the band, with the solo album he did every aspect of it. So with the solo project it was a question of taking advice but actually following through on a lot of the work. It was more a case of having a vision and following it, rather than coming to a band with some ideas and then the band taking things forward.

For the solo album, Martin had a picture of what he wanted to do. He had never had that before. He always just had songs; he would bring the songs to the band and, when they had finished enough for an album, it was an album; whereas, with the solo project, it was the first time he had written an album. He approached it as an album that ties together lyrically. He always likes to leave things to be formed by the recording process to a certain extent, but in terms of lyrics, he wanted it to be a much wider landscape than the De Rosa music. He finds the lyrics often guide the album, and when they can be seen as a group, he can start to think about tying the threads through it and revising just enough so that it flows as an album. The band's music was intensely personal, whereas the solo album had a mixture of the 'everyday moments' Martin sang about on earlier work but also had euphoric highs. There are some 'dancy' moments, and then some really 'focused' moments. He regards the dance stuff as 'almost too poppy', but quite likes that. He is really into pop music and dance music, as well as folk and guitar music.

As a songwriter, Martin generally starts with the lyrics. The music then responds to what is written. He generally waits to see what is written down lyrically, because he finds it hard to visualise music. Apart from the main melodies and chords, it is only when he is in the recording process that he has much of an idea about what he wants it to sound like. It is then a question of responding to what 'has been put down in terms of vocal melody and guitars'.

Martin sees himself as 'always moving from one thing to another' with records. On *The Other Half of Everything*, he listened to 'chunks and bits and pieces' over the course of the year it took to make it. For him, the album is better for that kind of process, rather than being recorded at, say, a six-week stretch. He would go in, play guitar and vocals, and then come back to revisit it six months later. There was a lot of revisiting, which could lead to some things being scrapped, others being 'layered up' and others taken in a different direction. Some of the work originated while he was working with De Rosa, but did not fit in with the band's work.

The solo album received a good reception in the press, especially the Scottish press, and was Bandcamp's 'Album of the Week'.

Leadership and professionalisation

Looking back, Martin feels that because he had some bad experiences early on he perhaps became too diplomatic. He regrets that he did not take more of a lead at times, rather than just blending in as 'one of the guys' and doing his bit. There was not the same DIY culture back in the beginning as there is now. He saw himself as a signed artist, and therefore able to focus on writing music. He expected the labels and the people around the band to do most of the marketing and publicity work. He has gained inspiration from talking to other musicians and reading other people's blogs. He regards himself as 'probably a late bloomer' in terms of leadership. De Rosa never had a live agent. They had good contacts with European and regional promoters and were able to book European tours, two or three weeks at a time, back then. Nowadays, Martin finds it more difficult to book extensive tours in the same way, as the contacts have changed in the years since.

Whenever he is at home, he is trying to make money through supply teaching to pay the bills, while writing songs in between, and trying to get gigs booked before going away again. This feels like 'complete chaos'. There is no routine. The idea of having a routine is very attractive, and he misses it, although he might quickly come to hate it. He would love to be able to write songs as a routine, because he finds it frustrating otherwise. He is grabbing time in the evening to work on ideas. He would love to be able to treat it like a job: to have an office to go to where he could write songs. Ideally, he would like to treat it 'completely professionally', but it has always been a kind of hobby. From his point of view, working in the music business is 'chaotic and unplanned' much of the time: 'in fact, lack of organisation is the key characteristic'. There is a dependency on other people, but they are often in heavy demand and he is not always sure when they will be available. It can be 'frustrating and then suddenly very surprising when good things happen, sometimes at very short notice'.

He tries to keep music the priority. When he got married and was trying to get money together for a house, it was difficult. He experienced feelings of guilt as the returns from music were so low compared to teaching, his 'day job'. He worried that he was simply trying to prolong an adolescent passion. Apart from primary school supply teaching, which gives him some flexibility, he does commercial photography (he is an art school graduate), as well as some training, using his teaching skills. He does some voluntary work for Gargleblast Records. As Martin puts it: 'It is like managing five or six occasional jobs, you know, in order to be able to make music when I need to make music.'

Key lessons

- Working through relationships in the band has a significant impact on the musical possibilities that are created/stifled (see Chapter 6).
- Going through changes can mean that there are 'resistance' and fall-outs, which can be dramatic and lead to break-ups, or which can, on other occasions, be coped with (see Chapter 5).
- Juggling different versions of the self, epitomised in alternative jobs, creates identity tensions (see Chapters 3 and 15).
- For an artist/musician, trying to go professional is one of the most challenging things you can do. It requires high levels of artistic, psychological, economic and social resilience (see Chapter 6).
- Leading and/or organising musical groups is a complex challenge, which requires handling of subtle combinations of personal and professional relationships (see Chapter 14).
- A member of an artistic, creative or musical group needs to have a clear and balanced understanding of how their skills contribute to the group and what they gain from the group (see Chapter 16).

Discussion questions

- What qualities does it take to be an effective leader of (a) a creative and (b) specifically a music group or band?

344 Martin John Henry and Daragh O'Reilly

342 Martin John Henry and Daragh O'Reilly

- What issues might arise in balancing both friendships and working relationships within a creative or musical group?
- What are the economic issues for musicians and other artists who wish to pursue their art on a professional or semi-professional basis?
- What might be some of the main differences between working in a solo creative project and collaborating on a collective task?
- How might artists and musicians cope with the unpredictability in their creative projects?
- How can musicians or artists hold on to their dreams in the midst of creative and economic challenges?
- Should musicians and artists be more organised?

For more information, visit:
www.facebook.com/martinjhenry
www.martinjohnhenry.bandcamp.com/
www.gargleblastrecords.bandcamp.com/album/the-other-half-of-everything
www.chemikal.co.uk/artists/de-rosa/

Musical identity: solo artist and band projects

Ben Talbot Dunn and Kevina Cody

Introduction

Ben Talbot Dunn is a singer, guitarist and songwriter, originally from Australia but now living and working in Scotland. He is currently the lead singer and guitarist with his band, Open Swimmer. The following charts his journey between these two countries, not just musically but from the perspective of someone who has negotiated the fluid, but often contentious, borders between his identity as a musician, frontman and band member.

Family ties – the genesis of his musical persona

Ben's alignment with band membership and musicianship began at just 15, when he and his brother toured Australia with their band, Ruby's Grace. For six years, Ben experienced and lived out his adolescence and young adulthood as a member of this band, allowing it to dictate what direction his life and subsequent experiences took. Even at a young age, Ben had a strong sense of how he wanted his musical identity to develop. Both he and his brother were inspired by another Australian band, The Waifs. The Waifs had chosen to eschew the traditional trajectory employed by record labels of using advertising and promotion to encourage a fan base. Instead they relied on building the fan base from the ground up by themselves, mainly through gigging and touring. They admired this approach to becoming a successful band, as opposed to focusing energies and creative efforts on making recordings that just got sent to record labels and were perhaps never heard by the public.

The unavoidable consequence of such a grassroots strategy was the lack of clout inherent in the promotional industry, which would have got them mainstream radio play. They had to accept that building a fan base themselves would mean a lack of presence on radio stations and other commercial channels. Social media were not present at the time, and even websites were not developed enough to represent any kind of advantage or benefit for the progression of their music. Posters and word of mouth were the primary means through which they could create an impact on the general public. They released an EP, a single and a live studio album. Then, the year before they broke up, they released a studio album, which Ben admits is something that he would not now be comfortable listening to, so far does he feel his current music has come from that point.

Stepping out of the cocoon

The demise of the band was not credited to any breakdown in communication or relationship between the two, but was rather the result of a desire by Ben to experience adulthood outside the confines and demands of the band. Although ready to leave the band, the move to Glasgow meant that Ben had to redefine his musical identity. Part of that process involved understanding the music scene in Glasgow and how it differed from Melbourne.

Fundamentally, Ben asserts that as a musician in Melbourne there was an acceptance of myriad different musical genres and tastes, and a permeable border between them. Musicians in Melbourne freely interacted and engaged with each other's projects, regardless of ascribed genre. Glasgow, although diverse, appears to Ben to epitomise a predominantly rock background, with various subgenres such as dance and jazz evident. In the midst of this Glaswegian music scene, Ben began to forge a solo musical persona. For the first four years of his time in this city, he performed and released an album as Ben TD. Ben recounts how he made a conscious decision to make accessible the 'people person' aspect of his personality in order to establish himself in this new musical environment. Doing open mic nights at local pubs, regularly introducing himself to new circles of people and generally existing in a 'social, open space' meant that Ben soon found himself playing regular gigs and being approached by potential managers. However, he soon became disenchanted with this managed solo career. He found that the managers 'spread themselves thin', trying to organise the careers of too many artists on their books. Eventually, Ben's frustrations at their lack of ability to book shows and festivals for him and actively promote his album led him to leave this arrangement and focus on managing his career himself.

Aside from the management issue, Ben soon found himself missing the collective identity and experience of band membership. He describes his eventual boredom at going to see solo musicians with acoustic guitars, and how this led him to realise that if he was bored watching something that he did himself, it was time to evolve his musical persona. Ben argues that

singing solo with his guitar was too easy for him to do, and that considering the plethora of similar artists on the Glasgow music scene, it was
time to once again engage with the prospect of playing with and in a band.
He wanted a challenge, but argues: 'I did not turn Open Swimmer into a
band to challenge myself, I did it because of the sound; I was fed up with
the sound of the acoustic guitar.'

Negotiating self and collective identities – the era of Open Swimmer

The formation of his new band, Open Swimmer, happened retrospectively, in the sense that Ben had already recorded an album for the band by
himself in Melbourne with a group of musicians, and on his return to
Glasgow formed a band around this album. Ben recalls how, at the
beginning when he formed his new band, he saw it as a completely
separate musical identity, entirely disconnected from his sense of a musical self as 'Ben TD'. This separateness was reinforced through the fact
that, at first, Ben avoided playing his solo material with the band.
However, as he once more evolved into a band member, he felt more at
ease using material from his solo gigs.

Ben's experience in Open Swimmer vividly illustrates an oscillation
between individual and collective musical identities. He clearly identifies himself as the leader of the band 'because I wrote all the music
and made the album without any of the band members', but concurrently he acknowledges that it is now a band sound – a 'group of
musicians as opposed to one guy'. Another significant factor that under-
lines the individual element of the group's identity as Open Swimmer
is that each member of the group plays in more than one band. Ben
explains that this is down to the diversity and multiplicity of music
in Glasgow, and that, in fact, he has 'come to realise that it is unfair to
even imagine that they would not be'. Ben himself cites membership
of another band called Kettle of Kites. However, he is clear that this
is something he is happy to do only until Open Swimmer goes further
as a band.

From a logistical point of view, the balance between Open Swimmer
and the musicians' other group commitments is managed on a 'first in,
first served' basis. In other words, if a gig has been booked, all members
must commit to it, even if another gig arises in the meantime. So he
acknowledges that this results in a lot of juggling, ensuring that if the
band is booked for a gig or festival, each band member must inform the
others if they are free or not: once confirmed and put in the diary, all band
members must commit if they are available.

Building the band's identity

Ben explains that succeeding as a band involves not just being approached to do gigs but proactively building the band's image and fan base by trying to secure gigs themselves. In stark contrast to Ben's adolescent experience with Ruby's Grace, where social media and web promotion in general were nonexistent, harnessing the power of social media is now a vital component of the band's progression; in particular, streaming websites such as Soundclub, where interested parties can hear the band's music online.

However, despite the importance of this outlet, Ben stresses that securing a festival slot is top of the band's current agenda. Within the festival scene, a hierarchy is quite visible to Ben. Some festivals are smaller but enjoyable to play, while the bigger festivals represent a serious opportunity to solidify the band's presence on the national – if not global – music scene. But with such opportunity comes a more significant challenge, in that the bigger festivals are quite regimented, with a specific process in place to secure a slot for your band. Ben explains the 'BBC introducing' stage, which they have at many festivals around the UK. Essentially, no band will secure a place on a festival stage unless they have gone through the 'BBC introducing' process and format – for example, of the radio shows. Even though Ben is quite clear about the importance of this structured route to gaining access to the festival outlet, he still insists that, regardless of process, the importance of being liked is also a significant factor. 'No one ever talks about it but they have to like you – it is like people, in the end it comes down to the people and whether they like you and want you to play.'

Counting coins – musician as an occupational identity

In the midst of the band's pursuit of continued success is the more grounded issue of income and money from their musical endeavours. As yet, the band hasn't made any substantial amounts of money. Their manager, Tristan, is entrusted with keeping track of any income that does come the band's way. Tristan himself does not get paid on a regular basis. He is more passionate about doing the job itself than receiving any pay for it. However, Ben points out that whenever the band does find itself in situations where money is available, Tristan will always get a percentage of it. For Ben, paying Tristan is a priority, in that the band members see themselves as musicians who just want to play music, whereas Tristan is doing a job for them all and will always get paid before the band members themselves. The band currently re-invest any money that is made from gigging back into promotion, as well as covering expenses they incur while on the road.

Understanding this dynamic faced by many musicians in the industry – pursuing a passion while trying to make a living – is a reality for Ben and Open Swimmer. Ben's ultimate focus and drive is making music, but he concurrently acknowledges that some opportunities to play with his band must be considered carefully, as they can end up costing the band members money. In addition, there are some gigs that may involve investing money but represent serious opportunities for exposure among industry figures, and Ben insists that those gigs are always important. Therefore, it is a genuine tightrope that must be walked between pursuing a passion regardless of economic return, while at the same time making money to ensure that this same passion and dream can live on in a commercially oriented world: 'the only reason it is about the money is so that I can do it'.

Crafting the band's identity – independent versus label release

As this point, Open Swimmer have not released the album they have recorded. They are grappling with the decision of whether to be a brand new band and try to secure a label to release it, or alternatively to explore the possibility of an independent release. Regardless of the outcome of this decision, the band are fervently pursuing rehearsals and live gigging, as they are acutely aware of the importance of being a good live band, so difficult is it to make money from album sales alone in the current musical environment. However, Ben simultaneously acknowledges that in order to get a profile of listeners and fans you need a body of work – an album. Not having a release and yet continuing to gig to establish fans is not the traditional way a band would operate, Ben concedes, so they are trying to put a taster album together for fans, which would be a more economically viable way of getting their recorded music out there. He is quite proud of the fact that they can boast an increasingly established profile as a band in Scotland – playing on the 'BBC introducing' shows, headlining one of the King Tut's winter night shows and selling out small gigs in Glasgow – without yet having actually released any material.

Releasing material inevitably involves a choice between independence and label involvement. The band would regard a decent British label as an attractive option, as it would prevent them being pigeon-holed as just a Scottish band by music fans down south: 'it gives you more opportunities, and you are not seen as something that is limited or stuck in Glasgow'.

Ben acknowledges that Scotland's musicians tend to keep to themselves because of the vibrancy and self-sufficiency of their music scene, but that this can often result in disconnectedness from the national music market.

The only way to ensure that you have a presence nationally is to take some risks: play gigs, no matter how insignificant, and in time the persona of the band will evolve to having an identity on a national scale. In this pursuit of national recognition, the importance of getting a booking agent is central. The competition among bands playing the circuit is so intense that now many venues are only dealing with booking agents to source bands; therefore, not having a booking agent excludes you from many opportunities. In part because of his frustration with this process, Ben reflects on the current state of the music scene in Australia. Although acknowledging that his frustration probably leads him to idealise what is going on back home, there appears to him to be a more open music scene there, with bands not having the same corporate restrictions when it comes to establishing a profile and getting considered for gigs and venues.

Ownership and leadership – the band 'façade' and project Ben

Ben explains that a characteristic of the contemporary music scene is a tendency for band members also to have active solo pursuits as musicians. Being in a band involves a negotiation of solo and group identities. At first, Ben explains that Open Swimmer regard themselves primarily as a band more than a group of solo artists, despite Ben's acknowledgement that he writes the songs and has made albums without the band. In articulating the identity of the band, however, Ben reveals an undecidedness about its solo or collective essence. In other words, although he had until this point considered Open Swimmer to be primarily a band, he equally sees it as a one-man project with a team behind it. Comparing Open Swimmer with groups like Sam Bean and Iron and Wine, which are decidedly individual projects with a group of musicians supporting them, Ben concludes that perhaps there is still a strong element of that attached to the band's identity.

As a measure of whether the band's identity is fundamentally individual or collective, Ben considers the possibility of collaborating with the band on another album. This is something he concedes would not entirely materialise. Although he consults other band members for variations on piece arrangements, he admits: 'mostly I do dictate how it is going to sound and I guess if it does not sound like how I want it to sound, then it is not going to happen'. This almost dictatorial relationship with his band has nothing to do with exerting power, however. Ben's sole motivation and reward is the music. More than anything else, he wants the output of the band – its musical persona – to be his. This pursuit of individual creative fulfilment, encased within the semblance of a group, leads Ben to conclude: 'maybe the band thing is a bit of a façade of wanting to seem like a band'. Wanting a band, for Ben, means wanting its sound, but also its profile on the music scene.

Regardless of ambiguity and blurred boundaries around its core identity, fundamentally Ben sees Open Swimmer as involving collective activities. However, this collectivity doesn't extend to decision-making, as several band members are not interested in being part of the decision-making process, partly because they already occupy this role in other bands. Being in Open Swimmer for some means focusing solely on the music and leaving the organisation and logistics to other members.

Ben is now comfortable with the centrality of his role in the band's identity and his established leadership of its activities. This was not always the case. Ben admits struggling at first within Open Swimmer with the issue of highlighting that it was his music the rest of the group were just playing, even to the extent of feeling uncomfortable being the one at the front of the band, singing. However, this – Ben's ownership of the group's musical outputs and the recognition of that – is now something that is openly acknowledged and accepted by all band members. The band gives Ben enough separation from being a solo artist to enjoy the collectivity of making music in a group and creating that sound but, at its heart, Open Swimmer is Ben, and he is not 100 per cent aligned with the ideologies of a band and a collective essence. However, although comfortable with the one man and his band analogy, Ben does feel that there must be an element of commitment to a band identity as, psychologically, musicians don't invest in a situation where they feel it is just them supporting an individual musical pursuit. So perhaps calling them a band was more for the reassurance of those around him than any definitive alignment with a group identity.

Each member of the band appears to have a different understanding of its identity. Band member Ritchie, for example, is happy for Ben to take ownership of the group, and reassures Ben that it is ultimately his music and that he is part of the band because he wants to play Ben's sound. Ben continues to play solo gigs as Open Swimmer. A central part of Ben's understanding of Open Swimmer as essentially his project with the aid of a group of musicians is reinforced when Ben discusses his latest musical outputs. For the first time, Ben is 100 per cent comfortable promoting his music and believing in his music, so that even if the current band was no more, he would be willing to hire people to play with him to ensure the continued pursuit of his musical endeavours.

This reveals a fundamental understanding for Ben – people are the vehicle for him to perform the music he is writing. The band identity is a collective that acts not like a group but as a mechanism for Ben to continue producing, performing and enjoying the music that he alone creates. Despite Ben's insistence that the group dynamic is still appealing to him – being on the road with the band, rehearsing as a group and sharing music – it is still his music and his musical identity that is shared and at the forefront of the group's persona.

Ben has now returned to Melbourne and continues to perform both in the band Open Swimmer and solo under that same name.

Key lessons

- Negotiation of solo and group identities: the current landscape of the music industry requires that many band members are also concurrent solo artists or members of other bands. Therefore, one of the primary organisational tasks of any band is to negotiate how this solo/group/ other group dynamic is going to affect each member and each band's activities. Open Swimmer's strategy of 'first in, first served' is an example of their attempt to formalise an approach to managing the band and its composite solo and group identities (see Chapters 6 and 15).
- Ownership and leadership: the corollary of the oscillation between solo and group identities and activities is a conflicted, non-linear under-standing of ownership and leadership within the group. In the case of Open Swimmer, Ben's integral role in creating the music for the group has lent itself to a natural inclination to assume the leadership role in the group's organisation. However, this is also supported by the other group members, who are happy to view Open Swimmer as a group in which they can take a step back from decision-making and leadership.
- Organisational process of the music scene: Ben's account gives a vivid insight into the rigid, sometimes bureaucratically oriented process whereby bands gain an opportunity to gain mainstream exposure. His reflexive account of trying to secure a slot in a festival designed to introduce new groups ironically being an easier thing to do once you've established your profile illustrates a central contradiction at the heart of how this industry is organised (see Chapters 12 and 13).

Discussion questions

- List, explain and discuss the implications of both avoiding and embrac-ing commercial practices throughout Ben's musical career thus far.

- Discuss whether fitting the band Open Swimmer retrospectively around an already created album had an effect on the everyday organisation, as well as the identity, of the band and its members.
- Ben recalls how he saw the formation of Open Swimmer as a musical identity entirely disconnected from his sense of a musical self as 'Ben TD'. Discuss whether you agree or disagree with this.

For more information, visit:
www.myspace.com/bentdmusic
www.openswimmer.com/

An embodiment of a band

Duglas T. Stewart, Charlotte Gilmore and Peter Keenan

Introduction

The BMX Bandits have stood at the epicentre of the Scottish pop music scene for over two decades. However, despite helping launch the careers of influential indie bands ranging from Teenage Fanclub and Eugenius to the Soup Dragons, and being the band of which Kurt Cobain of Nirvana once said: 'if I was to be in any other band, it would be the BMX Bandits', the group itself never grew beyond the confines of a fervent cult following. They were essentially the vehicle of singer Duglas T. Stewart, who formed the band in 1985, selecting the name 'BMX Bandits' out of his belief that the band would fall apart after one gig. Instead, the group has been playing and recording on and off for twenty-seven years, and has made fourteen albums. The band has seen members come and go: there have been twenty-six members in their twenty-seven years, aside from the lead singer Duglas. The following is Duglas's story of his band.

Duglas

Duglas grew up in Bellshill, which he describes as 'a sort of ex-industrial sort of town, where the major industries were coal and steel and when they left the town was probably drained of a lot of life blood and possibly, for a lot of people, hope and stuff like that'. However, for Duglas this environment stimulated his creativity, insofar as it motivated him to escape, albeit mentally, by creating a more 'beautiful world' for himself. 'It is really in your mind that you are transporting yourself to a kind of more beautiful world, or you are trying to create a more beautiful world . . . think I have always been driven by creating.' Throughout his life, Duglas has also been driven by provoking a reaction, something which began at school: 'I had a strange kind of fearless quality up until, you know, up until probably well into my adulthood, I am sort of – that is from a school in Lanarkshire, Bellshill Academy and I would hang around smokers' corner, wearing a Sherlock Holmes hat and lighting up a pipe to actually be an irritant and provoke reaction.' This 'fearless quality' and desire to 'provoke reaction' have carried through into his on-stage performances:

I always had a slightly kind of fearless thing like, even like when the band started the notion of again, similar to school, the fact that there would be a certain percentage of people in the audience, who you knew always wanted to kill you but actually I liked that, I liked the fact that it would be strange for them that I was not acting like the, if you like, the archetypal rock male ... there was always a big kind of proportion of men wearing like Whitesnake or Doors t-shirts with moustaches, who were very threatened by the idea of you.

A short history of the BMX Bandits

His personal qualities also made Duglas the obvious choice as the front-man when he first formed a band:

I formed a group and Norman [Blake] was involved and Sean [Dickson] who ended up being in the Soup Dragons, Frances [McKee] and some other friends, and just straight away I found myself in a position, it was not like, oh what will Duglas do, it was just obviously he will be sort of the front person, even although technically I might be the worst singer out of all of those – it is not really down to being the best singer, it is about having the ability to make a positive impact.

This group was the Pretty Flowers, which stemmed from Duglas and Norman making music in each other's bedrooms when they were young.

I was performing when I was little, funny songs and stuff from about eight, but Pretty Flowers was the first, I guess, sort of formal, thing. It kind of came about, well, my friend Norman, who went on to be in Teenage Fanclub and was in early BMX Bandits, and I used to kind of go to each other's houses and make like an album a night – not an album that was ever going to be released, but you know we would just get some like Tupperware dishes and a casserole and Norman would have a guitar that he had borrowed and we would just make up, we would fill a tape with songs, we were very good at just making up on the moment, and playing back in fits of laughter.

The Pretty Flowers was disbanded, but with some its members Duglas formed the BMX Bandits, and in 1986 their debut single 'E102' launched them to the forefront of the C86 uprising (C86 was a cassette compilation released by NME in 1986, featuring new bands licensed from British independent record labels of the time). After a series of subsequent singles and roster changes, the BMX Bandits released their long-awaited debut LP, C68 Plus, in 1990. In 1992, the BMX Bandits signed to the Creation label, where they issued the autobiographical single 'Serious Drugs'. Released in 1993, Life Goes On was the band's next LP, followed up by 1995's Gettin' Dirty, which was an album inspired by the Beach Boys.

After the group released *Theme Park* in 1996, Duglas split off to make a solo record, *Frankenstein*. In 2006, after a long period of musical inactivity, the group released Duglas's favourite Bandits album, *My Chain*, followed up by with *Bee Stings* in 2007. In 2009 the band released a compendium of 'hits' and lost songs called *The Rise and Fall of the BMX Bandits*, before returning with a new studio album, titled *BMX Bandits in Space* in 2012. Duglas describes this most recent album as:

... sort of little snapshots of love stories from my own life and stories that I've been affected by about others but sometimes misremembered, half remembered or altered to be how my romantic mind wanted things to be. So I'm drifting in space in a sort of dream replaying these little scenes over and over in my mind and trying to find my way back home.

The BMX Bandits *is* Duglas

In an interview for the cultural and arts magazine *The Skinny* (23 November 2012), the journalist Michael Pedersen asked Duglas to describe what it meant to him to be a BMX Bandit. Duglas replied:

It's pretty much everything I am. It can make everyday life a bit tricky to navigate, but I don't think I really have a choice any more. For other people I think it's put quite well by something Norman Blake said. He said, 'to be a BMX Bandit you need to be unafraid of being ridiculed or thought foolish by others'.

Similarly, in the feature-length documentary produced by Jim Burn marking the twenty-fifth anniversary of the BMX Bandits, *Serious Drugs: Duglas and the music of BMX Bandits*, the title of which is a reference to the band's most celebrated song, 'Serious Drugs', Duglas said: 'Outwith [the band] I don't really exist, I don't know who I am outwith that ... I don't know who I am except a BMX Bandit'.

The BMX Bandits songs mix melodic qualities and humour with, at times, raw and heartbreaking pathos: 'nearly all BMX Bandits songs are, you know, it is like the world according to Duglas'. Duglas gave the example of the album he wrote after breaking up with someone: 'The album *My Chain* you would think would just be an album of pain and it is not, there is a lot of humour in it – I mean, I could see the funny side of my misery sometimes.' So for Duglas, escaping to 'a world of beautiful songs' allows him to both express and escape struggles with depression. Writing songs let him 'turn things that are negative into positive things', as these excerpts from his diary entries describe:

Sometimes the real world is much too real for me to face and so I run away and hide in another place, a world of beautiful songs ... things seem better there.

There is so much darkness and sometimes it feels like I'm drowning in it ... but there's also beauty there.

He also alluded to the connected nature of these feeling within his interviews, and how he needs to express the 'darkness' within himself in his songs.

DUGLAS: 'I will do things like put myself in the worst possible situation to make things really painful for myself ... but I can be really quite down and I can be the opposite, so high I cannot sleep for three days.'
INTERVIEWER: 'Do you write songs in those extremes?'
DUGLAS: 'Yes, I think that is the only place I can ... it would always be when I would be in a more heightened state [of real pain] ... captured in the notes, the rhythm and in the sound and I guess that has always been my kind of obsession ... but it is always a struggle...'

In the BMX Bandits documentary, one of Duglas's band members acknowledged this investment as he talked about Duglas 'really lay[ing] himself bare [...] The thing is about Duglas ... he is so consumed with the idea of being an artist and what it means to be an artist...'. Leaving himself vulnerable is something Duglas acknowledges:

I sort of think sometimes being on stage if you are singing very emotional songs, you are almost lying there naked and saying you can tell me that I am okay or you can come up and kick me and humiliate me. David Scott actually said to me, 'Being in the BMX Bandits one thing you need to be, is not be frightened of being humiliated' ... and I think it is because this sort of thing that you could be laughed at, you know, because there is humour in it [the songs], also because it is nakedly honest and if you are nakedly honest some people can go, 'Ha, ha, ha, look at him he is crying' ... so it is almost like that thing of actually putting yourself in a vulnerable position and just trusting people not to kick you.

Duglas and his band family

While Duglas has written many of the group's works solo, including 'Your Class', 'The Sailor's Song' and 'Doorways', he has also collaborated with many of the other members. Stewart's most regular songwriting collaborators have been Francis McDonald, Norman Blake and, more recently, David Scott of The Pearlfishers. Duglas's lack of technical music ability means that he also needs collaborators in order to create his songs. However, despite this need, Duglas was clear that BMX Bandits is his 'form of expression', and during the band's lifetime he has asked two members to leave. The first was guitarist Sean Dickson, who went on to form the Soup Dragons: 'this is my form of expression: other people may take a part in it ... and contribute ... but it couldn't be Sean's form of expression'.

Similarly, creative differences with his songwriting collaborator and drummer of eighteen years meant that Duglas asked Francis McDonald to leave the band. The struggle there was rooted in their differences over the band's creative direction:

There came a point a few years ago where Francis I think was wanting BMX Bandits to go one way and I was wanting them to go in another way, and it came to the point where we could make albums where there would be tracks that were like what I wanted BMX Bandits to be and there would also be tracks that Francis wanted them to be. And unfortunately, and Francis would totally admit it, it could not be what Francis wanted it to be. Francis was a massively significant player in the group, he was in the band for eighteen years and probably the person I wrote most songs with, but if he left the band it could still be BMX Bandits. But if I left the band it would not be BMX Bandits and I think everybody would sort of see that. People like long-term members of the band Norman [Blake] and David [Scott] and Sushil [Dade] have all said in interviews, 'oh, BMX Bandits *is* Duglas'. I think that is a kind of confusing statement because it is sort of true on one level but on another level it is not true. It kind of sounds like it is belittling all these other people's contributions that I could not exist without, but I think in a way it is almost, to me, like if you think of Duglas as a being, I am not just this internal thing and Duglas who has had these people as parents, who went to this school, who was friends with David, who was friends with Norman, so all these other people are a part of me as well so that is why, I guess, you could also say the band is Duglas because Duglas is made up of David, Norman, Francis, living in Glasgow, falling in love with this person, so it is almost like, I guess, a kind of ongoing portrait of me and my life.

This sense of the BMX Bandits and its members being a part of who Duglas is, is also reflected in his *Skinny* interview (23 November 2012):

Well, BMX Bandits has become not so much a group but more an extended musical family. People who've played with us in the past haven't completely left and could sometimes still pop up on new recordings or at shows. Norman has played on every album since he officially left the group in 1991. On the new album [*BMX Bandits in Space*] Sean Dickson and I have written our first track together since 1986. I sometimes worry everyone might grow tired of me and leave me but I'm glad they seem to be happy giving so generously of their time and talent to my vision.

Key lessons

- Identity struggles influence a musician and these are expressed through music-making (see Chapters 6 and 15).
- Creative leadership and collaboration influence band relationships (see Chapter 7).

• A musician can be the embodiment of a band: 'Outwith [the band] I don't really exist, I don't know who I am outwith that . . . I don't know who I am except a BMX Bandit'.

Discussion questions

• Reflect on Duglas's personal experiences: how do they influence his songwriting?
• The BMX Bandits have achieved acknowledged artistic success but not significant commercial success. Why do you think this is?
• How do you think Duglas's leadership style and vision have influenced the band? What type of leader is Duglas?

For more information, visit:
   www.myspace.com/bmxbanditsgroup

Rock music on the big stage

Jim Prime and Peter Keenan

Introduction

Jim Prime is the keyboard player and co-songwriter with Scottish rock-pop band Deacon Blue. From 1987 to 1996, the band had seventeen Top 40 hits and three No.1 albums that totalled more than six million in record sales until they (temporarily) split in 1996. Jim initially played as a session musician with Scottish pop band Altered Images as they charted in the UK and US at the beginning of the 1980s. Still in his early twenties, he then played alongside Eric Clapton, Phil Collins and John Martyn. He spent two years in French icon Johnny Halliday's band, and he has worked with many other established musicians such as Scottish folk artists Phil Cunningham and Eddie Reader. He has also held musical director roles in two Scottish theatre companies. The following is Jim's story of his journey as a musician, spanning over three decades, where he reflects upon the trials and tribulations in creating and maintaining musical success, as well as the personal impact of its absence that required readjusting to 'everyday life'.

In preparation for going on the big stage

Jim's early years were important in preparing him for a career in songwriting and live performance. He received piano lessons from the age of 7, followed by encouragement from an enthusiastic music teacher, who persuaded him to get involved in school theatre and shows. The appeal of the theatre hall had an immediate effect on him: 'If it was empty, I just felt incredibly privileged to be allowed in it and standing there. Then I am backstage, and I can see all the workings of it. That was just heaven ...'

Jim started his first band as a teenager, but with his background working in theatre, 'where you have to turn your hand to any style', he soon developed into an accomplished session musician in different music forms ranging from traditional to jazz to 'songs for Christmas parties'. As he could play by ear, his musical repertoire soon widened as he also discovered that 'music was quite a good tool to wheel out at parties as you get popular that way'.

Despite his early successes as a session musician, Jim took the decision in 1983 to 'quit playing music in bands because he could not make any money out of it'. He resorted to working in a bank in an IT role in an attempt at 'joining the human race'. His 'time out' with the bank was 'a very strange period' and turned out to be 'absolute hell'. After two years he moved on to work in a bar where Glasgow's media and entertainment set hung out. At this time, he described himself as 'always having delusions of writing a song, but not really managing to find the right person to sing it'. He felt he needed a singer-songwriter partner, and while working in the bar one night, a local radio DJ called Mark Goodier handed him a demo tape by a singer-songwriter called Ricky Ross. 'I met up with Ricky, I loved his songs and found I could write with him. We struck up a good relationship and the rest is history.'

Jim and Ricky initially 'piecemealed' a band together to play several gigs, but eventually 'found the musicians that were going to give them a little bit more'. The band soon signed a record deal with Columbia Records in 1986 and subsequently released six albums and nineteen singles throughout the following decade.

Writing and recording the songs to go on stage and perform

Deacon Blue's songwriting process often started with Jim 'having the song worked out in his head' and 'coming up with the chords and the tune first'. He would then play it on the piano to Ricky 'until he starts singing, jotting down one-liners, phrases, anything that comes into his head ... and I will start reacting to the way that he is singing it, and I'll begin thinking about instrumentation'. On other occasions, Ricky initiated the process as he would 'write differently' by bringing 'five different songs every week' and Jim would then 'search the tune for a "hook line"'. Jim found this worked well, as 'Ricky knew he could just ask me to play something, and I could play it'.

Both of these approaches to writing songs highlighted the different roles Jim and Ricky held and the contributions they each made. On the one hand, Jim described himself as having the 'pop sensibility' because he had been in Altered Images and he knew 'what a "hook line" was and the notes that you are going to remember the song by'. Whereas Ricky's poetic sense and literary qualities were drawn from being an English schoolteacher, which suggested 'he was quite good at writing lyrics'.

An important element of both approaches was Jim and Ricky's ongoing interaction and discussions with each other about constructing their songs. This involved some 'to-ing and fro-ing'. With the band's hit 'Fergus Sings the Blues', Jim recalled, 'it was the first time we ever used brass, and I would go up to Ricky and say "this is what I'm thinking about"'. Ricky's lyrics mattered a great deal to Jim in terms of their local places references but also that they should carry some cultural and political meaning to them:

What excited me was that we were singing songs about Glasgow and not about some place in Tallahassee, you know? We were singing songs about Buchanan Street, songs about the Mitchell Library and places I knew. Glasgow was also quite militant at the time we started, so the first song I wrote was called 'Loaded' and it talked about the wealth in England's south east while Margaret Thatcher was imposing the poll tax on Scotland without understanding the differences up here.

As their relationship evolved, Jim assumed the role of 'band organiser' and 'musical director', with Ricky emerging as 'musical educator' and ultimately 'bandleader'. Jim felt that he had to 'play catch up for quite a while', as he had 'missed a whole lot of bands like The Blue Nile and The Associates that profoundly influenced most of the 80s thing'. Indeed, it was Ricky who began introducing Jim and the other band members to artists such as these. Jim recalled: 'Ricky is so knowledgeable about the history of music and he has an enormous record collection. I had never heard of any of people like Gram Parsons or even Springsteen.'

Decisions within the band were also deferred to Ricky, who 'called the shots'. 'It was easier that way', argued Jim, who was 'happy to be second in command' because this still allowed him to direct the rest of the band on the basis of his technical expertise in a way that Ricky was unable to. Jim found that he was 'good at organising the troops in the band to play as well as they can, to understand the song and how Ricky wanted to get it up to scratch and up to speed'. Although he acknowledged Ricky's role as bandleader, Jim still had an important communication role to play because 'Ricky did not really know how to talk to a bass player, how to talk to a drummer and how to get him to do this and do that. And I did.'

Jim was also actively enforcing some degree of stylistic conformity on other members who did not share Ricky's tastes and ideas. For example, 'there were tensions because our guitar player was good but in a different way, as he was into jangly kind of pop and not really into Ricky's music'. Despite this, the band still managed to integrate some diverse and varied musical influences, but Ricky 'generally' always had the final say.

Deference towards Jim and Ricky seemed to emerge and be maintained for historical reasons; namely, they were the founder members of the band. As for Jim himself, he fully advocated the order of things within the band that deferred final decisions to Ricky, and he strongly believed that 'knowing your place' was important for the band's stability and progress:

> You recognise your roles and responsibilities in any group and where you fit in the band hierarchy. There is no such thing as a democracy in music. It does not work. So, I would sit down and listen to them squabbling over what the set list should be and eventually I'd just have to say, 'Look guys, let's just accept one thing, this is what we are doing'.

Order would soon be restored as the band acquiesced to Ricky's position.

After the songs for an album had been written, the recording process itself was very closely tied to the band's technical competence and the eventual touring and live performance of the songs.

> One of the key things we learned early on was that whatever we record, we have got to be able to play it live. So when we record, we record as a band. We will spend time in rehearsal studios and we will get the song sounding as good as we think it will sound live and then go into a studio and play it that way. Loads of bands do it like that. It is the best way to get a performance on the track. A really good performance is first and foremost, before you actually record a song.

Yet despite the band's time and effort in mastering the playing of new songs, the songs were 'deconstructed' and 'taken apart' by a record producer, 'who basically comes in and says "that is crap"'. The initial songwriting process may previously have been in the hands of Jim and Ricky, but the song's development was now firmly in the hands of someone else, who demanded: 'they have got have got to play more of this and start doing less of that' prior to then 'piecing it all back together in a form that he thinks is going to sell lots of records but also be the better for that song'.

This was a process that the band became accustomed to when recording. Jim learned that a producer's intervention and contribution was important for the band to then stand back in order to allow producers 'to do their magic'. From bitter experience, Jim found that 'if you give Deacon Blue too much of a lead, or too much room to manoeuvre, then it tends to be a complete mess and a waste of money as we found out when we went to America for two months and came back with eight absolutely useless tracks'.

He attributed this partly to 'sitting in jacuzzis, driving open-top cars, and going to the beach', as the recording process felt like 'a holiday'. Too leisurely and relaxed a recording environment was unproductive for Deacon Blue, so they began retreating to the studio during the winter months, where they could be 'all locked up inside as there was nothing better to do'. Living in residential recording studios helped the band 'go to work' in a structured environment. This helped them to 'just try to get a vibe, and that can be at 2pm or 8pm or 10pm ... it just depends'. The band found this was 'the best approach' to recording as they were 'just immersed in it' and focused solely on their songs.

What also helped the band record was excluding the record company from coming 'anywhere near the studio' as 'it is bad karma'. At that stage of the process, Jim found that the band and the record company held very different and sometimes competing priorities: 'All they are interested in is getting a record that they think they can make money out of, whereas you are thinking about artistic qualities, about sounds, textures, and creativity'.

Who to go on stage and perform with

Throughout the period of Deacon Blue's success, the band comprised both 'core members' and 'session musicians ... who were outsiders in a way'. This issue of 'core' versus 'outsider' group status was something that Jim identified with personally, because he had at different times in his career held both of these positions. Distinctions were made between being an 'independent' session musician with temporary membership and a 'core member', who was signed and contracted to the record label and 'institutionally managed'. Session musicians were considered to have different priorities, responsibilities and concerns. For example, 'jobbing musicians have also got to be managing themselves towards their next job, how they are making money and how they are paying the bills at home'.

The commercial aspect and long-term benefits of the band playing well, promoting the album and touring successfully were not considered to be concerns of session musicians from Jim's perspective:

They are part of the band during rehearsals, and they are 'our' band on stage, but they argue over different things. We will be arguing about recording, the attitudes of the record company and having to meet with people like press and promotion, and they don't. I am a core member and managed with a record label, a publishing company. And managed in the sense that we want to maximise sales and ticket revenues. But when you are on tour, you maybe have four musicians that are self-employed. They basically turn up and do their job.

'Doing the job' was a euphemism for 'doing what you were told'. Jim understood this from his own experience when recalling: 'Altered Images hired me and told me not to *play* too much because it was not cool to do anything flowery'. Ironically, Jim adopted a similar stance with session musicians himself as a 'core member' of Deacon Blue. Session musicians essentially played a functional role in his view and they remained detached from the song development process. Jim directed them and he held no expectations of session musicians contributing to songs with any creative ideas or suggestions. If anything, this was often discouraged.

Before, during and after touring

Although touring was a time to receive public acclaim from adoring audiences and music media alike, Jim found life on the road 'very hard', as it involved relinquishing all personal responsibility for his daily schedule to a tour manager; 'trying to get used to this was a common cause of stress on tour'.

The tour manager's role was a multifaceted one that involved coordinating timetables across America, Europe, Australia and Japan. He needed to know exactly how many people had paid for tickets so that what the band got paid for was 'properly accounted for and put in the bank'. He also had to hold together the relationship with the road crew, who were 'very mercenary creatures that basically keep the whole thing going'. Although the crew had no allegiance or loyalty to the band, the success of the tour was completely dependent on them. In addition to the organising, negotiating and financial role, the tour manager had 'the great responsibility' of providing the band's 'rider' and 'making sure that all the right drinks, crisps and all that crap is in the dressing room'. Furthermore, he was required to adopt the role of guardian by 'making sure that we don't go off and get completely drunk and throw ourselves off a bridge somewhere'. In this respect, Jim found that different tour managers had alternative 'parenting styles' as providers, consolers and 'listening to you moaning about how you get stage fright'.

It was during his time as a touring musician that Jim felt his role was not solely a creative one, as he often re-evaluated the significance and value of his role in the wider scheme of things: 'Being managed takes a long time to get used to as it is not a real existence. You think, "This is not for real: you are not really that important". It is just that you play tunes that people like and that is it.'

Adapting to touring was challenging because it was a period of being 'detached from reality'. Its routine involved 'getting out of your bed, and getting on the bus' with the tour manager, who was 'like a holiday rep as they will be the ones who will be organising golf trips or things to do, so they'll have you busy on your days off'. Although being taken care of in this way was initially welcomed and enjoyed, this kind of work arrangement became complicated when Jim was also trying to manage and cope with the pressures of family life back home. At these times, Jim found that there was 'no support for creative musicians when they are facing distress on tour and maybe facing marriage break-ups'. What to do in such situations was both confusing and frustrating. As Jim describes:

I have done the rock 'n' roll bit, and I have also done the coping with having a baby whilst I am on tour at the height of the band's career as well. These are things that there is just not a support manual for, and there is not any support within the creative industries for people who secretly struggle.

It was problematic for Jim 'fitting back in after touring' and returning to his wife and family, largely because it required assuming full personal responsibility for his daily life again. It also meant conforming and re-adjusting to the structure and demands of family life. Coping with life at home again was not so straightforward. For example:

When you come home, you cannot crack open a bottle of beer at 3pm as you have got to go and pick your kids up. You have got to go and do the shopping, and you have got to cook food that the family wants to eat. As we are not doing anything while we are away on tour, musicians come home and their partners are like their new managers but they have not got the time to deal with them.

The freedom, dependency and self-indulgence of the touring musician suddenly needed to be abandoned. For Jim, this was easier said than done.

Parting ways, then going down that old path together once again...

By 1996, the band felt some resignation that 'there was nothing more they could do here' with the limited success of their latest releases. They had achieved enormous commercial success over a nine-year period, but 'it was not really going anywhere as the record company had gone on to hipper new things' with the emergence of Brit-Pop. Jim recalled: 'Everybody hated us. Deacon Blue were a 1980s band. It was your uncle's music by the time you got to 1996. Stuff your mum whistled in the kitchen. So we called it a day.'

While reflecting on his success with Deacon Blue during the 80s and 90s, Jim said:

My goals were to be on a stage playing to an audience and them loving it. I achieved that. If somebody asked me what the high point in my career was, it would be listening to 220,000 people on Glasgow Green [in 1990] singing the words to your song ... because they know it. That is the biggest thrill in the world.

In 2010, the band reformed to play a small music festival in Ayrshire. They were soon playing live again by popular demand: 'We could not sell any records, but we could sell tickets, so that is what we started doing.'

Nevertheless, by 2012, Deacon Blue had released a new album (*The Hipsters*) to critical acclaim, and in 2013 they embarked on a sixteen-date tour, playing old and new songs to large audiences in major venues such as the Royal Albert Hall.

Key lessons

- Commercial success is often time-limited, even for famous and established bands. It is rarely marked by continuing success over decades, and its absence can often be influenced by what other current musical and cultural trends are emerging at the time (see Chapter 2).
- Autocratic decision-making appears to work well for some bands that defer 'the final say' to one individual or bandleader (see Chapters 5 and 14).
- Identity: there are issues of 'in group' and 'out group' membership of bands with 'core' and 'session' players. The identity of Jim's role was fluid and temporal in this respect (see Chapters 6 and 15).
- Deacon Blue's success was lengthy, then absent, yet they returned to a '40-something' audience for live performances, and to fans who subsequently demanded a new album (see Chapters 8, 9 and 10).

Discussion questions

- Should bandleaders be self-designated or appointed by others? Do bands need a leader at all? Can 'democracy' exist in a rock-pop band?
- How might the 'core' versus the 'session' membership status of a band both help and hinder the creative process?
- What emotional and social resources might musicians draw upon in order to readjust to 'real life' after touring?

For more information, visit:
www.deaconblue.com

Playing in the Royal Scottish National Orchestra

Lance Green, Katy MacKintosh and Charlotte Gilmore

Introduction

Lance Green is a trombonist who joined the RSNO in April 1982. Katherine (Katy) MacKintosh is currently Associate Principal Oboe with the RSNO. The following describes Lance and Katy's experiences of working in an orchestra.

Background

Katy grew up in a musical family: 'my dad always played a lot of piano and so basically we were brought up with music, and I sort of played the piano when I was about 1, really'. She became serious about her music early on, and aged 5 she went to the Royal Scottish Academy of Music and Drama (RSAMD) to play the violin and piano and sing. When she was 14, she 'realised that it just was not happening with the violin', and so she took up the oboe: 'I am quite a late starter for the oboe; my piano teacher said you look like an oboist, I did not know what I was taking up'. Katy progressed with the oboe quickly because she knew how to read and play music. After the Junior Academy at the RSAMD she went to the Royal Academy in London and studied there for four years. Katy had won the Woodwind Final of the Young Musician of the Year before she went down to London; because of that, she felt 'very much squashed, I guess, because there were great oboe players and I wasn't the next big thing, I think'. For Katy, being in London was a difficult experience: 'it felt like you were on a conveyor belt and constantly competing against everyone else who played your instrument and I just craved being back in Scotland'. Despite finding living in London difficult, Katy felt that she had to stay there after graduating from the Academy in order to:

prove myself as a player, thinking if I went back up to Scotland that was not really making it ... I think the RSNO is sometimes regarded as not as good as London orchestras simply because it is not in London – it is that straightforward, and I don't agree with it. I think that there are some really strong sections in the RSNO and I think our woodwind section is really one of the strongest in the country but I felt at the time that I needed to prove myself.

Initially, Katy taught music and did freelance gigs. She then began to get a lot of well-paid session work on, for example, TV jingles and west end shows. However, she decided to move back to Scotland, after thinking she 'would get bored playing the same music day in and day out, but it was a good thing', and she secured a position with the RSNO.

Lance started playing the cornet at a young age and then took up the trombone. Lance's father was a military bandsman, playing the clarinet, so Lance started learning the cornet within the band. He then progressed on to the trombone: 'there was a great teacher who said, "He is not a natural musician, he is an animal – give him an animal's instrument, the trombone"'. Lance trained at the Royal Academy of Music, but before going he did a business degree. 'My parents had said, you are not doing music, we are not going to let you do music, so I did a business studies and admin for four years, but all the time I kept the music going in the brass band and National Youth Orchestra and teaching myself.' At the Academy, Lance studied classical music 'simply because I was frustrated and I wanted to know about that stuff. It was good to play [in the brass band] but you did not play very much but you had to use your brain. I used my brain a little bit until I went to the Academy in London; I did everything through natural instincts.'

RSNO education work and music in hospitals

Lance and Katy are both involved in the RSNO's education work. This gives them a chance to improvise and play different styles of music from those played within the orchestra: 'education work, it is a completely different skill I think to pitch it to the children'. The need for 'completely different skills' from those required to perform in an orchestra 'scares' a lot of the players, and so 'there are a lot of people in the orchestra who would not touch it with a bargepole, but then there are a lot of people who do a lot of it, me [Katy] included'. Some of the musicians who choose not to do education work also just want a complete break from the whole orchestra, given the workload that this entails. However, Katy talked about really getting a 'buzz' out of it, because she is able to connect with her audience, something that is more difficult playing with the orchestra:

Take my education work away from me, and I will be unbearable really, because working face to face with someone ... actually getting a real, proper interaction with someone means the world to me . . . [in the orchestra] when you play to a sea of faces you don't know what effect you have on them, you cannot see that. When you play to a group, a smaller group of people you are really close to them and you can see the way the music is affecting them.

Katy also plays music in hospitals, and was working as part of a trio in Yorkhill hospital in Glasgow for a decade:

I guess we were specialising, we were trying to specialise in the cancer ward because you have kids in there for quite a while, so you can build up a relationship and do projects with them, and I was getting really interested in working with kids who have been in road traffic collisions, so maybe they were in a coma. I think that music is really interesting in that situation.

Lance works at the Royal Scottish Conservatoire, and he talked about getting a real buzz from teaching students, with whom he could identify as a musician 'struggling to get a living' as he had in his young playing days:

I get a buzz from teaching at the Scottish Academy because students for me are great people, and I really identify with them struggling to get a living. They work hard, they keep me on my toes because they are constantly demanding lots of things, have you heard this, have you seen this . . . I won't have heard it, I won't have done it, I am not up to date and I respect them.

Recruiting in an orchestra

Normally, musicians audition for a job and then, 'if you are interesting enough', the musician gets a trial position with the orchestra. This often lasts a long time, because 'it is more than just finding the right player, it is finding the right personality to fit in with the section as well and it gets all personal and everyone has got their own kind of thoughts on the way it works'. Because the positions are so specialised it often takes an orchestra years to fill them when a vacancy arises. 'Personality, the standard of playing, everything has to be researched. You have got such a specialised job to sell that there are not many candidates out there, or the calibre are not out there, or the standard is not high enough and you just have to keep going on until you find the right person.' While there were a large number of musicians applying for each position, as Lance describes – 'in the 1960s a tuba job was filled and there was one excellent candidate. A tuba job has just gone in the last year and there were 120 in for it; that is what has changed in the last forty to fifty years' – finding the right calibre of musician was difficult. This was because a lot of the 'high-flying student musicians' were going into other professions because the wage levels in orchestras are not as high as in other professions. 'The money in this game, people are reluctant to have a job in the art world, because it is not moving properly in the same sphere as other professions ... the money isn't there for the type of pressure you have to deal with.'

Both Lance and Katy felt it was a situation specific to the music business, but this type of reward structure is starting to be challenged:

I think we are just so far behind in the music business, because people seem to think that it is not a business and that it is music so it is, so we can have our own rules and this goes and that goes. And so the section carries on because it is somehow acceptable because it is not a normal business ... it is certainly being eradicated.

The conductor–player relationship

The conductor's job was described by Katy as 'a lonely job ... they spend their lives in hotel rooms for starters, they have a very limited social life, I guess, because they are always away touring'. From the payers' perspective, conductors are an:

... interesting breed, in that they tend to be bi-polar or something – when they don't have a baton in their hands they can be the loveliest, kindest people. The moment they pick up the baton they feel that they need to make sure that they are completely in control, they are completely controlling people so you are never really on an equal level with them.

Some conductors are:

... control freaks and want to control every aspect of a solo, for instance, that you are playing, and then others will let you take the major, let you deal with it, but that – unfortunately – is rare. If the conductor mucks up and you question something he is doing in a rehearsal – you would not want to do that too often, honestly ... I mean, I questioned him [the conductor] today and for the rest of the rehearsal he has been trying to fault me because he just wanted to make things difficult.

However, while conductors are musically trained, they not trained in the way the orchestral players are, 'and that is the problem', because they do not understand how it feels to play the particular instrument, and so they cannot provide the support that the musician needs. They also may not know what each musician is capable of, and so '... often we have to use our initiative really to figure stuff out ourselves'.

Conductors communicate with an orchestra in various ways, some more effective than others: 'whether it is your fingers, your eyes, but most it is from the mouth, you get a lot of verbal diarrhoea, very much so. The stage manager tries to motivate his actors; they have learned their lines and are somehow trying to sort of direct it.' Rather than using a 'flashy' technique, the conductor and orchestra relationship was thought to work best when the conductor 'kept things simple': 'to do things that are magical, keep them very simple and that makes concerts happen and rehearsals happen too. The whole relationship works.'

The players talked about 'bailing out' the conductor when things go wrong in a performance – this was the job of a principal player: 'It will be a principal player that will correct something if the whole orchestra is not quite sure what it maybe is, or the conductor has added an extra beat in a bar, the conductor missed the beat, then one player just with an instrument plays it.' The players talked about the conductor learning 'through' the orchestra: 'if you think of the gig tonight you will probably find that we had to bale him [the conductor] out somewhere, he learns stuff through us, so he will play stuff over and over again until he figures out how to do it'.

The orchestra dynamic and performance

The orchestra was comprised of players from a wide range of ages and diverse backgrounds: 'every class, from all walks of society'. There was also a spectrum of struggles, needs and wants:

... we have got players who keep themselves to themselves, players who struggle every time they go on stage to get themselves on stage, they are suffering from nerves, it might be drink, they might take beta-blockers, they will do whatever they need to and they build up a profile and get on with it ... You have got people that worry about the reviews being wonderful that night and they will go and chat up reviewers and all that stuff ...

The players talked about hiding their emotions after a performance, whether it was a good or bad one for them.

A lot of the time, you know what, don't show that it worked for you because that is not cool ... There is a lot of good hiding going on in an orchestra ... you have got to turn on that feeling based on that. But inwardly you are going through hell. Or you could be going through absolute bliss, joy. You just don't want to show your emotion, and unfortunately there were times when it is not possible to hide it ... Sometimes I still get that, I feel really vulnerable.

Within an orchestral performance a good performance was based on the individual players' experience, and there were often 'huge differences of opinion of how they feel. They might be judging it on the strength that they did not play so well themselves, and others might be "oh that was completely shit" – you are always treading this fine line. With eighty to a hundred musicians you never get unanimity.'

The players felt little direct connection with the audience: 'Well that is a funny word, "connection" with the audience – they are so far away.'

Rather, the players' relationship with the audience was based more on giving them the best live orchestral experience, and on allowing them to escape their everyday worlds. As musicians, the performance was a job of work, and they had to concentrate on playing their piece:

I go there because that is exactly what I want, I want the peace and quiet, I want to escape what I have been doing during the day, I want to see live music, I don't want to hear it on the radio, I don't want to hear it on the TV, I appreciate that . . . but a musician cannot afford to let that happen to them because you have got to concentrate, you have got to focus on what you are playing, sometimes you can escape and think, 'Wow, it is all happening', but for most of the time no, you have got a job of work to do and you have got to get from the start to the end.

Key lessons

- There can be tensions between the conductor and the orchestral players, depending on the conductor's style of leadership (see Chapter 5).
- Different skills are required within different playing contexts – for example, between Lance and Katy's improvisational education work and their orchestral work. Katy and Lance place value on working with children and students, compared to playing within the orchestra (see Chapter 16).
- The nature of orchestral playing is specialised, and the low wages within the 'art world' discourage 'high-flying students' from orchestral playing (see Chapter 7).

Discussion questions

- Consider the differences between Lance and Katy's work in education and their orchestral playing. What skills are required within the different contexts?
- Reflect on the nature of the relationships within the orchestra, and with the conductor and audience. How do you think this affects the orchestra's performance?
- What kind of 'hiding' goes on in the orchestra? Why do you think this is?

For more information, visit:
www.rsno.org.uk

Reflections of a gigging musician

Ian Smith and Charlotte Gilmore

Ian Smith manages the portfolio for music, intellectual property develop-
ment and content ownership at Creative Scotland. He joined Creative
Scotland with a long history in the UK and international music industry.
Ian was Head of Music at the Scottish Arts Council, following twelve years
as the Scotland and Northern Ireland organiser for the UK Musicians'
Union, where he founded the folk, roots and traditional music section.
For more than twenty-five years he was a professional musician working
with the Royal Scottish National Orchestra (RSNO) as Co-principal
Horn. He was the founder of Scottish Brass and served as a Governor of
the Royal Scottish Academy for Music and Drama (RSAMD; now the
Royal Conservatoire of Scotland) and as a member of the executive board
of the Musicians' Benevolent Fund. Ian is currently a member of the
executive board of the European Music Council. In this section, Ian
reflects on his experiences as a 'gigging musician'.

Background

Ian was a gigging horn player for almost thirty years. He started playing
with the Scottish National Orchestra (SNO) – or Royal Scottish National
Orchestra (RSNO) as it is now – at the end of 1971, at a time when he was
just beginning his third year at the Royal Academy for Music in London.
Ian recalled that he:

did an audition and they offered me a job on the same day, which is very rare; Alex
Gibson – or, as he became, Sir Alexander Gibson – who founded Scottish Opera,
was the Principal Conductor of the SNO for twenty-five years and appointed me to
the horn section.

Now you would have to do weeks of trialling. I was completely taken by surprise
because I knew nothing about anything, at only 20 years of age and, as I said, I was
starting my third year of college at the Academy in London. I phoned my horn
teacher in a bit of a panic saying, 'What do you think I should do?' He was
Chairman of the London Philharmonic Orchestra (LPO), and he said, 'Just do it

for a couple of years – it will be a good experience, and then come back to London'. Instead, I spent twenty-two years in the RSNO; I was very lucky.

I was Co-principal, so during my time in the orchestra I picked up lots of other work as well, because I was a very enthusiastic fan of music, orchestral music and particularly jazz. I started getting work with what was then the BBC Radio Scotland Big Band, which is sadly no longer.

I was working with great arrangers, playing arrangements by people like Stan Kenton, working with people like Brian Faye – who was then the director of that orchestra and a very well-known and respected arranger – John Gregory, Adrian Drover: just a really rich time for lots of varied work going on. That is the reason why I, as a student, was playing in one of London's top orchestras, because there was a lot of opportunity and if you had the right connections (like your teacher was chair of the orchestra) you could get work.

My first professional gig was at 19 years of age with the LPO, and then I played a lot of jazz, a lot of sessions and a lot of jingles and bits and bobs whilst I was still in the orchestra, which was very, very good for me. But then I got the offer to play with the London Symphony Orchestra (LSO) just because someone who had worked with the SNO went to the LSO, and then I started getting offers to play with them. So for ten years I was a regular deputy player with the LSO. I was working in Scotland with the SNO and in London with the LSO, and I was just very, very lucky.

Horns in Poland

'In those early years we did a lot of touring, and one of the first tours I did was in 1976 to the Autumn Festival in Warsaw, Poland. The Autumn Festival is a famous contemporary music festival.' For Ian, the most telling memory of the tour and of that time was: 'for the first time in my young professional life, understanding what freedom really meant: you know, freedom of the press, freedom of expression, musical freedom, ability to work wherever you were good enough to work, rather than where the state allowed you to work'. At that time in Poland, 'when you went into the airport it is all staffed by military personnel and I mean military personnel – and very restrictive. So that was my first introduction to living within a closed party regime.'

One evening, while at the festival, the players were all sitting in the band room getting ready for a performance. Ian was sitting next to his colleague, Charlie Floyd, warming up and practising their horn duets. The two horn players from the Polish Chamber Orchestra, an orchestra of high repute, which at that time was conducted by Jerzy Maksymiuk, came into the band room to speak with Ian and Charlie. Ian recalled:

Horn players are very cliquey, it is a bit like a club, so we started talking to them but they were looking at the horns we played on. It is like 'What car do you drive?' if you are interested in cars or 'What motorbike do you ride?' if you are interested in motorbikes, and so there is kind of anorak conversations start about 'What horn do you have?', and they got out their horns and these horns are literally held together by solder and string.

Ian and Charlie realised that because the Polish players were not allowed out of Poland, they could only have what was available to them in the country or on tour, and these players could not afford the sort of instruments that Ian and Charlie played on:

I was 25–26 and I already had the best instrument that you could buy and did not think anything of it – that is what you bought because you are professional, you have the best equipment, you would mortgage your house to buy an instrument before you bought a house, you know. And to cut a long story short, we could just see that they were in need of equipment which we carried out in our crates: we carried spares around because a horn is a mechanical object – things break, things wear out, so all the spare parts, if you like, a bit like going rallying, you know, in the van is a spare car, a spare engine, bits of body work, it is the same thing. So we just handed them all our spare equipment and they started crying, and that was so moving because we were not saying, 'Look, we have got loads of money', we were just saying, 'We are colleagues/friends, we have it, you have it. You cannot get this so you have it, because when we get back we will get this for free, the manufacturer will send it to us, we will just make a phone call and say we need some more valve oil grease and they will send it to us because they endorse us using their products.'

Chernobyl

One of the next tours for Ian involved playing in Berlin in the Philharmonie, 'one of the great concert halls of the world'. Behind the Philharmonie was part of the Berlin wall, and the musicians could look over the wall into East Germany.

We could look across the divide, which was mined with traps and all that stuff, but the guy in the observation post in East Germany was looking at us and I am looking through, you know, a camera lens . . . and he is waving at me and I am waving at him, and I was thinking what is this about, we are the same. It was the same experience that we had in Poland with the horn players; we are the same, we are just the same, and it is not about colour or religion, we are just the same, we are human beings but in that case we are musicians.

It was during this tour, while the musicians were in Berlin, that Chernobyl happened. Ian remembers:

. . . going back to the hotel after the rehearsal and the television was on and the news presenter was talking about which areas were worst hit by the fall-out from Chernobyl, and the location worst hit was in the middle of where we were, over that part of Europe in which Berlin sits. We are idiots and we did not think anything of it, so the whole brass section went out the next morning wearing shower hats, saying this would protect us from the nuclear fall-out – I mean how ridiculous: we were just comedians. I mean, we would all be laughing now if we were disabled in any way! As many people were, near the site of the blast ... no one took it seriously.

Hairspray

Over the years Ian had 'the great privilege of playing in Symphony Hall, Chicago, Carnegie Hall, New York, with Claudio Arrau'. Claudio Arrau was then around 80 years old, and at that time 'one of the world's gods of piano ... and he was coming towards the end of his career'. Arrau toured with the RSNO and they played Carnegie Hall, New York. Ian notes:

If you are a horn player, and if you are on great form the two concertos you want to play are the two Brahms piano concertos because they are, depending on which seat you are sitting on, like mini horn concertos. So it is either a great day at the office or a funny way to give your notice, and fortunately it was a great day at the office. At the end of the concert in the Carnegie Hall in New York, having this elderly man just look up to the horn section – to you – and give a bow, it does not come any better.

Ian talked about another 'great day at the office', in one of his very first concerts with the SNO, which was a gala concert with Artur Rubinstein, who was then in his middle-to-late 80s.

He came to the keyboards with Alex Gibson and I had never played with someone of that repute, and he sat at the keyboard, and he was playing the Grieg *Concerto* and the Beethoven *4th Concerto*. He sat, and he had a little bag, and sat at the keyboard and got out of his bag a huge can, an aerosol can and sprayed up and down the keyboard. Because it is Artur Rubinstein, it is like Albert Einstein has come into the room: you can do what you like, I am in the presence of genius, and he put the can back in his bag and zipped it up. He sat and looked up, and of course we are all going, 'What the hell is he doing?' And he said to Gibson, 'Ah, this is my wife's hairspray – I am an old man so I like the keys to be sticky!' Well, the audience that night, and I absolutely kid you not, at the end of the performance he played a Chopin piece as an encore that every piano student, and myself included, would have struggled with. He was an old man but he played Chopin beautifully, and when he got to the end you could actually hear people crying, you know, before the applause started. Now that does not happen very often. You will never see or hear this man again and of course a few years later he had died, but these moments are so, so very special.

Good conductor

Ian talked about what he looked for in a good conductor:

Well you want to look up and you want them to be clear, and we saw it with Järvi, and I worked with Maazel and Previn and Tilson Thomas, and what you had from them was clarity of vision; you knew what they wanted. They did not all have the great stick technique but it goes beyond that. Maazel has very small movements; Klemperer, very small movements. They did not swish the air, but you did not need a lot of movement because you knew what was required, and most professional orchestras can work without a conductor. Often, you will find that the leader takes a very predominant role if there is a bad conductor on the box, because the strings can mostly see him or her, and a nod or a gesture is enough. The great conductors are very rare, they really are. The ones through my career, there was probably half a dozen, no more, that actually made a real, real difference to what you did.

I am one of the lucky ones. It is not just about luck, but luck plays a part. One of the most important things you must never lose is your enthusiasm and your passion for what you do, because don't forget that a lot of the success that I and other musicians have had is because your hobby in a way becomes your profession. It is a hard life: you have got to keep your professional practice absolutely at the very, very top. It is like football, it is like athletics, you know: muscle tone when you are a brass player or a wind player. You know the physiognomy of the lips, for example, is what I paid my mortgage through using, over many years. You are in serious trouble if your muscle tone starts to deteriorate, and it happens – it happens with age, it happens with muscular problems like dystonia, which affects a lot of players, the equivalent to repetitive strain injury. A lot of people, a lot of professional musicians have no 'plan B', and if something goes wrong then they are lost. I absolutely planned for 'plan B': I got to a certain age and said, 'Right, I am now going to actively find a route out of playing whilst I am playing well. No one is going to tell me, "I think it is time that you should go" – I am going to make that call', and I was lucky enough to be able to make that choice at the end of 1993/94. I joined the Musicians' Union, so I was still working within the music industry but I was working from a completely different perspective, and that is really when I started to learn about the industry. I knew a lot about playing and I knew a lot about the mechanics of making music and performing music. But everything that was behind that, I did not know so much. I think I am a more complete professional now than I would have been if I had stayed in playing. You cannot play at the level I played at, at my age now. I mean, there are exceptions, but they are literally on the fingers of one hand, and I was not about to let that happen.

Key lessons

• Taking opportunities to play with experienced peers and a range of styles of music enables development as a musician.

• Good instruments and equipment, in addition to a conductor with clarity and vision, can make a difference to how a musician plays (see Chapter 17).

• It is important for a musician to have passion and enthusiasm for playing: 'your hobby in a way becomes your profession. It is a hard life: you have got to keep your professional practice absolutely at the very, very top.'

Discussion questions

- What were the cultural differences Ian experienced when going to Poland and Germany, and how do you think these affected him?
- Reflect on Ian's experiences as a musician and his work within the Union and now Creative Scotland. How do you think the earlier stages of Ian's career could, or should, influence his role now? Should managers and policy-makers be musicians?
- If you were a professional musician, what would your 'plan B' be?

For more information, visit:
www.creativescotland.com

20 Next steps in the dialogue: insights for practising and theorising

Charlotte Gilmore and Nic Beech

Our purpose in this chapter is to reflect on the empirical examples in order to stimulate an ongoing dialogue. As we said in the opening chapter, our aim is not to provide overly normative prescription, but to explore 'promising practices' (Delbridge et al., 2007). We regard these as resources that may be useful to others, in that readers can select ideas, react to them and adapt them to inform practice in new contexts. In the constructionist mode (Cunliffe, 2008), people can pick up 'snippets' of other people's stories and use them in composing their repertoire of future action (Sims et al., 2009). The repertoire does not need to be replicated mimetically, but is an expanding pool of resources, which can be combined and recombined to fit new situations. This style of learning is experimental, in that it deliberately moves into the unknown, but it does so with a set of supportive ideas that become moulded into the style of the actor, such that it is possible to analyse and produce possible actions in a reflective but speedy way (Beech and MacIntosh, 2012). The dialogue, in this sense, is not necessarily with other people in the room, but is conducted between the self and the stories and ideas of others – what might be termed 'absent presences'. It is future-oriented, as it engages with the possible reactions of others in the real-life situation, and is experimental in deciding on particular courses of action and working out how they have been received and what impact they have had. Subsequently, further actions can be taken on the basis of how those earlier steps have worked out. It is also imaginative – drawing in the vicarious experience of others and learning from it.

What we offer here is a set of patterns, discernable in the empirical chapters, that are derived inductively. They are not the only patterns, but they are ones we found helpful, which – we hope – will be of use to others. They are arranged in four sections: (A) Orientation, (B) Operation, (C) Reaching out and (D) Reaching in. Each section contains two or more questions; the empirical snippets presented beneath them offer ways of engaging with, and finding one's own answers to, the questions.

A.   Orientation

In this section we are concerned with how people orient to the process of organising music-making. As people approach the tasks, what do they aspire to? What assumptions do they make? What are the practical implications of their approach? From a constructionist perspective, this is significant because the meanings that people (selectively) perceive and make relate to their orientation to the social world. The two questions posed are how do we choose the balance between art and commerce? And where do we strike the balance between collaboration and competition? Both of these can be answered at various positions along a sliding scale, and it is normal for people to move along that scale as a result of feedback, experience and learning. They may also take up different positions on alternative projects (for example, ones they are leading as opposed to ones they are joining) and at different career stages. We would contend that it is potentially useful to recognise and understand one's own position in any particular setting, and to be able to recognise the orientations of others, in order to interact and manage the situation effectively.

A1.   How do we choose the balance between art
and commerce?

The art versus commerce dichotomy has been debated for many years, and it relates to values – what people see as being most important – and to what has become almost a moral hierarchy. The pure pursuit of art might be regarded by some as superior to the transient and self-oriented pursuit of wealth. However, as Oswick (Chapter 4) indicates, this may be too simple a way of constructing the debate. Both Hackley (Chapter 10) and Bradshaw (Chapter 12) deconstruct the simple separation of economic and aesthetic markets and the role of production and consumption in society (see also Mason, Chapter 8; and Saren, Chapter 9). The focus on aesthetics that Strati (Chapter 2) brings does not remove music to a 'pure' realm away from the physical, embodied experience – and such experience is embedded in the social and economic world, which enables certain experiences and restricts others. Changes in technology enable some access to the production and consumption of music in a less resource-intensive way but, ultimately, the important issue is the values that underlie the productive process – are the people involved doing it for the music, monetary reward, a combination of these two or a broader set of purposes? There are occasions when music-making is simply financially instrumental, and times when it is only about music, but most of the stories presented above incorporate a broader set of values – including being part of a community, expressing the self or important messages and making beauty more accessible to people who might not otherwise have access to it. Given a portfolio of activities, it is likely that there will be different emphases in values that orient participants to those activities, and this does not appear to present strong contradictions – rather, people seem to seek a balance over time and over different areas of the practice (see Bilton and Cummings, Chapter 7; Nicolini and Greig, Chapter 17).

Simon Webb (Chapter 18, pp. 251–7), discussing economic and artistic priorities in decision-making within the City of Birmingham Symphony Orchestra (CBSO), sees them as 'inseparable' in 'strong' decision-making. Artistic/creative organisations like the festivals and orchestras need to balance their 'practical', 'hard-headed' business objectives with their 'creative' objectives:

I think only that the two are inseparable: there is no single part of the operation that you could consider either as artistic or operational or whatever the tag we give to it ... Whenever somebody is making a very strong economic point we would always bring in the artistic balances and vice versa, and that is how you make the strong decisions.

For many of the other indie bands, 'hard-nosed commercialism' does not fit with the image of an indie band (see Cloonan, Chapter 18, pp. 226–35). Indeed, there is a tendency for bands to pursue their passion, regardless of economic return: 'the only reason it is about the money is so that I can do it' (Talbot Dunn and Cody, Chapter 19, pp. 343–51). This sentiment is reflected in the discourse the musicians use when discussing the 'business side' of their music, as they 'hated to sound corporate' (O'Sullivan and Chillas, Chapter 19, pp. 317–25). However, the indie bands also recognise that they need to get 'business savvy' if they want to 'get their music beyond their bedroom walls' (ibid.). Very few of the indie bands are fully self-sustaining – that is, making enough money so that they do not need 'day jobs', such as working in bars and cafés or teaching music. Digital downloads have made producing albums financially loss-making, but bands need the albums in order to tour, and unsigned bands needed to pay to record and produce an album themselves. Thus, for the musicians, grappling with the creative and business elements of the music industry involves determination and hard work. As Cloonan (Chapter 18, pp. 226–35) notes: 'art and commerce are not opposed – they just sometimes take a while to get into bed with one another'.

For a band, being signed to a label means that the label will release and promote the album, with the band's agent being responsible for organising a promotional tour. On entering a contract with a label, bands need to grapple with the impact of the business side of the industry on their creativity. Getting a record deal on such a label means that bands feel the risk of losing creative control. It comes with a 'weight of expectations', and bands feeling pressure to comply with market forces outside of their control – for example, choosing which track on the album will be put out on radio as a single, when the band's choice of preferred song is different from a radio plugger. The label has to try to sell albums, which in turn has effects on the creativity of musicians. There are tensions between labels that are 'too interested in numbers' and the band that is interested 'in the art form'.

Another route for bands is releasing on DIY labels such as Olive Grove Records (Chapter 18, pp. 245–50) and Song, by Toad (Chapter 18, pp. 285–9), which are considered 'a step up from self-release'. The fact they are independent is seen by the musicians as advantageous in terms of not being for profit – the label gives the band the time to develop musically and to build a following:

They [Song, by Toad] give us a lot of support actually because they are independent, it is like: 'Oh right, your first album, it was okay, but we are going to stick with you for the second and let you kind of get your fans and blah, blah, blah, whatever' – that is business talk, but it has been really good. (O'Sullivan and Chillas, Chapter 19, pp. 317–25)

For Lloyd at the Olive Grove label, 'going in thinking that you are going to make money out of it [music] is a recipe for disaster at the moment'. Rather, the ethos behind these labels is to cover costs and return any profits to the band that makes the music. For Lloyd (Chapter 18, pp. 245–50) and Matthew (Chapter 18, pp. 285–9), the boundaries between music and work are somewhat blurred, but they are cognitively reconciled (i.e. conceptually blended): music is both work and play (see Chapter 3 on the integration of stories and Chapter 15 on the integration of identities). The altruistic ethos behind these DIY labels, run by music enthusiasts like Lloyd and Matthew, means that while the bands pay for everything involved in putting out a new release, organisationally the label 'does everything for them'.

A2.   *Where do we strike a balance between collaboration and competition?*

A characteristic of the contemporary music scene is a tendency for band members also to have active solo pursuits as musicians. Being in a band and in an orchestra involves a negotiation of solo and group identities (see

Coupland, Chapter 6), but in different ways. Artists tend to collaborate on a number of projects at the same time (see Bilton and Cummings, Chapter 7), and collaborations come about as a result of an individual's reputation and networks. The Fence Collective (Chapter 18, pp. 218–25) is an example of musicians collaborating to form a record label and festival identity: a small, independent 'cottage industry record label'. But within bands, while there is a level of musical collaboration when it comes to the arrangements of the songs, for example, as with Jim Prime and Ricky Ross (Chapter 19, pp. 358–65), the main songwriter assumes the mantle of leader. This role of leadership can also be seen in orchestras – for example, the BBC Philharmonic (Wigley and Gulledge, Chapter 18, pp. 258–61) emphasises the need for clear decision-making by those in leadership positions, particularly during times of (perceived) crisis.

Louise Mitchell (Chapter 18, pp. 213–17), who has organised both Celtic Connections and the Edinburgh Festival, discusses the collaborative approach one needs in working on festivals, where managing relationships involves dealing with people both internal and external to the organisation. Louise talks about a 'no blame culture' and always backing her colleagues: relationships, reputation and collaborative practices are absolutely essential as they build trust. This is borne out by Nod Knowles (Chapter 18, pp. 205–12), who emphasises the need for networks in running festivals, but also acknowledges the competition with other festivals for audience numbers. Similarly, artistic decisions are somewhat, but not totally, collaborative within the large orchestras. For example, a board of trustees oversees the running of the CBSO (Chapter 18, pp. 251–7), while its chief executive officer (CEO) and a small management team deal with strategic matters and day-to-day operational activities. In terms of the artistic programme, the CEO, working closely with the music director and the principal guest conductor, has the final decision on programming. In contrast to the indie bands and labels, the repertoire decision-making for orchestras consciously balances artistic with commercial considerations – programming new, neglected pieces that challenge players alongside large-scale repertoire that aims to attract a full house. Collaborations between orchestras tend to be done on a project-by-project basis, and one project at a time (Chapter 18, pp. 251–7; pp. 258–61). Such collaboration between orchestras or with a particular conductor is again based on reputation. As Michael Downes (Chapter 18, pp. 270–7) describes, when orchestras identify partners who have an equal interest in developing the provision on offer, creative and rewarding collaborations can be stimulated.

B.   Operation

The enactment of music-making and its organisation pose a range of challenges. One is the question of how the right skills and knowledge are marshalled to perform effectively. These skills include songwriting and composition, arranging and orchestration, rehearsing and enabling others to perform, and a set of organisational skills in leadership and the ability to join and maximise the utility of networks, which are themselves dynamic and frequently political in nature. The orientation taken (e.g. to be more collaborative or more competitive) has an impact on how these tasks are approached, and the enactment of the practices also reflects on the overall style and identity of the performer/organiser. For example, adopting a democratic leadership style can be achieved alongside a political and com-petitive approach to networking (see Hibbert, Chapter 14), but it is possible that the politicking can have an impact on how project members view the style of leadership – is it regarded as genuine or merely instrumental (see Thomas, Chapter 5)? Equally, there are cases where a fairly authoritarian approach to leadership is adopted, but the overall ethos is one of team-working and comradeship. In such circumstances, the crucial elements are to understand how skills are being deployed in the particular practice (e.g. leadership), and how this deployment will be interpreted by others (e.g. in a network). Hence, in operation – as in orientation – the organiser/performer is in the midst of a process of balancing a range of demands, interpretations and pulls in different directions (see Nicolini and Greig, Chapter 17).

B1.   How should the division of labour be managed?

For orchestras and the festival organisers there are formal structures in place to manage the division of labour. A key feature of managing labour within these organisations is establishing trusting relationships between the managers and their teams. For example, for Louise Mitchell (Chapter 18, pp. 213–17) the key aspects of managing labour within the organisation of a music festival are the importance of trust and of building relationships; providing space for innovation and improvisation within her team; and promoting a collaborative approach.

Managing relationships in this way leads to 'everyone pulling in the same direction', as with the CBSO's successful programming of *St Matthew Passion* conducted by Sir Simon Rattle. Simon Webb (Chapter 18, pp. 251–7) puts this down to 'knowing what we were setting out to do and putting all the pieces in place well in advance and everyone pulling in the same direction. It was classic management stuff but that was what happened.' Similarly, Cloonan (Chapter 18, pp. 226–35) describes a clear separation between his managerial tasks and the band's musical tasks, although there are shared values and a close affinity.

Although it would seem that the organisation of the DIY labels, managers and bands is improvisational and ad hoc, in terms of organising a band's artistic trajectory, most of the indie musicians we talked to think strategically about their trajectory and have informal 'loosely formed' roles in place to operationalise their progression. The different organisational tasks are distributed among the band members according to their personal skills and interests. For example, in Jill O'Sullivan's band, Sparrow and the Workshop (Chapter 19, pp. 317–25):

Gregor has often done the driving on tour and contributed merchandising ideas such as posters for gigs, fake tattoos and flower pot shots. Nick is the 'tech boy', recording and mixing demos. He also does all the admin for the band's tours, giving festival promoters advance material and specs for the sets. Jill's role is to keep on top of emails, deal with press crews and maintain social networking sites and fan interaction.

The musicians also note that on tour they face the challenging task of 'being both a musician and working as a t-shirt salesman': 'we are the roadies, we are the merchandise sellers, we are the musicians, we do it all ourselves...' (Panagopoulos and Chillas, Chapter 18, pp. 236–44). Similarly, in some organising practices there is considerable overlap between operations and marketing (see Donald and Greig, Chapter 18, pp. 262–9; Hunt et al., Chapter 18, pp. 278–84, for examples).

B2. *What approaches to leadership can be adopted?*

As Hibbert notes (Chapter 14), the approaches and practices of leading are dependent on context. Among the singer-songwriters there is a desire to be emotionally bonded and musically engaged with the band, but there is also a fear of losing artistic control. As such, there is a tendency towards being dictatorial (as the artistic director of a major festival put it: 'democracies in bands do not work; someone needs to be the driving force'), and this often results in these leaders wearing 'some in the band down a bit' with their determination to be the artistic 'driving force'. Indeed, all the lead songwriters tend to identify themselves as leading on the artistic decision-making: 'because I wrote all the music ... mostly I do dictate how it is going to sound and I guess if it does not sound like how I want it to sound, then it is not going to happen' (Talbot Dunn and Cody, Chapter 19, pp. 343–51). Many of these musicians need to 'dictate' to band members the artistic direction of the songs and music. Where there is artistic conflict and tension within the band, band members are sometimes asked to leave by the 'artistic leader', who tends to embody the band, and define its identity. For example, Duglas T. Stewart (Chapter 19, pp. 352–7) says of Francis McDonald of the BMX Bandits: 'if he [Francis] left the band it could still be BMX Bandits. But if I [Duglas] left the band it would not be BMX Bandits and I think everybody would sort of see that'. However, Duglas does acknowledge that as a leader he: 'sometimes worries everyone might grow tired of me and leave me, but I'm glad they seem to be happy giving so generously of their time and talent to my vision'. Thus, among some of the singer-songwriters there is a tension between being a collaborative person, identified with the band, and being separate from and in control of the band.

In contrast, the leadership practices within orchestras are much more collaborative once the repertoire has been selected. As Chris Stout (Chapter 19, pp. 298–304) puts it: 'A good conductor will lead the orchestra but still allow them the freedom to perform.' The freedom to perform ultimately means the freedom to contribute to leading (Hibbert, Chapter 14). In this way, and in contrast to the singer-songwriters, the CEO of the CBSO – with ultimate responsibility for the orchestra's artistic vision – does not purely dictate; rather, he 'feeds on' the opinions of those working in the organisation that he leads. There is a somewhat participative style of management:

... the artistic vision is very much owned by the Chief Executive. He is very keen to listen to the range of opinions that feed into that and I think that this is the crucial part of it: it is not in any way a dictation, it is absolutely he will feed on that and quite often, you know, he will find himself making a decision which, on a personal level, he might disagree with but he can hear the volume of opinion. (Webb and Dowling, Chapter 18, pp. 251–7)

Taking this a step further, for the Fence Collective (Chapter 18, pp. 218–25), 'the adoption and popularity of the idea of the Collective "grew out of the fact that there was no one who was a gang leader" and no one artist on Fence Records was breaking out and selling lots of records. Therefore, the Collective name was "stronger than each individual name".'

Thus, choices about leadership entail difficult juggling acts. There is often a need for clear artistic purpose and direction (see Strati, Chapter 2), but this needs to be embedded in the taste and judgement of a practising community (see Beech et al., Chapter 1), so there is both individuality and collectivity in arriving at artistic decisions. The enactment of the artistic vision incorporates both technical activities that can fit together easily and activities that may be contested to some degree (see Thomas, Chapter 5). So there is a role for moments of directive leadership – see Lori Watson's story (Chapter 19, pp. 290–7) for an example where greater direction might have been helpful – alongside leadership aimed at facilitation: bringing the best out of others by giving them the supportive context for performance – see the role of the producer in Jenny's story (Chapter 19, pp. 310–16).

B3.   *How should we operate in a network?*

Networks are fundamental to the operation of the music industry both for musicians building careers and for the organisational side of venues, festivals and groups (see Beech et al., Chapter 1; Bilton and Cummings, Chapter 7). The operation of networks relates to the balance in orientation towards collaboration or competition, and it is clear that in many situations the same people collaborate on some projects and events while competing on others. This means that there is a need to be able to cope with the emotional and psychological pressures of ambiguous relationships, and to be able to operate in line with the espoused artistic values, even when there are (potential) differences and tensions. On the whole, the tales of experience presented above tell of a positive orientation to networking and a broadly collaborative orientation.

As we see with Ian Smith (Chapter 19, pp. 372–7), being integrated into a network of talents and well-connected musicians is an important part of a musician's learning and career trajectory:

I was working with great arrangers, playing arrangements by people like Stan Kenton, working with people like Brian Faye – who was then the director of that orchestra and a very well-known and respected arranger – John Gregory, Adrian Drover: just a really rich time for lots of stuff going on. There was a lot of work. That is the reason why I, as a student, was playing in one of London's top orchestras, because there was a lot of work and if you had the right connections, like your teacher was chair of the orchestra, you could get work.

Within her story of dealing with the crisis with the opening night of Celtic Connections, Louise Mitchell (Chapter 18, pp. 213–17) also discusses the value of building and maintaining a good network of relationships. She talks about always trying to network, even without an immediate purpose or agenda. Louise reflects that within her career she has built up a reliable network of people. This networked collaborative approach reflects in itself the nature of working on festivals. This is illustrated particularly within the Fence Collective's Homegame (Chapter 18, pp. 218–25), in which the community helps with the organisation of the festival, resulting in a complex network of 'stakeholders', whose roles, relationships and responsibilities contribute to the festival. The network is held together by a sense of cooperation and co-dependency, ensuring the sustainability of the festival.

For DIY indie bands and labels, starting out is very much an ad hoc 'learn as you go' process, very often learning from other, more experienced members of the live music network. Making connections with other bands that are already established in the touring music scene, building friendships with other bands in this network, is integral to becoming established on the live music scene. Recognition matters, mainly from other well-known and respected artists in the 'scene' – hence the importance of networking – and this is the same for orchestral collaborations with different orchestras and conductors, as Ian Smith (Chapter 19, pp. 372–7) describes in his story.

The network of bands are just 'like-minded individuals who all like the same kind of music and a bit of banter'; building friendships with other bands 'is just what you do' in order to become established (Panagopoulos and Chillas, Chapter 18, pp. 236–44). However, despite this informality, networks are vital for learning how the music industry works. R.M. Hubbert (Chapter 19, pp. 305–9) describes how the roles he played organising albums and tours for his own bands and others helped him develop the knowledge he needed to become a solo artist, because he had an in-depth understanding of how bands organised a DIY label. Like the musicians, managers and those running these DIY labels need to be well connected into the network of contacts and up to date with all the upcoming bands and new releases on the national music scene. Similarly, in Cloonan's (Chapter 18, pp. 226–35) experience as a manager, the 'learning as you go' process means, for example, being aware of the different venues' fees and equipment, and knowing how to arrange tickets and where to get posters printed.

Just like the young indie bands trying to get gigs and into the network of musicians, starting a DIY label is very much an improvised 'learning as we go' process. There is a lot of 'pulling in favours' from friends made within the network and taking advice from those more experienced in the DIY network – for example, Matthew (Chapter 18, pp. 285–9) asked advice of Johnny from Fence Records (Chapter 18, pp. 218–25), one of the more established independent labels on the music scene. Like the independent bands, although these labels give the impression of being improvised and self-managing, a high degree of careful organisation and specific practices go into ensuring the independent identity is maintained.

C.   Reaching out

Clearly, a significant part of the purpose of music-making is to reach audiences. However, audiences are mixed in what they expect and hope for, so in most cases it is unlikely that one performance, in mode and content, will delight all. There are phases of early career when audiences may be lacking and there is a need to grow the market for a performer (see Mason, Chapter 8). This can be done by joining with established performers, gaining access to high-profile venues or by use of more generic marketing techniques such as the use of social media campaigns. Alternatively, there can be an effort to make a new market. This might be done by developing new forms of performance, or bringing performance styles that are successful in one culture into another. Celtic Connections (referred to in Chapter 1 and Chapter 18, pp. 213–17), is one example in which an educational programme accompanying concerts over a decade in effect brought up a generation of school pupils to be aware of a form of music they might otherwise have had little access to. Some of those young people have gone on to be part of the long-term audience, and even to become players. Similarly, it is common for orchestras to undertake educational and 'outreach' activities to take music to new potential audiences and break down socio-cultural barriers (see Green, MacKintosh and Gilmore, Chapter 19, pp. 366–71). In other circumstances – for example, when a career is well advanced – it is possible for the audience to become limiting: still wanting to hear the old hits rather than new material. However, for most of the performers cited here, connection with the audience is a highly significant part of what makes the process meaningful.

Another aspect of reaching out is to other players and participants in networks. This is a significant aspect of operational practice, and while it is commonly regarded as essential, it is also difficult to achieve (see Smith and Gilmore, Chapter 19, pp. 372–7, for example). One way of considering networking practices is to understand the role of legitimacy – that which makes others take you seriously. Legitimacy might be gained through notable performances, having particular skills that are valued by others, being associated with successful projects and being able to imitate the received norms of the social group (among others). Fortunately, faking these things is not as easy as it sounds, and although pretence might be maintained for a short while, it is difficult to maintain over time. For the actors in the tales told above, legitimacy among peers and with others in the industry has been established over time and entailed trust-building as they became recognised.

C1.   How do we engage with audiences and markets?

Saren (Chapter 9) discusses the connections between consumption and production. In the music field, and perhaps in the 'creative industries' more generally, these connections are emphasised. Those who go on to become musicians have typically had a strong interest and amateur involvement early in life. Similarly, those on the organisation and management side often have very strong interests and are also consumers. The nature of the 'markets' (as Hackley, Chapter 10, and Bradshaw, Chapter 12, point out) is that they are not simply based on the exchange of products or services for money. Rather, the meaning of the 'service' is co-created with the audience, who are part of the energy of a live event and who have an impact on the modes of promoting and distributing both recorded and live music through social media and technology.

The initial years of a band's trajectory are typically spent 'basically trying to figure out how to get people to the concerts' (Panagopoulos and Chillas, Chapter 18, pp. 236–44). Marco's band United Fruit did this through making connections with bands who were already established in the music scene, building friendships with these bands, and by touring. In so doing, there came a point where 'the power shifted and we became one of those bands that other bands were asking to do that' (ibid.).

Bands need the experience of playing in order to become 'a good live band' (Cloonan, Chapter 18, pp. 226–35). Getting a gig often involves a promoter 'taking a chance': 'we just had to keep begging for gigs and then eventually someone took a chance' (Panagopoulos and Chillas, Chapter 18, pp. 236–44). Gigs are also important for bands to develop a fan base, for exposure to the music media and bloggers, and to be seen by promoters and A&R record company people.

For the musicians, the most important element in playing live is the audience. The best gigs are 'when you feel you are not just doing it, that you are actually engaging, when people come up to you after and say that they got something out of that, they felt good' (O'Sullivan and Chillas, Chapter 19, pp. 317–25). Engaging and connecting with the audience through their music is crucial to a 'successful' performance. In addition, within a band, the connection and trust among the musicians is also important to a successful performance, as Chris Stout (Chapter 19, pp. 298–304) notes:

. . . when you all grow as a group together, live on stage, you show that the situation is as important as the music you are making; the audience are involved in that – your relationship in the concert for the last hour has helped that improvisation because you are all happy and you can just pour yourselves out. You are also all in tune with each other as well, and you know what the audience wants to hear.

At the Homegame and Away Game festivals (Chapter 18, pp. 218–25), the boundaries between musicians and audiences – which are tangible at larger, more commercially driven festivals – are broken down and blurred. In contrast, for orchestral players, rather than achieving a connection with the audience through a performance, they can feel 'distanced' from the audience because of the traditional orchestral set-up. The players have to find other ways of directly connecting with an audience through their music. For example, Royal Scottish National Orchestra oboist Katy MacKintosh (Chapter 19, pp. 366–71) does hospital and education work:

Take my education work away from me, and I will be unbearable really, because having working face to face with someone ... actually getting a real, proper interaction with someone means the world to me ... [in the orchestra] when you play to a sea of faces you don't know what effect you have on them, you cannot see that.

In a somewhat contrasting example, Lori Watson (Chapter 19, pp. 290–7) describes a situation where, before she became well known, she took part in a concert that showcased new composers. This type of industry activity can be very significant in helping musicians reach new audiences, and although that particular story was not one of unmitigated success, that type of practice – along with competitions – is nonetheless crucial in enabling new artists to get exposure.

C2.   How do we achieve and maintain legitimacy?

Legitimacy, as McCusker-Thompson (Chapter 11) argues, is not just a matter of being in the right place at the right time, but rather of being the right person at the right time. Carrying social capital, being seen as a member of the community with standing (see Beech et al., Chapter 1) and operating effectively in the network are all part of gaining and building legitimacy. As Coupland (Chapter 6) comments, threaded through the tales of experience are accounts of the self as a legitimate player, as a rightful member of a community. Martin Cloonan (Chapter 18, pp. 226–35) describes a way of indie bands 'legitimising' themselves by getting a manager: 'the move to appoint a manager is also a statement ... we're serious, this is not just pissing about'. Bands also gain 'legitimacy' progression by being signed to a label as opposed to self-releasing: 'being signed to a label is more like a seal of approval'. A disadvantage of the self-releasing strategy is that the wider music-listening public may not take bands seriously; some audiences perceive bands to be 'more legit if they're on a label'.

The venue that bands and orchestras play is also a way of achieving and maintaining legitimacy. The venue names are code for size of audience and sometimes niche of interest. In the main, the larger the venue, the further up the hierarchy a band can position itself in terms of fan base size, pulling power of audiences and earning potential. However, some venues are notably and deliberately small but have a reputation, for example, as

places record label scouts frequent or for attracting a particularly discerning audience such as music scholars, and are therefore imbued with
symbolic value. As Marco Panagopoulos (Chapter 18, pp. 236–44)
notes, although it is hard work to get into a venue the first time, 'when
no one knew who we were', after a successful show, 'the next time you
make friends, you see people, you legitimise yourself'.

Within the festival scene, there is also a hierarchy – some festivals are
smaller but enjoyable to play, while the bigger festivals represent a serious
opportunity to solidify the band's presence on the national if not global
music scene. Despite the importance of this structured route to gaining
access to the festival outlet, the value of being liked by 'the right people',
such as notable DJs or programmers, is also a significant factor.

In orchestral playing, having the right sort of training (and often where
you trained) is important as a starting point. But following this, passing the
audition – which may have changed over time (see the contrasting examples
of Lance Green and Katy MacKintosh, Chapter 19, pp. 366–71, and Ian
Smith, Chapter 19, pp. 372–7) – entails not only technical excellence but
also a degree of fit with the orchestra and the section. This includes the
sound produced together but also personal fit, and hence auditions and
trials may last over an extended period as people work out how good the fit
is. Similarly, conductors may spend time as temporary, sometimes one-off,
guests before being selected (or not) to have more formalised connections
with the orchestra, but even the more formalised versions of the job are
often time-limited and non-exclusive (see Webb and Dowling, Chapter 18,
pp. 251–7). Hence, in this context, having trained in the right place, being
introduced by the right people and performing (both technically and
socially) during a trial period are all parts of gaining legitimacy. As a career
develops, these same factors remain in play, with the addition of reputation,
as a player or conductor becomes known for their specialisms (for example,
in particular styles of music or the interpretation of particular composers)
and their abilities to work with others and attract an audience.

D.   Reaching in

Music is an intensely personal thing, as well as being a form of public
art. For many of the songwriters and composers, the music they produce
is, at least in part, a form of self-expression (see Hoedemaekers and
Ybema, Chapter 15). For some of the bands in the tales above, the lyrics
of songs are revelatory, and over a career fans trace life events that, for
others, would be private matters. Those running festivals and orchestras
might become known for an association (and expertise) in a particular
genre. Hence, music-making is a form of 'reaching in' to the self,

expressing and rewriting one's identity, and developing relationships with others that become part of life. Clearly this is not trivial, and so it is unsurprising that it is often emotionally charged and a big part of people's life stories (see Sims, Chapter 3). Working in groups over time to produce personal work leads to both very strong bonds and significant break-ups.

Few aspects of performance can remain static. For most, as we see with Ian Smith's experience as a young musician (Chapter 19, pp. 372–7), there is a progression over time, and this entails learning:

My first professional gig was at 19 years of age with the LPO, and then I played a lot of jazz, a lot of sessions and a lot of jingles and bits and bobs whilst I was still in the orchestra, which was very, very good for me. But then I got the offer to play with the London Symphony Orchestra (LSO) just because someone who had worked with the SNO went to the LSO, and then I started getting offers to play with them. So for ten years I was a regular deputy player with the LSO.

As this example shows, the learning may be deliberate and overt, or it may result from accrued experience, through which performers hone their craft and are challenged, as we see with Simon Rattle in the pro-gramme of *St Matthew Passion* (Chapter 18, pp. 251–7). As Simon Webb describes: 'It was everything that the CBSO was about in that it was celebrating the development of talents that had been nurtured by us as well as very high-quality performance ... It pushed our musicians really to the limit, so it was challenging for them'. Either way, learning occurs as people reflect, pick up tips from others and sometimes receive quite direct feedback.

D1.   *What happens to personal and group identities?*

As cited in Coupland's chapter (Chapter 6): 'Identity is not seen as a thing that we are, the property of an individual, but as something we do. It is a practical accomplishment, achieved and maintained through the detail of language use' (Widdicombe and Wooffitt, 1995: 133). This is reflected in the personal nature of many of the songs written by the singer-songwriters. They included political message songs, songs of love and loss, songs of desolation and confusion, and sometimes story songs. Hence, a lot of the self is expressed in the songs. The style of writing, the 'sound', is also part of the identity of the singer-songwriters. As such, identity can play an especially significant role for them, since their output is often seen as an extension of the inner world of its creator(s) and a symbol of their identities, both by the creators themselves and by audiences or consumers. Like any product of our professional, artistic or commercial endeavours, for a singer-songwriter making and performing music is a project of self-realisation (see Hoedemaekers and Ybema, Chapter 15).

Being in a 'dark place' in order to be able to write is also a common theme. The songwriters deliberately put themselves into such emotional situations, even though they find it painful, because that is where they are able to write what they have to. In order to be the writer they see themselves as, they have to be there. Indeed, being a songwriter can entail intrinsic struggles. In another part of her interview with Shiona Chillas, Jill O'Sullivan said: 'my songwriting would go down the tube if I ever became happy'. It appears to be a self-perpetuating process, driven by a desire for creative 'perfection' and failure once they reflect on their work, and a repeating of the cycle. Hence, there is an unfulfilled striving as part of the self as writer. Being unhappy and unfulfilled appears to be part of what they need to be in order to strive for fulfilment and self-expression.

Many of the singer-songwriters are humanistic, often with left-leaning political opinions, and this is part of who they are as indie musicians. They are very close to their bandmates and have generally developed relationships that provide a safe context to 'try anything' (Reeve and Gilmore, Chapter 19, pp. 310–16; Prime and Keenan, Chapter 19, pp. 358–65). For some, there is a very strong identification with the band. For example, in a documentary marking the 25th anniversary of his band, entitled *Serious Drugs: Duglas Stewart and the music of the BMX Bandits*, Duglas talked of not existing outside of his band: 'I don't know who I am, except a BMX Bandit' (Chapter 19, pp. 352–7). Also, as we see in Martin Cloonan's story (Chapter 18, pp. 226–35) and the demise of Zoey Van Goey, managers too can identify strongly with a band and their music:

I still love all the members of the band. And I smile and cry a lot to their music. I always knew that these were the days we'd look back on and tried desperately to enjoy it while it lasted. It was often fucking hard work, especially for them. But making moments of rare beauty often are. Other than missing the Paris show, *je ne regrette rien*.

The collective identity of the Fence Collective's Homegame and Away Game (Chapter 18, pp. 218–25) is central to ensuring the sustainability, and thus the future, of the festivals. Hence, the organisers' vision of the future is not one of ever-increasing economic profits but of maintaining the boutique nature of their festivals, which involves the community of Anstruther.

D2.   What learning do we derive?

In a creative field, innovation and learning are constantly present. Although some parts of the more commercial market may thrive on predictability and replicability of product – such as reunion tours of bands and mainstream repertoire in orchestra (see Bilton and Cummings, Chapter 7) – innovation comes from taking risks and exploring demanding repertoire, be it contemporary (e.g. with the BBC Philharmonic: see Wigley and Gulledge, Chapter 18, pp. 258–61) or baroque (see Downes, Chapter 18, pp. 270–7). Learning can derive from material differences (e.g. the use of period instruments and their impact on singers: see Downes, Chapter 18, pp. 270–7) or from new ways of reaching audiences for classical music in airports (see Donald and Greig, Chapter 18, pp. 262–9). As Sims (Chapter 3) points out, learning is not only about taking such risks and seeking to innovate but also about the conclusions one draws for future practice. The process of reflexivity that links experience and future action (see Hibbert, Chapter 14) can itself be challenging, as it can entail learning from the things that did not go well as well as the successes, and it can entail a radical questioning of the self.

As we learn in Lori Watson's story (Chapter 19, pp. 290–7), where there is not strong artistic leadership, or there is a sense of the structure not being in place to take the lead 'from the front', it can be detrimental to the performance. In addition, it can negatively affect the confidence of the artist in progressing creatively, in terms of composing. However, Lori's reflexive account of her Distil story illustrates that she has sought to draw learning from the event to apply to her current practice. Not repeating the same mistakes is an important part of learning.

The learning may be more collective and formal in other settings – for example, in the orchestras described above (see Webb and Dowling, Chapter 18, pp. 251–7; Wigley and Gulledge, Chapter 18, pp. 258–61). Here, profiling past concerts and doing cost–benefit analyses to assess popularity and risk is part of the normal routine. 'The Artistic Forum – a senior group involving trustees, CBSO senior management, players and conductors – analyses and discusses every concert, looks at the marketing figures, balances competing perspectives (e.g. the players did not like a particular guest conductor but he brought in a huge audience) and so on.' This information is accumulated over time and provides considerable input when considering future programming possibilities. In Jane Donald's example of the orchestral flash mob (Chapter 18, pp. 262–9), learning and reflection are written through the whole story. The idea occurs from an open team discussion and drawing in ideas from external contacts. The execution of the idea requires the orchestra to step outside of its 'comfort zone' into the unknown. In so doing, they learn from external experts from different (theatrical and airport promotion) contexts. This means being open to foreign and challenging ideas and questions, and being willing to work through their consequences – on both sides (for example, the musicians playing without the score and airport security allowing sharp objects to be used). The feedback was very positive, but there was also learning from criticism. Some players and others involved in the orchestra thought that the recorded sound quality was not good enough and that this was something that would need to be addressed in future similar activities. More generally, having taken this risk, there was a degree of social learning in the orchestra about how it might (or might not) step outside its comfort zone in the future.

Chris Stout's learning trajectory has helped him develop the confidence 'to reach out' of the tradition of traditional music and develop a 'style of his own':

I think I have a style of my own because it has evolved through time and I have allowed it to be influenced by so much . . . I don't feel that I need to bend my style so much now to accommodate other styles. I have never played traditional music in a purist way. I have allowed my music to be influenced by whatever musical style I have come into contact with; I have allowed it to influence my style directly, whether it be Brazilian music, jazz or classical. I come from a place where the tradition is very, very secure, and in safe hands, so I have the confidence to reach out.

Learning also comes with establishing and maintaining the creative integrity and identity of bands, festivals and orchestras. For example, with the Homegame and Away Game festivals, Johnny and Kenny were approached to do something on a much bigger scale than these boutique festivals, starting with an audience of 1,000 and increasing anywhere up to 10,000, with the support of an additional event manager. While they initially thought, 'this could be quite cool, we could make a bit of money out of this', they then recognised that they would have to surrender much of their control over, and involvement in, the event. Control, in this case, is not over the minutiae of organisation, but of the identity and experience of the event. So they decided that increasing the size of any of the festivals would run the risk of a loss of their identity, which has been the unique selling point 'not only with our audience, but with the other artists that want to be part of our collective, and other artists who want to play a set'. Hence, it is possible to learn about one's identity and core market by reflecting on decisions made and the rationale/emotion of those decisions.

Concluding comments

The intention behind this book was to facilitate a generative dialogue that brought together ideas and practices from related but separate fields of organising and music-making. There is an argument that the two fields are radically different, holding separate values (means–ends commerce versus end-in-itself art), different forms of legitimacy (financial success versus qualitative artistic success) and practices that are almost oppositional (the highly structured versus creative and unpredictable). In practice, these differences do exist to some extent, but they are not always as dichotomous as might be presumed. Organisation theory has moved radically in the last two decades, and is now far more concerned with dynamism, social construction, nuance and uncertainty than its stereotype would lead us to believe. Similarly, music-making is concerned with producing 'output' that will be heard by an audience, that achieves certain artistic and other aims, and that, for some at least, produces sufficient financial return in order to keep doing it. The ways of thinking may be different in certain technical aspects – for example, the technicalities of composition are different from the technicalities of accounting or programming. These differences may be accentuated when there is a significant division of labour, as is the case with orchestras, bands on the big stage and festivals. However, this is not true of small 'entrepreneurial' groups and individuals, who carry out a range of tasks from composing to financing.

One of the most striking areas of contiguity is in personal and professional values. The musicians who have contributed to this book clearly value the music that they and others produce. In some cases, they put so much value on this that they are willing to make considerable financial and personal sacrifices in order to be musicians. The story is not so different with managers. They also really value the music. In some cases, managers have made personal investments in bands and other aspects of music-making, with the full expectation of making a financial loss. While not being the philanthropists of old (see Beech et al., Chapter 1), they do display considerable altruism in their commitment. Similarly, people working in the management of orchestras in many cases could earn far more utilising their skills in other industries. They are passionate, highly informed and 'on the side' of art and the artists. Likewise, musicians want things to run effectively and efficiently for their message to get out and be heard, and they want to be able to work in complex, multiple project teams – which is where much organisation theory is currently focused.

Therefore, the stage is set to continue and enhance the dialogue. One step is to recognise the contiguities, and another is to value the differences for what they bring to the party. A third is to engage in continuous learning – from experience, reflection and experimentation. We hope that holding in mind some of the balances presented above will help with this endeavour. The issue is not to choose doing the 'right thing' over the 'wrong thing' – rather, the question is: How should we proceed under conditions of uncertainty? Framing such choices by an awareness of the balances and tensions within orientation, operation, reaching out and reaching in may not always generate ideal outcomes, but it can enable a thoughtfully active way of engaging with the possibilities of organising and making music.

References

Beech, N. and MacIntosh, R. (2012) *Managing change*. Cambridge University Press.

Cunliffe, A. (2008) Orientations to social constructionism: relationally-responsive social constructionism and its implications for knowledge and learning. *Management Learning*, 39: 123–39.

Delbridge, R., Gratton, L., Johnson, G. and the AIM Fellows (2007) *The exceptional manager*. Oxford University Press.

Sims, D., Huxham, C. and Beech, N. (2009) On telling stories but hearing snippets: sense-taking from presentations of practice. *Organization* 16(3): 371–88.

Index

414   Index

Printed in the United States
By Bookmasters